MW01259833

Loyal but French

Loyal but French

The Negotiation of Identity by French-Canadian Descendants in the United States

Mark Paul Richard

Michigan State University Press · *East Lansing*

Copyright © 2008 by Mark Paul Richard

⊖ The paper used in this publication meets the minimum requirements of ANSI/NISO
Z39.48-1992 (R 1997) (Permanence of Paper).

 Michigan State University Press
East Lansing, Michigan 48823-5245

Printed and bound in the United States of America.

14 13 12 11 10 09 08   1 2 3 4 5 6 7 8 9 10

LIBRARY OF CONGRESS CATALOGING-IN-PUBLICATION DATA
Richard, Mark Paul, 1960–
Loyal but French : the negotiation of identity by French-Canadian descendants in the
United States / Mark Paul Richard.
p. cm.
Includes bibliographical references and index.
ISBN 978-0-87013-837-9 (pbk. : alk. paper) 1. French-Canadians—Maine—Lewiston—Ethnic
identity. 2. French-Canadians—Cultural assimilation—Maine—Lewiston. 3. Immigrants—
Maine—Lewiston—Social conditions. 4. Lewiston (Me.)—Ethnic relations. 5. Lewiston
(Me.)—Social conditions. 6. French-Canadians—United States—Ethnic identity. 7. French-
Canadians—Cultural assimilation—United States. 8. Americanization. 9. Immigrants—
United States—Social conditions. 10. United States—Ethnic relations. I. Title.
F29.L63R53 2008
305.811'4074182—dc22
                                2008015734

Cover design by Erin Kirk New
Book design by Sharp Designs, Inc., Lansing, MI

Front cover photos of Jacques Cartier Institute members with a team of horses and La
Grande Hermine (*upper*) and of Alfred Auger on Saint-Jean-Baptiste Day (*lower*) are used
courtesy of the Franco-American Collection at USM/ Lewiston-Auburn College.

g green press INITIATIVE Michigan State University Press is a member of the Green Press Initiative
and is committed to developing and encouraging ecologically responsible
publishing practices. For more information about the Green Press Initiative and the use of
recycled paper in book publishing, please visit *www.greenpressinitiative.org*.

Visit Michigan State University Press on the World Wide Web at *www.msupress.msu.edu*

Contents

Illustrations

Acknowledgments

The intellectual journey that culminated with this book began in the fall of 1992, when I introduced myself to C. Stewart Doty, professor of history at the University of Maine. A pioneer of Franco-American history, Doty offered me the opportunity to study the history of the group of which I was part but about which I knew little. Five minutes into our first meeting, Doty became my advisor, and our encounter set the direction of my career. Robert Babcock, Jacques Ferland, Paula Petrik, David Smith, and Raymond Pelletier of the history and French departments nurtured my interest in Franco-American history and culture, and they helped me to develop the intellectual, methodological, and language skills I needed to pursue successfully my Master of Arts degree.

John Herd Thompson's invitation to study North American history at Duke University allowed me to continue honing the skills I needed to research and write this manuscript. I profited immensely from Thompson's thoughtful guidance and constant support as my graduate advisor. Thompson read and commented upon multiple earlier drafts of this manuscript, helping to shape the ideas and the prose of my dissertation so that I could most effectively tell my story. I can only hope to emulate with my own students his many contributions as an advisor and mentor. While at Duke, I also benefited from my coursework and discussions with Alexander Keyssar, Lawrence Goodwyn, Wendy Wall, Edward Tiryakian, Suzanne Shanahan, and Paol Keineg of the history, sociology, and French departments.

Numerous other individuals—librarians, archivists, members of religious communities, and the staff of public and private organizations—assisted me as I completed the research for this manuscript. I would especially like to thank Sheryl Whitmore, Lizette Leveille, Susan Grant, and Sr. Renee Turcotte of the Lewiston Public Library; Mary Pollard of the Office of the Clerk of the Superior Court of Maine at Auburn; Madeleine Roy and Donat Boisvert of the Franco-American Collection at Lewiston-Auburn College; Sr. Therese Pelletier of the Chancery Archives of the Roman Catholic Diocese of Portland, Maine; Rev. Albert Dumont of the Archives of the Dominican Order of Montréal, Québec; and Janet Roberts of the Maine Newspaper Project at the Maine State Library. Roberts provided me access to *Le Messager,* the French-language newspaper of Lewiston, literally as she and her staff produced the microfilm from the original publications. I sincerely appreciate the access that she—and all of the individuals representing the repositories cited in the bibliography—provided to the sources I needed for this project.

This book would not have come to fruition were it not for the generous financial support I received to conduct my research and to write the narrative. I am grateful to the Ford Motor Company endowment fund, administered by the Duke University North American Studies Program, for summer research funds in 1998 and 1999; to the Coca-Cola Foundation for funding my Fulbright Research Grant to Canada in 1998–1999, a grant administered by the Canada–U.S. Fulbright Program; to the Duke History Department for the financial assistance it provided so that I could devote my energies on a full-time basis to drafting the manuscript from 1999 to 2001; and to the Lucien E. and Georgiana M. Martin Memorial Scholarship Fund, administered by l'Association Canado-Américaine in Manchester, New Hampshire, for support in 2000–2001.

Finally, I am also grateful to my parents, Roger and Claire, for their encouragement to pursue my graduate education. They also supplied many helpful anecdotes from their own experiences, sharing them generously during the course of my research and writing. I dedicate this book to them.

Introduction

In 1855, arsonists twice damaged the Catholic church of Lewiston, Maine. Allegedly members of the Know-Nothing political party, which opposed immigration and especially Roman Catholics, they registered their intolerance by burning the church of the Irish-Catholic immigrants who had come to work in this burgeoning industrial town.[1] Their actions established the cultural context that would greet the next group of immigrants, French Canadians, who began arriving in Lewiston in the late 1850s. Through the second half of the nineteenth century and into the twentieth, French Canadians confronted discrimination. Yet, in this context of persistent pressure by nativists in the United States to anglicize and to become assimilated Americans, most individuals of French-Canadian birth and background in Lewiston retained their French language, their Catholic faith, and many of their French-Canadian traditions through the first half of the twentieth century; some have maintained them to the present day. This monograph traces the process by which French-Canadian immigrants and their descendants joined U.S. society from the mid-nineteenth century to the contemporary era. Its central argument is that French speakers of Lewiston actively negotiated the terms of their entry into U.S. society.

In recent decades, the field of migration history has attracted growing scholarly attention, in large part due to the work of the ethnic and labor historians who have tried to situate their studies in a broader, more global framework. To a larger degree than in the past, scholars are now also considering the non-European sources of migration to the United States. One sending society still greatly neglected by scholars is Canada, a nation that has contributed proportionally more of its population to the United States than any other donating country. During the century prior to 1930, from 2.5 to 3.0 million English- and French-speaking Canadians migrated to the United States. Underscoring Canada's major contribution as a sending society, its native-born population totaled 3 million in 1871 and 8 million in 1931. The proximity of Canadian-born immigrants to their homeland, their exemption from U.S. immigration restrictions until 1930, and their relative slowness in becoming naturalized citizens of the United States have made their experiences different from those of immigrants from outside of North America. Though significant to the histories of both Canada and the United States, the international migration of Canadians during the nineteenth and twentieth centuries has not received sufficient historical attention. On the one hand, this scholarly neglect reflects U.S. perceptions that few differences exist between English Canadians and Americans; on the other hand, it reflects Canada's discomfort with the large emigration of its people to the United States, for not being American is a defining element of the Canadian national identity. While English Canadians may have blended more easily into existing communities in the United States, language, religion, and the formation of ethnic enclaves distinguished French-Canadian immigrants. Consequently, francophone immigrants have received comparatively more attention from scholars than have their former, anglophone compatriots.[2] These French-speaking Catholics also received more attention from nativists in the United States.

French Canadians emigrated to the United States as part of the Québec diaspora in which nearly one million persons took up residence in the U.S. Northeast by the start of the Great Depression. Most *Canadiens*, as the French Canadians called themselves, settled relatively close to home in New England's industrial centers, such as Lewiston and Biddeford, Maine; Manchester, New Hampshire; Central Falls and Woonsocket, Rhode Island; Lowell, Lawrence, and Fall River, Massachusetts. In these textile mill towns, the *Canadiens* succeeded the Irish as the predominant source of unskilled labor after the Civil War.[3] They and their offspring eventually made up a substantial proportion of the population of the industrial centers of the Northeast. In Lewiston, for example, people of French-Canadian birth and background made up nearly half of the city's residents by 1900, and an estimated 65 percent by 1930.[4]

Studies of French Canadians in the United States have focused primarily on their migration, settlement, and formation of ethnic communities. Consequently, we know little about their experiences after the opening decades of the twentieth century. Moreover, we know little about how French-Canadian descendants joined the host society.

Almost universally, accounts of French speakers in the United States present their history as a continuing struggle between assimilation and *survivance* (the preservation of the French language, Roman Catholic faith, and French-Canadian traditions).[5] Historians of other immigrant groups likewise tend to oversimplify ethnic preservation and assimilation by depicting them as binary opposites. Rather than struggling between the two, Lewiston's francophones negotiated their identity in the United States: they often challenged, rejected, or redefined the norms of the host society. Thus the process by which they joined U.S. society involved twists and turns and was anything but linear, challenging notions that the Americanization process takes place in a straight-line fashion leading to what we call "assimilation." While learning English and becoming naturalized citizens and voters, French-Canadian descendants demonstrated greater cultural persistence than most other ethnic populations. Given their steadfast use of the French language, their consistent practice of Catholicism, their preference for endogamous marriage, their founding of ethnic institutions, and their adoption and reshaping of French-Canadian traditions in Lewiston, the term "acculturation" rather than "assimilation" better describes the process by which they engaged the host society.[6] This monograph, in short, offers a new lens through which to view the history of French speakers in the United States. Moreover, in positing that ethnic retention and acculturation can serve as intertwined goals, and in underscoring the way in which an ethnic group negotiated its identity in the host society, this study offers a new conceptualization of the process of Americanization.

To examine how individuals of French-Canadian descent refashioned their identity over the past century and a half, this work utilizes the vehicle of the community study. Lewiston was once a major industrial center in the state of Maine and region of New England. This monograph explores how the identity of individuals of French-Canadian birth and background in Lewiston changed over time. It explores the values, traditions, and collective coping strategies that francophones brought from Canada to the United States, and it examines the extent to which Lewiston's French-speaking population continued to rely upon models and resources available in Canada after the emigration experience. In analyzing the processes of acculturation—such as adoption of the English language, intermarriage between individuals of French-Canadian descent and those of other ethnic backgrounds, and the growth and decline of French-Canadian institutions in Lewiston—this study also considers the role of Catholic clergy in facilitating or delaying the Americanization of French speakers.

In this work, "French Canadians" will designate the French-speaking populations of Québec and other Canadian provinces in both the nineteenth and twentieth centuries. Along with "*Canadiens,*" the term "French Canadians" will also refer to the francophone immigrants and their offspring who lived in the United States during the nineteenth century. "Franco-Americans" will refer to individuals of French-Canadian birth and background in the United States during the twentieth century, for this population began calling itself Franco-American around the turn of the century.[7] "French-Canadian descendants" or "individuals of French-Canadian birth and background" may be used from time to time, particularly when referring to multiple generations of French speakers in the United States.

From the late nineteenth century through the twentieth century, French-Canadian descendants made up one of the three largest population groups of Lewiston. The other two groups were the Irish and native-born Americans, or "Yankees." Lewiston's three major ethnicities were not hermetically sealed; individuals and families moved between them, and the meaning of each ethnicity changed over time. The city's French-language newspaper, *Le Messager* (*The Messenger*), provides an example of the permeability of ethnic lines. After commenting that William Curran had three sons serving in the U.S. Navy during World War I, *Le Messager* stated: "Although of Irish origin, Mr. Curran is native of the Province of Québec, is married to a French-Canadian woman, and is rightly considered as one of us."[8] To distinguish members of Lewiston's three major population groups, I will employ the terms "American," "Irish," and (depending upon the century) "French Canadian" or "Franco-American." Lewiston's ethnic groups used these terms to define themselves and each other for much of the period under study.

While examining the contributions of elites, this monograph emphasizes the experiences of ordinary French Canadians and Franco-Americans. They made up a substantial proportion of Lewiston's working-class population in both the nineteenth and twentieth centuries. Since they generated few records of their own, this study, of necessity, pieces together a wide variety of sources to reconstruct their history, including naturalization records and materials from religious archives, sources historians have thus far underutilized.

Descriptive statistics provide portraits of Lewiston's changing population in 1880, 1920, 1960, and the 1990s. These years marked turning points in the history of French-Canadian immigrants and their descendants. Briefly, from the 1880s, French-Canadians began demonstrating population stability in Lewiston.[9] The 1920s represented the final decade of the migration/settlement/community-formation period. During the 1950s and especially the 1960s, external forces such as the closing of textile mills in Lewiston, the advent of television, and changes in the Catholic Church, along with forces internal to the community, sped up the acculturation of many of the city's French speakers. Finally, data from the 1990s provides a contemporary portrait of Lewiston's Franco-Americans and what remains of their culture and institutions as they entered the new millennium. Throughout each of these periods, individuals of French-Canadian birth and background confronted different permutations of the cultural intolerance nativists promoted in Lewiston in 1855. The chapters that follow examine how francophones managed these outside pressures to become Americans of French-Canadian descent.

Creating a Mosaic

Catholic Immigrants in a Protestant Mill Town, 1850–1880

In 1873, a reporter for the *Lewiston Journal* trailed a group of French Canadians walking to their new church; hearing them chatting in French caused him to reflect: "To all intents, one feels himself in a foreign city." What Protestant Americans (Yankees) observed inside the church bemused them all the more: "It seemed like a scene in another land," one journalist reported at Christmas in 1882, "the monks in long, white habits and black over-robes, coming and going at intervals; the gray nuns, replenishing the tapers and decorating the altar, with a genuflection each time they passed and re-passed the host."[1] Like the Irish immigrants who had arrived before them, French Canadians diversified the Protestant mill town of Lewiston, Maine, in the nineteenth century. Besides their Catholic faith, French-Canadian immigrants brought another language and different traditions to the Spindle City, vastly changing its character in the eyes of natives. This chapter examines the arrival of French-Canadian immigrants in Lewiston in the nineteenth century, highlighting the religious, ethnic, and economic differences that distinguished them from the Americans and, to some extent, from their Irish coreligionists. For French Canadians, these differences led to ethnic segregation from 1860 to 1880, but even as they developed ethnic solidarity during this period, French Canadians began to adopt some traits of the host society.

When Governor Samuel Adams signed the act incorporating Lewiston as a town in 1795, it was an isolated, agricultural village of Massachusetts. The advent of manufacturing and railroads ended Lewiston's isolation, causing it to evolve into an industrial city by the mid-nineteenth century. Local businessmen, taking advantage of the power generated by the thirty-eight-foot falls of the Androscoggin River, organized Lewiston's early manufacturing operations. They opened a woolen mill before Maine gained its statehood in 1820, and they established the Lewiston Falls Cotton Mill Company in 1845. After a railroad line reached Lewiston in 1849, Boston capitalists built additional cotton and woolen mills in the town. The largest plants—the Bates, Hill, and Androscoggin mills—each had fifty thousand spindles by 1872. In that year, Lewiston's nine cotton and five woolen mills produced over 32 million yards of cotton cloth and nearly seven hundred thousand yards of woolen cloth. Incorporated as a city in 1861, Lewiston became Maine's foremost textile center in the mid-nineteenth century.[2]

The textile industry dominated Lewiston's economy until the mid-twentieth century. In 1883, it provided employment for over 6,000 persons; at the turn of the century, 70 percent of the city's work force labored in its mills. Although Lewiston's textile industry, like the rest of New England's, declined after the First World War, it survived the Great Depression. Capitalists with national concerns purchased the Bates, Hill, and Androscoggin mills, which had planned to close in the late 1920s, in order to safeguard their investments in the utilities that sold power to these mills. In 1937, Lewiston's textile manufacturers employed 5,000 men and women—approximately half of the state's textile workers. Not until the permanent decline of most of Lewiston's mills in the 1950s did this one-industry city begin diversifying its economy.[3]

The initial source of labor for Lewiston's mills was young, native-born farm women, who typically worked long enough to accumulate the funds they needed to finance further education, repay family debt, or establish a dowry. Irish immigrants, who had arrived in the United States between the mid-1840s and early 1850s to escape the potato famine in Ireland, succeeded the American women as operatives in Lewiston's textile industry. The Irish had come to the Lewiston area to build the railroads and dig the canals that diverted water from the Androscoggin River to power the mills. When the native-born women went on strike in 1854 to back their demand for an eleven-hour work day, mill managers replaced them with Irish workers.[4]

In that same year, the Know-Nothing political party came to Maine. It had formed in New York in 1852; when questioned about the organization, members sworn to secrecy typically quipped, "I don't know," thus giving the party its name. The Know-Nothing movement spread to each state and territory of the United States, amassing one million members by 1854. In Maine, the movement took root in coastal and river towns, where much of the state's Irish population had settled. In 1854, anti-Catholic sentiment fomented by the Know-Nothings led to the burning of Catholic churches in the coastal communities of Bath and Ellsworth, Maine, and to the tarring and feathering of Ellsworth's Catholic priest. The state's Protestant ministers helped spread the Know-Nothing movement, which drew its membership from the middle and lower classes. By the fall gubernatorial election, up to one-fifth of Maine's voters either belonged to the party or sympathized with it, estimates historian Allan R. Whitmore. With approximately twenty-seven thousand members, Maine's Know-Nothing Party reached the height of its popularity in 1855, the year the state received its first Catholic bishop.[5]

That same year, nativists twice torched the Catholic church of Lewiston. Albert H. Kelsey helped repair the structure after the first fire, and he fought in vain to save the building during the second one. When he arrived at the scene, he "found five or six hundred Lewiston people standing on the street opposite the burning building. They were hooting and yelling and jeering," he told an interviewer nearly half a century later. After fire engines arrived, someone cut their hoses. Kelsey procured another hose from the nearby Bates Mill, and he stationed people along the hose to prevent it from being cut; he then sprayed the gathering crowd before attempting to douse the enflamed structure. Kelsey blamed the Know-Nothings for the blaze. "There was a feeling of bigotry abroad in those days," he remembered. A contemporary witness, "An Irish Catholic" letter writer to the *Democratic Advocate*, stopped short of indicting the Know-Nothing Party, but attributed the fire to "a few misguided men" within the movement. In its report of the fire, the *Democratic Advocate* charged: "Here are more of the practical workings of Know-Nothingism. Our place [Lewiston] will soon compete with Bath and Ellsworth, in their unenviable notoriety." Indignant, the rival *Lewiston Falls*

Journal contended that the *Advocate*'s allegation was "unfounded," and it defended the Know-Nothings as "high-minded and honorable men." The *Journal* did not, however, condone the church burning, and it asked readers: "Will not some one move in reference to repairing the chapel which has been thus maliciously and wickedly destroyed?" Whether Know-Nothings were directly responsible for the two fires at Lewiston's Catholic church in 1855 is not certain; they were responsible, however, for creating in Maine an anti-Catholic climate that made possible the church's destruction. Whether the church burnings represented working-class Yankee protest against Irish strikebreakers is also not certain, though it is possible. By 1850 the Irish made up nearly one-fourth of Lewiston's residents and 75 percent of its unskilled labor supply. When they entered the mills, they constituted an economic threat. The poverty of Lewiston's Irish immigrants, their involvement in petty crimes, the sanitation problems they caused the city by building shacks on vacant lots, their lack of temperance despite Maine's prohibition laws, and their Catholicism must have led Know-Nothings and other native-born Americans to view them as a social threat as well.[6]

The agent of the Franklin Company served, however, as a patron to Lewiston's Irish population, and he helped Catholicism take root in the city. Boston capitalists created the Franklin Company in 1854, and it acquired ownership of the water power of the Androscoggin River, the canals, and several hundred acres of land. As its agent, Albert H. Kelsey built the Bates, Hill, Androscoggin, Lewiston, and Continental mills, and he planned city streets as well as the common, earning the titles "the man who built Lewiston" and "godfather to the prosperity of the Spindle City" by the time of his death in 1901. Class and ethnicity intersected in Lewiston in complicated ways, as this elite Yankee agent supported members of the Irish working class. Not only did Kelsey sell the Irish their church building, but he also helped them repair the damage after the first fire; probably again with Kelsey's assistance, the Irish rebuilt their church after the second fire. Later, Kelsey sold the Irish one of the Franklin Company's finer lots. The Irish had asked the company to sell them land for a new church on terms similar to those it had granted Protestant denominations, but the company's Boston-based board of directors had twice refused to sell to these Catholics. In 1863, Kelsey simply penned a deed and slipped it among routine paperwork requiring official signatures from Boston. "I realized how important it was to encourage Catholicism for the sake of the people who were flocking to our city," explained Kelsey. On the lot the Irish purchased, they built Saint Joseph's, the "Mother Church" of the six parishes Catholics founded in Lewiston through the early 1920s.[7]

Lewiston's next immigrant population, French-speaking Catholics from Canada, began arriving in the city in the mid-nineteenth century. Naturalization records reveal that at least two French Canadians lived in Lewiston before 1860. One of them, Charles Voyer, resided in Lewiston for six months around 1857–1858 before moving to Biddeford, Maine, and eventually back to Lewiston in 1868. The other, Noel Gravel, arrived in Lewiston in 1859, but he does not appear in the 1860 census. Nor does Georges Carignan, who French-language accounts claim was the first French Canadian to establish residence in Lewiston.[8]

Not until the 1890s did Lewiston's French speakers embrace Carignan as their founder. In 1892, two years after Carignan's death, *Le Messager* first claimed in its Saint-Jean-Baptiste (Saint John the Baptist) Day edition that Carignan had arrived in Lewiston in 1860 and had been its first French-Canadian resident. When the city celebrated its centennial in 1895, *Le Messager* published in its souvenir edition the biographies of notable French Canadians, and it included Carignan for his role as the city's first French Canadian.[9] These celebratory accounts featuring Carignan as a founding figure served to convey a sense of longevity (and not of transience) to the French-Canadian presence in Lewiston; they also served to advance the argument of French speakers that they had exercised a role in the city's history. As we will see in chapters 2 and 3, francophones contended—and offered credible evidence—in the 1880s and 1890s that they had a stake in the host society, contrary to the assertions of nativists. Promoting Carignan as their Lewiston founder served a role, therefore, in the identity-making process of these French Canadians in their country of adoption.

French Canadians had migrated to various parts of Maine since the 1830s. According to geographer James P. Allen, they had traveled in two different migration streams. In one stream, French Canadians living on the south shore of the Saint Lawrence River, from opposite the city of Québec downriver to counties near Kamouraska, had moved eastward to the upper Saint John River valley in northern Maine (see map). In the other stream, those living along the Chaudière River in Beauce County had migrated to central Maine on the Kennebec Road to pursue seasonal work in ship-yards, on farms, and in the woods.[10] These pre-railroad migration patterns influenced population flows from Canada to Lewiston after the development of rail transportation.

Located about thirty miles south of Lewiston, the city of Portland, Maine, became the winter port of Montréal, Québec, when the Atlantic and Saint Lawrence Railroad (later part of the Grand Trunk Railway system) connected the two cities in 1853. In the mid-1870s, a railway extension linked Lewiston to the Grand Trunk line, a development that significantly increased the French-Canadian population of the city. According to historian Yves Frenette, only the Carignan family resided in Lewiston in 1860, compared to 689 children and adults in 1870, and 4,475 individuals in 1880. By the late nineteenth century, the city of Lewiston had the largest number of French speakers in Maine, and in 1900 French Canadians made up almost half of the city's 23,761 residents.[11]

As Lewiston's French-Canadian population expanded beyond the city's industrial section, francophones also moved across the river to Auburn. They resided primarily in the area known as New Auburn, within walking distance of Lewiston's ethnic enclave, Petit Canada (Little Canada). Auburn, however, attracted far fewer immigrants than its twin city. In 1880, for example, Auburn had less than half the population of Lewiston, and over nine-tenths were native-born; by comparison, under two-thirds of Lewiston's residents were native-born. In contrast to Lewiston, which had ten Protestant and two Catholic churches, Auburn had fifteen Protestant and no Catholic churches in 1880.[12] Auburn was the bastion of Anglo-Saxon Protestants and, as we shall see, a wellspring of anti-Catholic activity.

Just as Lewiston became known for textile manufacturing, its sister city gained its industrial reputation for shoe production. Auburn's shoe industry began with two small factories in 1836, and by 1859 the city had twenty-three shops that produced over 271,000 pairs of shoes. The industry employed about 3,000 in 1876, and employment peaked at 8,000 in 1922. In 1935, Auburn's shoe industry had 6,500 on the payroll and produced over 12 million pairs of boots and shoes. Together, Auburn and Lewiston became known as the "Industrial Heart of Maine" in the twentieth century. Their burgeoning factories from the nineteenth century became the major employers of French-Canadian immigrants and their descendants.[13]

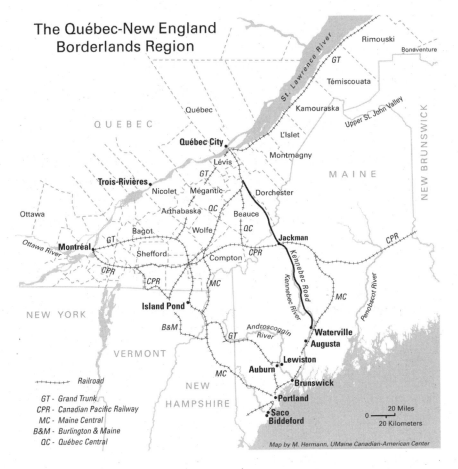

The Québec-New England Borderlands Region

Railroad
GT - Grand Trunk
CPR - Canadian Pacific Railway
MC - Maine Central
B&M - Burlington & Maine
QC - Québec Central

Map by M. Hermann, UMaine Canadian-American Center

The emigration of French Canadians to the Lewiston-Auburn area was part of the Québec diaspora in which hundreds of thousands of franco-phones moved to the United States between the end of the Civil War and the start of the Great Depression. Around 1860, French Canadians increasingly opted to emigrate to the United States rather than to rural western Canada. Speaking to the Maine Bar Association in 1923, Lewiston attorney F. X. Belleau, who had migrated east to Maine from Québec's Shefford County in 1876, explained: "In the days of my youth rural Canada offered very little advantage to young people in its towns or villages. It was the case of either going West or coming East. The best opening for many youths was then the New England States to which we came in large numbers." People moving to the Canadian West needed capital to purchase land, and they had to pay higher railroad fares than to nearby U.S. states. Moreover, the industrializing cities of the northeastern United States offered jobs.[14]

The opportunity for waged work was an important consideration for French-Canadian emigrants. Economic and demographic changes affecting the rural and urban populations of Québec created conditions of unemployment and distress during the second half of the nineteenth century. Agriculture became increasingly specialized and farmers less self-sufficient. Usury was a significant problem: indebtedness, incurred during years of poor harvest, was difficult to repay even in years of good crop yield—a situation that led to discouragement and precipitated emigration, particularly among the young who despaired about continued prospects of working for little or nothing. Because industrial development in Québec's cities did not proceed at a pace rapid enough to absorb the province's surplus rural population, much of it needed to migrate elsewhere. During periods of recession, urban dwellers likewise had to migrate to earn the funds they needed to repay debt. Given the prevailing philosophy that they had to help themselves, French Canadians pursued jobs in the United States.[15]

Nineteenth-century naturalization records reveal that Lewiston's French-Canadian immigrants came predominantly from the Province of Québec. Of the 1,188 French-Canadian men of Lewiston who became citizens from the 1870s through the 1890s, only 1.3 percent were born outside of Québec, and most of them were from the neighboring Province of New Brunswick.[16] Acadians, French speakers from the Canadian Maritimes, tended not to settle in textile mill towns like Lewiston but in Maine towns with paper mills. These migration patterns probably helped the state's francophones to retain distinct regional identities as French Canadians and Acadians, identities occasionally noted in Lewiston.[17]

No more than 8.1 percent of the men who naturalized in the Spindle City in the nineteenth century had been born in Québec counties north of the Saint Lawrence River. Of this group, two-thirds had come from the three largest cities on the river: Québec City, Trois-Rivières, and Montréal.[18] The largest cities of Québec were not major suppliers of Lewiston's naturalizing francophones.

The remaining French Canadians who naturalized in Lewiston through 1899 had places of birth widely dispersed among Québec counties south of the Saint Lawrence River (see map). They were not concentrated in any one county. No county, for example, supplied more than about 12 percent of the immigrants who naturalized while living in Lewiston. Two regional patterns emerge, however. Témiscouata and Kamouraska, located directly north of Maine along the lower Saint Lawrence River, together supplied as much as one-fifth (19.4 percent) of Lewiston's naturalizing males in the late nineteenth century. To Maine's west, a south-shore belt of Beauce, Mégantic, Wolfe, Arthabaska, and Nicolet counties probably furnished over one-third (36.1 percent) of Lewiston's naturalizers.[19] These regional clusters appear as enlargements of the migration fields to Maine that existed before the extensive development of railroad transportation between Québec and the northeastern United States.

James Allen argues that railroad development largely accounts for the wide distribution of the places of origin of Lewiston's French-Canadian population. He points out that central Maine towns like Augusta and Waterville, which had pre-railroad connections to Beauce County, drew two-thirds of their French-Canadian population from Beauce after rail transportation connected them. Another central Maine town, Brunswick, received more than half of its French-Canadian residents from towns in four contiguous counties of Québec within fifty miles of l'Islet County, according to William N. Locke. Settled by francophones principally after the construction of railroads, Lewiston had a wider migration field than Augusta-Waterville or Brunswick because railways facilitated the spread of information and contacts to this larger and faster-growing city, Allen maintains.[20]

Naturalization records provide information on the migrant journey of about 6 percent of the French Canadians from Lewiston who naturalized through 1899. To take one example, Flavien L'Heureux had been born in Sainte-Rosalie (Bagot County) but had emigrated to the United States from Weedon (Wolfe County), a town in a noncontiguous county due east from his place of birth. Like L'Heureux, at least 40 percent of the nineteenth-century naturalizers—for whom we have information about the migrant journey—had lived in more than one Québec town before crossing the border to the United States.[21] Perhaps the geographic mobility of emigrants prior to leaving Québec, coupled with the wide distribution of their places of origin, explains why French Canadians did not exhibit village or county identities once in Lewiston.

Court clerks processing naturalization papers provided more thorough information on the migration patterns of Canadians after they entered the United States. Over three-fourths (78.7 percent) of the French speakers who naturalized through 1899 had migrated directly to Lewiston after crossing the border, one-tenth (9.5 percent) had arrived at other locations in Maine before proceeding to the Spindle City, while another tenth (10.8 percent) had stopped first in other U.S. states, mostly in the Northeast; the place of arrival of the remaining immigrants (1.0 percent) was unknown. Flavien L'Heureux had arrived in Lewiston in 1872 and had lived there until his naturalization in 1885. His behavior appears typical of nineteenth-century naturalizers, for the large majority of French Canadians who had migrated directly to Lewiston had remained in the city until they became U.S. citizens.[22] The records suggest, then, that the French-Canadian men of Lewiston who opted to become citizens in the late nineteenth century had demonstrated considerable population stability within their adopted country prior to taking out final naturalization papers. This demographic stability, however, was a late-nineteenth-century development.

Unlike the seasonal migrations that had taken place prior to the Civil War, the French Canadians who arrived in the United States after the mid-1860s came in greater numbers, stayed for longer periods of time, and brought nuclear and extended families in a "chain migration." In fact, Yves Frenette finds that over 90 percent of Lewiston French Canadians who appeared in the federal censuses in 1870 and 1880 lived with other family members; their family migrations stand in contrast to the migrations of other ethnic groups, where men generally migrated alone. Until the 1880s, these post–Civil War migrations of French speakers did not usually lead to permanent settlement. Like Charles Voyer, the French Canadians who migrated to Lewiston before 1880 typically moved on to other industrializing cities of the United States or back to the Province of Québec. Sixty-seven percent of the French Canadians listed in the 1870 Lewiston census did not appear again in the 1880 census, Frenette finds. As a temporary stopping place for the majority of its French-Canadian residents, Lewiston did not have a stable francophone population. Not until the final two decades of the nineteenth century did they begin settling in the Spindle City on a permanent basis.[23]

One of the first steps in the settling-in process was acquiring a parish of their own. During the 1860s, French Canadians worshiped with the Irish.

In 1869, when Lewiston's French speakers numbered about one thousand, they began holding their own masses in the basement of Saint Joseph's Church, with a Flemish priest, Clement Mutsaers, as celebrant. Assigned a French-Canadian priest in 1870, Lewiston's francophones subsequently formed their own "national" parish, initially renting from the Irish the chapel they had rebuilt following the nativist attacks of 1855. The pastor, Edward Létourneau, was a native of Beauce County and from the diocese of Saint-Hyacinthe, regions from which many French Canadians had come. Throughout the late nineteenth and early twentieth centuries, other Catholic immigrants who settled in the U.S. Northeast and Midwest replicated the same pattern as Lewiston's French Canadians: they celebrated mass with the ethnic group that preceded them, then held their own services in the church basement or chapel under the direction of an appointed foreign-born priest, and later founded their own parish.[24] Through this process, French Canadians and other Catholic immigrants rooted themselves in the United States.

As sociologists Robert E. Park and Herbert A. Miller argued in the early 1920s, the formation of tight-knit ethnic communities functioned as an integral part of the rooting process. Anti-Catholic hostility in the United States often worked to promote ethnic solidarity among new immigrant populations. Whether Reverend Létourneau encountered anti-Catholic sentiment in Lewiston has gone unrecorded. As pastor of Maine's first French-Canadian parish, he stayed in his post only a little over a year, leaving under suspicious circumstances. His successor, Saint-Hyacinthe native Pierre Hévey, had difficulty finding lodging in the city on account of anti-Catholic, anti-French-Canadian sentiment on the part of its native-born residents.[25] This negative experience probably only further motivated the French-Canadian pastor to promote ethnic solidarity among Lewiston's French-speaking population.

In January 1872, several months after arriving in Lewiston, Hévey facilitated the founding of a national society. He asked the men of the parish to join him in a meeting after vespers one Sunday at which Charles Lalime of Worcester, Massachusetts, discussed the advantages of forming a mutual-aid association. Within a week, Lewiston's French Canadians founded the Saint-Jean-Baptiste Society, named and modeled after one in Québec that nationalists had organized to unify francophones and to provide them (and, consequently, their families) with social assistance in times of illness, disability, or death.²⁶ Divisions within the Lewiston society led a group of French Canadians to form l'Institut Jacques-Cartier (the Jacques Cartier Institute) in May 1874 as a literary club and alternative association. The following month, members of l'Institut traveled to Montréal along with over ten thousand French-Canadian immigrants living in the United States to celebrate Saint-Jean-Baptiste Day, in honor of the patron saint of French Canadians, and to *fête* the fortieth anniversary of the city's Société Saint-Jean-Baptiste. Its ethnic pride aroused by the event, l'Institut decided to organize Lewiston's own celebration the following year. By merging with the local Saint-Jean-Baptiste Society, l'Institut Jacques-Cartier strengthened its forces in June 1875, and it organized in that month Lewiston's first public celebration of Saint-Jean-Baptiste Day.²⁷ Founded during Hévey's tenure, l'Institut Jacques-Cartier became an important national society in Lewiston, one that both provided social assistance to francophones and promoted their ethnic cohesion.

During the decade in which Hévey ministered in Lewiston, he also helped French Canadians establish their own church, school, cemetery, and other societies. In 1872, they built Saint-Pierre (Saint Peter) Church. Rather than continuing to share the final resting place of the Irish, they opened their own cemetery in 1876. Two years later, Hévey founded the first bilingual school in Maine, staffed by the Soeurs Grises (Grey Nuns) of Saint-Hyacinthe, so named because of the color of their habits. In 1879, he formed les Enfants de Marie (the Children of Mary), a religious association for young women, and l'Union Saint-Joseph (the Saint Joseph Union), another mutual-aid society that the men of the parish could join. Uniting French-Canadian men who had come to Lewiston from different parts of Québec and who did not know each other was the central goal of l'Union Saint-Joseph. Frenette argues that Hévey's efforts in promoting solidarity among Lewiston French Canadians led to the creation of an ethnic network that helped root this previously mobile population.²⁸

Ethnic isolation characterized the community-building of the 1870s. To establish their own parish, school, societies, and cemetery, Lewiston's French Canadians broke away from their Irish coreligionists. In life as in death, these French speakers lived apart from the city's Protestant-American and Irish-Catholic residents, segregating themselves in their Petit Canada. In the early 1870s, the *Journal*, the newspaper of Lewiston's native-born

American population, reported that the city's French Canadians were "quite clannish" because of their language, and that they patronized their own grocers, physicians, and hackmen. It noted, however, that the children spoke a mixture of French and English, taking "to English, like a duck to water," and that their skills enabled them to serve as interpreters for older family members. While expressing mild concern that French Canadians had purchased little property in Lewiston and that they sent their earnings back to Canada, the *Journal* complimented them for their religious devotion, work ethic, temperance, and for how rarely they required police or court intervention. The *Journal's* articles served to introduce Lewiston's French-speaking residents to its anglophone population and to explain how the city was becoming, in its word, a *"mosaic."*[29] The articles also reveal that by acquiring English-language skills, French-Canadian children had begun the process of acculturation.

While the ethnic isolation of French Canadians aroused the curiosity of Lewiston's American majority in the 1870s, there appears to have been little conflict between the two groups or between the French Canadians and the Irish during this decade. This impression arises, however, from English-language sources. Written accounts in French detailing the state of ethnic relations in Lewiston, such as chronicles by clergy or journalists, first appear in the 1880s. Available evidence suggests that only after French Canadians achieved population stability in the Spindle City, and began actively to participate in the political process, do we find tangible evidence of ethnic competition and conflict between them and Lewiston's American and Irish populations.

Data compiled from the 1880 federal manuscript census provides a portrait of Lewiston's francophones at the start of the decade during which they began to form a stable population. In revealing the extent to which French Canadians differed from the rest of Lewiston's residents, the census data serves as a baseline from which to compare changes in this population over historical time. For 1880, the data particularly highlights the economic and ethnic divisions of the Spindle City.

French Canadians made up the second largest ethnic group of Lewiston in 1880. Americans made up less than half (47.8 percent) of Lewiston's total population, while French Canadians made up one-fourth (24.8 percent) of the city's residents, followed by the Irish, who made up one-sixth of the population (16.9 percent). Members of the other ethnic and racial groups together constituted one-tenth (10.6 percent) of the city's residents and will not be included in the discussion that follows.[30]

French-Canadian households were larger than those of the other, most populous groups of Lewiston. French Canadians had larger nuclear families. In addition, while they did not extend their households with kin to the same degree as the Irish or Americans, a greater proportion of them took in boarders, the majority of whom (59.3 percent) were women. The nine-member household headed by Onesime Pepin serves as an example. In 1880, he and his wife, Octavie, had six children living at home and one boarder, a woman.[31] While economic need probably underlay the practice of French Canadians to extend their households with boarders and kin, religious and cultural explanations likely account for the larger size of their nuclear families.

In fact, data from the 1880 census points particularly to cultural practice. The data suggests, for example, that French-Canadian children married at a younger age than Irish or American children. Religious practice, then, did not solely account for the larger size of French-Canadian families, for Irish Catholics in Lewiston likely heeded the same religious teachings against limiting family size. Instead, the cultural practice of marrying at a younger age than Lewiston's other ethnic groups, hence increasing the potential years of reproduction, better accounts for the larger size of French-Canadian families in 1880. This cultural practice had its origins in Québec. Historian Bettina Bradbury has found, for example, that French-Canadian men and women from Montréal tended to marry at a younger age than Irish Catholics for much of the second half of the nineteenth century.[32]

Lewiston in 1880 was predominantly working-class. Over 80 percent of the male and female workers from each ethnic group held blue-collar jobs. Although primarily working-class, American men and women enjoyed a greater variety of occupations, and they were far less tied to industrial work than Lewiston's other ethnic groups (see table 1). As a visiting woman religious observed, textile mills employed most of Lewiston's Catholics, ringing a bell at 4:30 each morning to wake them and ringing it again at 5:45 A.M. to announce that only fifteen minutes remained before the start of their twelve-hour work day.[33] Less tied to mill work, Americans had higher socioeconomic standing in Lewiston in 1880.

Table 1. Occupational Distribution of Lewiston's Ethnic Groups in 1880 (in percentages)[a]

	AMERICAN	IRISH	FRENCH-CANADIAN	ALL OTHER
Men (*N* = 241)				
WHITE COLLAR				
Self-governing professional	3.6%	0%	0%	0%
Salaried professional	0	0	1.5	0
Small business and managerial	1.8	0	0	0
Semiprofessional	0.9	0	0	0
Clerical and sales	11.6	2.4	3.0	9.5
BLUE COLLAR				
Self-employed	0.9	0	0	0
Nonindustrial	26.8	7.1	4.5	19.0
Industrial	42.9	90.5	87.9	71.4
Primary sector	11.6	0	1.5	0
Unknown	0	0	1.5	0
NUMBER	112	42	66	21
Women (*N* = 148)				
WHITE COLLAR				
Self-governing professional	0%	0%	0%	0%
Salaried professional	9.6	0	0	0
Small business and managerial	0	0	0	0
Semiprofessional	0	0	0	0
Clerical and sales	1.9	0	0	5.9
BLUE COLLAR				
Self-employed	0	0	0	0
Nonindustrial	21.2	20.6	2.2	1.8
Industrial	67.3	79.4	97.8	82.4
Primary sector	0	0	0	0
NUMBER	52	34	45	17

Source: Derived from every twentieth household in the U.S. Census, 1880.
a. Columns may not add up to 100.0 percent on account of rounding.

In that year, only a small proportion of married women worked. But the proportions differed by ethnic group. Over one-fourth (27.3 percent) of the Irish wives worked outside of the home, compared to over one-tenth (11.9 percent) of the American and under one-tenth (8.1 percent) of the French-Canadian wives. Most married women, then, did not serve as secondary wage earners in Lewiston's families in 1880. Because American men held Lewiston's better jobs, most of their spouses probably did not need to supplement their wages. That was not the case in the Irish and French-Canadian households. Ethnicity, though, differentiated the ways in which these women contributed to their family's economy: Irish wives tended to work outside of the home more often than francophone women, and the latter more often took in boarders than their Irish counterparts. This was Octavie Pepin's situation. "Keeping house" was her occupation, and the boarder residing in her home brought additional income to her family. In brief, the low incidence of married women working outside of the home was not a phenomenon relegated to Lewiston's middle class during the second half of the nineteenth century.[34] It did, however, necessitate other strategies to supplement the income the men brought to Irish and French-Canadian families.

One strategy was to have children work. Over one-third of the Irish and French-Canadian household heads (35.5 and 39.4 percent, respectively) had working single children under the age of twenty-one. This was the case in under one-seventh (13.0 percent) of the households headed by Americans. Francophone working children, all Canadian-born, made up the largest proportion (44.9 percent) of Lewiston's work force between the ages of ten and twenty, inclusive. These children were part of a labor migration to the United States. Census data reveals that sixty (60.6) percent of Lewiston's French-Canadian households in 1880 had arrived in the United States with children. In fact, all six children living with Onesime and Octavie Pepin in 1880 had been born in Québec; the oldest five—two sons, ages eighteen and twenty-three, and three daughters, ages eleven to fourteen—all worked in cotton mills.[35] For French Canadians, as for the Irish, child labor served as a family strategy to ensure survival.

Because so many French-Canadian and Irish children needed to contribute to their family economies, they did not have the same opportunity for education as American children. While nearly two-thirds (65.0 percent) of the individuals who attended school during 1879–1880 were

Americans, one-tenth (9.5 percent) were French Canadians, and one-sixth (16.8 percent) were Irish. These ratios reflect that American children attended school in excess of their ethnic group's proportion of the city's total population, unlike the underrepresented French Canadians. The percentage of Irish school children matched the group's proportion of the total population, probably because Irish wives served as secondary wage earners in far more cases than French-Canadian wives. But other evidence reveals limits to the educational opportunity of Irish children. When census takers came around in 1880, only Americans had children over the age of seventeen who had attended school during the previous twelve months. Among the Irish children who had gone to school, there were no boys over age eleven and no girls over fifteen; similarly, among French Canadians, no boys over age thirteen and no girls over fourteen had attended school. In the Pepin family, only the ten-year-old son, Edmond, had attended school during the census year; none of the older children had.[36] In addition to economic need, religion and ethnicity account for these differing patterns of school attendance. Sending children to public schools, where they would not receive religious instruction, was not an attractive option for Irish and French-Canadian Catholics. Religious and ethnic (particularly language) considerations led French-Canadians to found their own parish elementary school in 1878; the Irish followed suit, establishing one of their own in 1881.

One-fifth (19.7 percent) of Lewiston's population aged ten and above were illiterate in 1880.[37] Unsurprisingly, the French Canadians and the Irish constituted most of the persons lacking literacy skills in that year. Over 60 percent (61.1) of the men who could not read and/or could not write were French-Canadian, 25 percent (25.9) were Irish, and 2 percent (1.9) were American. In each of these ethnic groups, women outnumbered men who could not read and/or could not write. Onesime and Octavie Pepin were an exception, for the census taker recorded that Onesime could neither read nor write, while Octavie could do both. Nonetheless, among women lacking literacy skills, half (50.6 percent) were French-Canadian, while close to one-third (30.4 percent) were Irish, and only a small proportion (6.3 percent) were American. Premigration experience in part explains why French Canadians made up the majority of Lewiston residents lacking literacy skills in 1880, for the Province of Québec had no compulsory education laws before

1942, and students in the nineteenth century frequently left school around the age of ten or eleven, following their first communion.[38]

French Canadians were also more prone to unemployment than Lewiston's other large ethnic groups. Exactly half (50.0 percent) of the French-Canadian working men in the city had experienced unemployment at some point during the twelve-month period from June 1, 1879, to May 31, 1880. Among these men were Onesime Pepin, a laborer, and his son Ludger, a cotton mill worker; they had been out of work for nine and two months, respectively, during this one-year period. Over one-third (38.1 percent) of the Irish and under one-sixth (15.0 percent) of the American working men had bouts of unemployment during the same year. These figures point to a labor queue among men, and it existed among working women as well. French-Canadian women had the greatest incidence of unemployment (28.9 percent), followed by the Irish (23.5 percent) and the American (13.5 percent) women. Each of the three Pepin daughters had herself been out of work from two to nine months during the previous year.[39] While Lewiston's working women had generally experienced less unemployment than men of the same ethnic heritage, they too had been subject to a labor queue in which ethnic groups—in reverse order of their arrival in Lewiston—had endured the most frequent incidence of unemployment.

Census takers did not record more instances of illness or disability among any particular ethnic group on the day of their visit in 1880. Between 2 and 3 percent each of the Irish, French-Canadian, and American residents of Lewiston were maimed, crippled, bedridden, otherwise disabled, or ill when enumerators came around. Thus, general health did not appear to differ by ethnic group. This finding stands in contrast to the annual reports that the city physician filed during the 1870s. He argued that poor-quality housing, inadequate ventilation, overcrowding, and unemployment had led to illness and death among the city's Irish and French-Canadian residents. In 1878, he pointed out a correlation between consumption and factory work. As occupational data from the 1880 census reveals, Lewiston's Irish and French-Canadians were the most heavily represented in the city's factories.[40] The poverty of these ethnic groups led to the health concerns the city physician expressed in his yearly reports.

Ethnicity led to social segregation in Lewiston, as the choice of marriage partners demonstrates. The census reveals that 98.6 percent of American household heads had American wives, 94.7 percent of the Irish heads had Irish wives, and 100.0 percent of French-Canadian heads had wives of Canadian descent, presumably of French-Canadian heritage. Because the 1880 census does not indicate whether enumerated Canadians were English or French speakers, and because it does not provide the maiden names of spouses, one cannot know with certainty that all wives were French-Canadian. But other evidence confirms that there was little exogamy among Lewiston's French-Canadian population. In 1880, 92.6 percent of the marriages celebrated at Saint-Pierre Church were between *Canadiens*. The others were mixed marriages. Perhaps most French Canadians marrying other ethnics in 1880 had their marriages consecrated outside of the city's French Catholic church. None of the marriages that took place at the Irish Catholic church in that year involved French Canadians, however. Data compiled from a marriage index at the Lewiston City Clerk's office, which may be incomplete because Maine did not require marriage licenses before 1892, reveals that 85.7 percent of French Canadians married a spouse of the same ethnicity in 1880. By comparison, French Canadians in Fall River, Massachusetts, exhibited the same rate of intermarriage (14 percent) in that year. While confirming a high rate of endogamy among French Canadians, the marriage records of Saint-Pierre Church and the city of Lewiston also suggest that a small number of the city's French Canadians—divided nearly evenly between men and women—engaged in mixed marriages once in the United States.[41]

During the 1880s and 1890s, French Canadians continued to build their ethnic community in Lewiston. Unlike the immigrants who had arrived in the 1860s and 1870s, the new immigrants transformed their surroundings so that Lewiston no longer was a Protestant mill town. As data from the 1880 census reveals, French Canadians in the Spindle City were at the bottom of the city's social and economic pyramid. Joining U.S. society became the strategy by which to improve the position of the group; for French Canadians in Lewiston in the late nineteenth century, ethnic preservation and acculturation proved not to be dichotomous goals.[42]

❧

The Rooster Crows

French Canadians Become Naturalized Citizens and Democratic Voters, 1880–1900

In 1884, the *Lewiston Evening Journal* proclaimed the victory of the Republican candidate for mayor by featuring a crowing rooster at the top of its election report. French Canadians of Lewiston complained during that election of Republican dirty tactics, and *Le Messager* warned: "Change tactics, Republican sirs, or otherwise it is quite likely that the *Journal* will not have occasion for a while to place a rooster at the head of its columns, because we will be 500 voters next year."[1] Guided by Dominican priests and other local elites, Lewiston's French-Canadian immigrants became naturalized citizens and voters in the late nineteenth century. These *Canadiens* demonstrated their agency as they joined the host society and as they evolved into Democratic partisans by the start of the twentieth century.

Through their newspaper, Lewiston's francophone elites staunchly defended the interests of French-Canadian immigrants in the United States. Founded in 1880 by Dr. Louis J. Martel, a native of Saint-Hyacinthe whom Reverend Pierre Hévey had invited to Lewiston to practice medicine, *Le Messager* reached 500 subscribers during its first month of publication. It appeared twice weekly in 1891 and had 3,000 subscriptions by the turn of century. The French-language newspaper's motto made clear its chief concerns: "Religion and Nationality." Thus it served as an instrument for elites to perpetuate the three pillars of *survivance*, or ethnic preservation: the French language, the Roman Catholic faith, and French-Canadian traditions.[2]

During the first year of publication, editor J. D. Montmarquet wrote numerous columns to support the decision that tens of thousands of Québec residents had made to emigrate to the United States. He often deflected criticism from nationalist clergymen and journalists in Québec who considered those depopulating the province traitors and "rabble." Montmarquet took issue with suggestions that French Canadians should colonize new lands in northern Québec or western Canada, rather than emigrate to the United States, because doing so required capital that few had. He complained that the Canadian government spent large sums of money to encourage immigration, particularly of people of English and Scotch ancestry, but did little to help the *Canadiens* who lived in poverty. Emigration, he claimed, was the only logical choice for scores of French Canadians.[3]

Through his columns, Montmarquet dismissed the arguments of French-Canadian nationalists that emigration to the United States threatened *survivance*. Given the lack of opportunity in Québec, he contended that there was little possibility that francophone Canadians would return permanently to their native land. Consequently, Montmarquet wrote editorials to promote naturalization, arguing that by gaining the right to vote, French Canadians could exercise influence in their adopted country. In response to charges from Québec that the *Canadiens* would lose their language, religion, and ethnic identity as a result of taking the oath of allegiance to the United States, Montmarquet insisted: "No naturalization law requires us to sacrifice our national character, and no law of the United States demands that of us." Countering arguments that French-speaking immigrants would lose their language in the United States, *Le Messager*'s editor maintained that the same danger existed in Canada. He pointed to complaints by the Québec press that English was the language of legislative bodies, businesses, and passenger trains north of the border. Americans posed no greater danger to the language, culture, and traditions of French Canadians, Montmarquet contended, than did English-Canadian groups like the Loyal Orange Lodge or the Young Britons in Canada. Those who naturalized, he asserted, could continue speaking French and preserving their ethnic traditions.[4]

Cultivating the ethnic and political consciousness of Lewiston's franco-phones became the central goal of *Le Messager*'s editor and of other French-Canadian leaders. Six months after *Le Messager*'s founding, when Lewiston had only about one hundred French-Canadian voters, Montmarquet helped organize le Club National, an association designed primarily to promote naturalization, and he became its first president. Like Montmarquet, but unlike most of Lewiston's French-Canadian population in 1880, the other five officers of the organization did not hold industrial jobs. J. E. Cloutier, first vice president of le Club National, was a carpenter. Léon Lefebvre, the second vice president, was the first French Canadian elected to municipal office in Lewiston; a member of the Common Council in 1880, he worked as a carpenter in 1883 and probably had done so in 1880. Among the other members of le Club National, secretary Wilbrod Filiatrault was a clerk, treasurer Magloire Phaneuf a grocer, and Charles Sabourin, the sergeant at arms, operated a boot and shoe business from his home. Open only to men of French-Canadian ancestry, le Club National boasted 150 members by January 1881. Unlike similar clubs that French Canadians had organized in other cities of the northeastern United States, Lewiston's Club National was nonpartisan. This probably reflected Montmarquet's influence, for it was his editorial policy that *Le Messager* favor neither Democrats nor Republicans in national and local political contests.[5] Montmarquet played it safe by adopting a nonpartisan stance, it seems, to avoid creating divisions within Lewiston's francophone community.

In addition to promoting naturalization, le Club National served as a forum to discuss ethnic and social concerns. It debated whether French-Canadian children should be educated in French or English, and whether the *Canadiens* should blend in with Americans or work to preserve their French-Canadian ethnicity. Unfortunately, *Le Messager* did not report on the substance of these deliberations. On occasion, individuals from Lewiston's other ethnic groups attended meetings of le Club National, most likely when the organization considered questions not directly related to French-Canadian identity. For instance, *Le Messager* reported that American and Irish residents of the city came to the January 1881 meeting, at which various members of le Club National played roles (including doctor, lawyer, farmer, journalist, a wealthy individual, and a poor person) to consider which station allowed one to be of greatest service to society.[6] Through its activities, le

Club National served to raise the ethnic and social consciousness of Lewiston's French-Canadian immigrants as they pondered their integration into the host society.

The organization's leader proposed and presided over a statewide convention in Waterville that had the same goals. Organized around Saint-Jean-Baptiste (Saint John the Baptist) Day in June 1881, the first convention of French Canadians and Acadians of Maine considered ways to preserve the ethnic heritage of the state's French speakers as they joined U.S. society. Bishop James Augustin Healy sang mass at the convention and encouraged French-Canadian immigrants to naturalize so that Catholics could gain influence in the country. The bishop strongly recommended that francophone youth receive instruction in English in all subjects other than religion. While the convention's francophone delegates adopted a resolution favoring naturalization, they also pushed for the preservation of the French language. These elites promoted the establishment of French Catholic schools to help children maintain their French, and they called upon francophones throughout the state to speak French in their parishes, schools, societies, and homes. Resolving that the interests of Maine's French-speaking population did not rest with either the Democratic or Republican parties in particular, they maintained political neutrality and urged francophone voters to exercise their conscience at the polls.[7] Under the leadership of the president of le Club National, the Waterville convention gave statewide voice to many of the club's concerns. In Lewiston, the organization received a significant boost from the Dominican priests who arrived in the fall of 1881.

Anticlerical measures of the French government, such as forbidding members of religious orders from living together in communities, motivated the Dominicans to emigrate to North America. They especially wanted to serve in the United States. But, after considering calls from the archbishop of New Orleans, Louisiana, and the bishop of Saint-Hyacinthe, Québec, the Dominicans chose Saint-Hyacinthe as their North American base in 1873, believing it offered greater potential to furnish recruits to the order. As we shall see, the Dominicans' decision to locate in Québec had considerable impact on the preservation of French-Canadian ethnicity in Lewiston. Once established in Québec, the Dominicans looked for missions in the United States. When Catholic prelates in Boston and Providence did not accept their offers to serve, they approached Maine's bishop.[8]

Financial considerations and finesse on the part of Bishop Healy and the Dominicans led Pierre Hévey to resign as pastor of Saint-Pierre (Saint Peter) Parish during the fall of 1881. Hévey's unorthodox financial arrangements had worried the bishop since the latter's appointment in Maine. The French-Canadian pastor had financed construction of Saint-Pierre Church by organizing "a Savings Bank in which he was allowed to use all but 10 per cent of the deposits," reported the *Lewiston Journal* in 1873. Established with the approval of Maine's first bishop, David Bacon, Hévey's savings bank raised over $100,000 for church projects from 1872 until his departure. After meeting with Hévey in 1875, bishop-elect Healy recorded his concerns that Lewiston's "Canadian Church" had $40,000 of debt, and that "the priest has also received deposits from Canadians— This may at any time prove to be a strange & startling embarrasment [*sic*]." Six years later, Healy's concerns apparently materialized. According to Dominican sources reportedly originating from Hévey himself, and for reasons that went unrecorded, Saint-Pierre parishioners withdrew their savings from the pastor's bank in 1881, leaving him $22,000 in debt. When the Dominicans approached Healy for an assignment in his diocese in that year, he sent the order's representative to visit Lewiston and Auburn. The Dominican priest called upon Hévey. Recognizing the bishop's intention, Hévey subsequently negotiated the terms of his resignation with the prelate and the Dominicans.[9]

Given the tenuous situation the Dominicans had faced in France, they were sensitive to religious and political issues in the United States after they arrived in Maine. As forced emigrants, the French Dominicans were acutely conscious of American hostility toward Catholic immigrants. Consequently, they did not wear their robes outside of the church and monastery of Lewiston, as they had in Europe and Canada, but instead dressed in laymen's clothing when appearing in public. At the Saint-Jean-Baptiste Day picnic in 1885, the Dominican provincial, who had traveled from Saint-Hyacinthe to Lewiston for the occasion, spoke of the unease he felt as a foreigner in the United States. He expressed discomfort at appearing in public without his habit, and he underscored the irony that the United States, a nation that claimed to value religious liberty, showed little tolerance for different religious traditions. The Dominicans attributed this climate of intolerance to New England's Puritan roots.[10] It undoubtedly motivated them to help

Lewiston's French-speaking Catholics solidify their ethnic network as they sought to gain influence in the city.

A year after arriving in Lewiston, the Dominicans opened a multilevel, utilitarian structure, called the Dominican Block, which provided space for businesses on the ground floor, classrooms on the middle floors, and an assembly room on the top floor. Upon hearing plans for the proposed structure, the *Lewiston Journal* likened it to a "French city building" or, according to *Le Messager*'s interpretation of the remark, a "City Hall *Canadien.*" As anglophones suspected, the building became the center of French-Canadian activity in Lewiston. For example, le Club National held meetings, and school children and the French-language societies put on musical and dramatic productions there.[11] The structure functioned as a space in which the Dominicans could develop further the ethnic network Hévey had begun, while simultaneously promoting the acculturation of French Canadians.

The Dominicans facilitated the development of ethnic networks in Lewiston by establishing additional associations for their French-Canadian parishioners. In 1886, a Dominican priest founded l'Association Saint-Dominique (the Saint Dominic Association) for young men, in order to keep them occupied "usefully and honestly." To channel constructively the intellectual and physical energy of its members, l'Association set up a library and gym by 1892, and it formed a baseball team in 1896. In 1888, the organist of Saint-Pierre Parish organized a musical association for young boys, known as la fanfare Sainte-Cécile (the Saint Cecilia band), that offered concerts and participated in parades. The Dominicans founded la Ligue Catholique (the Catholic League), a religious society for married men, in 1897. Parish women also had their own associations. They included the religious society les Dames de Sainte-Anne (the Ladies of Saint Anne), created for married and widowed women in 1888, and an auxiliary of l'Union Saint-Joseph (the Saint Joseph Union), established in 1899. Although a mutual-benefit society, the latter had religious and ethnic goals: "Their principal goal is the maintenance of religious practices and the French language in their families."[12] These societies, for which the Dominicans served as directors or chaplains, expanded the ethnic network of Lewiston's francophones in the late nineteenth century.

The parish schools the Dominicans oversaw helped French Canadians to preserve their native tongue and to learn the language of the host society.

Before emigrating to North America, several Dominicans had traveled to England to learn English; once in the United States, they continued to take language lessons. They similarly wanted parishioners to develop a facility in English, so they promoted its teaching in the parish schools. When the Dominicans started a night school program in 1883 for working children who could not read or write, they designated English as the language of instruction in a couple of classes. Because there were not enough Soeurs Grises (Grey Nuns) to educate the growing number of schoolchildren, the Dominicans brought les Petits Frères de Marie from France to teach the boys of the parish in 1886. Since many of the Marist brothers had received their education in England, they could teach their students in English and French. As girls and boys gained competency in English, they participated in dramatic and musical productions in both English and French at the *séances* (performances) organized at the end of the school year; they also answered exam questions in both languages, something which drew the praise of *Le Messager*. In February 1890, Bishop Healy sent the Dominicans a school program calling for more instruction in English, and they decided to adopt it. The pastor immediately traveled to Canada to search for additional sisters and brothers who could teach well in English. After finding some new educators, the Dominicans divided instruction in the parish schools, probably equally, between English and French.[13]

To continue this bilingual education, the Dominicans brought les Dames de Sion (the Ladies of Zion) of France to the local area in 1892. These sisters staffed the school the Dominicans opened for francophone youth in Auburn, and they replaced the French-Canadian Soeurs Grises who wished to concentrate their efforts on charitable works. Additional Dames de Sion took over for the departing Marist brothers in 1893. This French order had houses in England, enabling it to provide sisters to the Lewiston-Auburn area who could teach in English.[14] Assisted particularly by religious orders from France in the late nineteenth century, the Dominicans encouraged both the preservation of French and the adoption of English-language skills, the latter facilitating entrance into U.S. society.

Until the end of World War II, clergymen and journalists wrote the history of French-Canadian descendants in the United States, and they consistently emphasized *survivance* as the dominant theme of their migration experience.[15] The history of Lewiston's francophone community reveals the surprising finding that joining the host society was of tantamount importance. In fact, French-Canadian descendants viewed entrance into U.S. society and ethnic preservation as compatible objectives. In Lewiston, French Canadians who wished to plant roots in their country of adoption found their French-Canadian leaders and the French Dominican priests willing to assist.

Politics keenly interested the Dominicans during the 1880s and 1890s. From time to time, they made brief comments and inserted French- and English-language newspaper articles about them into their monastery's chronicle. When Maine resident and Republican presidential candidate James G. Blaine made a campaign stop in Lewiston in 1884, three Dominicans attended the reception, and one took the opportunity to shake his hand.[16]

But the Dominicans were not merely observers of politics. They encouraged and assisted French Canadians in becoming U.S. citizens so that these immigrants could gain influence in the host society. In February 1882, five months after his arrival in Lewiston, Pastor Alexandre-Louis Mothon attended a meeting of le Club National to urge the men of the parish to naturalize "in the interest of their situation and of their influence in the United States." To set an example, he and another priest took out papers to declare their intention to become U.S. citizens. The basic requirement for citizenship was that male immigrants had to have lived in the United States for five years; women did not naturalize on their own, but acquired derivative citizenship from either their fathers (if they were minors) or their husbands. Prior to a local election in 1883, the Dominicans met with French-Canadian leaders J. D. Montmarquet, J. E. Cloutier, Stanislas Marcous, L. J. Martel, F. X. Belleau, P. X. Angers, and William Sabourin; as we shall see, each of these men was politically active in the late nineteenth century, and five of them gained an elected or appointed office in the Lewiston city government in 1883. The Dominicans worked closely with le Club National in its naturalization campaign. At mass one Sunday, Mothon invited parishioners to attend a meeting of the organization at which he and other French-Canadian leaders made a strong pitch for naturalization. The Dominicans gave le Club National access to the parish lists and even paid some of the court costs of parishioners who filed naturalization papers. As a result of the concerted efforts of the Dominicans and le Club National, nearly eighty parishioners naturalized in time for the spring 1883 election.[17]

Their efforts did not go unnoticed by Republicans who held political power. Entries in the chronicle of the Dominicans indicate that over fifty French Canadians had traveled from Lewiston to Portland to naturalize in 1883. This was an unusual development: No French Canadians from the Spindle City had ever taken out final naturalization papers in Portland before that year. In fact, naturalization records reveal that only the municipal court of Lewiston and the Supreme Judicial Court in Auburn had granted final papers to Lewiston's francophones in 1882 and prior years. Why, then, would French Canadians travel thirty miles by train to Portland in 1883, when two local courts could have processed their papers? *Le Messager* explained. Republicans controlled local politics, and they worried that French-Canadian voters would help Democrats remove them from office. To avoid pressure from Republicans, French Canadians chose to travel to Portland to process their naturalization papers. That way, they did not have to have Republicans accept their witnesses and administer their oaths, and they felt more at liberty to vote their conscience, according to *Le Messager*.[18] In short, these French Canadians wished to acquire U.S. citizenship under circumstances with which they felt comfortable.

Lewiston's francophones continued periodically to use the courts of Portland after 1883. At times, they had little choice. In January 1884, *Le Messager* complained of unspecified irritations by the municipal court judge that forced French Canadians to go to the federal court in Portland to process their naturalization papers. Around 1893, the Republican-controlled state legislature passed a law denying municipal court judges the authority to naturalize foreign nationals, relegating this responsibility to superior court judges. Because these state court judges did not have the time to process naturalizations, assigning them the task was a Republican strategy to hinder citizenship acquisition, contended *Le Messager*. When over one hundred French Canadians were ready to naturalize at the state court in Auburn prior to the spring 1894 elections, the judge "simply refused to mix them [into the schedule]," and they had to travel to the federal court in Portland. *Le Messager* charged that the judge's action represented a ploy by Republicans to retain power: "They have tried all means to make us vote with them, and seeing that they could not succeed, they took this step to attain their goal." As a result, only one of Lewiston's French Canadians naturalized in Auburn in 1894; eighty-one others obtained their final naturalization papers

in Portland. In all, over one-fifth (21.3 percent) of the Lewiston French Canadians who naturalized in the 1880s and 1890s traveled to Portland to
gain their U.S. citizenship.[19] Entrée into U.S. society sometimes exacted a
price in inconvenience.

Yankees had reason to worry about the political weight of naturalized
French Canadians. Specifically, the records reveal that only two of the city's
French Canadians had naturalized prior to 1880, whereas naturalizations
exceeded five hundred during the 1880s, and they surpassed six hundred
in the 1890s. The absolute number of naturalizations demonstrates the increasing stability of Lewiston's French-speaking population from the 1880s
onward.[20] These figures attest to the willingness of French Canadians to
naturalize, and to the considerable efforts of the Dominicans and local elites
in providing them with information and practical assistance to overcome
political and other impediments to citizenship. Among other activities, le
Club National organized fundraisers to help francophones pay the court
costs associated with naturalization. French-Canadian attorneys like F. X.
Belleau and P. X. Angers (the first a Democrat and the second a Democrat
turned Republican) helped French speakers process their paperwork prior
to their court appearances, and these attorneys also assisted francophones at
the courthouse. When Maine changed its constitution to require that candidates for naturalization demonstrate the ability to read the U.S. Constitution
in English beginning in 1893, *Le Messager* alerted readers to this obstacle
and encouraged them to naturalize before the law went into effect; in 1892,
228 of Lewiston's French Canadians took out final naturalization papers, a
figure unsurpassed in any other year in the nineteenth century. In fact, naturalizations did not hit triple-digit figures again in the 1890s, likely due both
to challenging economic times and to the English-language requirement,
which excluded unilingual francophones.[21] Despite the obstacles, Lewiston's
French speakers acquired U.S. citizenship in significant numbers in the late
nineteenth century, dramatically increasing the number of French-Canadian
voters in the Spindle City.

Naturalization records provide us with a collective portrait of the
francophone men who became eligible to vote. Eighty (80.3) percent of the
French Canadians who naturalized in Lewiston from the 1870s through the
1890s had arrived in the United States under the age of eighteen. This large
percentage illustrates that most of those who embraced U.S. citizenship had

spent a portion of their formative years in their adopted land, presumably developing ties to the United States that made remaining permanently much more conceivable to them than it did to adult immigrants. Most of the men who naturalized in the late nineteenth century appear to have come to the United States as part of a child-labor migration, for over sixty (62.9) percent had arrived in the United States between the ages of ten and seventeen, inclusive.[22] Both the lack of opportunity in Québec and the jobs that the textile mills and shoe shops of Lewiston and Auburn provided these young immigrants must have motivated them to shed their British citizenship.

Proximity, then, may actually provide a major reason why French Canadians became U.S. citizens. Historian Elliott Robert Barkan has argued that the proximity of French-Canadian immigrants to their homeland explains why they have demonstrated greater reluctance than non–North Americans to become naturalized citizens and to assimilate into U.S. society. But nearness to Québec helped French Canadians in New England to keep abreast of the economic conditions in their homeland and may actually have encouraged their assimilation, Gerard Blazon contends.[23] The "proximity thesis" Barkan espouses therefore cuts two ways. The lack of opportunity in Québec, which precipitated mass migration in the 1880s and 1890s, and the availability of jobs in the industrial center of Maine made it much more likely for French Canadians who had emigrated to the United States at a young age to naturalize in the late nineteenth century.

U.S. legal requirements also help explain why those who had crossed the international border under eighteen made up the lion's share of naturalizers. In short, the process of gaining U.S. citizenship was easier for them: If they met the five-year residency requirement, they could take out (final) naturalization papers after reaching their twenty-first birthday. They did not have to go through the two-step process of declaring their intention to become a U.S. citizen and then filing their final naturalization papers at least two years later, the process required of other individuals.[24] In 1889, an English-language newspaper indicated that the two-year wait between filing first and final papers hindered the naturalization of French Canadians because it caused them to lose interest in pursuing U.S. citizenship. "As a consequence," it reported, "it is chiefly the young people who become citizens." Because naturalization requirements were less stringent for those who had entered the United States under the age of eighteen, and since they were more likely than older French Canadians to know English (an important consideration after 1892), it is possible that French-Canadian leaders seeking to expand their political armies prior to municipal elections each spring targeted the young in their naturalization drives. In fact, over three-fourths (77.2 percent) of the French-Canadian men who became U.S. citizens from the 1870s through the 1890s were thirty years of age or younger.[25] For the ethnic group with the least power in Lewiston, political expediency may have dictated pursuing young voters.

French-Canadian men did not wait particularly long to become citizens. Francois Ouellette, for instance, migrated to the United States at age fifteen, and he naturalized at twenty-two, one year after reaching the age of eligibility. Like him, over ninety (92.8) percent of those who had crossed the border under the age of eighteen naturalized within the first ten years of eligibility, that is, within ten years of their twenty-first birthday. Those who had entered the United States at age eighteen or older were a little slower to become U.S. citizens, yet over 80 percent of them (84.2) naturalized within the first ten years of eligibility. Isidore Morin, for example, had arrived in the United States at age forty-seven, and he naturalized fourteen years later; given the five-year residency requirement, he became a U.S. citizen within nine years of eligibility.[26] While we do not have figures on the proportion of Lewiston's French-Canadian immigrants who became U.S. citizens, the nineteenth-century naturalization data does challenge longstanding impressions, stemming from oft-made allegations, that French Canadians were especially slow about gaining citizenship.

Once French Canadians obtained U.S. citizenship, few gave it up. Letters loosely inserted into the bound volumes of naturalization records reveal that only five of the 1,188 francophones from Lewiston who naturalized through 1899 later repatriated in Canada. All were men in their seventies who relinquished their U.S. citizenship about fifty years after acquiring it. Geographer Ralph Dominic Vicero has estimated that about half of the French Canadians who had emigrated to the United States in the nineteenth century later returned to Canada.[27] Quite unlike them, the preponderance of the French Canadians of Lewiston who became U.S. citizens in the late 1800s made a conscious decision to modify permanently their ethnic identity.

Scholars have long assumed that the process of Americanization reduces intergroup competition and conflict. On the contrary, argues sociologist

Susan Olzak, integration into U.S. society leads to ethnic competition, which in turn leads to ethnic conflict. This study corroborates her argument. As Lewiston's French-Canadian men sought political citizenship by becoming naturalized citizens and voters, ethnic tensions increased in the Spindle City. When they demanded a share of influence, ethnic competition and conflict resulted.[28] As we will see, the experience of French Canadians in Lewiston demonstrates that, contrary to prevalent views, an ethnic group's political participation in U.S. society serves not to mitigate ethnic competition and conflict, but to accentuate them.

The 1883 Lewiston municipal election served as the opening round of the political battles that took place between French Canadians and Yankees. The election results gave the city's francophones a huge boost. Six of them won local office as members of the city's Common Council, the school commission, and the voter registration bureau. Their election doubled the number of French Canadians who had won office in the previous year. The six officials held some of Lewiston's better jobs. J. D. Montmarquet was editor and proprietor of *Le Messager*, J. E. Cloutier was a carpenter, Arthur Reny was a bookkeeper, and the others were businessmen: J. N. L'Heureux sold books and stationery supplies, and Stanislas Marcous and Frank Pelletier sold groceries. Two French Canadians gained appointments (made by the mayor with the approval of the Board of Aldermen and Common Council) as city physician and council secretary. The two appointed officials were professionals: L. J. Martel was a physician and F. X. Belleau an attorney. Most, if not all eight, of the elected or appointed French-Canadian officials had played an active role in promoting naturalization in Lewiston in 1883. Montmarquet and Cloutier were founding officers of le Club National, while L'Heureux, Marcous, Martel, and Belleau had each traveled to Portland to serve as witnesses to a number of Lewiston francophones who had naturalized there prior to the spring election; if Pelletier and Reny had played a role in promoting naturalization in Lewiston, it was a less prominent role than the other six French Canadians. Significantly, each of the eight elected and appointed French-Canadian officials was a Democrat. According to the Dominicans, French-Canadian votes in the 1883 election tipped the political balance in Lewiston toward the Democrats, helping them to dislodge the Republican administration that had presided over the city for the previous five years. Thus the fears of Yankee Republicans had been borne out.

Reflecting increasing confidence as well as a measure of partisanship, *Le Messager* claimed that Lewiston's Republicans had paid the price for treating the French-speaking population with indifference, and it warned them that greater numbers of French Canadians would vote in the future.[29]

Le Messager also seized the opportunity to rebut formally the accusations of Carroll Wright, the Massachusetts Commissioner of the Bureau of Statistics of Labor. Wright had provoked French Canadians throughout New England in 1881 by criticizing them for not establishing permanent ties to the United States. Wright had written:

> With some exceptions the Canadian French are the Chinese of the Eastern States. They care nothing for our institutions, civil, political, or educational. They do not come to make a home among us, to dwell with us as citizens, and so become a part of us; but their purpose is merely to sojourn a few years as aliens, touching us only at a single point, that of work, and, when they have gathered out of us what will satisfy their ends, to get them away to whence they came, and bestow it there. They are a horde of industrial invaders, not a stream of stable settlers. Voting with all that it implies, they care nothing about. Rarely does one of them become naturalized. They will not send their children to school if they can help it, but endeavor to crowd them into the mills at the earliest possible age.

Data on Lewiston compiled from the 1880 federal census and from nineteenth-century naturalization records demonstrates the accuracy of some of Wright's criticisms; yet even as he wrote his famous polemic, French Canadians in Lewiston and other cities had made it out of date. They had already taken steps to form stable communities in the northeastern United States. Not surprisingly, they reacted angrily to Wright's charges. Delegates to the June 1881 convention in Waterville adopted a formal resolution protesting against "the insults" Wright had heaped upon francophones of the Northeast. That fall, both the founder and the editor of *Le Messager* joined approximately thirty French-Canadian delegates from throughout New England at meetings in Boston to counter Wright's charges. Still smarting from Wright's criticisms in 1883, *Le Messager*'s postelection headline proclaimed: "This is what the Chinese of the East can do, when they are goaded!"[30]

Religion intersected with politics in 1883, when francophone Catholics sought resources from the Lewiston city government. In December, *Le Messager* complained bitterly that the municipal government chose not to pay for the night school the Dominicans were organizing. It reported that a local officeholder who headed a large financial institution had voiced concerns that educating French Canadians would cultivate political adversaries. *Le Messager* viewed his remarks and the city's denial of funding as part of a national trend of anti-immigrant hostility, and it directed its anger at both the Republican and Democratic parties for not supporting the school that nine hundred French Canadians had indicated an interest in attending. "The beaver is the symbol of our nationality, and we know how tenacious and persevering this animal is," wrote *Le Messager*, and it further warned: "We want what we are due, and be assured we will get it." That December, the monthly meeting of le Club National attracted five hundred people, including Irish politicians who wanted to unite Irish and French-Canadian voters.[31]

Two months later, Lewiston's Board of Aldermen apparently divided over religious lines as it debated whether or not to allow the Dominicans free use of the city hall for a bazaar to raise the funds they needed to finance the evening school.[32] In the end, the Dominicans won on this issue. They soon recognized that the interests of Catholics in Lewiston depended largely upon Democratic victories, something they acknowledged in their chronicle after the spring 1884 election.[33]

During that election, Lewiston's French-Canadian voters overwhelmingly supported Democratic candidates. Several prominent *Canadiens* voted with the Democratic Party for the first time, *Le Messager* reported, and in the end, Republicans mustered only ten of the three hundred French-Canadian votes. The newspaper also announced that all five French Canadians vying for positions on the Common Council and School Committee had won office. This election proved to be a turning point, bringing political battle lines into sharper focus for much of the French-speaking population. As *Le Messager* saw it, Republicans had treated French-Canadian residents with condescension and had insulted them, both by calling them "foreigners" and by trying to buy their votes; moreover, Republicans had opposed granting the Dominicans free use of the city hall. The Democrats, however, had treated the French-Canadian population more kindly because they wanted its votes, indicated the French-language newspaper. Although a Republican won the mayor's race, something the *Lewiston Journal* touted by placing a crowing rooster at the head of its election report, Democrats retained a majority of seats on the Board of Aldermen. After the election, *Le Messager* taunted Republicans and their mouthpiece with its prediction that French-Canadian voters would number five hundred in the following year, and that the *Journal* would not have reason to celebrate with a crowing rooster atop its election reports.[34]

Not surprisingly, *Le Messager* became a Democratic newspaper. Its founding editor resigned in November 1883, and under new editorial direction, the newspaper evolved into a Democratic publication during the 1884 presidential campaign. In June, *Le Messager* published a complimentary piece on Republican presidential candidate James G. Blaine, but did not endorse him. The following week, the newspaper claimed to be independent and counseled French Canadians to vote according to the merits of the political parties. In August, *Le Messager* abruptly changed course, publishing several articles criticizing Blaine. Besides profiting personally from his support for railroads as Speaker of the House of Representatives, wrote the editor, Blaine had supported the Know-Nothings, he had called French Canadians ignorant, and he had suggested that French-Canadian votes were for sale. Worse, *Le Messager* charged, he represented a political party that was anti-immigrant and anti-Catholic. Following the state elections in September, the newspaper claimed that French-Canadian Republicans prevented political unity among Lewiston's French speakers and were, in fact, "traitors." The newspaper was no longer neutral in its political-party preference. By October, *Le Messager* editorialized in favor of Blaine's Democratic opponent, concluding its piece with the request: "French Canadians, vote all for CLEVELAND and HENDRICKS." On January 1, 1885, *Le Messager* made clear its political-party affiliation, but gave itself some latitude: "In politics we will be Democrats, but independent Democrats." The newspaper indicated that it would support the Democratic Party as long it gave French Canadians a fair share of influence (that is, municipal patronage) and did not adversely affect their interests.[35] Democratic political partisanship became central to the identity-formation process.

Through the end of the nineteenth century, *Le Messager* worked to unite Lewiston's French speakers behind the Democratic Party. The newspaper encountered a number of obstacles. Influential French-Canadian Republicans were a significant one. French-Canadian attorneys were probably the motivating force behind the francophone Republicans. In 1895, two of Lewiston's three French-Canadian lawyers were active in the Republican Party; as *Le Messager* noted in the obituary of one of them two years later, P. X. Angers's efforts had served to divide Lewiston's French speakers in the late nineteenth century. In February 1887, French-Canadian Republicans organized an alternative newspaper, *La République* (*The Republic*), because they perceived "in a word, a gap to fill, that of serving the interests of all of our nationality." They also formed a political club called les Gardes Lafayettes (the Lafayette Guards) in 1888. While their newspaper survived only a few years, and their club probably not much longer, their presence and influence did. French-speaking Republicans, however, were few in number. In 1894, *Le Messager* challenged the *Journal*'s account that two hundred French Canadians planned to organize another Republican Club, because it did not believe there were two hundred francophone Republicans in Lewiston. Despite their small number, French-Canadian Republicans maintained a political presence in the Spindle City. During meetings they held at the Dominican Block, they put forward candidates to compete in caucus for the chance to run for office on the Republican ticket. In 1896, four French-Canadian Republicans won city government seats, while only two Democratic *Canadiens* gained local office in an election that returned the incumbent anglophone Republican to the mayoralty. The four French-Canadian Republicans were grocer William Sabourin, who won election to the Board of Aldermen; medical student Azarie Provost and druggist Emérilde Béliveau, who both gained seats on the Common Council; and insurance agent Philippe Lebrun, who became a poll warden. While scolding the *Canadiens* for supporting Republicans in that election, *Le Messager* congratulated Sabourin for winning a seat on the Board of Aldermen, and it expressed its trust that he would work to advance the interests of French Canadians. In complimenting Sabourin, the French-language newspaper proudly noted: "He speaks perfect English."[36] Even though Sabourin stood on the opposite side of the political aisle, *Le Messager* held him up as a model to francophones; French Canadians apparently were proud when one of their members spoke English well. From the limited evidence, we can only infer that francophone Republicans like Sabourin were business and professional men sufficiently proficient in English to find themselves comfortable in an anglophone milieu; perhaps they even depended upon the business of anglophones to make their living. For *Le Messager*, however proud it might be of men like Sabourin, Republicans constituted a political impediment.

The *Lewiston Journal* was perhaps a lesser obstacle. It tried to capitalize on the lack of unity among francophones—and their apparent lack of a French-language Republican newspaper—by offering a column in French beginning in December 1889. Entitled "Les nouvelles canadiennes" ("Canadian news"), the column carried announcements of supposed interest to Lewiston's French-Canadian population, such as birthdays, death notices, church and mill news. But the *Journal* was not interested only in selling copies, for it made its political intentions clear around elections. Prior to the September 1890 elections, for example, it asserted: "Keeping the Republican party in power is to assure to our beautiful and grand republic an era of prosperity without precedent in its history."[37] The French-language column disappeared about one month later.

Yankees in the Maine state legislature posed another obstacle to curbing the growing political power of French-Canadian Democrats. The Republican-dominated legislature passed a law in the early 1890s requiring the creation of local registration boards to revise voting lists. *Le Messager* saw this law as a Republican tactic to reduce the voting strength of francophones, and it offered credible evidence to support its view. Because Republicans made up a majority of the Registration Board's Lewiston members, they did not allow Democrats to collect the names of voters from the different wards of the city in late 1893, and Republican canvassers used the opportunity to intimidate French-Canadian voters. After asking French Canadians whom they had supported during the spring 1893 elections and whom they intended to vote for in the 1894 elections, the canvassers lectured them if they had voted Democratic, urged them to vote Republican, and if they said they would not, threatened that the state legislature would pass a law requiring them to do so in the future! Prior to the spring 1894 municipal elections, *Le Messager* pointed out that a large majority of the 723 names the Registration Board had dropped from the voting lists were Democrats, and it published the names of French Canadians removed from the lists so that they could re-register, typically by showing proof of their U.S. citizenship. Republican tactics did not end there. Republicans kept the Registration Board open only a few days each year to limit the time French Canadians and other ethnic groups could register to vote, and the board further hindered registration by asking francophones impertinent questions that wasted time, complained *Le Messager*. Prior to the spring 1894 elections, the newspaper taunted the Registration Board: "Those poor Republicans, they are so afraid to lose on Monday that they do not want to register voters."[38]

When Democrats lost elections in the 1880s and 1890s, *Le Messager* suggested explanations for the cross-party voting behavior of Lewiston's French-Canadian Democrats. It partly blamed Republican mill agents. U.S. tariff policy probably was of central concern to them, for mills benefited from protectionism. Occasionally, the agents frightened French-Canadian workers into backing Republican candidates. After Republicans won the fall 1888 elections, *Le Messager* charged that mill agents had told employees that "if they voted for the Democratic ticket, they would not be able to earn enough to provide one meal each day to their children." Such talk by one foreman caused a number of working children to return to their homes crying, complained *Le Messager*. In 1892, the newspaper reported that six workers had lost their jobs because they had voted Democratic. Two years later, when six hundred French Canadians voted against Dr. L. J. Martel, causing him to lose his second bid for mayor, *Le Messager* contended that mill agents had frightened workers into thinking that a Democratic administration in Lewiston would have led to salary reductions and to unemployment.[39]

The newspaper offered additional reasons why French-Canadian voters sided against one of their own in 1894. *Le Messager* reported that some French Canadians chose not to join forces with the Irish. Others traded their votes to Republicans for alcohol and for promises of jobs on the police force, thus revealing that French-Canadian votes could at times be bought.[40] Ethnic friction in the Democratic Party and false hopes of patronage impeded *Le Messager*'s efforts to promote Democratic Party unity.

So, it appears, did national character. Unlike when Democrats gained office, French Canadians typically received few of the patronage appointments that Republican administrations doled out, causing *Le Messager* to push Democratic candidates at all levels of government and to chide francophones who supported Republicans. After Republicans won local elections in 1895, *Le Messager* placed an upside-down rooster atop its election reports. When French Canadians again received few of the spoils, the newspaper scolded: "We hope that the lesson will be understood and that in the future we will set aside the petty hatreds which, up to now, have divided us." Here the newspaper hinted that national character sometimes prevented French Canadians from uniting. Later in the year, it explicitly stated that the lack of unity "is a weakness based somewhat upon nationality, one must admit." *Le Messager* felt divisions among French Canadians existed on both sides of the international border and were not particular to those living in the United States. When asking Lewiston's French Canadians to set aside their differences to join forces politically in 1896, it made reference to Honoré Mercier, a nationalist and former premier of Québec who had visited Lewiston several years earlier: "Let us heed the advice of the great Mercier: 'Let us end our fratricidal struggles, let us unite.'"[41] The newspaper hoped that appeal to a nationalist francophone leader from the homeland would help Lewiston's French Canadians to overcome differences that might be rooted in their national character.

Despite the influence of some notable French-speakers, the Republican Party did not attract more than a small proportion of Lewiston's French-Canadian population. In 1892, *Le Messager* estimated that 80 percent of Lewiston's French-Canadian voters were Democrats. This was not the case in all New England communities with large French-Canadian populations.[42] In Lewiston, however, *Le Messager* engaged francophones in a dialectic; through this process, French Canadians perceived their own self-interest and fashioned their political identity in the United States as Democratic Party loyalists.

Thus the ballot box became a center of ethnic competition and conflict in Lewiston in the late nineteenth century. As French Canadians became solidly Democratic voters, they helped Lewiston to evolve into a Democratic Party stronghold in the twentieth century. *Le Messager* continued to promote the Democratic Party in the twentieth century and to publicize the patronage appointments that Franco-Americans gained following Democratic victories in local elections. To acknowledge those victories, the French-language newspaper typically featured at the head of its election report a rooster crowing, "KOKORIKO!!"[43]

Not Foreigners but Americans

French Canadians Negotiate Their Identity in the Spindle City, 1880–1900

On June 24, 1897, the feast day of Saint-Jean-Baptiste (Saint John the Baptist), an estimated two thousand French Canadians paraded through the streets of Lewiston, Maine. Ten bands accompanied them. Flags of France and the United States adorned the city; huge decorated arches curved above its streets. On this day, Lewiston's French speakers also celebrated the twenty-fifth anniversary of their mutual-benefit society, l'Institut Jacques-Cartier (the Jacques Cartier Institute). After attending mass at Saint-Pierre (Saint Peter) Church, three hundred uniformed members of the society marched alongside a replica of the ship Cartier had sailed to the New World. The procession passed through the magnificent evergreen archway l'Institut had constructed in front of its meeting hall. A banner on the structure stated emphatically: "Not foreigners but Americans, Let us be fair."[1] It was on Saint-Jean-Baptiste Day that French Canadians in Lewiston typically argued that maintaining their language and their traditions did not preclude them from being loyal residents of the United States.

Commonly heard and seen during Saint-Jean-Baptiste Day celebrations in the 1880s and 1890s, the slogan *Loyaux mais Français* (Loyal but French) made two important statements.[2] It announced that French Canadians were modifying their social identity in the United States; more significantly, it asserted that francophones were doing so on their own terms. This chapter examines how individuals of French-Canadian birth and background negotiated their identity in the United States during the late nineteenth century, as nationalists in Québec attempted to pull them in one direction and as nativists in the United States attempted to pull them in another. Guided by Dominican priests and other local elites, Lewiston's *Canadiens* demonstrated their agency as they evolved into Franco-Americans by the start of the twentieth century.

Like the ballot box, French-Canadian institutions became a source of ethnic competition and conflict in Lewiston in the nineteenth century. The city's anglophones wanted control over the education of children. In 1884, a year after French Canadians had had to finance their evening school themselves, the city of Lewiston began to appropriate funds for public evening schools. While *Le Messager* lauded this decision, it did not, of course, support the efforts of local officials to undermine French-Canadian schools.[3]

In 1890, Lewiston officials tried to do just that. In August, nearly half a year after the Dominicans had increased the amount of instruction provided in English in the parish schools, Lewiston's superintendent of schools met with the Dominican pastor to ask him to send French-Canadian children to the city's public schools. He even offered to have Catholic teachers provide religious instruction before and after school and to provide some instruction in French. Changing demographics motivated the superintendent. From 1880 to 1890, the number of school-aged children of so-called American ancestry dropped by over 450, and those of Irish heritage declined by about 50, whereas the number of French-Canadian children of school age increased by over 1,700 in Lewiston. Because French Canadians did not send their children to public schools where they would receive instruction in English and mix with students of all backgrounds, the November 1890 Lewiston school report suggested that they lacked loyalty to the United States. "Our relations must be more closely interwoven. There must be more 'serious Americanism' and federation of common interests," argued Edward H. Hill, president of the School Committee. When Hill went on to note that schoolhouses in Lewiston had declining enrollments, one had been sold, and five others were no longer in use, he revealed another reason for his interest in recruiting French-Canadian students to the public schools. *Le Messager* pointed out that the school report did not criticize the Irish for sending their children to parish schools. The newspaper also argued: "The American Catholic episcopacy has signaled the danger of public schools and has ordered clergy to create parish schools," thus referring to the 1884 decree of the Council of Baltimore to promote parochial schools in the United States. While asserting the right of French Canadians to maintain their French language and their Catholic faith, *Le Messager* further contended that French speakers could indeed be good U.S. citizens and pointed out that they were, in fact, learning English.[4]

What *Le Messager* saw so clearly is precisely what anglophones did not comprehend: Lewiston's francophones were growing new roots in their country of adoption, but they were not interested in allowing their old roots to wither or die. "While adopting the political and social ideas of their new country and vowing profound affection and a sincere devotion," pastor Alexandre-Louis Mothon wrote of his French-Canadian parishioners in 1893, "they hope to preserve their traditions and their language, which they consider inseparably tied to their religious faith."[5] For French speakers in the late nineteenth century, ethnic retention and entrance into U.S. society were interconnected goals. Willing to modify their identity, French-Canadian immigrants wanted, however, to choose the terms of their entry and participation in the United States.

In 1891, Lewiston school officials embarked upon more aggressive strategies to increase the enrollment of French-Canadian youth in the public schools. After city officials agreed to let a French-Canadian woman run a private Catholic school for francophone youth in a schoolhouse that had remained vacant for eight years, the School Committee decided to use the building again to open a new school of its own, even though two other schoolhouses on the same street remained only partially occupied. Consequently, the Dominicans allowed the woman to teach her class in the assembly room of the Dominican Block before they built another school in Little Canada to accommodate her students. In September 1891, Lewiston's school superintendent placed ads in *Le Messager* informing parents that one of the city's public schools would offer instruction in French and English, and another had a teacher who spoke both languages. The superintendent emphasized in the ad that the public schools did not charge tuition. The strategy to open a bilingual public school did not succeed because the school did not enroll enough students, the Dominicans recorded in their chronicle. Over the next year and a half, the public schools probably attracted enough French-Canadian youth to worry the pastor, for he announced at masses in January 1893 that parents sending their children to public schools would not receive absolution; he made exceptions, however, for those who lived far from the Catholic schools, or whose children continued their education beyond the grades offered in the parish schools.[6]

Another French-Canadian institution, a hospital, created considerable religious and ethnic competition in Lewiston-Auburn during the late nineteenth century. Lewiston built a public hospital in the late 1860s that initially received little use; by 1876, the overseers of the poor felt that the facility was inadequate for a hospital and decided to close it rather than expand it, preferring instead to treat the sick at the City Farm, which also housed the destitute. A decade later, English-language newspaper articles argued the need for a local hospital, citing support for the idea from mill agents and doctors. To meet this need, the Sisters of Charity of Saint Hyacinthe, or Grey Nuns, opened a hospital in Lewiston in 1888, after having raised funds for it through bazaars they had organized with the support of French-Canadian societies. In founding the hospital, the sisters continued in the United States a practice they had begun in Québec of institutionalizing social services for French speakers.[7] Several non-francophone physicians supported the Sisters' Hospital. No sooner did the sisters organize their hospital in Lewiston than Protestants began discussing plans to build an alternative facility. Protestant women and ministers from Auburn, along with the non-francophone doctors who had originally supported the Sisters' Hospital, led the charge to build a competing institution. The *Lewiston Journal* published numerous articles about their proposed hospital, which, the Dominicans perceived, had a clear anti-French subtext: "Always without saying it officially, it is against us that this [hospital] is being planned."[8]

French Canadians believed their hospital adequately met local needs, and that opening a second hospital in Lewiston would only jeopardize the success of their institution. Consequently, after a Republican state legislator from Lewiston sponsored a bill in 1889 to allocate $40,000 for the proposed Central Maine General (C.M.G.) hospital, the Dominicans organized French Canadians to protest against the measure. At masses, they asked parishioners to join them in a meeting at the Dominican Block to discuss the issue, and eight hundred French Canadians, Democrats and Republicans alike, showed up. Following the meeting, *Le Messager* expressed its pleasure that although politics had divided French Canadians in recent years, they showed "harmony and unanimity" on the question of opposing the creation of C.M.G. hospital. One notable French-Canadian Republican did not attend the meeting. He was J. E. Cloutier, a former Democrat who had sponsored the appropriation for C.M.G. Twenty-five French Canadians from Lewiston traveled to the state capitol in Augusta to lobby against Cloutier's bill. A French-Canadian state representative from Biddeford spoke favorably to the legislature about the Sisters' Hospital, helping to defeat Cloutier's bill. Among the epithets hurled at Lewiston's French Canadians for their opposition to C.M.G. was that "the French will not Americanize." Less than two weeks after the state legislature denied funding to C.M.G., the Dominican pastor called for another meeting at the Dominican Block, this time to push more *Canadiens* to naturalize.[9]

Religious and ethnic prejudice against French Canadians led to the establishment of C.M.G. hospital in Lewiston. In November 1890, the Dominicans noted in their chronicle that individuals of American—and especially of Irish—ancestry continued to push for the creation of a second hospital in the Spindle City. At a state hearing in Augusta, an Auburn doctor complained that his patients would not go to the Sisters' Hospital because people spoke French there. An Irish man testified that "he did not want it to be understood that this was a 'Catholic' hospital. It was a 'French Catholic hospital,'" he insisted. A non-francophone doctor raised other complaints: the hospital also functioned as a home for orphans and the sisters, a chapel existed above the patients' wards, and physicians did not have a role in managing the institution.[10] The latter complaint subtly acknowledged the doctor's discomfort at seeing women enter the male sphere of medicine as directors of a medical institution, and it reveals gender discrimination as one motive for creating the new hospital in Lewiston. Thus, religious, ethnic, and gender biases of the late nineteenth century together conspired to create Lewiston's C.M.G. hospital, built after promoters secured state funding for the institution in 1891.[11]

So acute was the competition between C.M.G. and the Sisters' Hospital that it surfaced in a local contest for a music box. In December 1892, Peck's department store in Lewiston sponsored a contest whereby for each twenty-five-cent purchase, customers could cast a ballot favoring an institution of their choice. The one receiving the most votes would win the music box, valued at $200. By mid-December, Lewiston's two hospitals were among the top three institutions with the most votes. As the contest neared its end, English- and French-language newspapers regularly informed readers of the daily voting results. *Le Messager* implored readers to cast their ballots for the Sisters' Hospital; if they did not want to bother walking upstairs at Peck's to place them in the ballot box, they should hand them to a francophone clerk, the newspaper suggested. In the end, C.M.G. hospital won the contest, with 28,291 votes to the 26,627 the Sisters' Hospital received. French-Canadian elites recorded their dismay. A disappointed Dominican priest acknowledged that the contest's result was not "a defeat for the French-Canadian hospital," but wished he could have celebrated a loss by "the rival institution!!!" *Le Messager* expressed its disappointment by admonishing readers: "If all of the French Canadians who had made purchases at this store had voted, there is no doubt the result would not have been the same." It then conveyed the thanks of the Grey Nuns to those who had supported their hospital during the contest.[12] Certainly, neither of Lewiston's two hospitals needed a music box. The contest for it gave expression to the intense ethnic and religious competition that existed between French and English speakers in the late nineteenth century.

Competition and tension between Lewiston's Irish and French-Canadian Catholics surfaced in different ways in the late 1800s. As noted in the last chapter, sometimes they joined forces in the Democratic Party, and at other times members of each group crossed over to the Republican Party when ethnic friction prevented political unity. Competition between the French Canadians and the Irish appeared in religious works as well, although it was usually more subtle. When French Canadians made plans for a bazaar to raise funds for their parish in 1882, the Irish pastor, Thomas Wallace, scheduled one for Saint Joseph Parish to coincide, "probably to eliminate the temptation of his parishioners to spend money at the bazaar of the French Canadians!" the Dominicans noted. On July 6, 1884, the Irish pastor and his assistant joined the Dominicans and bishop for lunch, but were conspicuously absent from the afternoon ceremony to bless the new bells of Saint-Pierre Church. Less than two weeks later, Saint Joseph Parish ordered a church bell a thousand pounds heavier than any other found in Lewiston, causing the Dominicans to observe wryly: "It seems that Father Wallace has taken a liking to bells!" Wallace headed the Lewiston School Committee in 1886 and protested against the decision of the Board of Aldermen to let the Dominicans use two public-school buildings; as a result, the city allowed the Dominicans only one building, making it difficult for them to accommodate the growing number of French-Canadian schoolchildren. In 1892, when the Grey Nuns visited different parishes in the state to solicit funds for a boys' orphanage they planned to open, Wallace chose not to hold a special collection for them in his parish. As the French-Canadian population of Lewiston expanded and competed for resources, Wallace worried about the position of the Irish in the city. Consequently, in 1886, he made arrangements with Bishop Healy to erect a second Irish church in Lewiston, named Saint Patrick's, which he hoped would serve all of the English-speaking Catholics of Lewiston and Auburn. Wallace served as pastor of both Saint Joseph's and Saint Patrick's from 1890 until 1894, when the two became separate parishes with their own pastors, a development he deplored. He felt it divided the strength of Lewiston's Irish population. While scolding Saint Joseph parishioners for having requested their own pastor, he reportedly stated, "In a very short time this city would become a cananadian [*sic*] city."[13] This same concern must have underlain Irish support for C.M.G. hospital.

The religious and ethnic competition between francophones and the Irish Catholic and Protestant American populations of Lewiston likely motivated the Grey Nuns to promote integration rather than ethnic isolation in the charitable institutions they founded in the Spindle City. As Maine's first Catholic hospital, the Sisters' Hospital from the beginning admitted patients without regard to religious background or to ethnic origin, something Central Maine General Hospital acknowledged in its first report. Organized by Dr. Martel in 1893, the original medical staff of the Sisters' Hospital included doctors without French surnames; in 1898, about two-thirds of the attending, consulting, and adjunct physicians of the hospital had non-French names. Women of all religious or ethnic backgrounds could join the association of hospital patronesses, which, as in Canada, periodically gathered women together to sew for patients. The Men's Hospital Association, or patrons, formed in 1899 to work with the patronesses to organize concerts and dramatic productions for the benefit of the hospital, and it had French-Canadian and Irish men serving as copresidents; selected as honorary presidents were the Anglo-American state governor, the Irish bishop, a French Dominican priest, and an Irish pastor of Lewiston.[14] Given the ethnic and religious competition that surrounded the hospital's founding, building bridges between ethnic and religious groups undoubtedly worked to ensure the institution's survival.

The Healy Asylum, an orphanage founded by the Sisters of Charity in 1893, facilitated integration and Americanization. This likely explains why the institution did not encounter opposition from Protestant Americans; in fact, they supported the orphanage and attended a bazaar to raise funds for it in 1893. The sisters admitted boys, including juvenile offenders, of different religious and ethnic backgrounds to Healy Asylum. The 1896 report the francophone nuns wrote on the institution demonstrated an eagerness to illustrate Americanism. Written entirely in English, this report reveals that the sisters followed a curriculum similar to that of the public schools, and it stresses that they worked to help each boy under their care "to become an honorable and useful citizen." The picture they included of the kindergarten class prominently displays two U.S. flags. Thus, while administering a French-Canadian institution, the sisters wished to demonstrate their loyalty to, and integration into, U.S. society. Through their charitable works, by accepting people of other religions and nationalities, and by embracing American values, the Grey Nuns gained acceptance for their institutions.[15]

The actions of the sisters reflected political astuteness that helped them to obtain necessary funding. With the assistance of F. X. Belleau, a Democrat who represented Lewiston in the state legislature, the Sisters' Hospital and Healy Asylum received state appropriations in the 1890s. C.M.G. hospital, however, received more generous financial support from the state legislature than the hospital of the Sisters of Charity.[16] Although mitigated, prejudice against the hospital francophones had founded in Lewiston persisted through the turn of the century.

Ethnic and religious rivalry probably helped Lewiston's francophones, particularly its elites, to sympathize with Louis Riel in the late nineteenth century. A man of European and Native American ancestry, Riel had helped lead other *Métis* from the Canadian Northwest in an 1885 insurrection against the Ottawa-based federal government. Although Riel was insane, the federal government tried and hanged him for treason—actions that divided English and French Canadians. French Canadians from Québec protested vigorously against the federal government's handling of Riel, expressing anger at the treatment of such francophone Catholics outside of the Province of Québec. Throughout 1885, *Le Messager* published numerous articles on Riel and his trial. After his execution, French Canadians in Lewiston requested a mass for him, which the national societies attended. In June 1886, *Le Messager* joined voices with other French Canadians in the United States, arguing that "Riel's execution is a flagrant insult against our nationality that we can never forget." Francophone elites did not soon forget him. An editor of *Le Messager*, Dr. F. P. Vanier, wrote a play entitled *Louis Riel*, which was held at Lewiston's Music Hall and directed and acted by local French Canadians, including Dr. Martel, who played Riel. On the tenth anniversary of Riel's execution, *Le Messager* reminded readers of his fate.[17] The controversy in Canada over Louis Riel's execution revealed deep religious and ethnic divisions within the nation-state; the controversy likely resonated with francophones in Lewiston subjected to discrimination on the basis of their religious and ethnic background. Concern over Riel's plight connected French Canadians, at least emotionally, on both sides of the international border in the late nineteenth century.

Perhaps one measure of that emotional connection was the enthusiastic reception Lewiston francophones accorded Honoré Mercier in 1893. Mercier rose to power in Québec by capitalizing on the discontent of French Canadians with the Canadian government's handling of Riel; as premier, Mercier pushed for greater autonomy for the Province of Québec. Two years after leaving office, Mercier visited Lewiston during a speaking tour of French-Canadian centers in New England. According to *Le Messager*, Mercier wanted to see how French Canadians in the United States were doing, and he wished to promote the issue of Canadian independence from Britain. In introducing Mercier to a Lewiston audience of at least three thousand, including American and Irish individuals, attorney P. X. Angers called Mercier "Canada's [George] Washington." Speaking in both English and French, Mercier suggested that francophones in the United States, through their industry and toil, had gained some prestigious positions and the respect of Americans, but he expressed his belief that francophones in Canada, for the most part, lacked both prestige and the respect of anglophones. Mercier contended that problems between English and French speakers concerning religious and linguistic issues in Manitoba and New

Brunswick served as evidence that the English were not preserving minority rights in the provinces outside of Québec. The solution, he suggested, was for Canada to gain its independence from Great Britain. *Le Messager* paraphrased Mercier: "Only independence can give Canada true liberty." While the French-language newspaper—and perhaps Mercier himself—did not elaborate on how Canadian autonomy might improve the situation of French Canadians, the remarks of "the apostle of Canadian independence," as *Le Messager* called Mercier, must have drawn a sympathetic response from Lewiston's French speakers.[18]

Other ties existed between francophones in Lewiston and Québec. Sending young men to Québec's *collèges classiques* (classical schools) connected French speakers of Lewiston to their sending society after the emigration experience and helped them to preserve their French-Canadian ethnicity in the United States. Clergy provided secondary-level instruction in the *collèges*, training young men of approximately twelve to eighteen years of age to join the ranks of the elite in such capacities as physicians and clergymen.[19] Young francophone men seeking a classical secondary education during the late nineteenth century had to travel to Canada, because Lewiston's parish schools offered only an elementary education and New England did not then have its own *collège classique*. Periodic announcements in *Le Messager*'s local news column indicate that some of Lewiston's French-speaking youth did attend the *collèges* of Québec, but the newspaper did not provide sufficient information to determine enrollment patterns.

The yearbooks of Québec's classical schools supply the necessary information. By consulting them, geographer Robert G. LeBlanc determined that Saint-Charles Borromée in Sherbrooke and the Collège de Saint-Hyacinthe together had the largest proportion (about one-third) of the enrollments of French-Canadian descendants from the United States between 1865 and 1965. Raw data shared by LeBlanc reveals that the enrollments of Lewiston's French-Canadian youth at these two institutions increased as the nineteenth century progressed. Specifically, the two *collèges* had three enrollments from Lewiston in the 1870s, thirteen in the 1880s, and twenty-two in the 1890s. These increasing numbers reflect that more French Canadians in Lewiston had ascended the ladder of economic class high enough to be able to afford sending their sons to the classical schools of Québec. As we shall see, Lewiston's enrollments at these schools continued to increase in the early twentieth century. Training elites at the *collèges classiques* helped communities like Lewiston to maintain their ties with Québec and to preserve their French-Canadian traditions, French language, and Catholic faith—the three pillars of *survivance*.[20]

Trips to Québec provided Lewiston's French Canadians the opportunity to maintain regular contact with family and friends. Summer pilgrimages to Sainte-Anne de Beaupré in Québec, which the Dominicans organized around the saint's feast day in July, typically drew hundreds of Lewiston francophones. These pilgrimages, as well as individual trips, afforded the opportunity to visit relatives in Québec, surely providing a welcome respite from the hot mills during summertime. So many from the Androscoggin Mill took part in summer excursions during 1898 that a number of looms could not operate, and the mill had to bring in Polish workers to meet the shortage of labor.[21] When Lewiston's mills closed temporarily during periods of industrial crisis, French Canadians traveled to Canada for the length of their unemployment, spending it with family in Québec—presumably on farms where subsistence was easier than in an industrial city, for they had few savings on which to rely during difficult economic times. This happened in 1893, when eight hundred of Lewiston's French Canadians left for Québec one day in August; by early December, when the Bates Mill reopened, most of the nearly one thousand *Canadiens* who had departed during the mill's four-month shutdown had returned to Lewiston. The city's *Canadiens* also traveled to Québec for reasons not tied to religion or economics, such as a trip to Montréal's winter carnival by the snowshoe club "le Lewistonnais" in 1889.[22] Proximity to Québec allowed French Canadians to return temporarily, whether in times of need or leisure, to the networks they had in their society of origin.

The formation of a branch of the Société des Artisans (Society of Artisans) in Lewiston served to unite francophones on both sides of the international border in a mutual-benefit society in 1898. Les Artisans had their headquarters in Montréal, and they sent their inspector general to Lewiston in that year to persuade francophones to join this Canadian organization. In a meeting held at the Dominican Block, the speaker emphasized to the one hundred attendees that founding a branch of les Artisans in Lewiston would not supplant existing societies, but would serve instead as an additional resource for the city's French-Canadian population. Over seventy-five joined the organization, which boasted twelve thousand members in Québec and the United States in 1898.[23]

Celebrations of Saint-Jean-Baptiste Day also connected French speakers in the United States and Canada in celebration of their common heritage in honor of their patron saint. Periodically, French Canadians on both sides of the international border fêted together, as francophones from Lewiston and other New England cities traveled to Québec to join festivities organized in *le pays natal* (the native country). On one such occasion, which took place in Québec City in 1889, Dr. Martel underscored the shared roots of North America's francophones by calling the provincial capital "the cradle of our nationality." Speaking at the same event, Québec premier Honoré Mercier urged French Canadians in the United States to maintain their language and their faith: "Speak French and be Catholic; the English and the Americans always respect the French who have the courage to speak their language and to profess their faith." Sometimes, as in 1885, clergy from Québec came to preach in Lewiston on Saint-Jean-Baptiste Day. In 1896, Lewiston's celebration culminated with eight hundred viewing the play *Félix Poutré*, which focused on problems between anglophones and francophones in Canada during 1837—a theme that must have resonated with Lewiston's French speakers.[24] Whether in Québec or in Lewiston, *survivance*—in the face of domination by anglophones—always was a central theme of Saint-Jean-Baptiste Day.

In Lewiston, French Canadians also tried to observe other religious and ethnic customs they had practiced in Québec. Bishops and employers in the United States did not always make allowances for them, however. Celebrating Christmas with a midnight mass was a cherished French-Canadian practice. But Bishop James Augustin Healy, an Irish prelate who served in Maine from 1875 until his death in 1900, refused to accord French Canadians this privilege. As in Québec, New Year's Day was a special occasion. Lewiston's French Canadians would visit with family and friends on this day, often enjoying music they created with fiddles and accordions. But the factories at which many of them worked usually remained open. Sometimes French Canadians took matters into their own hands. In 1884, for example, a weaver told the *Lewiston Journal* that thirty-eight French-Canadian women risked losing their jobs when they informed employers that they would not work on New Year's Day. In 1889, French Canadians closed the local mills on New Year's Day simply by not showing up to work; some francophone workers had even left the factories early on New Year's Eve by escaping through the windows.²⁵ Preserving ethnic customs in a Protestant mill town occasionally necessitated taking risks.

Perhaps because French speakers in New England cities like Lewiston made the effort to maintain French-Canadian traditions and ties to Québec francophones, the attitude of Québec nationalists changed in the late nineteenth century. *Le Messager* pointed out in 1888 that the Canadian press looked more favorably than it had in the past upon the compatriots who had emigrated to the United States. In 1895 it published an article, presumably written by F. X. Belleau (then serving as U.S. consul in Trois-Rivières, Québec), that asserted that French Canadians now respected the francophones who had emigrated to the United States and, in some cases, even envied them.²⁶ This change of attitude on the part of Québec nationalists must also have reflected the reality that hundreds of thousands of French Canadians living in the United States probably would never repatriate.

Through newspapers like *Le Messager*, French-Canadian elites in the United States served as a significant obstacle to the colonization and repatriation efforts of the governments of Québec and Canada.²⁷ In 1886, *Le Messager* publicized reports that a Canadian colonization agent, Charles Lalime of Worcester, Massachusetts, had indicated that families needed at least $1,000 to relocate to Manitoba, Canada; the newspaper felt that the *Canadiens* in the United States simply could not afford the cost. *Le Messager* argued in the same year that French Canadians had established national communities with churches and schools in New England, and they risked a great deal if they migrated to the Canadian West in order to found French-speaking colonies as a "patriotic work." *Le Messager*, whose existence depended upon francophones remaining in Lewiston, consistently argued in the late nineteenth century that French Canadians were better off in the United States. By the end of the century, *Le Messager* contended that French Canadians living in the United States "were not built to become colonizers." Colonizing lands in Canada with children born and raised in New England's manufacturing centers was not practical, it asserted. A French-Canadian priest, who had formerly worked as a colonization agent to attract New England francophones to the Matapédia Valley in Québec, told the *Lewiston Journal* the same thing in 1898. "Thirty years in Lewiston has created a new generation that is not French-Canadian. They are French Americans, and have no claim upon Canada," the clergyman said. "They are a textile class, and are unfitted for farm work by their labor in the mills here. Their fathers may have been farmers, but they are cosmopolitan . . . and are unfit for subduing the wilderness." In arguing against repatriation, *Le Messager* itself echoed the geopolitical designs that Québec nationalists had come to adopt for New England in the late nineteenth century, writing: "Canada [i.e., Québec] is French, the United States is perhaps still far from being French, but New England is in the process of becoming French, thanks to us."[28]

In the late nineteenth century, French Canadians on both sides of the international border participated in the trade-union movement. Founded in 1869, the Knights of Labor became the first national labor organization in the United States, and it established itself in Canada in 1881. Called les Chevaliers du Travail by French speakers, the organization in Québec concentrated primarily on the city of Montréal, where it opened an assembly in 1882. Led by Cardinal Elzéar-Alexandre Taschereau, Québec's Catholic Church opposed les Chevaliers du Travail beginning in 1883, according to Fernand Harvey, because it felt that the organization challenged the Church's authority as the guardian of traditional cultural values, rooted in the province's rural past. After consulting Rome, Taschereau officially condemned les Chevaliers du Travail on February 2, 1885. Maine's Catholic bishop quickly followed suit. Healy, who opposed the Knights of Labor as a secret society, condemned the organization in his letter of February 18, 1885, written in French and English and read at masses throughout the state. Those who joined the Knights of Labor, the bishop threatened, would not receive the sacraments. Unlike Cardinal James Gibbons of Baltimore, who eventually persuaded Rome to change its position on the Knights of Labor, Healy, who had attended seminary in Québec for three years, apparently felt comfortable with the stance of Québec's prelates; he continued to maintain contact with them in 1885 to learn of the activities of les Chevaliers du Travail in Québec, and to keep informed of communications from Rome concerning the organization. Notwithstanding the opposition of Québec's Catholic hierarchy, les Chevaliers du Travail dominated the worker movement in the Province of Québec in the late nineteenth century.[29]

In Lewiston, French Canadians joined the Knights of Labor despite Bishop Healy's opposition. Ossian C. Phillips, a leader of the organization, indicated in March 1886 that Lewiston's francophones "comprise not a small portion of the Order," an observation *Le Messager* confirmed later in the year when it noted that "a large number of our readers belong to this association." When Phillips made his comment, the Knights of Labor was in the midst of a labor dispute that involved French-Canadian workers at Lewiston's Bates Mill. Details of their specific involvement are sketchy, however, likely due to secrecy on the part of both the Knights of Labor and the francophone Catholics who belonged to the organization. What we do know is that one French Canadian joined four other weavers in signing a published letter asking management to rehire a loom-fixer, allegedly fired for belonging to the Knights of Labor. According to the Dominicans, up to one-third of the 1,800 Bates Mill employees were French-Canadian. Some apparently were involved in the strike, precipitated by the firing of the loom-fixer and expanded by demands for a salary increase; at mass one Sunday, the Dominican pastor urged strikers to exercise caution and restraint. In its local news column, *Le Messager* informed members of les Chevaliers du Travail, who were in need on account of the strike, that they could make application for assistance to a French-Canadian man in Lewiston. Catholic clergy must have reprimanded *Le Messager*, for it subsequently expressed regrets for publishing the announcement. But it did so in a mocking tone, suggesting its sympathies lay with workers and not with the Church on this issue. "We saw no wrong there, *although the money came from the Knights of Labor*," the newspaper wrote, "and we hope that God will not *curse us with the pox* in order to punish our subscribers for having read this announcement exposing Canadian values too much [to those] in the United States."[30] *Le Messager*'s sarcastic tone, the participation of Lewiston French Canadians in labor protest, and their membership in the Knights of Labor despite its condemnation by the bishop all counter persistent impressions in the literature that French Canadians in the United States were unusually subservient to Catholic clergy and nearly always avoided striking.[31] Participation in the Knights of Labor in 1886 appears to have signified the development of working-class consciousness among Lewiston French Canadians, revealing the intersection of their ethnic and class interests in the host society.

Additional evidence from the late nineteenth century points to greater participation in the labor movement and in protest activity. *Le Messager* encouraged workers and offered them guidance. In 1887, the newspaper informed readers whom to contact to organize a "National Union of French-Canadian Workers of Lewiston," and by 1895, if not sooner, there existed a Union of French-Canadian Weavers in the Spindle City. Participation in such trade unions likely led to the demise of the Knights of Labor in Lewiston by the mid-1890s. One can infer from accounts in *Le Messager* that some francophone shoe workers also belonged to unions in 1893. During shoe strikes in Auburn in that year, the newspaper urged other *Canadiens* not to undermine the efforts of these unions by offering to work for lower wages than the strikers, thus undercutting the efforts of the working class; with such advice *Le Messager* reflected, and sought to shape, the working-class consciousness of French Canadians. In 1895, French speakers took part in a strike at the Continental Mill to pressure employers to return wages to the levels of previous years. *Le Messager* sided with Continental Mill workers, imploring in August 1895 "that the strikers remain united for several more days and we are convinced that their reasonable demands will be realized." Less than a week later, after one month of striking, Continental Mill employees returned to work without having won their demands. The Dominicans recorded in their chronicle: "Perhaps our people will not strike again in this way for nothing."[32] Unlike the Dominicans, *Le Messager* proved itself particularly friendly to the development of working-class consciousness among French Canadians in the late nineteenth century, encouraging their participation in improving the conditions of their work lives in the United States.

This was evident in the Androscoggin Mill strike of 1898, one for which *Le Messager* provided extensive coverage. Because of this reporting, the Androscoggin Mill strike serves as the best-documented example of the intersection of ethnic and working-class consciousness among Lewiston French Canadians in the nineteenth century. A depression in the cotton industry in 1898 led 150 mills in New England to slash the wages of 125,000 workers, precipitating strikes in various cities, including Lewiston. French Canadians took part in the three-month strike, participating in ways that revealed their reliance upon their ethnic networks and their ethnic traditions. Their mutual-benefit societies, l'Institut Jacques-Cartier and l'Union Saint-Joseph, raised money for strikers by organizing musical programs at the local opera house. Committees of men and women collected contributions for needy workers, and sympathetic employees of other mills provided assistance. Rebutting the *Lewiston Sun*'s contention that 150 *Canadiens* had returned to Canada during the first few weeks of the strike, *Le Messager* claimed that only seven families had done so. The option to return to Canada would enable francophones to hold out for their former wages, a French-Canadian weaver told the *Lewiston Journal*. Probably bluffing more than a little, he stated that Canadian colonization agents would assist francophones with "a pass to Montreal, and from there to the unsettled regions of Lake St. John where we have 100 acres of good land given to us, and we can have work upon the government roads . . . to keep us while we are clearing our land." The weaver further suggested that French Canadians could sit out the strike longer than "Yankees," because they lived more modestly. Two months into the strike, *Le Messager* reported that there were about 500 strikers, and they met at the Dominican Block to decide to continue striking. When Dominican pastor Raymond Grolleau announced at masses during the last Sunday of March that the Androscoggin Mill would reopen the next day, and that workers could return if they chose, the chronicler recorded: "He knows he is walking on hot coals." As parishioners left church, some indicated that the pastor should not get involved, others suggested that the mill agent had paid him off, while some felt that the pastor was more concerned with how the strike would affect Easter collections. But *Le Messager* informed readers that the fathers of families no longer able to purchase groceries after two months of unemployment had asked the pastor to see if he could get the mill to reopen; the pastor had then spoken with the mill's agent, who had agreed to reopen the Androscoggin Mill on condition that workers accept a cut in wages.[33] The poverty of Lewiston's French Canadians began to diminish the resolve of some to continue striking.

As some French Canadians returned to work, the *Lewiston Journal* published sensational stories about the actions of strikers. Fifty women, "enraged amazons," threw a French-Canadian woman into a gutter because she had resumed working at the mill, reported the *Journal* on the last day of March 1898. While the *Journal* did not indicate the ethnicity of the fifty women, *Le Messager* had the clear impression that "the American colleague" writing for the *Journal* meant French-Canadian women. A fabricated story, charged the French-language newspaper. It also argued that the *Journal* had exaggerated reports of strikers tossing sticks and stones at police, stories written "without doubt to prejudice the cause of workers." The American reporter offered such fabrications or embellishments, *Le Messager* further contended, simply because "the strikers have committed the wrong of being poor French Canadians!" After working all day at the Androscoggin Mill, Jean-Baptiste Labeau crossed the canal bridge to return home one evening in early April, and strikers chased him, yelling "Kill him!" and "Do him up!" The chase ended when Labeau reached his home, whereupon his wife emerged to throw wood at her husband's badgerers, asserting that he would continue to work. That was the *Journal*'s account. *Le Messager* reported that Labeau was well-off financially, something that annoyed those continuing to strike, and they followed him home blowing horns. "It was funny," deflected *Le Messager*. While acknowledging that Labeau's wife had thrown wood, the French-language newspaper indicated that an officer had let her know no harm was coming her husband's way. *Le Messager*'s explanation implied that the event constituted a charivari, a cherished French-Canadian practice used as an assertion of power against those violating norms of the community.[34]

In early April 1898, strikers returned to the Androscoggin Mill after nearly three months of unemployment during winter months. *Le Messager* suggested that women felt more strongly than the men about continuing the strike, not only because they believed that victory was imminent, but also because the strike had been so costly to their families that they wanted results. The French-language newspaper indicated that the workers had lacked organization. The only hint of any outside organizational assistance came from the *Lewiston Journal*, which published its suspicion that a man dressed in a "long coat and colored glasses," "a French Canadian who had formerly worked in Montreal," counseled strikers. While ethnic networks had helped sustain French-Canadian strikers for several months, their poverty forced them in the end to return to the Androscoggin Mill, "accepting the cruel conditions of management"—conditions the French-language newspaper did not spell out.[35]

The 1898 Androscoggin Mill strike, which *Le Messager* covered more extensively than any other labor action by local French Canadians in the late nineteenth century, gave evidence of the effort of French speakers to improve their economic conditions in the United States. Participation by francophones in this strike contravenes notions of the passivity of French-

Canadian men and women in the world of work. These notions originated with their anglophone contemporaries, such as Carroll Wright, and have since permeated the historiography on French Canadians in the United States. One anglophone contemporary, Bowdoin College professor William MacDonald, wrote in 1898 that "docility is one of his most marked traits," when describing the attractiveness of the French-Canadian worker to mill managers. "Above all, he is reluctant, as compared with the Irish, to join labor unions, and is loath to strike," contended MacDonald. The actions of French Canadians in the Androscoggin Mill strike counter the impressions of such nineteenth-century contemporaries and those of scholars who have repeated their assertions; in their view, the ethnic consciousness of French Canadians trumped their consciousness as members of the working class. The actions of francophones in the 1898 Androscoggin Mill strike demonstrate a strong measure of commitment to improving their lot in the United States and not returning to Canada.[36] Their actions also reveal an emerging identity in the world of work, just as one emerged in politics and other spheres as French Canadians joined the host society.

Le Messager seized every opportunity to encourage French Canadians to participate in the host society. Sometimes French speakers took part in distinctly U.S. holidays in the late nineteenth century. In 1892, anglophone organizers included French Canadians in Lewiston festivities commemorating the four hundredth anniversary of the founding of America by Christopher Columbus. Festival organizers had children from the public and parochial schools celebrating together, and they surprised the Dominican pastor and Dr. Martel by asking them to speak in French during, respectively, the afternoon program for children and the evening program for adults. In addition, l'Institut Jacques-Cartier paraded with the American societies during this celebration. As early as 1887, French-Canadian musicians took part in Lewiston's Fourth of July parade. In 1895, when Lewiston celebrated its centennial on Independence Day, several French-Canadian societies joined the parade, as did the children of Saint-Pierre School, who carried flags of the United States and France. Prior to the event, *Le Messager* coaxed French Canadians to participate in the celebration by publishing an article, most likely written by F. X. Belleau, arguing that the slogan "Let us be loyal but French" need not prevent French Canadians from joining in the festivities. The newspaper also urged: "Let us show we are Americans, and let us all decorate our homes." In the late nineteenth century, French Canadians typically observed another American holiday, Thanksgiving, which was not a workday, by attending mass at Saint-Pierre Church.[37] To the extent that Lewiston's French Canadians celebrated American holidays in the late nineteenth century, they did so in ways consonant with their ethnic and religious customs. In this way, they reshaped their identity in their country of adoption.

Nothing made clearer how French Canadians negotiated their identity in the United States than their annual public celebrations of Saint-Jean-Baptiste Day. While scholars have focused on these celebrations in the United States as illustrations of *survivance*, French- and English-language sources from the 1880s and 1890s reveal the surprising finding that Lewiston's French Canadians also used this feast day to assert their ties to the United States. They expressed it with the slogan "Loyal but French," or the variation "Loyal but French-Canadian."[38] By emphasizing their U.S. ties, French Canadians in the northeastern United States departed from those in Canada.

Emphasizing ties to France during Saint-Jean-Baptiste Day celebrations represented another departure on the part of francophones in the United States from their kith and kin in Québec. French Canada had lost its ties to France after the British conquest of 1759–1760, but French speakers in Lewiston found it expedient to resurrect those ties in the late 1800s. While the practice may have reflected courtesy on the part of French Canadians wishing to be inclusive and respectful of their French-from-France religious leaders, the custom of paying homage to France predated the arrival of the Dominicans in Lewiston. During the first local celebration of Saint-Jean-Baptiste Day in 1875, for example, the decorations on the speakers' platform included the flags of France and the United States, and the band played "la Marseillaise" during the afternoon picnic. Identification with France served as a way for Lewiston's French-speaking residents to highlight the shared roots and patriotism of the Americans and the *Canadiens*. During Saint-Jean-Baptiste Day celebrations, parades included allegorical chariots featuring French-Canadian, French, and American themes. For example, a young boy dressed in lambskin portraying Saint-Jean-Baptiste typically stood next to a lamb on one float, while on another, as in 1890, local French Canadians might pose as Revolutionary War figures the Marquis de Lafayette and George Washington, even though French Canada had rejected both the

French and American revolutions. In addition to the symbols, the discourse of Lewiston's francophone population underscored the historic ties between the French and American peoples. On Saint-Jean-Baptiste Day in 1897, Dr. Martel noted: "When this nation was yet in childhood and struggling for her rights, for her independence, Canada's mother, France, came to the aid of the thirteen colonies." Martel also pointed out that the French had played an important role in exploring New England's coast and other areas of what eventually became the United States. By harking back to their French roots, French-Canadian elites, like Dr. Martel, argued for acceptance in the United States. During the 1882 convention of French Canadians and Acadians of Maine, which Lewiston hosted in conjunction with the feast of Saint-Jean-Baptiste, Dr. Martel contended: "We believed it would always be permissible in the United States to speak the language of Lafayette without being considered strangers."[39] Making reference to a notable French figure from the U.S. Revolutionary War served to buttress Martel's argument that French Canadians could maintain their ethnic identity while being loyal to the United States. In brief, identification with France during Saint-Jean-Baptiste Day celebrations helped French Canadians to appropriate the historic connections of French speakers to the United States. This strategy helped Lewiston French Canadians more forcefully make the argument that *survivance* and acculturation did not represent dichotomous goals. This strategy also gave evidence that their identity as French Canadians was evolving in the United States in ways that distinguished them from francophones in Canada.

Neither the Province of Québec nor the country of Canada had an official flag until the mid-twentieth century. To symbolize their French heritage on Saint-Jean-Baptiste Day, Lewiston's French-Canadian residents typically hung the Tricolor of France throughout the city. They also symbolized their loyalty to the United States by decorating their homes and businesses with the Stars and Stripes. Thus the flags of France and the United States symbolically expressed the noncompeting loyalties—the intertwined identities—of Lewiston's *Canadiens*.[40] As the blue-white-red colors of France overlapped the red-white-blue ones of the United States, Lewiston francophones conveyed that retention of ethnicity and participation in the host society represented the same goal.

During the 1897 Saint-Jean-Baptiste Day celebration, attorney Emile H. Tardivel explained what he felt French Canadians most wanted in the United

States: "What we want, above all things, is to conserve our language and our traditions in private life and to speak the language of the country and to submit to American institutions in public life." He asserted that French Canadians had the right to preserve their ethnicity, just as Anglo-Americans had the right to preserve their heritage: "We intend to remain French Canadian just as the descendants of the first English colonists of New England have remained Puritan, that is to say by tradition, by love for ancestors." Contending that the strength of the United States lay in its diversity, Tardivel argued against those who tried to make the United States heterogeneous: "In effect, each nationality, with its distinctive qualities and its own activity, contributes to the material and moral development of the Union." As an example, he raised the question: "What would New England industry be, I ask you, without Irish and French-Canadian workers?"[41] Saint-Jean-Baptiste Day celebrations provided the forum through which Lewiston francophones negotiated their place in the host society.

As French speakers grew more numerous in the Spindle City, non-French-Canadian businesses and politicians also became involved in Saint-Jean-Baptiste Day events. By the mid-1880s, if not earlier, American businesses employing French-Canadian clerks decorated their establishments for the occasion. Civic leaders, including Lewiston's mayor and members of the Board of Aldermen and Common Council, often joined the parade and lakeside picnic, as well as the evening ceremonies usually held at Lewiston City Hall. The participation of local anglophone politicians and businesses in Saint-Jean-Baptiste Day activities testified to the growing economic and political influence of Lewiston's French-Canadian population at the end of the nineteenth century. So did signs proclaiming *Ici on parle français* ("French is spoken here"), which appeared in the shop windows of American businesses.[42] Change was not unidirectional: it did not take place only among the immigrant population.

By the mid-1890s, it appeared that Lewiston's anglophone population was beginning to understand genuinely what francophones meant by the slogan "Loyal but French." When Lewiston celebrated its centennial in 1895, the *Journal* complimented "the patriotic French Americans" for the large and beautiful evergreen archway they had erected over a street, and for flying the U.S. flag above it. The *Journal* pointed out that while various ethnic groups populated Lewiston, the city's "cosmopolitan" character was most evident during annual celebrations of Saint-Jean-Baptiste Day: "Lewiston for the day loses its Americanism, almost, and one might believe himself transported to a French province and witnessing a religious *fete* [*sic*] across the seas." "The Tricolor abounds on that day, as does the motto 'Loyal mais Francais [*sic*],'" the *Journal* reported. The newspaper also commented that most French Canadians in the city were U.S. citizens, and that they rarely created disturbances at their public and private celebrations. Concluding its celebratory edition, the *Journal* noted: "Each nationality has brought with it some of its peculiar habits or its religious rites that it mingles with its Americanism."[43] Although written about all immigrant groups living in Lewiston, these words suggest that the city's large francophone population had made its impact.

Perhaps that is why the *Journal* complained in January 1896 that the distribution of anti-Catholic literature in Lewiston by the American Protective Association (APA) served to foment discord at a time when the newspaper felt that the city's residents were enjoying harmonious relations. According to the *Journal*, the APA established a branch in Auburn and held weekly meetings. There is little additional information about the local doings or the membership of the organization. Founded in Iowa in 1887, the APA sought to reduce the influence of Catholics in labor and politics in the United States; at its height in 1894, the APA had about half a million members nationwide, though its strength lay in the Midwest. Nationally, one of the organization's strategies was to promote anti-Catholic propaganda, usually sensational (and fabricated) stories about the actions of men and women religious. The APA did not spare Lewiston. In a June 1895 article, the *Boston Daily Globe* described the new Catholic church the Dominicans were planning in Lewiston, which would have the largest seating capacity of any New England church; it reported that the Dominicans were also erecting a monastery, a home for their janitor, and new stables. Six months later, the APA distributed anti-Catholic literature through the mail in Lewiston. In February 1896, *Le Messager* reported that a California woman had heard APA allegations that Lewiston's Dominican priests persecuted in the basement of a newly built castle any Catholics who did not submit to their authority. She contacted Lewiston's mayor to ask that he intervene on behalf of the tortured Catholics. *Le Messager* responded by poking fun at the APA, suggesting it had stumbled upon "a colossal idea, or rather they have made a discovery that cannot but assure their immortality."[44]

Besides humor, *Le Messager* used reason to counter the nativism of the American Protective Association. When the organization appeared again in Lewiston in June 1896 to promote public schools, the French-language newspaper questioned why the United States claimed to maintain separation of church and state when such separation did not exist in the minds of groups like the APA. Its advocacy of public schools, *Le Messager* believed, was merely an attempt to promote Protestantism. Several years earlier, *Le Messager* had published an article suggesting that the APA lacked gratitude toward descendants of those who had helped the United States gain its independence from Britain. The author, probably a local physician, harked back to ties between France and the United States: "Lafayette and Rochambeau, in taking up arms to free the young America," the individual questioned, "did they expect that a century later this same America would seek to repudiate the great-grandsons of these French soldiers, whose great valor helped it to achieve its liberty?" The question turned the issue of loyalty back to nativists. In a perspicacious conclusion, the article's author suggested that the United States constantly searched for enemies: "Today, it is the Catholic faith that falls [under attack], and whose turn will it be tomorrow?"[45] Joining the United States did not preclude one of its least powerful groups from openly critiquing the host society's idiosyncrasies.

At the end of the nineteenth century, the Spanish-American War tested the loyalty of Lewiston's French-Canadian population, heightened ethnic tensions in the city, and highlighted some of the idiosyncrasies of the United States. Although there was no conscription during the Spanish-American War, *Le Messager* acknowledged that a small number of French Canadians had returned to Canada to avoid participating in the war effort; it complained, however, that the English-language press exaggerated the estimates of those who had left the United States. *Le Messager* argued that French Canadians often returned to Canada during spring to plant crops, and some had returned in 1898 because of hard times. The newspaper vigorously defended francophones against allegations by Americans that they feared participating in the war. It countered these charges both by pointing out that U.S. draft dodgers had moved to Canada during the Civil War, and by indicating that two French-Canadian men were organizing young francophone volunteers to join the war effort. Periodically, it reported on the number who signed up to fight. For his part, the Dominican pastor encouraged French Canadians not to flee the United States but to remain to fight in the military conflict; he later found himself working against identification with war heroes when he reminded parishioners of the Catholic custom of christening children with the names of saints, and not with names like "Dewey" or "Sampson." The desire on the part of some French Canadians to christen lads with such American names as Commodore George Dewey's or Admiral William T. Sampson's only provided further evidence of their fondness for their adopted country. Following the successful conclusion of the war, *Le Messager* published a couple of articles chafing at notions then rampant of the superiority of Anglo-Saxons, arguing that the United States constituted a mixture of immigrant populations that formed Americans, not Anglo-Saxons.[46]

Such arguments gave evidence that Lewiston's francophones had evolved from *Canadiens* to Franco-Americans by the turn of the century. The term "Franco-American," in fact, began to appear in *Le Messager* in the mid-1890s.[47] In expressing the loyalties of Lewiston's French speakers, this self-designation conveyed that they were playing an active role in constructing their social identity in the United States.

Through the late nineteenth century, then, French Canadians of Lewiston actively fashioned their own brand of Americanism. They chose to maintain their French language, their Catholic faith, and many of their French-Canadian customs, while simultaneously learning English, becoming naturalized citizens and voters, founding charitable institutions, participating in elective office, joining trade unions and labor protests, and taking part in U.S. holiday celebrations and wars. From the 1880s, French-Canadian leaders and the French Dominican priests linked community-building activities to the efforts of French speakers to gain a stake in their adopted country. As French-Canadian immigrants contended with pressure from nationalists in Québec on the one hand, and with pressure and discrimination from U.S. nativists on the other, elites helped Lewiston's French speakers to pursue *survivance* through participation in U.S. society, arguing convincingly that the two did not represent dichotomous goals. The slogan "Loyal but French" served to affirm this. Carrying flags of the United States and France in parades commemorating U.S. or French-Canadian holidays also gave evidence of the evolving French and American identities of Lewiston's francophones. So, too, did self-identification as Franco-Americans.

Contrary to what historians have emphasized, modifications in the identity of French Canadians in the United States did not result principally from the social, cultural, economic, and technological changes of the twentieth century.[48] Not only did the identity reformation take place earlier, but it also sprang from forces within the francophone community. In short, the changing identity of French Canadians had its origins in the late-nineteenth-century actions of French-speaking immigrants who sought to improve the conditions of their lives in the host society.

The process of French-speakers joining the host society served to increase ethnic competition and conflict in the Spindle City, as French Canadians grew in number and sought a measure of resources and influence. Religious differences between themselves and Protestant Americans proved to be the greatest source of competition and conflict for Lewiston francophones in the nineteenth century. As French-speakers increasingly participated in U.S. society in the early twentieth century, the Catholic Church became the predominant battleground within which ethnic differences were contested.

Playing Chopin

French Speakers Celebrate the Demise of Lewiston's Republican Majority, 1900–1920

During a June 1901 meeting of the Lewiston city government, the Anglo-American mayor asked Franco-Americans to cancel their Saint-Jean-Baptiste (Saint John the Baptist) Day celebration because he feared delegates from across the state might bring smallpox to Lewiston. A Franco-American on the Board of Health, Vital Ouellette, supported the idea. Then he asked about the planned Fourth of July celebration that would follow two weeks later. "On this question there is silence and quietly the subject changes," reported *Le Messager*. By the turn of the century, individuals of French-Canadian birth and background made up 46 percent of Lewiston's population.[1] By becoming naturalized citizens and voters, French speakers gained access to city posts, allowing them in the early twentieth century to exert their influence in the conduct of local affairs and to continue preserving their ethnic traditions in the Spindle City. They also helped Lewiston to evolve into a Democratic stronghold in the state of Maine.

During the first two decades of the twentieth century, as in the late 1800s, Lewiston's French-language newspaper worked hard to persuade francophones to remain in the United States and to become naturalized citizens. *Le Messager* had a challenging task because Québec's—and

Canada's—economy had improved, reducing emigration and making repatriation more attractive. Whereas net emigration from Québec to the United States stood at 150,000 during the 1880s and at 140,000 in the 1890s, it dropped to 100,000 during the period from 1900 to 1910, and to 80,000 in the period from 1910 to 1920. According to historian Yves Roby, not only did an improvement in Canada's and Québec's economy account for the reduced emigration in the early twentieth century, but strikes and child-labor legislation in the United States also made emigration less appealing than in the past and encouraged remigration to Canada.[2]

All of these elements likely reduced the incentive for French-Canadian immigrants to give up their British citizenship. Indeed, the number of French-speaking immigrants of Lewiston who naturalized during the first two decades of the twentieth century dropped significantly from the late nineteenth century. Whereas 1,186 had naturalized during the 1880s and 1890s, only 684 francophones from the Spindle City became U.S. citizens during the period from 1900 to 1919.[3] Other reasons also account for this drop. First, U.S. naturalization laws became more stringent with the passage of the Naturalization Act of 1906 and the creation of the Bureau of Immigration and Naturalization in the same year. This significantly affected the volume of naturalizations. Seventy (70.3) percent of the 684 men who naturalized during the first two decades of the twentieth century did so before September 27, 1906, when the new regulations went into effect. Second, and paradoxically, given the opposition of French Canadians to Canada's participation in World War I, the world conflict also suppressed the number of naturalizations. Not until World War I ended did naturalizations again approach pre-1907 levels.[4]

The francophones who naturalized in Lewiston from 1900 to 1919 had come from the same general regions of Québec as those who had naturalized in the late nineteenth century. Only a tiny minority—4.1 percent—had been born outside of the Province of Québec. As in the late nineteenth century, Lewiston's newest francophone citizens in the early twentieth century had come predominantly from areas of Québec south of the Saint Lawrence River. Less than one-tenth (between 7.0 and 8.9 percent) had been born in counties north of the Saint Lawrence, and most of these individuals had come from the cities of Montréal, Québec, and Trois-Rivières. Two regions of Québec again provided the largest number of new Lewiston citizens. The counties of Témiscouata and Kamouraska contributed up to 15 percent of the city's naturalizers during the first two decades of the twentieth century; Beauce and counties to its west (Mégantic, Wolfe, and Arthasbaska) as well as counties to its north (Dorchester, Lévis, and Québec) together provided up to 42.3 percent.[5] Thus, while the French-Canadian immigrants of Lewiston who naturalized from 1900 to 1919 had come from the same general regions of Québec as in the late nineteenth century, their migration fields now reflected greater numbers from counties north of Beauce.

Because naturalization records from 1907 consistently reported the place from which immigrants had come to the United States, we have some information on the journey that French speakers had taken within Canada before crossing the border. Arthur Grandmaison, for instance, had been born in Hull (Ottawa county), and he emigrated to the United States from l'Isle Verte (Témiscouata County). Like him, one-third (33.5 percent) of the 203 French speakers of Lewiston who naturalized from 1907 through 1919 had made at least one stop within Canada before crossing the international border. None of the persons who naturalized during this period appeared to have migrated to a different Canadian province before entering the United States.[6]

Naturalization records suggest that French-Canadian immigrants did not exhibit a great deal of geographic mobility in the United States before becoming citizens. They reveal that 90.4 percent of the francophones who naturalized from 1900 to 1906 had migrated directly from Canada to Lewiston, and under one-tenth had arrived in the United States at other locations in Maine (2.5 percent), other states in New England (3.1 percent), or in states outside of the New England region (1.0 percent).[7] Naturalization records after 1906 offer no information on the place of first U.S. residence. Other data on these naturalization forms, however, gives us a glimpse of the migration patterns of francophones within the United States. Shoemaker Philippe Neri Beaudet, for example, completed his first naturalization papers in Salem, Massachusetts. In all, only seven out of the 203 persons (3.4 percent) who naturalized from 1907 to 1919 had filed their declaration of intention in U.S. cities other than Auburn or Portland, Maine, the cities where Lewiston's French-Canadian immigrants all filed their final naturalization papers during this period. To take another example, the two oldest children of shoemaker Alphonse Bilodeau had been born in Lynn, Massachusetts, while his third child had been born in Norway, Maine, and his fourth in Lewiston. Only twelve of the 203 naturalizers (5.9 percent) had children born in the United States outside of the twin cities of Lewiston and Auburn.[8] In short, the records suggest there was little geographic mobility in the country of adoption by French speakers who naturalized during the first two decades of the twentieth century.

The records also suggest that there was little migration back and forth across the international border by these naturalizers. The places of birth of the children of immigrants sometimes provide evidence of their return migration to Canada. For example, the two oldest children of Joseph Lachance had been born in Michigan in 1892 and 1893, while his seven youngest children at the time of his naturalization had been born in Québec between 1894 and 1906. Lachance, however, was the only one (0.5 percent) of the 203 men of Lewiston who naturalized from 1907 to 1919 for whom the places of birth of his children reveal such migration back and forth across the border prior to his naturalization.[9]

How French-Canadian immigrants traveled from Canada to the United States appeared on naturalization records after 1906, when the Bureau of Immigration and Naturalization revised and standardized record-keeping operations. Although Québec shares a long border with Maine, and eight of its counties at the turn of the century lay along the state's western and northern borders, 89.7 percent of the Lewiston francophones who naturalized from 1907 to 1919 had entered the United States in Vermont, most of them at the town of Island Pond. This is what Arthur Grandmaison had done, even though Témiscouata County shares part of Maine's northern border; the reason for his circuitous route to Lewiston was that French-Canadian immigrants traveled to the Spindle City almost exclusively on railway lines that passed through Vermont. Ninety-nine percent of those who naturalized from 1907 to 1919 had crossed the international border by train—most, like Grandmaison, completing all or part of their journey on the Grand Trunk Railway, typically over the course of one day.[10]

For these immigrants, returning to their place of origin was relatively easy. Hundreds from Lewiston took part in yearly excursions that Saint-Pierre Church, their local societies, and the railroad companies organized to Québec.[11] But pilgrimages to Sainte-Anne de Beaupré, and trips to visit family and friends in the Province of Québec, did not typically lead to repatriation.

Although *Le Messager* regularly informed readers of visits and talks in Lewiston by colonization and repatriation agents working for the Province of Québec or the Canadian federal government, it stressed in other articles that better economic and social conditions generally prevailed in the United States. In January 1902, *Le Messager* argued against returning to Canada to work in the manufacturing sector, contending that "we will have to work much more and be less paid." In 1906, the newspaper contended that French Canadians did not live a better life farming in Canada, claiming, for instance, that individuals colonizing areas of northern Québec found that "the wood merchant . . . is the veritable lord." It instead advised those who wished to return to the land to purchase farms in New England, where they could combine farming with a cash income from industrial work. Problems between Catholics and Protestants in the United States had declined significantly as Catholics had grown in number, the newspaper suggested, indicating (without evidence) that "our religion is more honored and more respected here than in Canada"—a suggestion that challenges contemporary national-identity myths that Canada treated minorities better than did the United States. The French-language newspaper periodically published brief announcements of French Canadians who returned to Québec or who moved to western Canada to establish farms. *Le Messager* also did not pass up the opportunity to point out examples of French Canadians emigrating from Canada to Lewiston for a second time. While the newspaper acknowledged that colonization and repatriation agents acted out of a patriotic duty to make Canada a strong country, it felt that the possibility of repatriation was a significant obstacle for the francophones seeking to make progress in the United States.[12]

Consequently, *Le Messager* strongly encouraged French-Canadian immigrants to naturalize. It particularly argued that naturalized francophones could wield more political influence in the community—an influence proportionate to its numbers. The newspaper insisted that a larger Franco-American electorate could demand an increasing share of the patronage appointments made after every municipal election. Disarming those who maintained that a tension existed between the preservation of French-Canadian ethnicity on the one hand and entrance into U.S. society on the other, *Le Messager* contended that naturalization was not incompatible with French-Canadian identity. Indeed, naturalized francophones could better demonstrate their ethnic pride by advancing the interests of their group in the United States.[13]

In 1902, *Le Messager* conveyed this message with a bit of humor. Tongue-in-cheek, it asked women, who did not yet have suffrage, to do their part to get the men of the community to naturalize. It suggested that they introduce a patriotic dimension to their courtship rituals:

When a young man asks a young woman:
————Do you love me?
She should respond:
————Are you naturalized?
Then we would certainly expand the number of our voters, and our influence would increase.
Come on, young ladies, a little shock to the heart; it's in your interest since it will help our nationality.[14]

In its efforts to promote naturalization, *Le Messager* periodically detailed in its columns the laws governing, the costs associated with, and the steps involved in the naturalization process. The newspaper regularly published information about evening classes designed to help francophones learn English and to prepare them for the exam on U.S. history and government instituted by the Bureau of Immigration and Naturalization. It even supplied—in English—the questions naturalization examiners often asked, along with the correct responses. This French-language newspaper routinely reported on the efforts of the individuals (usually attorneys) and the societies that organized naturalization clubs and drives and that helped French speakers process the paperwork necessary to become citizens. Occasionally, it would suggest the number of compatriots eligible to take out first or final papers, urging them and the French-language societies to take steps to ensure their naturalization. It also publicized the numbers as well as the names of those who had taken out naturalization papers. Readers of *Le Messager* never lacked information or even prodding to become U.S. citizens. *Le Messager*'s concerns about the possibility of remigration suggest there were two immigrant groups in Lewiston: sojourners and naturalizers. Shortly before the Canadian national elections in 1911, the newspaper announced that an unspecified but sizable number of French Canadians from the local area planned to return to Canada to cast votes for the incumbent Liberal prime minister, Wilfrid Laurier.[15] Such announcements reveal the challenge the newspaper faced in creating one francophone community in Lewiston—one willing to give up its British citizenship to become citizens of the United States.

Le Messager was not above pressuring French-Canadian immigrants to naturalize. Sometimes the newspaper published the names of persons who had previously filed their declaration of intent to become U.S. citizens, but who were slow about taking out their final papers. It warned them that they faced having to start the process over if they did not complete it within the allotted seven years. During World War I, *Le Messager* wanted Lewiston's francophone men to demonstrate their loyalty to their adopted country by beginning or completing their naturalization and by serving in the U.S. military. It informed readers that immigrants who did not initiate the naturalization process would be considered deserters by Canada, and those with first papers over seven years old would be considered aliens by the United States.[16]

Unlike in Canada, there was no conscription crisis in the United States among individuals of French-Canadian birth and background during World War I. At that time, Canada did not have autonomy, and it entered the world conflict with Britain in August 1914. Henri Bourassa, the editor of Montréal's *Le Devoir* and an outspoken critic of Canada's participation in World War I, visited Lewiston during a 1915 speaking tour of New England. According to *Le Messager*, Franco-American elites helped fill the city-hall auditorium, even though some disagreed with Bourassa's politics, including his opposition to Canada's entry into the world conflict. *Le Messager* was among the Franco-American newspapers that criticized French-Canadian nationalists like Bourassa during the anti-conscription riots that took place in Québec in 1918, when French Canadians objected strenuously to being forced by Anglo-Canadians to take part in an imperial struggle they felt did not concern them. In that same year, Canadian and British officers tried to expand the number of enlisted men by recruiting Franco-Americans. They established offices in Portland and Lewiston, hoping to attract at least five hundred Maine men to the war effort. They placed ads in *Le Messager* depicting soldiers at the front lines—ads that indicated "these men are stopping the Huns" and that asked Franco-Americans: "Why not help them?" Recruiters spoke in English and French about the war, drawing one to two thousand people to rallies at Lewiston's city hall. But they appear to have attracted few actual volunteers. Only eleven men joined the Canadian army as a result of a rally in May 1918, reported *Le Messager.*[17]

Lewiston Franco-Americans opted instead to fight the war under the U.S. flag. It probably helped that draft registrars included French speakers, one of them a Dominican priest. According to l'Institut Jacques-Cartier (the Jacques Cartier Institute), Franco-Americans provided the largest number of volunteers to the war effort before the United States imposed conscription. Participation in the U.S. armed services demonstrated loyalty to the country of adoption. In all, approximately eight hundred Franco-Americans, representing about half of the total enlistees from Lewiston, served in the First World War.[18]

Robert G. LeBlanc has argued that the cultural survival of French Canadians and Franco-Americans in their respective countries necessitated different responses to participation in the world conflict. A minority in Canada, increasingly agitated by the treatment of francophones outside of the Province of Québec, French Canadians resisted being forced by Anglo-Canadians to take part in a war to defend the "mother countries" of England and France, with which they felt no bonds. For their part, Franco-Americans intent upon preserving their ethnicity in the United States needed to demonstrate their loyalty to the host society. Their different reactions to participation in the war, according to LeBlanc, led to a "cultural divergence" between French-Canadian and Franco-American elites.[19] The basis of this divergence was that ethnic retention and acculturation composed the same goal for Franco-Americans; this was not the case for French Canadians who felt no need or desire to acculturate in Canada.

Assisted by publicity in *Le Messager*, Franco-Americans continued in the early twentieth century to organize themselves for naturalization. They formed their own naturalization clubs, sometimes creating new ones when they felt existing clubs lacked sufficient drive in promoting U.S. citizenship. In 1903, for example, a new club decided to help French-Canadian immigrants pay the costs of naturalization in order to improve upon the results of the existing naturalization club. Franco-American attorneys continued to offer assistance at no cost to francophones who needed help to process their papers. Most of these attorneys were politically active and likely expected recompense on election days. Unlike in the nineteenth century, the Dominicans played little role in the naturalization efforts of the early twentieth century, other than serving as examples for the city's francophone population by becoming U.S. citizens themselves. Franco-Americans could join other naturalization clubs, such as the Democratic Club organized by city employees. But Lewiston's French speakers tended to rely upon their own clubs, the help of their own elites, and the resources of francophones to gain U.S. citizenship.[20]

In the early twentieth century, French speakers continued to face obstacles to political participation in the United States. As in the late nineteenth century, about one-fifth (21.5 percent) of Lewiston's francophones traveled to Portland, Maine, to take out their final naturalization papers during the first two decades of the twentieth century. All but one did so before the Bureau of Immigration and Naturalization began overseeing immigration. While *Le Messager* did not comment specifically on the reasons for traveling to Portland after the turn of the century, local officials probably made it difficult for Lewiston francophones to naturalize at the county courthouse prior to municipal elections. Newspaper announcements and naturalization numbers suggest this. For example, announcements of organized trips to Portland to process naturalization papers appeared in *Le Messager* in February 1905 and 1906, just a couple of weeks before the municipal elections. *Le Messager*'s 1901 announcement and advice that the Auburn court's sitting judge "is well disposed toward our people; let us profit by it" no longer seemed to apply. In fact, only five francophones from Lewiston naturalized at the county courthouse in Auburn in 1905 and 1906, while 112 others traveled thirty miles to Portland to take out their final naturalization papers.[21] This inconvenience, it appears, continued to be the price exacted to join the U.S. political process.

New U.S. laws significantly impeded the naturalization of French-Canadian immigrants.[22] Beginning in September 1906, those who had entered the United States as minors under eighteen had to file a declaration of intention (first papers) and to wait two years before filing their final papers to become U.S. citizens. Unlike in the past, they now had to follow the same two-step naturalization procedure as those who had entered the country as adults. In addition, candidates for citizenship had to demonstrate that they could speak English. These requirements, along with improved economic conditions in the sending society, caused French-speaking men to take longer to naturalize in the early twentieth century than they had in the late nineteenth; this was especially evident among those who naturalized during the second decade of the century. Arthur Grandmaison again serves as a case in point. He arrived in the United States before his fourteenth birthday in 1898 and declared his intention to become a U.S. citizen in 1913; because he did not naturalize before new federal regulations went into effect in September 1906, he had to complete both first and final naturalization papers and to meet the English-language requirement. Grandmaison therefore became a citizen in 1919, at age thirty-five, fourteen years after reaching the age of eligibility. In spite of the new naturalization regulations and improved economic conditions in Canada, a large majority of the French-Canadian immigrants who became U.S. citizens in the early twentieth century, whether they had crossed the border as minors or adults, nevertheless naturalized within ten years of their eligibility.[23]

Twentieth-century naturalization records suggest some of the occupational and family variables that affected the decision of French-speaking men to become U.S. citizens. Beginning in 1904, naturalization forms provided the occupations of candidates for citizenship. The data reveals that a majority of the French-Canadian immigrants of Lewiston who naturalized in the early twentieth century held industrial jobs: from 1904 to 1909, 65.8 percent were industrial workers, compared to 54.1 percent between 1910 and 1919. Lewiston's French speakers had experienced some upward occupational mobility from the first to the second decade of the twentieth century. Arthur Grandmaison, formerly a mill operative, had become a clerk by the time of his naturalization in 1919. White-collar workers made up more than one-tenth (12.4 percent) of the francophones who naturalized during the first decade of the twentieth century, and over one-fifth (22.4 percent) of those who became citizens during the second decade.[24] Like Grandmaison, those with better jobs had more incentive to remain in the United States. Another explanation for the increase in the proportion of white-collar job holders who naturalized is that they probably had more experience speaking English than industrial and other blue-collar workers. Grandmaison probably had to speak English more frequently in the course of his work than the Franco-Americans employed in the local textile mills and shoe factories. Like other white-collar workers who naturalized during the second decade of the century, Grandmaison must have been less intimidated than industrial workers by the English-language requirement instituted by the Bureau of Immigration and Naturalization and tested by its naturalization examiners.

After the bureau standardized naturalization documents, the forms provided information about the marital status and families of the male immigrants who became citizens. Data for the period from 1907 to 1919 reveal that a preponderance (72.4 percent) of the Lewiston men who naturalized in the early twentieth century were married, and nearly thirty (29.3) percent of the married men had U.S.-born wives, something which must have encouraged these men to naturalize. But the birthplace of children appears to have been a more decisive factor. Over half (57.6 percent) of the men who naturalized from 1907 to 1919 had children, and in 80.3 percent of these cases, their offspring had all been born in the United States; an additional 12.8 percent of these married or widowed men had some children, but not all, with birthplaces in the United States. Thus, over 90 percent of the naturalizing men with children had some offspring who had acquired U.S. citizenship at birth. As these children grew up, they undoubtedly developed ties to the United States that made it difficult for their fathers to contemplate relocating them to Canada, providing the impetus for these men to remain permanently in the United States. In Arthur Grandmaison's case, his wife and the four children they had by the time of his 1919 naturalization had all been born in the United States, a situation which surely must have influenced his decision to become a U.S. citizen.[25]

Self-reported data recorded by federal census takers in 1920 confirms the patterns discerned from the naturalization records and also reveals other variables that may have prompted French-Canadian men of Lewiston to become U.S. citizens. As demonstrated in table 2, having first or final naturalization papers correlated positively with the ability to read and write, the ability to speak English, and having children who had been born in the United States. Though the patterns were not as pronounced as with the other variables, engagement of the citizenship process also correlated with younger age of arrival to the United States and with longer residency.

It appears not to have correlated with marital status. An alien in 1920, Vénérand Vallé represents the flipside of most of these patterns. He had

Table 2. Variables Correlating to the Naturalization of Adult Male French-Canadian Immigrants in 1920 (in percentages)[a]

	NATURALIZED OR HOLDING FIRST PAPERS	ALIENS
LITERACY		
Able to read and write (N = 75)	70.7	29.3
Unable to read and write (N = 11)	27.3	72.7
Unknown (N = 1)	100.0	0
ABILITY TO SPEAK ENGLISH		
English-speaking (N = 76)	68.4	31.6
Non-English-speaking (N = 10)	40.0	60.0
Unknown (N = 1)	100.0	0
LENGTH OF U.S. RESIDENCE		
Under 10 years (N = 12)	50.0	50.0
10–19 years (N = 29)	62.1	37.9
20–29 years (N = 22)	86.4	13.6
30–39 years (N = 16)	50.0	50.0
40–49 years (N = 7)	71.4	28.6
50–59 years (N = 1)	100.0	0
AGE AT MIGRATION		
under 10 years (N = 22)	68.2	31.8
10–19 years (N = 39)	71.8	28.2
20–29 years (N = 14)	71.4	28.6
30–39 years (N = 5)	60.0	40.0
40–49 years (N = 5)	0	100.0
50–59 years (N = 1)	0	100.0
Unknown (N = 1)	100.0	0

arrived in the United States in 1911 at the age of forty; his wife and seven of the nine children living with them in 1920 had been born in Canada, and, although he spoke English, he was illiterate.[26] In short, Vallé's older age at arrival, the shorter period of his U.S. residency, the Canadian birth of his wife and most of their children, and his lack of literacy skills probably all held him back from becoming a naturalized citizen.

	NATURALIZED OR HOLDING FIRST PAPERS	ALIENS
CHOICE OF SPOUSE		
Canadian-born Franco-American (*N* = 52)	59.6	40.4
U.S.-born Franco-American (*N* = 10)	90.0	10.0
Non-Franco-American (*N* = 2)	100.0	0
No spouse (*N* = 23)	65.2	34.8
PLACE OF BIRTH OF CHILDREN		
All U.S.-born (N = 41)	73.2	26.8
Canadian- and U.S.-born (N = 6)	66.7	33.3
All Canadian-born (N = 8)	12.5	87.5
No children (N = 32)	68.8	31.3
HOME OWNERSHIP		
Owned (*N* = 10)	60.0	40.0
Rented (*N* = 50)	64.0	36.0
Resided in another's home (*N* = 25)	76.0	24.0
Unknown (*N* = 2)	0	100.0
OCCUPATION		
White-collar (*N* = 10)	90.0	10.0
Blue-collar (*N* = 68)	66.2	33.8
None (*N* = 9)	33.3	66.7

Source: Derived from every thirtieth household in the U.S. Census, 1920.
a. Of the 88 French-Canadian immigrants in the sample who were eighteen years of age or older (the earliest age at which they could take out first naturalization papers), 39 were naturalized, 18 had first papers, and 30 were aliens; one whose citizenship status was unknown was excluded.

Census records from 1920 also reveal that occupational and home-ownership status did not correlate as strongly with naturalization as other variables. The men holding first or final naturalization papers had predominantly blue-collar jobs. Ninety percent of those with white-collar occupations had taken steps, however, to change their citizenship status by the end of the second decade of the century. Homeownership did not

correlate positively with adoption of U.S. citizenship, for the large majority
of men with first or final naturalization papers either rented or lived in the
household of another person.[27] In brief, owning a home and holding one
of Lewiston's better-paying jobs did not appear to influence the decision to
pursue U.S. citizenship to the same degree as noneconomic variables. For
first-generation Franco-Americans of Lewiston, language skills and family
considerations seemed to be more important.

The efforts of Le Messager and local elites to promote naturalization
in Lewiston, and the desire of francophones to acquire citizenship, seem to
have yielded significant results. Based upon the 1920 census, 44.3 percent
of the city's adult male French-Canadian immigrants had naturalized by
1920, and another 20.5 percent had declared their intention to become
U.S. citizens. Nearly two-thirds, then, of Lewiston's first-generation adult
male French speakers had begun or completed the naturalization process by
the end of the second decade of the century. The proportion of Lewiston's
francophone men who had naturalized or taken out first papers by 1920 exceeded the state average for French-Canadian immigrant men of Maine and
for all other New England states except Rhode Island. Hard-fought gains
were kept. Official letters attached to the naturalization records reveal that
only two (0.3 percent) of the 684 men who became U.S. citizens in Lewiston
between 1900 and 1919 later repatriated in Canada. The tiny percentage of
repatriates stands in sharp contrast to global estimates of remigration. About
half of the individuals who had emigrated from Québec to the United States
in the nineteenth century remigrated to Canada, estimates Ralph Dominic
Vicero, and about one-third who had emigrated between 1900 and 1930
returned to Canada, estimates Yolande Lavoie.[28] The process of naturalization worked against these patterns, for the French-Canadian immigrants of
Lewiston who modified their ethnic identity by naturalizing in the United
States tended overwhelmingly not to relinquish their citizenship through the
affirmative act of repatriation.

As francophones became U.S. citizens and gained greater influence in
Lewiston, tensions arose over the French spoken in the Spindle City, and
language politics became a salient issue. Putting down the French spoken by
Franco-Americans was a means of social control, an effort to make French
speakers with Canadian roots feel inferior to anglophones and to persons
fortunate enough to have had ample access to education. Self-conscious

francophones began abandoning their mother tongue in the early twentieth century. This development worried Franco-American elites who derived their influence in the host society from French speakers. Their concern over the potential loss of the French language, which would point to a decline in the ethnic identity of French-Canadian descendants, helps explain why they engaged the Irish Catholic hierarchy and the French Dominicans in bitter ethnic disputes in the early twentieth century, as we shall see in the next chapter.

Periodically, *Le Messager* offered brief comments in its local news section illustrating that some Franco-Americans felt ashamed of the French language. These Franco-Americans tried to speak only English, even if they spoke it poorly. In 1905 *Le Messager* suggested that when Irish clergy heard this badly spoken English, it motivated them to push the anglicization of Maine's Franco-Americans. The newspaper coaxed those individuals reluctant to speak French by pointing out that French was still the language of diplomacy and was an essential part of who they were: "To be embarrassed to speak one's mother tongue is like scorning one's own goods." At the same time, *Le Messager* wanted to encourage Lewiston's Franco-Americans to improve the quality of their French, suggesting that they avoid "vulgar and wicked words" that denigrated the language and reflected a lack of education. French Dominicans of Saint-Pierre Parish apparently did, too, for they reproduced an article from *Le Messager* in the parish publication at the turn of the century that indicated that the French Dames de Sion (Ladies of Zion) "gradually transformed the language of our children" to "a French so pure."[29] It was a compliment they did not extend to the French-Canadian Soeurs Grises (Grey Nuns), who had taught in the parish schools before the arrival of les Dames de Sion and who still taught the children residing at the orphanages they directed. There existed a tension in Lewiston between so-called "Parisian" French and Canadian French—a tension that Franco-American elites fought but, on occasion, inadvertently fed.

Beginning around the turn of the century, *Le Messager* found itself defending the French spoken in Lewiston against comments by the *Journal* and educated Americans who put it down. One derogatory remark came from Bowdoin College professor William MacDonald, who wrote in 1896 that Maine's French-Canadian population "speaks no language save the barbarous Canadian French." In Lewiston, Americans learned what they considered to be "real Parisian French" at Bates College, *Le Messager* reported in 1898, but Parisians would chuckle upon hearing it, the newspaper insisted. *Le Messager* contended that Lewiston's French-Canadian descendants communicated perfectly well with the Dominicans from France, and it maintained that the difference between the French of both groups was small: "There only exists a small difference in the accent, just as one exists between the language of the English and that of the Americans." In perhaps the clearest and most succinct explanation of the reason for this difference, *Le Messager* quoted Benjamin Sulte, a French-Canadian historian, who had stated: "The form of our language is lost in France. We preserved it [in North America], and this old form has become our originality." When Bates College organized a French club in 1904 to provide opportunities for students to practice their French, it almost certainly did not take up *Le Messager*'s suggestion to work on "the French of Canada."[30] Spoken by Lewiston's working-class population, Canadian French offered no prestige.

Tension in the community over "Parisian" and Canadian French became an issue in the appointment of language teachers in the public schools. In 1913, attorney H. E. Holmes complained in a letter to the editor of the *Lewiston Journal* that the instructors who taught French at Lewiston High School were not native speakers, something that "results in the language being taught as a dead language." Holmes pointed out that Franco-Americans made up half of Lewiston's population, but there were no Franco-American teachers at the local high school. Hiring one of them to teach French would help students "learn to speak the language, and to speak it with a French accent," he maintained. Pleased by Holmes's efforts, *Le Messager* revealed in a front-page headline: "Attorney Holmes is fighting the stupid prejudice that we do not speak real French." In 1919, the Lewiston school commission debated whether or not to hire a Franco-American to fill a vacancy to teach French at the high school. A Franco-American doctor serving on the commission pushed for the appointment of a French-Canadian descendant, while a non-French-surnamed doctor voiced his adamant opposition to teaching Canadian French in Lewiston schools. Perhaps a compromise, a Bates-trained Franco-American gained the appointment; she was Adrienne Belleau, the first Franco-American woman from Lewiston to graduate from Bates College, and the daughter of politically prominent attorney F. X. Belleau.[31]

One means of preserving the French language in Lewiston was to acquire and read French books. In 1903, the Franco-American societies and les Dames de Sion together had about 2,500 titles that they allowed to circulate. Only after a Franco-American gained appointment to the board of the public library in Lewiston do we find indications in *Le Messager* and in the city's annual reports of the purchase of French books for local residents. In 1904, *Le Messager* reported that F. X. Belleau, a director of the public library, had been authorized to purchase from 300 to 400 French titles from Paris. The following year, the library planned to acquire several hundred more French books as a result of Belleau's efforts, the newspaper reported. Library trustees noted in 1907 that "the small collection of French books in the library has been read and reread by the French people, who have repeatedly asked if more volumes might be added to what we already have." Reports of the city librarian and the trustees in other years also reflected high demand for French titles in the early twentieth century. Literacy rates had improved significantly from the late nineteenth century: in 1880, 43.5 percent of Lewiston's French-Canadian population, age eight and above, either could not read and/or could not write, whereas in 1920 only 8.4 percent were illiterate. By 1918, if not sooner, the Lewiston Public Library also looked to acquire titles by French-Canadian authors, such as clerics Camille Roy and Lionel Groulx. Not until 1916 did the library hire its first Franco-American librarian, Ernestine Lemaire, the sister of the municipal clerk who won election as mayor in the following year.[32] As Belleau's influence in the selection of books at the public library reveals, when Lewiston's Franco-Americans gained political influence and obtained greater access to city positions, they increasingly had the opportunity to help the Spindle City's French-Canadian descendants preserve their ethnicity.

Franco-Americans gained political strength in Lewiston in the early twentieth century as the result of their concerted efforts to naturalize and to vote. In 1903, their 1,200 voters made up one-fourth of the city's voting population, and Franco-Americans increased their electoral strength by over 500 persons through 1916. Although the enfranchised Franco-American electorate was small in proportion to its overall population, it did make some significant political gains during the first two decades of the century. In 1907, Franco-Americans won three of the seven seats on the Board of Aldermen, the first time in Lewiston's history that they had gained so many seats. By 1914, Lewiston elected its first mayor of French-Canadian descent, and each year from 1917 to 1920 the city also elected a Lewiston-born Franco-American as mayor.[33]

To help achieve these results, *Le Messager* worked very hard in the early twentieth century to encourage Franco-Americans to overcome their differences and to unite politically. In 1902, the newspaper expressed its belief that doing so was a prerequisite to electing a mayor of French-Canadian descent. But Democratic, Republican, and Socialist political clubs headed by Franco-Americans competed for members and divided Lewiston's French speakers. Typically, *Le Messager* offered a brief announcement in its local news column that a new club had formed to promote the interests of a particular political party in Lewiston elections, and it usually named the officers and sometimes indicated how many members the club had attracted. From these periodic announcements of "new" partisan clubs, we can infer that they were more akin to ad hoc political-campaign organizations than to entrenched political machines. The Franco-American Socialist Club, which also sponsored candidates and tried to garner Franco-American support, had the least success in attracting votes. In 1904, for example, student Joseph A. Phénix won only 45 votes in his bid for a seat in the state legislature, while the Democratic victors from Lewiston each outpolled him by over 2,000 votes. Occasionally, non-francophone Republicans tried to capitalize on divisions among Franco-Americans. In 1900, for instance, Republican candidates vying for seats in the state legislature promised to vote funds for the planned expansion of the Sisters' Hospital in order to gain Franco-American votes. Factions within the Democratic Party, probably centered on personality conflicts, further split Franco-Americans in the early twentieth century.[34]

Despite these divisions within the French-speaking community, and perhaps because of them, *Le Messager* continued to promote the Democratic Party. It periodically reminded francophones that Republican administrations in Lewiston had refused Franco-Americans a fair share of patronage appointments. *Le Messager* was overt about patronage. It never passed up the chance to list the number of jobs, particularly in the police department or on the road commission, that Franco-Americans had gained following Democratic victories in local elections.[35]

Unity between Irish and Franco-American voters led to Democratic victories in Lewiston municipal elections. But Democratic gains also led to ethnic competition. In 1902, Franco-Americans overwhelmingly backed Irish-American D. J. McGillicuddy's bid for mayor, causing *Le Messager* to claim that his election was "essentially a French-Canadian victory." Because Franco-Americans had delivered 60 percent of the Democratic vote in that election, they expected a proportionate share of the patronage appointments. When francophones did not receive enough of the jobs, two Franco-Americans on the Board of Aldermen and five on the Common Council threatened to resign from their elected posts until McGillicuddy agreed to settle the matter to their satisfaction. Franco-Americans were determined to wield the political clout they had won to push for their share of the spoils. This act of self-assertion found parallels in religious matters, as we shall see in the next chapter. Through the first two decades of the century, cooperation and conflict characterized relations between Lewiston's Irish and Franco-American populations as they vied for the right to appoint members to local jobs.[36]

Le Messager's dream of having a mayor of French-Canadian descent in Lewiston came to fruition in 1914 when Dr. Robert J. Wiseman won the mayoralty. Wiseman's situation illustrates the permeability of ethnic lines in Lewiston. A native of Stanfold, Québec, he was the son of a Scotch father and Irish mother, and he married a woman of French-Canadian descent. Franco-Americans regarded him as one of their own; according to *Le Messager*, Wiseman was "a veritable Franco-American at heart and by nationality." Wiseman joined the Lewiston School Commission in 1908, gained appointment as temporary superintendent of schools in 1909, and won election to the Board of Aldermen in 1910. In both 1911 and 1913, he lost his bid for mayor in the Democratic caucus. After losing the Democratic nod in 1913, he decided to run as a Progressive candidate, but lost the general election to the Democrat who had defeated him in caucus. *Le Messager* interpreted the election result as an indication that Franco-Americans were still loyal to the Democratic Party. In a meeting at l'Institut Jacques-Cartier Hall in November 1913, Franco-American Republicans, Democrats, and Progressives asked Wiseman to run again for mayor in the spring elections. Americans and Franco-Americans supported Wiseman's candidacy, *Le Messager* reported, and he agreed to run. This time, however, Wiseman did not campaign on the Democratic ticket. Instead, he gained the Republican nomination and the support of the Republican *Lewiston Evening Journal*. During the spring

1914 election, he ran on three tickets: Republican, Progressive, and Citizen. Dissatisfaction with the incumbent Democrat's administration, which had left Lewiston with a large budget deficit, propelled Wiseman's candidacy. Although some Franco-American Democrats did not vote for Wiseman, a coalition of Americans and Franco-Americans helped him trounce his Democratic opponent. Because of ill health and the demands of his medical practice, Wiseman chose not to run again in the following year. *Le Messager* hoped Wiseman would seek the mayor's job during the spring 1916 elections, "but this time openly on the Democratic ticket."[37]

For four terms from 1917 through 1920, Lewiston-born Democrat Charles P. Lemaire held the mayor's office. When he won reelection in 1918, *Le Messager* was ecstatic, for it felt that Franco-American voters had demonstrated unity and had asserted their political power. Exuding confidence, the newspaper warned Republicans that they had little future in the city. Lemaire and the other Democrats celebrating his victory conveyed the same message in an evening torch-light parade. They marched through the city's Republican wards and in front of the *Lewiston Journal* offices. As they did so, the Saint-Dominique band "played part of the funeral march by Chopin to announce to them that they were actually dead, politically speaking."[38]

By 1920, asserted *Le Messager*, Lewiston had become "the Democratic fortress of Maine." This was true even beyond local elections. Every four years from 1904 to 1920, Democratic gubernatorial and congressional candidates gained a majority of Lewiston's votes, as did Democratic presidential candidates in the three elections from 1908 to 1916.[39] By the second decade of the twentieth century, Democratic partisanship in the Spindle City had become integral to Franco-American identity.

The Winding Road

From *Canadien* to Franco-American, 1900–1920

During Lewiston's centennial celebration in 1895, a French-Canadian letter writer expressed pleasure at how much relations between French Canadians and Americans had improved by century's end. In particular, the writer noted, "the enlightened and intelligent American no longer reproaches us now for speaking our language and for practicing the religion of our fathers." But, he warned, French speakers in the United States faced another danger: the hostility of New England's Irish prelates to the French language.[1] During the early twentieth century, Franco-Americans in Lewiston and elsewhere in Maine perceived the same hostility on the part of their Irish bishops, and they became engaged in heated ethnic controversies. In religious as in secular matters during the first two decades of the twentieth century, they found that ethnic differences still served as a source of competition and conflict. Even as their ethnic feelings intensified during conflicts with Irish bishops, Lewiston's French speakers continued to Americanize on their own. The road they chose from *Canadien* to Franco-American took various twists and turns, demonstrating that the process of joining U.S. society was anything but linear.

Pressure from Irish bishops to push the Americanization of Lewiston's French speakers resulted in ethnic controversies in which they joined other francophones from throughout the state to demand greater influence in Maine's Catholic Church. Until 1905, Lewiston's Franco-Americans had maintained cordial relations with Maine's bishops, all of whom had been of Irish descent. Though displeased by the appointment of another Irish bishop in 1901, and by the new bishop's subsequent appointment of an Irish vicar general as his assistant, *Le Messager* accepted these decisions calmly. When the *Woonsocket (Rhode Island) La Tribune* chastised *Le Messager* for its complacency, the newspaper explained: "Good Catholics must submit to the orders of the pope and to those of the bishop, his representative." In 1884 and 1895, Bishop James Augustin Healy had threatened to forbid Catholics from reading *Le Messager* because of critical articles it had published on church issues and on Catholic clergy in Québec and New England. Healy's rebukes had served to temper the French-language newspaper, particularly in its reporting of ethnic tensions and conflicts between Irish bishops and French-Canadian parishioners in different New England states.[2]

In 1905, however, *Le Messager* erupted. It reported the rumor that Maine's third bishop, William O'Connell, had told his diocesan council that he wanted to anglicize the French-language parishes of Maine. While the newspaper felt that O'Connell and other Irish clergy hoped to unify the state's Catholics, it strongly resisted the idea of "[forcing] us to speak the language of Protestants." Lewiston Franco-Americans, of course, wanted to learn English; after all, their parish school had been the first in Maine to offer a bilingual education. *Le Messager* expressed pleasure at the bilingual training of children; after observing them taking their French and English exams at the end of the 1902–1903 school year, it argued that a facility in English and French would help these children to obtain good jobs in Lewiston in the future. But when *Le Messager* learned of O'Connell's desire to anglicize Maine's French-speaking population, it reacted angrily, even disrespectfully. This was such a contentious issue for individuals of French-Canadian birth and background, because they viewed their French language and their Roman Catholic faith as inextricably intertwined. The saying *Qui perd sa langue, perd sa foi* (Whoever loses his language, loses his faith) well captured their sentiments. Following the report of O'Connell's remarks, *Le Messager* published a spate of articles complaining vociferously about the inferior position of Franco-Americans, particularly of their clergy, within the diocese.[3]

No longer willing to accept all decisions of Catholic prelates, Franco-Americans decided to fight publicly for the interests of Maine's French speakers. Lewiston's l'Institut Jacques-Cartier (Jacques Cartier Institute) quickly organized a committee on *la Cause Nationale* (the National Cause) to spearhead the fight. The committee wrote to Maine's Franco-American societies, asking for their support to thwart the efforts of Irish coreligionists who were working against the use of French in the Diocese of Portland. The societies subsequently began sponsoring fundraising events, such as whist parties, to raise money for la Cause Nationale.[4]

As la Cause Nationale gained momentum and planned a convention in Lewiston for francophone delegates from throughout Maine, the Irish vicar general and the Dominican priests of Lewiston tried to cool the movement. Acting on behalf of Bishop O'Connell, who was abroad, Monsignor Edward F. Hurley called Joseph Côté, the convention's secretary, to Portland; while the substance of their discussions remained secret, the vicar general must have pressured Côté to ensure that the convention's proceedings remained respectful of the Catholic Church and its clergy. Hurley also telegrammed the Dominican pastor: "You must accept the presidency of the large national convention of Lewiston," the Dominicans recorded in their chronicle. Hurley then visited the Dominicans in Lewiston and went to the hospital to see the ailing pastor, Alexandre-Louis Mothon. Following Hurley's visit, the Dominicans noted that they did not agree with all of the goals of la Cause Nationale as reported in *Le Messager*, "and we regard taking hold of it very important to give it direction." As the Dominicans expressed hope that Mothon would be well enough to do the job, they implied that they wanted to preserve the interests of Maine's Catholic Church in its conflict with Franco-Americans.[5] But, in seeking to disconnect religion from nationality, the French Dominicans parted with Franco-Americans who viewed them as inseparable.

Francophone elites attending the March 1906 convention highlighted the fact that Franco-Americans made up 80,000 of Maine's 106,000 Catholics. They called for priests of the same heritage in parishes where Franco-Americans constituted a majority, and they requested the appointment of a Franco-American or, at the very least, a French-speaking bishop to succeed O'Connell, who had recently been elevated to coadjutor archbishop of

Boston. While the convention acknowledged the importance of bilingual education in the parish schools, it argued the need to maintain the French language in order to preserve the Catholic faith of Maine's Franco-American population. *La langue est la gardienne de la foi* (Language is the guardian of the faith), convention delegates strongly believed.[6] In this respect, individuals of French-Canadian birth and background differed from Irish Catholics for whom no connection existed between language and faith. This difference was at the heart of the controversies that divided Irish and Franco-American Catholics in the early twentieth century.

Several Dominicans, including Mothon, attended the two-day convention, held at the hall of l'Institut Jacques-Cartier. The Dominicans chose not to serve on the committees organized "to deal with the difficult questions." *Le Messager* recognized the role the Dominicans played at the convention and, when it found itself embroiled in a dispute with them three months later, publicly alleged that Mothon had attended to inhibit the delegates and to spy for the Irish vicar general.[7]

La Cause Nationale continued to gain momentum after the convention, and it generated support from sympathetic Franco-American clergy. They fed articles to *Le Messager*, which coded their signatures as "x," "xx," or "xxx," to denote different priests. When Bishop O'Connell called individual clergymen to Portland in April 1906, the Dominicans suspected he was bearing down on those critical of his administration. The Dominicans wondered if the priests feeding *Le Messager* would be discovered and punished, and if the newspaper would be condemned.[8]

By summer, the Dominicans found themselves the object of *Le Messager*'s wrath. When a delegation representing la Cause Nationale went to Rome in June 1906 to plead for a bishop of French-Canadian birth or background for Maine, it learned that six years earlier, Dominican priests had asked the pope and cardinals not to appoint a "French Canadian" as Maine's bishop. This information turned Franco-Americans against the Dominicans from France who had administered Saint-Pierre Parish for a quarter century. Although Lewiston's Dominicans vigorously denied the allegations of representatives of la Cause Nationale, *Le Messager*, designated as the official organ of la Cause Nationale by its Comité Permanent (Permanent Committee), harshly attacked the order in a series of articles. The newspaper argued that the Dominicans were closer to the Irish than they were to Franco-Americans and they, like the Irish, harbored goals of anglicizing French-Canadian descendants in the United States. *Le Messager*'s proprietor, J. B. Couture, asserted "that they came to Lewiston to 'evangelize' us, just like one does the Indians or the Chinese." While not blaming local Dominicans, he repeated the complaint that the Dominican order had opposed the appointment of a *Canadien* as bishop of Maine in 1900, and he speculated that the order had done so again in 1906. From the time the Dominicans had arrived in Lewiston, Couture further complained, none of the monastery's superiors or their assistants had been of French-Canadian descent.[9]

Le Messager increasingly directed its attacks toward the French pastor. It challenged Mothon, for example, to explain why Bishop O'Connell had permitted the Dominicans to tear down Saint-Pierre Church to erect another, "a temple much too costly for our population." Suffering ill health, undoubtedly aggravated by the personal attacks, Mothon resigned in July 1906, after having served three separate stints, a total of seventeen years, as pastor of Saint-Pierre Parish.[10]

During the controversy between *Le Messager* and the Dominicans, the latter tried to undermine the newspaper. The Dominicans took away from *Le Messager* the job of publishing the bimonthly parish bulletin, *La Quinzaine* (*The Fortnightly*). They also asked the parish music director, Henry F. Roy, to launch a competing French-language newspaper. The Dominicans provided Roy with workspace, revenue from the publication of *La Quinzaine*, and some financial support, and *Le Courrier du Maine* (*The Courier of Maine*) made its first appearance on July 24, 1906.[11]

Thus the controversy over the preservation of the French language in Maine, precipitated by remarks reportedly uttered by the state's third Irish bishop, divided Lewiston's Franco-Americans from their French-from-France religious leaders. This dispute marked a defining moment in the history of Lewiston's francophone population. From that point, they increasingly looked to French Canadians to help them preserve their ethnic identity in the United States. No longer was it enough to have French-speaking religious leaders; Lewiston's French-Canadian descendants demanded *Canadiens*. This action represented a twist in the road from *Canadien* to Franco-American.

At a meeting of over seven hundred persons at l'Institut Jacques-Cartier Hall in July 1906, Lewiston Franco-Americans decided to ask the Dominican provincial from France to appoint a pastor of French-Canadian heritage to succeed Mothon at Saint-Pierre Parish. Delegates of the Permanent Committee of la Cause Nationale met in person with the provincial, and he granted their request. He split Mothon's position in two, appointing a French prior to head the monastery and a French-Canadian pastor to oversee the parish. *Le Messager* subsequently expressed its public thanks for a *Canadien* as pastor.[12]

The changeover to pastors of French-Canadian descent proved significant and long-lasting. From 1906 until 1986, when the Dominican order stopped administering Saint-Pierre Parish, all pastors were of French-Canadian birth and background; in fact, all but one were Canadian-born. These French-Canadian and Franco-American pastors helped Lewiston's francophone population to preserve its ethnicity through much of the twentieth century.

Several developments internal to the Dominican order also helped Lewiston Franco-Americans to retain their ethnicity. Shortly after the French Dominicans established themselves in Lewiston in the early 1880s, Mothon clashed with the provincial vicar for North America, stationed in Saint-Hyacinthe. Mothon wanted the Lewiston mission to develop not as part of the Canadian province, but as an autonomous American organization with an English-language ministry. The provincial vicar, also from France, instead saw the Dominican missions in North America as one administrative unit. Initially, the Dominican monasteries in Lewiston and Saint-Hyacinthe differed in that French-from-France Dominicans had assignments in Lewiston, and French-Canadian Dominicans had theirs in Saint-Hyacinthe. A controversy ensued when Mothon strenuously objected to the transfer of a French Dominican from Lewiston to Saint-Hyacinthe. The provincial vicar prevailed over Mothon in this dispute and won the authority to move personnel between missions in Canada and the United States.[13] This development ensured an infusion of French-Canadian clergy into Lewiston for over a century.

Separatist tendencies persisted within the Dominican order in the late nineteenth century. In 1887, Lewiston's Dominicans took over the administration of Sainte-Anne Parish in Fall River, Massachusetts, to help resolve an ethnic controversy in the Diocese of Providence. The Irish bishop, Thomas Francis Hendricken, had precipitated conflicts throughout his diocese by appointing Irish pastors to French-Canadian parishes, including Sainte-Anne.

Embroiled in disputes with French-Canadian Catholics, Hendricken had not offered the French Dominicans a mission in his diocese in 1880, when they had first approached him. His successor, Bishop Matthew Harkins, consulted Bishop James Healy of Maine for a peaceful resolution to the conflict in Fall River, and Healy pointed to the Lewiston Dominicans, whom Harkins subsequently invited to Fall River. Tensions did not immediately dissipate, however. As a Dominican historian wrote in 1973, "The French Canadians do not easily forgive the earnestness with which their French pastors associate with Irish pastors; for their part, the French priests have trouble getting along with their French-Canadian colleagues." This tension between French and French-Canadian clergy led to a secret struggle in the late nineteenth century in which French Dominicans from Fall River sought to separate the U.S. missions from the administrative control of Canada, in order to remain tied to the Province of France. As early as 1884, when the Lewiston mission had shown its separatist bent, the Dominicans in Canada had themselves hoped to achieve autonomy from France for the houses of North America. Due to anticlericalism in France, the Dominican missions in Canada and the United States gained their autonomy between 1908 and 1911 and together became la Congrégation Saint-Dominique (the Saint Dominic Congregation).[14]

This development facilitated the Canadianization of the francophone Dominicans in North America. The effects were visible in the composition of the Lewiston monastery. Whereas none of the six Dominican priests and brothers who took over Saint-Pierre Parish in 1881 had been French-Canadian, fourteen of the sixteen Dominican priests and brothers in 1920 were French-Canadian immigrants, and the other two were natives of Belgium and France. The establishment of a novitiate in Saint-Hyacinthe also promoted the Canadianization of the order. By 1889, aspiring Dominicans from Canada could pursue their religious studies in Québec and no longer had to travel to Europe for all or part of their training.[15] The location of the Dominican novitiate served to solidify and to perpetuate French-Canadian control over the Saint-Dominique province. Over time, the Dominican novitiate provided a large supply of French-Canadian clergy to the order, and their assignment to Lewiston played no small role in the cultural persistence of Saint-Pierre Parish. As we will see, the Dominicans became engaged in a private struggle with Maine's fourth consecutive Irish bishop in the early twentieth century, a struggle that stemmed from the public conflicts the bishop had with Maine's Franco-Americans.

Displeased by the appointment of another Irish bishop for Maine in 1906, Franco-Americans from Lewiston and other parts of the state expected to clash with Louis S. Walsh shortly after he arrived in the Diocese of Portland. Writing for *Le Messager*, J. L. K. Laflamme argued: "The elevation of Father Walsh to the episcopal seat of Portland . . . will not be a defeat for the Franco-American cause, but only a delay. The battle begins." In one controversy that Walsh inherited from his predecessor, French speakers criticized the division of Saint-François de Sales, a Franco-American parish in Waterville, Maine. They strongly protested the reassignment of 1,200 Franco-Americans to Sacred Heart Parish, newly created to meet the needs of 265 Irish Catholics and headed by an Irish pastor. Franco-American concerns centered on ethnic differences: based on what the Irish pastor and Irish bishop had said, Franco-Americans feared that English would become the only language used in the new parish, and they worried that francophones might not establish an easy rapport with the pastor. Church authorities settled the dispute in 1908 by establishing Sacred Heart as a bilingual, territorial parish—one to which all Catholics living within its boundaries would belong.[16]

In another, much larger controversy with Bishop Walsh, Franco-Americans wanted the state legislature to repeal an 1887 law establishing the bishop as sole proprietor of all Catholic Church properties in Maine. Instead, they wanted parishes to exercise control over their own institutions, just as the *fabriques*, or parish corporations, did in Québec. Because the bishop held title to their churches and schools, Franco-Americans feared he would use their funds to pursue the goal of assimilating them into U.S. society. They felt they had ample cause for concern. Besides dividing Saint-François de Sales Parish, Walsh had chosen an Irish priest to serve as his vicar general, he had selected Irish clergy to fill a majority of the seats on his Diocesan Council, and he had appointed Irish pastors to various Franco-American parishes in Maine; Walsh had also denied Franco-American pastors permission to sit in on the exams of parish children—exams administered by diocesan inspectors of Irish descent and which increasingly tested the English-language skills of francophone students. Furthermore, Walsh had upset Franco-Americans by insisting that a

Franco-American parish in Biddeford pay diocesan collections from parish funds—funds that would otherwise have been used to support the parish's institutions.[17]

At a 1909 convention in Brunswick, Maine, Franco-Americans charged the Permanent Committee of la Cause Nationale with the task of getting the state legislature to repeal the 1887 Corporation Sole law and to replace it with something akin to the Québec *fabriques*. Armed with 7,500 signatures collected by Lewiston's *Le Messager* and Biddeford's *La Justice*, Biddeford attorney Godfroy Dupré presented the Franco-Americans' case before the Judicial Affairs Committee in March 1911. He appealed to American principles to achieve Franco-American ends, arguing for "No taxation without representation."[18]

Because the 1887 law had made it easier for the Church to establish credit, Walsh opposed the efforts of Franco-Americans to change it, and he became the object of bitter attacks in the Franco-American press. Walsh fought back. He must have prevailed upon Lewiston's Dominican priests to support his position, because after he visited the Dominican order in late February 1911, the Dominican pastor spoke out against the Franco-American bill to overturn the Corporation Sole law. Pastor Dominique Jacques charged that the measure was anti-Catholic, and warned parishioners that those who signed the petition faced excommunication, *Le Messager* subsequently reported. A few days later, *Le Messager* issued a correction: those who signed the petition did not face possible excommunication; only those who drew up the bill and pushed it in front of the state legislature did. Testifying before the Judicial Affairs Committee in March, Walsh and bankers persuaded lawmakers not to overturn the Corporation Sole law.[19]

Two months later, Walsh interdicted the six members of the Permanent Committee "because of the grave public scandal given by their various words and acts in a recent attack on Church authority, Church property and Church law in the Diocese of Portland." This left the men, one of whom was the editor of *Le Messager*, one step removed from excommunication. Walsh publicized his decision through a letter written by the diocesan chancellor that he asked priests to read at masses in Lewiston and most likely throughout the diocese. In the letter, Walsh warned Catholic societies not to associate with the interdicted men lest they risk being "deprived of their rights and privileges as a Catholic Society in the Diocese of Portland."[20]

Le Messager refused to be intimidated, and it continued to show its disrespect for the Irish bishop. In June 1911, it indicated: "Monsignor Walsh advises French-Canadian Catholics not to read bad newspapers. We do not know which newspapers the Green Lord [Bishop] reads, but Le Messager must be one of them. Thanks all the same for the announcement." In January 1912, the French-language newspaper reported that Walsh had asked local pastors whether l'Institut Jacques-Cartier was sponsoring an upcoming meeting at city hall on la Cause Nationale; because two interdicted men from Biddeford, Godfroy Dupré and Alfred Bonneau (editor of La Justice), planned to speak at the event, the bishop threatened to excommunicate the society's members. Le Messager taunted: "The evening program is under the patronage of all French Canadians of Lewiston and Auburn, and Monsignor will have a lot to do [in excommunicating them all]." Lewiston Franco-Americans apparently were not worried. According to Le Messager, 1,500 people went to hear Dupré and Bonneau speak.[21]

Following Bishop Walsh's interdictions, la Cause Nationale became the central topic of Saint-Jean-Baptiste Day speeches for at least a half decade. Whereas past speeches had usually focused on the place of Franco-Americans in the larger U.S. society, they now centered on their minority status in Maine. Alfred Bonneau promoted la Cause Nationale in 1911, asking Franco-Americans of the Lewiston-Auburn area to withhold funds from the Diocese of Portland and to support instead their parish schools. At Lewiston's Saint-Jean-Baptiste Day celebrations in 1915 and 1916, Bonneau continued to promote la Cause Nationale. He argued in 1916 that the situation of Maine's Franco-Americans was similar to that of French Canadians in Ontario.[22] Bonneau's remark referred to legislation against the use of French by the francophone minority in the schools of Canada's most populous province. In short, the conflict with Bishop Walsh caused a shift in the principal theme of Saint-Jean-Baptiste Day speeches: rather than focus on the participation of "loyal" francophones in U.S. society, keynote speakers addressed the conflict with the Irish hierarchy of Maine, particularly over the issue of preserving the French language. Thus, Walsh's efforts to push the Americanization of French-Canadian descendants precipitated ethnic tension and conflict, and if anything, had the effect of increasing the determination of Lewiston's Franco-Americans to control the terms and pace of their entry into U.S. society.

Franco-Americans must have taken heart in October 1911, when they learned that the pope favored a system of parish corporations similar to those that existed in the state of New York, rather than a Corporation Sole as existed in the Diocese of Portland. Franco-Americans initially regarded the pope's decision as a defeat for Walsh. But the parish system that Rome recommended did not resemble the Québec *fabriques*; worse, it still gave the bishop control over parish funds. Undeterred, Franco-American elites pressed forward. *Le Messager* published ads asking readers whether they favored replacing the Corporation Sole law "by a law that will respect the rights of the laity like those of the clergy?" Franco-American leaders must have received an encouraging response. In 1913, they again asked the Maine state legislature to overturn the Corporation Sole law. Instead, the legislature approved a parish corporation system modeled after that of New York, whereby the bishop, vicar general, the pastor, and two parishioners (appointed by the three clergymen) would form the corporation.[23]

Perhaps the bitterest conflict in Maine's Catholic Church during the twentieth century, the Corporation Sole controversy ended nearly a decade after Bishop Walsh arrived in Portland. After the pope upheld Walsh's interdictions of six Franco-American leaders in 1912, the bishop worked through the Dominican pastor to get *Le Messager*'s editor, J. B. Couture, to make written amends to him. He warned the pastor that the societies to which Couture belonged could not take part in religious celebrations. Four of the interdicted men from Biddeford reconciled with the bishop, and the Corporation Sole controversy petered out about a decade after it began. As late as 1917, however, Bishop Walsh was still inquiring of the Dominican pastor whether Couture would agree to sign documents to absolve himself for the role he had played in the conflict.[24] Couture remained intransigent.

Like other Irish bishops in the United States, Walsh sought to Americanize the Catholic Church in the early twentieth century. This goal, coupled with Walsh's desire to assert his authority over the dissident francophones who challenged it, led him to attempt to curtail some French-Canadian practices in Maine. As a result of the Corporation Sole controversy, in which Franco-American societies played a central role, Walsh forbade the national societies from entering churches with their banners and insignias, something they typically did on French-Canadian feast days like that of Saint-Jean-Baptiste. After a synod in Portland in 1886, Bishop Healy had similarly refused French-Canadian societies entrance to Maine's Catholic churches. But after negotiations with Lewiston's Dominican priests and ethnic societies Healy agreed to consider the national associations as parish organizations, provided they accepted an appointed chaplain, submitted their bylaws to the bishop for approval, and gave the chaplain the authority to overrule decisions adversely affecting issues of faith or morals. Despite the 1889 decision of the Council of Baltimore not to allow societies to enter Catholic churches in regalia, Lewiston's Franco-American associations had continued to do so until Walsh's 1911 ban. In 1905, the year before Walsh became bishop, the only societies that could not enter Saint-Pierre Church as a group were those without a religious character, namely those that did not restrict membership to Catholics and did not have a chaplain who could overrule decisions. Walsh's ban, *Le Messager* complained, sought to separate religion and nationality—elements it viewed as inseparable, as the slogan on its masthead continued to proclaim. The ban also discriminated against Franco-Americans, *Le Messager* charged, because it did not apply to Irish, Polish, and other ethnic societies.[25]

One effect of Walsh's ban was to dampen enthusiasm for Saint-Jean-Baptiste Day celebrations during the second decade of the twentieth century. Unable to enter the Catholic Church as a group, Lewiston's national societies opted not to organize parades in some years. Celebrations consequently lacked the grandeur of the past. Sometimes, they even lacked a religious component. Preoccupied with *la Cause Nationale*, Franco-American societies simply lacked the energy and the resources to organize large and splendid celebrations in honor of the patron saint of French Canadians. After the conflict with Walsh subsided, Franco-Americans still lacked enthusiasm for the feast day. As *Le Messager* put it in 1917, "Would the narcotic of the Corporation Sole be taking effect, by chance?"[26]

Celebrating Christmas with a midnight mass was another French-Canadian custom that Walsh curtailed. Because the pope had asked Catholic churches worldwide to open the twentieth century in religious celebration, Saint-Pierre Church had offered a midnight mass on New Year's Eve in 1900. At the request of parishioners, Pastor Alexandre-Louis Mothon wrote Bishop O'Connell in 1902 for permission to offer a midnight mass on Christmas Eve, explaining that fears of disorder had prevented these celebrations in the past, but (he pointed out) that the midnight mass at the start of the new century had gone well. O'Connell granted his permission; he later received Mothon's report that no disturbances within or outside of the church had taken place, and he allowed Franco-Americans to hold midnight masses at Christmas through the end of his tenure as Bishop of Portland. Unlike his predecessor, Walsh permitted midnight masses only among men and women religious and not the laity.[27] While the reasons for Walsh's decision have gone unrecorded, he must have felt motivated to withhold ecclesiastical privileges from the ethnic group that challenged his authority as head of Maine's Catholic Church.

As illustrated earlier in the Sacred Heart controversy in Waterville, Bishop Walsh favored the creation of territorial rather than national parishes, so that Catholics of all nationalities living within a parish's defined boundaries attended the same church. But in 1907, Walsh had divided Saint-Pierre to create another national parish in Lewiston for Franco-Americans living in the downtown industrial section known as Petit Canada. Rather than support an expansion of Saint-Pierre Church, residents of Little Canada had asked for their own church as early as 1890, and French-Canadian descendants in New Auburn had made a similar request. In 1891, the Dominicans established a chapel-school in New Auburn, and they administered it until 1902, when Bishop O'Connell separated New Auburn's approximately 400 Franco-American families from the 2,000-plus families of Saint-Pierre to create the parish of Saint-Louis, thereafter administered by secular (that is, diocesan) clergy. When the Dominicans obtained O'Connell's permission in 1904 to build a larger church in Lewiston, ostensibly because the existing structure required major repairs, Franco-Americans in Petit Canada renewed their request for a church of their own, closer to where they lived, rather than supporting a new building for Saint-Pierre. Despite divisions within the Franco-American community over this issue, the Dominicans in 1905 tore down Saint-Pierre Church, built a temporary chapel, and began construction of the basement of the large church that stands today. Discontent with the decision persisted in Petit Canada, and its residents continued to push for a new parish. The displeasure of French-Canadian immigrants in this matter may have had roots in the *fabrique* tradition with which they were familiar. Under the leadership of the first Canadian-born Dominican pastor of Lewiston, who was probably also versed in the tradition, the order polled the residents of Petit Canada during the 1906 parish visit, and the Dominicans subsequently decided to recommend dividing the parish in order to end the squabbling in the francophone community.[28] Residents of Petit Canada also voiced their desire for a *Canadien* as pastor. In 1907, Walsh met with the individuals seeking a new parish, and he separated 825 Franco-American families from Saint-Pierre to create the national parish of Sainte-Marie (Saint Mary), to which he appointed a pastor of French-Canadian descent. While local Franco-American leaders and the Dominicans approved of the establishment of Sainte-Marie Parish, despite the ongoing construction of a new church for Saint-Pierre, Walsh likely had other motives for his decision. Some have speculated that he felt threatened by the plan of the Dominicans to build a cathedral-sized, Franco-American church in Lewiston.[29] Subsequent events suggest he may have agreed to create another national parish in Lewiston in order to limit the influence of the Dominicans in the Spindle City.

In a little-known aspect of Maine's Corporation Sole controversy, Bishop Walsh struggled privately with the Dominicans for administrative control of Saint-Pierre Parish during the public controversy and for long after it subsided. Because Reverend Joseph A. Dallaire, the first Dominican pastor of French-Canadian descent, had borrowed money on the parish's behalf and had changed architects and the plans for the new church without first securing diocesan approval, Walsh dismissed him. In 1912, when the Dominicans replaced the order's third French-Canadian Lewiston pastor, Walsh protested to the provincial in Saint-Hyacinthe that they had done so without first consulting him. Walsh further informed the provincial that they had to "reach some understanding in regard to the status of the Community in that parish" before he would consider the appointment of another Dominican pastor to Saint-Pierre. He asked the provincial to meet with him in Portland "and to bring whatever mutual contracts or signed documents there may be that have passed between the Bishop of Portland and the Congregation of St. Dominic."[30]

Walsh, it turns out, wanted the title to Saint-Pierre Church. The Dominicans maintained that Bishop Healy had granted them title to the church property in 1881 and that they, according to the terms of their convention with him, could hold it until the order left Lewiston. Walsh contacted Mothon, who as the first Dominican pastor of Saint-Pierre had made the arrangements with Bishop Healy. Mothon subsequently informed Walsh and the Dominican provincial in Sainte-Hyacinthe that Healy had later asked him to pass title to Saint-Pierre back to the Diocese of Portland, in order to conform to decrees of the Council of Baltimore about placing church properties under diocesan control. Mothon indicated that he had agreed to Healy's request, but various circumstances had prevented the two from signing the necessary paperwork prior to Healy's death. After receiving Mothon's letter, Walsh contacted the Dominican provincial to request the transfer of Saint-Pierre Parish property to the Diocese of Portland "as agreed upon by the late Bishop Healy and Father Mothon." When the provincial asked Walsh to let matters stand, Walsh dismissed the idea and proposed plans to take the matter to higher authorities in the Catholic Church; Walsh also threatened to withhold his approval for various needs of the parish: "The question of schools and further developments in the parish must certainly depend in a large measure upon the settlement of this matter." When the provincial did not agree to Walsh's proposal for a conference, Walsh informed him that he would withhold "favors" from the Dominicans, including his permission for "any other [Dominican] Fathers [to] come into the Diocese." Walsh steadfastly withheld approval for a new school for Saint-Pierre during this private struggle with the Dominicans for the rights to the parish property. When the Dominican master general in Rome asked Walsh in 1916 to approve plans for a new school for Saint-Pierre, he informed him that the Dominicans had decided to turn the church property over to the Diocese of Portland, but would reserve the property of the monastery.[31] Walsh, in turn, allowed the construction of the new school, but he and the Dominicans continued to dispute technical points about the transfer until his death in 1924.

Ethnicity was at the root of this private conflict between Walsh and the Dominicans. An extension of the Corporation Sole controversy that pitted French-Canadian descendants against their Irish bishop, this conflict led French-Canadian Dominicans to oppose the actions of the Irish bishop to exercise control over parish property. Correspondence from Mothon reveals that French Dominicans were more flexible in acceding to the demands of the Irish hierarchy than were French-Canadian Dominicans. Walsh implicitly recognized this fact: "The practical expulsion of the French Fathers from the Convent in Lewiston, the establishment of the new Province in Canada controlling the houses in the United States, and various local difficulties affecting the personnel and the administration of the parish in Lewiston," he wrote Mothon in 1913, "have all considerably and substantially changed the original purpose and spirit of their establishment." Frustrated with the difficulty he had in getting the French-Canadian Dominicans to cede parish property to the diocese, Walsh decided to ask the Dominican master general in Rome to change the ethnic composition of the Lewiston monastery, to provide priests "of all nationalities." Walsh received no response to this request.[32] He continued to struggle with the Dominicans—and with Franco-Americans—until his death in 1924.

• • •

The struggles between Lewiston Franco-Americans and Irish bishops during the opening decades of the twentieth century, and the competition that existed between Franco-American and Irish politicians to award patronage during this period, might seem to suggest that issues of ethnic identity preoccupied only the elites. But ethnicity also defined relationships for ordinary Franco-Americans. Scant reports in *Le Messager* reveal that this was true in sports. In July 1919, Franco-American and Irish residents of Lewiston and Auburn formed their own baseball teams to compete against one another. "To make spectators feel more comfortable and at ease," even the fans would be segregated, *Le Messager* announced in anticipation of the eagerly awaited game. One section of the stands would be reserved for the Irish, another for the *Canadiens*, and a large section between them for those who remained neutral, *Le Messager* explained. Over one thousand fans attended the game, which the Irish team won five to three. "The French-Canadian team was defeated by the errors and decisions of the Irish umpire," *Le Messager* complained. To avoid this problem at the next game, the manager of the Franco-American team hoped to have an American umpire, "in order to satisfy both teams." At the end of the second decade of the twentieth century, ordinary residents and elites alike continued to perceive three major ethnicities in Lewiston—a perception confirmed by census data, which revealed that American, Irish, and Franco-American residents together represented five-sixths (83.9 percent) of Lewiston's population in 1920.[33]

Census data from that year reveals that Franco-Americans continued to stand out in Lewiston in various respects. Eighty (79.5) percent of those who could not read and/or could not write were Franco-Americans, the majority (60.0 percent) of whom were women. Vénérand and Léontine Vallé were among them, for neither could read or write. Most (64.1 percent) of the Franco-Americans lacking literacy skills represented first-generation stock, with the second (12.8 percent) and later generations (2.6 percent) supplying smaller proportions. In contrast, no other ethnic groups in Lewiston reported a lack of literacy skills in 1920 by members beyond the first generation.[34]

The above figures belie the fact that in 1920, the large majority of Franco-Americans were able to read and write. Of the first- and second-generation Franco-Americans ages eight and above, 87.3 percent were able both to read and to write. They lagged slightly behind Lewiston's other groups, for 96.4 percent of the Americans, 94.7 percent of the Irish, and 92.7 percent of all other ethnic groups in Lewiston could read and write in 1920.[35] While individuals of French-Canadian birth and background had made significant educational gains since 1880, they still trailed the rest of Lewiston's population in the early twentieth century.

Two-thirds (66.1 percent) of the first- and second-generation Franco-Americans aged ten and older reported an ability to speak English in 1920.[36] The large majority (79.4 percent) of those who did not speak English were Canadian-born, and most were women. In the Vallé household, each of the seven children from ages ten to twenty-one could speak English, as could their father, Vénérand. Only the wife and mother, Léontine, could not. Women like her constituted 85.7 percent of the first-generation Franco-Americans who did not speak English. Among second-generation Franco-Americans, 55.0 percent of the non-English speakers were women.[37] While revealing increasing levels of acculturation with succeeding generations, the data also suggests that women played a significant role in the preservation of the French language in Lewiston.

Further analysis reveals that only 15.0 percent of the men and 7.8 percent of the women of French-Canadian descent who did not speak English in 1920 had employment outside of the cotton industry. All others did not work, worked at home, or made their living in cotton mills. For her part, Léontine Vallé did not work outside of the home.[38] Staying at home or working in the cotton industry appeared consequential to French-language retention in Lewiston.

In 1920, Lewiston largely remained a working-class community. But American and Irish women and men were less concentrated in industrial jobs than Franco-Americans and other ethnic groups (see table 3). While Franco-Americans had experienced some upward occupational mobility since 1880, the majority of the working men and women in 1920 held industrial jobs in the textile mills and shoe factories of Lewiston and Auburn. A modest measure of upward mobility had taken place with succeeding generations of Franco-American men. Whereas 87.7 percent of first-generation francophone men held blue-collar jobs in 1920, 76.3 percent of the second generation did. Franco-American women enjoyed no such mobility, for 93.8 percent of the second generation had blue-collar jobs, compared to 90.3 percent of the Canadian-born women.[39] Franco-American women more often than men lacked the ability to speak English and the ability to read and write—skills important to upward occupational mobility.

Unlike in 1880, married Franco-American women (33.3 percent) more often worked than American (22.2 percent) or Irish (9.1 percent) women, and these Franco-American wives supplied well over half (58.8 percent) of Lewiston's wedded working women in 1920. Franco-American wives in the United States were more likely to work outside of the home than were French-Canadian wives of Québec. According to historian Jacques Rouillard, married francophone women in Québec tended not to work for wages prior to World War II; as late as 1941, only 10 percent did. Rouillard points to cross-border differences to account for the differing rates of workforce participation by Franco-American and French-Canadian women. A higher demand for labor existed in New England, and Catholic clergy in Québec had more influence over their flock than they did in the United States, he argues. According to a Mrs. Lagace, who lived in Lewiston from 1903 to 1919, priests in the United States had many more parishioners than clergymen in rural Québec and were therefore unable to exert the same amount of influence over them.[40] Economic and demographic differences between Québec and New England thus led to increasing workforce participation by Franco-American women in the United States in the early twentieth century. So did the enactment of child-labor legislation and the subsequent, increasing rates of school attendance.

In 1920, Franco-Americans supplied 60.8 percent of Lewiston's young labor force, a percentage moderately larger than their proportion of the population. Yet, Sylvie Beaudreau and Yves Frenette find that only 16 percent of Lewiston's Franco-American children between ten and sixteen years

Table 3. Occupational Distribution of Lewiston's Ethnic Groups in 1920 (in percentages)[a]

	AMERICAN	IRISH	FRANCO-AMERICAN	ALL OTHER
Men (*N* = 277)				
WHITE COLLAR				
Self-governing professional	2.4%	4.2%	2.5%	0%
Salaried professional	2.4	0	0.8	0
Small business and managerial	14.6	8.3	5.0	7.7
Semiprofessional	2.4	0	0	1.9
Clerical and sales	12.2	12.5	7.6	3.8
BLUE COLLAR				
Self-employed	3.7	4.2	1.7	1.9
Nonindustrial	22.0	29.2	28.6	23.1
Industrial	34.1	41.7	52.9	61.5
Primary sector	6.1	0	0.8	0
NUMBER	82	24	119	52
Women (*N* = 177)				
WHITE COLLAR				
Self-governing professional	0%	0%	0%	0%
Salaried professional	12.2	12.5	0	0
Small business and managerial	0	0	0	0
Semiprofessional	8.2	0	0	0
Clerical and sales	26.5	25.0	8.5	15.4
BLUE COLLAR				
Self-employed	2.0	12.5	3.2	0
Nonindustrial	16.3	12.5	5.3	15.4
Industrial	34.7	37.5	83.0	69.2
Primary sector	0	0	0	0
NUMBER	49	8	94	26

Source: Derived from every thirtieth household in the U.S. Census, 1920.
a. Columns may not add up to 100.0 percent on account of rounding.

of age contributed to the family economy in 1920, in sharp contrast to 1880 when 72 percent did. Beaudreau and Frenette account for this drop by pointing to a 1907 Maine law forbidding the employment of children under fourteen, a law which the state enforced more strictly than previous child labor legislation; they also point to the unwillingness of parents to subject their children to the increasing intensification of textile production, and to an improvement in socioeconomic conditions in the early twentieth century. At the same time, they acknowledge that parents possibly falsified the ages of young working children to hide their noncompliance with child labor laws. In my sample, no Lewiston residents had reported having working children under fifteen in their households.[41]

Data from the 1920 census reveals that, of the persons who had attended school at any point since September 1, 1919, 32.0 percent were American, 49.1 percent were Franco-American, and 2.9 percent were Irish; the remaining 16.0 percent came from Lewiston's other ethnic groups. These percentages roughly reflect each group's proportion of the city's population. But data published in the 1920 Lewiston school report suggests that Irish and Franco-American youth did not enjoy the same access to education as the Americans. Specifically, the school report provides a census of school-age persons ranging from four to twenty-one years, and it reveals that Franco-Americans made up 69.1 percent of Lewiston's population of school age, the Irish 8.8 percent, and Americans 13.3 percent. Nonetheless, proportionately more Franco-American children attended school in 1920 than in 1880. Beaudreau and Frenette argue that this increase in school attendance led to a change in family strategies between 1880 and 1920 whereby more Franco-American mothers entered the workplace to supplement the income of their spouses.[42] The participation of married francophone women in the workforce appears to have been primarily a twentieth-century phenomenon. This helps to explain the lack of occupational mobility that existed in 1920 between first- and second-generation francophone women, for the U.S.-born probably lacked the experience as well as the skills to advance to better jobs.

While the differences between the Franco-American, Irish, and American populations of Lewiston declined from 1880 to 1920, various signs point to the Franco-Americans being less well-off than the other groups in the early twentieth century. Franco-Americans had more working mothers, took in more boarders, and held Lewiston's lowest-paying jobs. In addition, fewer of them owned property—only 17.5 percent of the Franco-American heads owned their homes in 1920, compared to 47.4 percent of the Irish and 32.9 percent of the American heads.[43] Although Franco-Americans had made educational and economic gains, they still lagged behind the other large ethnic groups of Lewiston in the early twentieth century. This may have motivated some to engage in labor activity.

Accounts of trade-union activity and worker protest in the early twentieth century suggest that ethnic identity and working-class consciousness developed simultaneously among Lewiston Franco-Americans. One sign of the growing consciousness of Franco-Americans as workers was their participation in Lewiston's Labor Day celebrations. In 1904, *Le Messager* reported that about seven thousand persons took part in the city's Labor Day activities. The events included a parade in which the Saint-Dominique band marched, various races and contests at the city fairgrounds in which seven of the twelve winners were Franco-Americans, and an evening ball at Lewiston City Hall. While *Le Messager* did not indicate how many of the participants were Franco-Americans, its brief report of the day's activities—and its assumption that readers would be interested in the events—suggest that some had, in fact, joined in the festivities. Reports of other Labor Day celebrations in the early twentieth century also suggest the participation of Franco-Americans. In 1911, for example, the *Lewiston Journal* reported that the Saint-Dominique band marched in the parade, and that Edmond Turmenne was among the organizers of the day's activities that drew thousands, including visitors from elsewhere in Maine. Turmenne, a Franco-American from Lewiston, was president of the Textile Workers of Maine and author of the "Colonne Textile" ("Textile Column") that appeared periodically in *Le Messager*, providing news of union activities and promoting unionization. In 1915, three Franco-American bands—Saint-Dominique, Brigade, and Union Musicale—participated in the Labor Day procession, and Franco-American (as well as non-Franco-American) individuals and businesses won awards for the workhorses they entered in the parade that also celebrated the opening day of the Maine State Fair.[44] These newspaper reports suggest that Franco-Americans may have been more active than previously thought in developing their identity as workers, and that although there were different class variations, Franco-American identity was elastic enough to encompass all classes in the community.

There were other signs of working-class consciousness in Lewiston. In 1904, l'Union Saint-Joseph organized an evening program of entertainment to raise funds for striking workers in Fall River, Massachusetts—a city that had a large Franco-American population. Lewiston-Auburn factories closed for Thanksgiving, and Franco-Americans had Requiem masses sung in 1904 for workers from different rooms or departments, just as they had in previous years. When Maine passed a law limiting the work week to fifty-eight hours in 1909, the Saint-Dominique band led Lewiston's parade, and two of the five members of the banquet reception committee were Franco-Americans. In 1911, carpenters from Lewiston and Auburn formed a local union, and all ten officers had Franco-American surnames. What these various details suggest is that the working-class and ethnic identities of a number of Franco-Americans had intersected by the early twentieth century.[45]

Accounts in *Le Messager* of union activity and labor protest add further evidence of the intersection of these identities. In September 1901, *Le Messager* reported that the Androscoggin Mill would reopen after having closed one month for repairs. After pillowcase makers learned that they would have to operate six looms instead of four, and that their daily wages would drop from $1.30 to $1.00 when the mill reopened, fifty of them initially decided to strike. One week later, *Le Messager* reported that sixty striking weavers had returned to work after agreeing to run six looms and accepting a daily wage of $1.07. "It is true that it is less than they were earning before," the newspaper sympathized, "but it is still more money than the mill agent wanted to give them when they went on strike." While *Le Messager* did not indicate the strikers were Franco-Americans, the fact that it reported the strike implies that they were. For its part, the *Lewiston Journal* offered no coverage of this labor protest. The Androscoggin Mill strike points to an important historiographic issue. The lack of coverage of small-scale worker protests in the English-language press, and the brief and incomplete reporting of the French-language press provide reasons why historians have not recognized the greater role Franco-Americans have played in labor activities in the United States. By teasing out evidence from brief and scattered reports in the French-language press, often short paragraphs in the local news column—which scholars have tended to overlook when focusing instead on editorials—we can develop a better understanding of the world of work for Franco-Americans.[46]

In its reporting of meetings to organize Franco-American workers and the various strikes in which they participated, *Le Messager* revealed that it was not solely the mouthpiece of Franco-American elites, but that it had the interests of workers at heart. In February and March 1905, the newspaper publicized efforts to organize shoe workers. Representatives of the International Boot and Shoe Workers Union, Alphetus Mathieu of Montréal and Philip J. Byrne of Boston, came to speak in French and English to shoe workers of Lewiston and Auburn. Large numbers of Franco-American men and women attended the meetings in both cities, *Le Messager* reported.[47] It did not specify exactly how many attended or how many joined the union. Nonetheless, the French-language newspaper's brief reports demonstrate that it included the francophone working class in its definition of the Franco-American community.

The reports also reveal the interest of Franco-American men and women in improving the conditions of their work lives. A shoe strike from December 1905 to January 1906 provides additional, though limited, evidence of this. About thirty leather workers at National Shoemakers of Auburn began the strike after asking for a salary increase and for the recognition of their union. According to the *Lewiston Journal*, an organizer named Byrne, of the Boot and Shoe Workers Union, instigated the strike. This must have been the Boston representative who had visited the Twin Cities earlier in the year. Unlike *Le Messager*, which stated that the demands of the shoe workers were reasonable, the *Journal* expressed its disapproval: "The general feeling seems to be that the action of the strikers is unwarranted and should not have been taken." About twenty employees of the National Shoe Makers' Lewiston factory joined the strike in January. In reporting this news, the author of an unsigned letter to *Le Messager*'s editor referred to the strike as "our strike" and asked: "Out of respect and for the integrity of our nationality, we would ask our compatriots to stay away from the factory and not to cause trouble, although in reality we are being treated as slaves." The letter writer thus revealed that Franco-Americans participated in the strike, something that reports in the *Journal* and *Le Messager* did not make clear. The letter writer further complained that management maintained a blacklist to prevent strikers from finding jobs in other local shoe shops. At least eighty-four shoe workers from Lewiston and Auburn went on strike before it ended in mid-January. When *Le Messager* reported that the strikers and management had reached a satisfactory agreement, it congratulated workers for having handled themselves well. Workers and manufacturers chose not to publicize the terms of their agreement, indicated the *Journal*, which also reported that nearly all strikers would regain their employment.[48] While we do not know how many Franco-Americans took part in the strike at National Shoemakers, what is significant is that they had a role in labor protest in the early twentieth century, countering impressions of their passivity at the workplace.

Other reports of labor protests present a mixed picture, one of both cooperation and a lack of unity in labor activity. In July 1906, seventy-five men working on the electric railroad in Lewiston struck; they demanded that their workday be shortened from ten hours to nine. *Le Messager* revealed interethnic cooperation in this strike: "The strikers are French Canadians, except for seven or eight Irish, but all are in agreement about demanding a reduction in the hours of work." The street railroad paid off the striking workers and indicated it would seek to replace them with Italian laborers. The strikers asked Mayor William E. Webster to help them in pressing their demands, and he agreed because the demands were reasonable, *Le Messager* reported. A Democrat, Webster surely recognized that the Irish and Franco-Americans were important sources of electoral support. Despite the mayor's efforts on behalf of the workers, the street railroad was not inclined to meet their demands. Encouraged when five Franco-Americans returned to work, it would not consider the offer of strikers to take a five-cent wage cut, for a daily salary of $1.60, in exchange for a shorter workday. It appears that local Franco-Americans were not the only ones complicating the strike situation. At one point, *Le Messager* expressed its hope that Franco-Americans from Brunswick, the former location of the railroad's central office, would not take the jobs of striking workers. Neither *Le Messager* nor the *Journal* appears to have reported the outcome of this strike.[49]

The strike of electric-railroad workers illustrates several important points nonetheless. It demonstrates a measure of cooperation between Franco-American and Irish laborers to improve their difficult working conditions, highlighting their identity as members of the working class in Lewiston. It also demonstrates that the lack of worker unity was not necessarily the product of ethnic divisions; most of the strikers were Franco-Americans, yet it was a handful of Franco-Americans who returned to work and therefore complicated the protest for the remaining strikers. The development of class consciousness did not proceed in a straight-line fashion among Lewiston's Franco-American population.

This was the case in the shoe strike of 1913, one for which *Le Messager* provided extensive coverage. In late September, about ninety shoe workers from Lunn and Sweet left the Auburn factory to protest the fines the company had assessed for mistakes they had made on the job; they argued that they could not support themselves on the resulting wages. A few of the strikers were Franco-Americans and the others were mostly Greeks, reported *Le Messager*. By early October, 135 shoe workers were on strike. When *Le Messager* learned that Franco-Americans were taking the jobs of striking workers, it argued that they were hurting other Franco-Americans and advised them not to do so. The newspaper (as usual) considered the demands of the strikers reasonable, and it argued that Franco-Americans would ultimately benefit if the labor protest succeeded in improving the wages of workers. *Le Messager* had to come to terms with the working-class consciousness of Franco-Americans, for they constituted the base of its readership, and it tried to give them direction in this strike. But the newspaper appears not to have succeeded. In mid-October, *Le Messager* reported that S. J. Pothier, the secretary-treasurer of the Shoeworkers Protective Union from Haverhill, Massachusetts, had arrived in Lewiston to lead the strike. About seventy-five Greeks escorted Pothier through several streets in a parade to the city's Central Labor Union Hall while playing Greek music.[50] In its reporting of this event, *Le Messager* seems to have missed the irony that the strike leader the Greeks so enthusiastically welcomed had a Franco-American surname and no Franco-American followers.

Ethnic conflict erupted between the Greeks and Franco-Americans in Lewiston. One evening, some Greeks called two Franco-Americans "scabs." The following evening, reported *Le Messager*, a group of Franco-Americans gathered together to ensure that it did not happen again. Consequently, upwards of thirty Greeks and Franco-Americans broke into a fight that lasted about a half hour. It ended only when police broke it up; had they not, claimed *Le Messager*, someone might have died. A letter to *Le Messager*'s editor suggested that past and current ethnic tensions between Franco-Americans and Greeks were at the center of the conflict. In the past, Greeks had tended to accept lower wages and to work as strikebreakers. Shoe-factory bosses encouraged the ethnic tensions, the writer pointed out, in order to manage their workforce. Yet, like the editor of *Le Messager*, the individual appealed to Franco-Americans to unite with the Greeks in this strike and not to serve as strikebreakers, so that all groups could benefit in the end.[51]

But that did not happen. About one week after the fight, Joseph J. Ettor, a national organizer for the Industrial Workers of the World, came to Lewiston. Ettor met with the Greek strikers. He also spoke with about a dozen Franco-American shoe workers who had returned to the factory to convince them not to go back until the strike was settled. A shoe-factory boss subsequently ventured into Lewiston's Petit Canada to try to persuade the shoe workers not to heed Ettor's counsel; the boss threatened that they would not have jobs after the strike if they did not return to work. Another incident reveals that some Franco-Americans continued to take the jobs of striking workers, causing ethnic tensions to persist between Greeks and Franco-Americans. On their way home from Lunn and Sweet during the fourth week of October, strikebreakers Henry Lupien, Joseph Albert, and J. Roy suffered head and leg injuries when "a gang of Greeks" attacked them with bricks and stones, reported *Le Messager*. Lupien required stitches to the head, and the other two sported bruises, indicated the *Lewiston Journal*. By late October, some Greeks had moved to Massachusetts to find work, and most other strikers, Greek and Franco-American, had returned to their jobs at Lunn and Sweet.[52]

The Lunn and Sweet shoe strike of 1913 reveals the competing roles of Franco-Americans in labor activity in the early twentieth century. Some Franco-Americans took part in the strike, but others interfered with it by serving as strikebreakers. Consequently, competition for jobs led to conflict, as Greek and Franco-American Lewiston residents engaged in fights. Whether conflicts took place between Franco-American strikers and francophone strikebreakers has gone unrecorded; reported conflicts were only between Greeks and Franco-Americans. Ethnic divisions, it appears, largely prevented the success of this strike. Such ethnic divisions in the world of work complicated the development of working-class consciousness among Franco-Americans. For ordinary Franco-Americans, as for the elites, ethnicity continued to establish the boundaries of relationships in the early twentieth century.

The small proportion of mixed marriages reflected this reality. High rates of endogamy persisted among each of Lewiston's three largest ethnic groups, but endogamy was particularly marked among Franco-Americans. Data compiled from the 1920 nominal census reveals that three-fourths of the American (76.5 percent) and Irish (75.0 percent) household heads had spouses of the same ethnicity, and over nine-tenths (93.5 percent) of the Franco-American heads had Franco-American spouses. Marriage records maintained by the City Clerk reveal that Franco-Americans continued in 1920 to choose spouses of the same ethnicity. Eighty (80.3) percent of the 346 marriages involving Franco-Americans in that year were with other Franco-Americans. Census data reveals that what little intermarriage existed among Lewiston residents of French-Canadian descent had taken place primarily among the American-born, for 88.9 percent of the second-generation heads in 1920 had Franco-American spouses, compared to 96.6 percent of those from the first generation.[53]

The membership of Lewiston's two Irish parishes in 1920 also reveals some intermixing between the Franco-American and Irish populations of the Spindle City.[54] In 77.6 percent of the fifty-eight families identified from the baptism registers of Saint Joseph's, neither the mother nor the father of the baptized child had a French name; 6.9 percent of the families had fathers with French surnames, 13.8 percent had mothers with French maiden names, and in only one family (1.7 percent) did both parents have Franco-American names. Slightly over one-fifth (22.4 percent) of the childbearing families of Saint Joseph's, then, had at least one Franco-American member, unlike in 1880 when none had. There was a much smaller Franco-American presence at Saint Patrick's. Of the seventy families identified, 92.9 percent were headed by parents who both had non-French names, 1.4 percent had fathers with French surnames, 5.7 percent had mothers with French maiden names, and there were no families where both parents had French names in 1920. Only 7.1 percent of Saint Patrick's families of childbearing age, then, had at least one Franco-American member in 1920; by contrast, no parents of baptized children had French names in 1892, the first full year that the parish celebrated baptisms.[55]

The data on the membership of Saint Patrick and Saint Joseph parishes in 1920 helps reveal the extent to which Lewiston remained ethnically segregated in the early twentieth century. At the same time, it demonstrates a measure of acculturation. The intermarriage of Irish and Franco-American Catholics led to a Franco-American presence in Lewiston's two Irish parishes by 1920.[56] That presence existed primarily among the wives of male parishioners. These Franco-American women perhaps viewed marriage to their English-speaking coreligionists as an avenue to social mobility.

Franco-American and Irish elites also intermixed in a Catholic club in early-twentieth-century Lewiston. In 1901, *Le Messager* reported that "many of our most distinguished French Canadians as well as the better class of Irish Catholics" were members of the local organization of the Knights of Columbus. In 1919, when the French-language newspaper reported with evident pleasure that "a good number" of Franco-Americans had joined this Catholic society, it argued that the intermingling of Franco-Americans with the Irish would help each ethnic group better understand the other as they worked on spiritual and temporal matters.[57]

The information on Franco-American membership in Lewiston's Irish churches and in the Knights of Columbus provides impressionistic evidence that individuals of French-Canadian descent in Lewiston first intermixed with other ethnics within Catholic institutions. If correct, this impression suggests several points. First, it indicates that Catholic (notably Irish) institutions helped facilitate the acculturation of Lewiston's Franco-American population. Second, for a fraction of Lewiston's francophone population, it suggests that identity as Catholics may have come to supersede ethnic identity, that religion possibly served as a more cohesive bond than ethnicity in identifying relationships. If accurate, this represents a change from the late nineteenth century, a possible evolution in the identity of the city's French speakers. Third, while ethnic retention and acculturation represented the same goal for the majority of Lewiston's Franco-American population in the early twentieth century, for a growing minority they appeared to be divergent goals. This, too, represents a change.

That French speakers acquired the English-language skills that allowed them to intermix with non-francophones in Lewiston was due in part to the arrival of new teaching orders to Lewiston in the early twentieth century—orders that helped the city's youth to preserve their French-language skills while they learned English. When the general chapter of les Dames de Sion (Ladies of Zion) decided that all houses had to observe the regulation not to teach male pupils, the order withdrew from the parish schools of Lewiston and Auburn in 1904, and the sisters departed for new assignments in Kentucky, Saskatchewan, and Brazil. Expelled from France in July 1903, on account of anticlericalism in the aftermath of the Dreyfus Affair, Domini-can Sisters agreed to emigrate to the United States to take over Saint-Pierre School. Because few of the French Dominican Sisters could speak English, they initially supplemented their teaching staff with Dominican Sisters from houses in England and the United States, forming a staff of thirty-two in Lewiston during 1904–1905. The sisters spent their spare time and school vacations studying English. Anglophone sisters from nearby Saint Patrick's School, who were members of the French-Canadian order of la Congréga-tion de Notre-Dame (the Notre Dame Congregation) of Montréal, gave the Dominican Sisters lessons in English each morning during the 1905 summer vacation. Beginning with the 1904–1905 school year, the Dominican Sisters taught religion, reading, and writing in French for the first half of each day, and they taught math and geography in English during the second half. Saint-Pierre School therefore continued to provide instruction in French and English on an equal basis after the arrival of the French Dominican Sisters.[58]

In 1916, the Ursuline Sisters arrived to teach at Sainte-Marie School. Sisters from this French-Canadian order had emigrated from Trois-Rivières, Québec, to Waterville, Maine, in 1888 to teach at the city's French-Cana-dian parish school. They studied English during school holidays, and they gained their autonomy in 1891 in part because Trois-Rivières could not supply English-speaking teachers to Waterville. The Ursulines of Waterville subsequently founded a novitiate, and the order grew. Six sisters of French-Canadian descent moved into a converted Lewiston mill building in 1916 that served as a convent-school.[59] During the first half of the twentieth cen-tury, the Ursulines divided instruction nearly equally between English and French at Sainte-Marie School. Their students learned to give presentations in English, and they put on musical and dramatic programs in both English and French.[60] Like the students of the Dominican Sisters, those at Sainte-Marie School had the opportunity to retain their French language while learning the language of the host society in Lewiston.

The experiences of Lewiston's Franco-Americans during the opening decades of the twentieth century highlight a number of important themes. To the extent that French speakers Americanized, they did so on their own. The actions of Irish bishops, to a large extent, and of nativists, to a lesser degree, generally intensified the ethnic feelings of Franco-Americans and, if anything, made them more determined to Americanize at their own pace; what happened in Lewiston therefore contradicts the common notion that outside pressures from nativists were primarily responsible for the Americanization of foreign-born persons and their children in the United States.[61] A related point, the process of joining the country of adoption, was not like traveling on a turnpike leading in a straight line to what we call "assimilation."[62]

The experience of Lewiston's Franco-Americans also challenges commonly held perceptions that the process of "assimilation" in the United States serves to mitigate ethnic conflicts. The ethnic controversies described in this and the previous chapter occurred during a period when the net immigration of French Canadians had dropped from previous decades; lacking the reinforcement of new immigrants, Franco-Americans chose to fight, even within the Catholic Church, to gain influence in proportion to their numbers. In the case of Franco-Americans, growing involvement in the activities of the host society increased, rather than reduced, ethnic competition and conflict.[63]

To resist assimilation into U.S. society, immigrants and their descendants had to join it to some degree. Learning English, naturalizing, and voting helped to advance the interests of Franco-Americans in their country of adoption.[64] So did developing their identity as members of the working class and the Democratic Party. Intermixing with other ethnics (notably the Irish) in Catholic institutions, including the institution of marriage, may have served the same ends. These elements all point to the evolution of the identity of francophones. In short, Franco-Americanism in the early twentieth century entailed accepting civic responsibility in the host society, learning its de facto official language, and participating in its institutions and wars, while being proud to speak the French language and to celebrate French-Canadian traditions. Like French-Canadian descendants in the late nineteenth century, most of Lewiston's Franco-Americans through 1920 continued to view their participation in U.S. society as a way to achieve *survivance*.

Franco-Americans nonetheless met significant opposition in making a place for themselves in the United States. Despite the efforts of francophone communities like Lewiston to acquire English, xenophobic tensions led Maine and other New England states to pass legislation pushing English-language instruction during and after World War I. Nativists in the Maine legislature passed a law in 1919 requiring English as "the basic language of instruction" in the state's public and private high schools. During a speech on Saint-Jean-Baptiste Day in the following year, attorney Fernand Despins pointed out the irony of U.S. involvement in World War I, ostensibly to promote democracy, while zealots pushing Americanization worked to deny those of French-Canadian descent the ability to speak French in the United States. Like his predecessors on Saint-Jean-Baptiste Day in the late nineteenth century, Despins argued in 1920 that preserving the French language and French-Canadian traditions was not incompatible with loyalty to the United States.[65] The affirmation *Loyaux mais Français* (Loyal but French) still rang true. To Despins and to most other Franco-Americans in Lewiston, preserving ethnic traditions and becoming participants in the host society did not represent dichotomous goals. This belief, and the resumption of heavy immigration from Québec, would fortify Lewiston Franco-Americans in the 1920s against the Americanizing push of Bishop Walsh and that of the Ku Klux Klan.

Competing Americanisms

The Bishops, the Klan, and the Intertwined Identity of Franco-Americans, 1920–1940

About one hour past midnight on August 10, 1924, a bomb exploded in Lewiston, Maine. Startled Lewiston residents awoke to confront a twelve-foot crucifix blazing atop one of the city's highest peaks, visible both in Lewiston and its twin city, Auburn. Ralph O. Brewster had won the Republican gubernatorial primary. The dynamite blast and the burning cross punctuated the victory celebration of the Ku Klux Klan. The organization had come to Maine in 1921, and by its height in the mid-1920s had enrolled up to 150,000 members.[1] The Klan in Maine represented a Protestant backlash against the growing number of Jewish and Catholic immigrants, and it pressured them to Americanize. But not only the KKK wanted French speakers to Americanize in the early 1920s: Bishop Louis S. Walsh of the Diocese of Portland also demonstrated little patience with Catholics who wished to retain their ethnic traditions. His brand of Americanization differed from the Klan's, of course, for his objective was to unify the Church against the anti-Catholic activities of groups such as the KKK. Yet through the 1920s and the Great Depression of the 1930s, despite pressure from the Roman Catholic Church and the Klan, Franco-Americans in Lewiston maintained their French language and many of their French-

Canadian traditions; at the same time, they reshaped their identity in the United States. They did not constitute an ethnic enclave. So secure were Franco-Americans that they defined their own place in the economic, political, and religious life of Lewiston.

In 1920, over 100,000 of Maine's 768,014 residents were foreign-born, and one-third (33.1 percent) of this immigrant population were French-Canadian. These French-Canadian immigrants joined the ranks of Maine's Catholic Church, which by 1920 had 150,000 communicants, nearly one-fifth of Maine's total population.[2] Because Franco-Americans retained their French language, Roman Catholic faith, and many French-Canadian traditions, they became subject to increasing pressure to Americanize following World War I. The unhappy consequence was that they continued to experience discrimination during the interwar period. The postwar Americanization movement found expression in two different forms in Lewiston—one within and the other without the Catholic Church. For his part, Bishop Louis Walsh continued his offensive against the Dominican priests in the early 1920s, and he continued pushing French speakers to shed their language and culture. Other Americanizers operated against the Catholic Church, and their anti-Catholic activities help explain why Bishop Walsh pressured Franco-Americans to abandon some of their ethnic traits. These Americanizers were the nefarious Ku Klux Klan.

Unlike during the post–Civil War era, the Klan in the 1920s expanded far beyond the South, forging a national organization between three and six million strong. The Klan had appeal beyond the South, not because it advocated white supremacy, as it had in the past, but because it had evolved into an organization that also embraced such themes as Americanism, nativism, Prohibitionism, and traditional moral and family values, contends Leonard J. Moore. If one looks beyond the Klan's rhetoric and to its activities, he argues, the Klan represented something more than a Protestant backlash against urban immigrants. In his view, the KKK functioned as a social and civic organization through which white Protestants tried to reassert control over their communities. Its strength lay in states like Indiana in which white Protestants consituted a majority of residents.[3]

The same was true in Canada. The Ku Klux Klan migrated north to Montréal in 1921 and then spread to the Maritimes, Ontario, and western Canada. The Klan allegedly burned Catholic buildings in Québec in 1922, but it did not develop into a strong organization in that province, where Catholics made up about 80 percent of the population. The Klan drew its strength from western Canada where white Protestant majorities existed. In Alberta and Saskatchewan, the Klan directed its energy against French Canadians as well as Catholic immigrants from Central and Eastern Europe, in order to assert a Protestant and British character over the western provinces.[4]

The growing Catholic population of Maine attracted the Klan to the state. In Bangor in March 1923, individuals collected signatures to hear the leader of Maine's Ku Klux Klan speak on the topic of Americanism; in Portland in June, the Klan held its first open meeting; in September in Milo, it conducted its first parade in New England. By the mid-1920s, Maine's Klan had admitted 150,000 individuals, a figure surpassing that of each of the other New England states. The Klan's rise in the Northeast in the 1920s is an aspect of nativism in the United States that has not attracted much attention from historians.[5]

The KKK first started recruiting in the Lewiston-Auburn area in 1923. Given the small number of African-Americans and Jews in Lewiston, it is clear that the Klan came to intimidate Catholics, the largest proportion of whom were Franco-American. *Le Messager* recognized the threat the Klan posed: "It [this sect] feels that the Franco-American people have wronged it simply because they are Catholic and it would like to reduce them to nothing." The French-language newspaper challenged the Klan's version of "Americanism": "But by what law does the Ku Klux Klan authorize itself to destroy Catholics? Does not the United States Constitution give every individual the right to practice his religion?"[6] With such discourse, Franco-Americans made clear that they knew their rights in their country of adoption, and their tone suggested that they would assert those rights.

The King Kleagle of Maine's Ku Klux Klan, F. Eugene Farnsworth, had been born in Maine but had lived his first thirty years in New Brunswick, Canada (which also had a Klan in the 1920s); he subsequently made his home in Massachusetts before returning to Maine. In March 1923, Farnsworth spoke at the Odd Fellows Hall in Lewiston against Roman Catholics and hyphenated Americans. Accounts in the English- and French-language press reveal that Farnsworth singled out Irish Catholics but not Franco-Americans in his remarks. Given Lewiston's demography, perhaps Farnsworth was being prudent. In its report of the meeting, *Le Messager* dismissed the Klan as a hollow threat, calling the KKK "quite simply a new kind of exploitation of public curiosity." It argued that English-language newspapers and local rumors had given the meeting more attention than it deserved. According to *Le Messager*, a local society had hired a private detective to attend the meeting, and he had counted 271 people there, among whom were two Franco-Americans, one businessman, and the rest, members of the working-class (presumably Yankees). Not all supported the organization, *Le Messager* argued, suggesting that many had attended out of curiosity, and pointing out that the Klan had collected less than $50 in contributions at the meeting. *Le Messager* also reported that Mayor Louis J. Brann, a Democrat, had stated that he would not allow the Klan to use Lewiston City Hall or other public buildings for meetings.[7]

In April meetings in Auburn and Lewiston, Farnsworth continued his attacks against ethnic groups that had brought to the United States religious traditions other than Protestantism. In Auburn, Farnsworth argued: "This is not an Italian nation, this is not an Irish nation, and this is not a Catholic nation, [sic] it always has been and always will be a Protestant nation." He voiced his concern that the Knights of Columbus in the United States was part of "the Pope's political machine," and he argued against parochial schools, contending that all children should be educated in the public schools. He complained that Masons in Lewiston feared to wear their insignias lest they lose business. Farnsworth did not mention Franco-Americans, but attacked Irish Catholics, warning that "7,000 shanty Irish micks" could have as much influence as 70,000 Protestants—an influence, in other words, far beyond their numbers. At a Lewiston meeting, Farnsworth similarly argued that as aliens gained political power in the United States, Protestants were losing control of the country.[8] Farnsworth's broad attacks against Catholics and the foreign-born, of course, represented indirect attacks against Lewiston's Franco-Americans, a population growing in number and political strength in the 1920s.

Louis-Philippe Gagné responded to Farnsworth in a front-page article in *Le Messager*. Against Farnsworth's notion that the United States was a Protestant nation, Gagné contended: "The separation of church and state exists in the United States and one does not have the right to say that the nation is Protestant." His discourse conveyed that Franco-Americans knew intimately their constitutional rights in the United States. Gagné went on to dismiss Farnsworth's assumption that people could not be both Catholic and American, and he chastised the KKK for corruption in its national ranks: "But when accused as criminal, as were some leaders of the Ku Klux Klan, one does not come make laws for the peaceful people of Maine."[9] As a defender of Franco-Americans, *Le Messager* never hesitated to assert the rights of francophones as U.S. residents, nor to point out the idiosyncracies of the host society. Gagné's defense made clear what nativists neither could nor would accept: the notion that ethnic retention proceeded hand in hand with participation in U.S. society.

In May 1923, *Le Messager* reported that the Klan was experiencing difficulty making inroads in Lewiston, and it felt that the nervousness of local Catholics about the Klan's presence had declined. Because Lewiston had a large Catholic population, demography worked in its favor against the Klan. The organization had difficulty renting a hall in Lewiston and ended up holding its meetings across the river in Auburn.[10]

Auburn was more receptive to the Klan. In contrast to Lewiston, which had four Catholic churches, one synagogue, and nine Protestant churches in 1920, Auburn had one Catholic church, one synagogue, and eighteen Protestant churches. Only 15.2 percent of Auburn's 1920 population consisted of foreign-born whites, unlike Lewiston, where they made up 32.3 percent of the city's residents. Men, women, and children of high school age attended Klan meetings in Auburn, and there the KKK held its first initiation ceremony at a secret meeting in May 1923. By late September, the *Sun* reported that the Klan had an estimated 1,700 members in Lewiston-Auburn, and that it planned to purchase land for a temple in Auburn. Either these numbers from the English-language press were greatly exaggerated, or the Klan had lost ground by the spring of 1924; despite Farnsworth's claim to be making inroads in Lewiston and Auburn, *Le Messager* reported in March 1924 that the Klan had only several hundred members.[11]

The hooded knights at first encountered resistance, even in Yankee Auburn. After the KKK petitioned the City Council to use Auburn's city building for meetings, the sole council member with a Franco-American surname asked the body to deny the Klan's request, and it complied with a 3–2 vote in November 1923. After Klan-backed candidates won three seats on the Auburn City Council in December, a cross burned to celebrate the Klan's victory near the site of the newly established Sacred Heart Catholic Parish, largely composed of Franco-Americans. Now in the minority, Franco-American city councilor George C. Bolduc cast in February 1924 the only vote against the Klan's use of Auburn Hall.[12] Winning approval to meet in the Auburn city building represented another victory for the Klan, giving it stronger footing in Lewiston's twin city.

Remarks by Klan leaders published in the English- and French-language press of Lewiston never revealed any direct attacks against Franco-Americans. The KKK, it appears, had a healthy fear of Lewiston Franco-Americans. Elsewhere in Maine, clashes took place in 1924 between Klansmen and Franco-Americans in Greenville in February, and in Biddeford in September. The Klan certainly seemed aware of Lewiston's demography. In April 1924, when ten Klansmen paraded in regalia for the first time during an open meeting at Auburn's Odd Fellows Hall, W. H. Cline, a Klan organizer from Ohio, "drew a comparison between the cities of Lewiston and Auburn relative to the Ku Klux Klan activities," reported the *Sun*. It continued: "The Klan[,] he stated[,] would not dare to parade in dress uniform in Lewiston, but intimated that such an act might be done in Auburn with impunity." About two hundred Klan members paraded in regalia in Lisbon Falls, a community near Lewiston, in early May 1924. When *Le Messager* reported this news, it pointed out that the KKK had not met in Lewiston for a year; it did note, however, that a thirty-foot cross facing the city had burned the previous week. Whether the cross burning was the Klan's doing or not, its purpose was to intimidate Lewistonians. According to the *Sun*, boys in Auburn may have burned it as a hoax. "It is true that we have a pretty lively set of boys up this way who like no better fun than to stir up a little excitement, and if they could give the impression that the Ku Klux Klan had at last captured Lewiston, I am sure they would enjoy the joke immensely," stated the *Sun*'s unidentified source, who lived near the scene. In mid-May, a cross burned from 9:30 P.M. until midnight in Auburn near the Lewiston Falls. Auburn police made no attempts to stop the burning, the *Sun* reported, and it implied that the KKK had set the fire.[13]

The presidents of Bates College in Lewiston and Bowdoin College in Brunswick joined a national committee called the National Vigilantes to curb the growing influence of the Ku Klux Klan in the United States. Despite their leadership, some students from the two colleges attended Klan meetings in Auburn. About thirty-five students from Bates and a few from Bowdoin participated in Klan meetings in November 1923. According to the *Sun*, the KKK intentionally changed the date of one of its scheduled meetings in order to thwart any efforts by Bates College officials to prevent its students from attending.[14] Perhaps Bates students themselves brought the Klan onto the college campus in August 1924.

That month, the English-language press reported, and *Le Messager* translated for its readers, the news that local Klan members planned to celebrate the Republican gubernatorial nomination of Ralph O. Brewster with a highly visible cross burning. On Sunday morning, August 10, 1924, they apparently did so. Lewiston residents awakened by the dynamite bomb saw a twelve-foot cross blazing atop Mount David, located on the Bates College campus and visible in both Lewiston and Auburn. Brewster went on to win the fall gubernatorial election, "supported by the K.K.K.," noted the Dominicans in their chronicle. Brewster won every Maine county except Androscoggin. In that county, Brewster won Auburn with 3,581 votes to his opponent's 1,883 votes; Lewiston, however, supported the Democratic opponent with over 4,000 more votes than the 2,116 it gave Brewster.[15]

Following Brewster's election came reports of more explosions, cross burnings, and Klan sightings in the Lewiston area. In September, *Le Messager* indicated that the English-language press had reported that the Klan had set off bombs near Sabattus, a community that borders Lewiston, and had burned a cross in Auburn. But *Le Messager* indicated that "some ordinary hoaxsters" rather than the Klan may have been responsible. The French-language newspaper contended that the results of the gubernatorial election should not be viewed as a Klan victory, pointing out that Brewster had denied ties to the organization. Perhaps persuaded by Brewster's denials, *Le Messager* may simply have been trying to protect Franco-Americans from the fear of being themselves in the face of increasing activity designed to intimidate them. Several days after *Le Messager*'s commentary, the *Sun* reported that Franco-Americans Arthur Dumais and George Bolduc had seen two hundred "white robed [sic] figures" in a remote section of Lewiston on Saturday night, that a cross burning had taken place around midnight the same evening on the Côté farm in another section of Lewiston, and that an explosion of dynamite bombs had preceded two other cross burnings that same Saturday night, one in Lewiston and the other in Auburn.[16] The

Klan, or those who wished to credit the Klan, made their presence felt in the Lewiston area.

Reported in the English- and French-language press in late 1924, divisions existed within the Klan of Lewiston-Auburn that diminished its ability to exert influence over the local community. The Klan did, however, maintain a presence in Auburn at least until mid-1926, when the City Council denied its request for permission to parade publicly in regalia. In that year, membership in Maine's Ku Klux Klan dropped to 61,136, and the organization thereafter collapsed. Its statewide membership declined to about 3,000 in 1927, and to 226 in 1930. Corruption within the state organization, a lack of financial support, as well as the national decline of the Ku Klux Klan, led to its demise in Maine.[17]

Sources make it difficult to judge the impact of the KKK on Lewiston's Franco-American population. If the experience of Theophile Bernier was at all representative, however, it would appear that the Klan did not substantially intimidate this ethnic group. According to grandson Pierre Vincent Bourassa, Bernier refused to allow the KKK to influence him adversely. Bernier voiced this opinion in English while in a hardware store, adding that "if the Klan did not like the way he felt they could pay him a visit to settle the problem." Assaulted one week later while returning home from his job at a textile mill, Bernier discovered nothing missing from his wallet. The attack, it seems, was his consequence for antagonizing the Klan. Bourassa indicates that his grandfather did not report the incident, because of the possibility that local police or judicial authorities belonged to the organization. The incident made Bernier more resolute about retaining his French-Canadian identity: "From that day on Monsieur Bernier refused to speak English, associated with few Protestants, and voted for the Democratic ticket."[18] From this limited, anecdotal evidence, we can speculate that the effect of the Klan on at least some Franco-Americans may have been for them to assert more forcefully their ethnic identity. Interestingly enough, that assertion, at least in the case of Theophile Bernier, found expression at the ballot box as well as in his choice of language and associates. While it revealed a measure of retrenchment (in his decision to speak only French and to limit contact with non-Catholics), it also gave evidence of his civic participation (he was a voter). Thus, in seeking to retain his ethnic identity and to express it by exercising suffrage, Bernier gave evidence of his decision to pursue political participation and *survivance* as intertwined goals.

Another indication that the Klan did not succeed in intimidating Franco-Americans in Lewiston was that they did not feel it necessary to avoid Brewster. Although it was an open secret that Brewster had been involved with the Klan during his 1924 bid for governor, Franco-Americans had such confidence—and sufficient electoral power—that they could invite him to their events and know he would feel compelled to attend. Franco-Americans invited the governor to their winter carnival in 1925 and to the Saint-Jean-Baptiste (Saint John the Baptist) Day banquet in 1927, receiving him at the banquet with "a veritable ovation." In 1930, *Le Messager* reported that Franco-American Republicans met with Brewster in Lewiston and supported his bid for the U.S. Senate. That same year, when the American Snowshoe Union held its installation ceremony at the Lewiston chalet of the Franco-American club le Montagnard (the Mountaineer), Brewster was among the politicians who spoke at the event.[19]

One effect of the Klan's presence may have been to prompt Franco-Americans to anglicize their names, but I have discovered no evidence of this in Lewiston in the 1920s. Only in 1930 did naturalization forms begin to provide a line for those wishing to change their name, and the records reveal there was little name-changing among Lewiston francophones. Only ten (1.6 percent) of the 612 men and women who naturalized from 1930 to 1939 modified their names. Half of the alterations involved individuals shortening their names, typically by selecting one of their three given names as their own. For example, Joseph Elzear Wilfrid Paradis shortened his name to Wilfrid Paradis. Under half of the name changes of the 1930s involved anglicizations. Two men and two women anglicized their given names but retained their French family names. For example, Raoul Leopold Cote became Ralph Leopold Cote, and Lucienne Levesque became Lucy Levesque. None of the individuals who naturalized in the 1930s anglicized his or her family name.[20] Name-changing is a topic that surfaces frequently in the literature on Franco-Americans, but it seems to have occurred infrequently in Lewiston. Because the city had such a high concentration of French speakers, most who naturalized in the 1930s probably did not feel the pressure or the need to anglicize their names in order to fit into the social milieu. Moreover, passing as non-francophone appears not to have been an important consideration for the French-speaking immigrants of this Franco-American city.

Interviews with elderly Franco-Americans may present a different picture of the effect of nativists like the KKK on Lewiston residents. But currently available sources, including published and taped interviews with Lewiston Franco-Americans, shed no further light on this matter.[21] What is clear, however, is that the presence of the Ku Klux Klan in Lewiston in the 1920s represented another cycle of anti-immigrant, anti-Catholic hostility in the Spindle City. That hostility originated with the torchings of the city's Irish Catholic church, allegedly by the Know-Nothings in the mid-1850s. It continued as discrimination by Protestant Yankees against French-Canadian Lewiston residents in the late nineteenth century, with the efforts of the American Protective Association in the 1890s representing but one manifestation of this cycle of hostility. That cycle repeated itself in Lewiston through the actions of the Ku Klux Klan in the 1920s, directed in large part against the city's Franco-American population. The KKK's presence in Lewiston thus perpetuated discrimination against Franco-Americans.[22]

Much of that discrimination was directed against the practice of speaking French. In a speech before the Maine Bar Association in 1923, attorney F. X. Belleau argued against nativists who wanted francophones to abandon their French language. "No one disputes the fact that English is the language spoken in this country and that it is to one's great disadvantage not to speak it," he stated. "But there is no necessity of forgetting the mother tongue," he contended as he promoted bilingualism. In 1925, the Maine state legislature considered, and later tabled, a bill to require public servants to use only English, and for public transactions to take place solely in English. Representative H. E. Holmes of Lewiston, the attorney who had advocated for Canadian French in the local schools in 1913, vigorously opposed the measure. He argued that French speakers had made a significant contribution during World War I, "and if the French language had been good enough to fight and to die, it should be good enough to be heard in the state of Maine," paraphrased Le Messager.[23]

French even came under attack at the local level. In 1926, the Lewiston Evening Journal reported that some of the eight boys charged with stealing coal from the Maine Central Railroad had required assistance translating into French the words of the judge and clerk of courts. The boys were students or former students of Sainte-Marie (Saint Mary) School. As public servants, the judge, the clerk of courts, and the attorneys should communicate with the public in its language, *Le Messager* asserted in defense of the boys. This was a different position from July 1925, when *Le Messager* had reported that five boys around fifteen years of age, all born and raised in Lewiston, had been unable to speak English when they appeared in municipal court to face their charges. At the time, *Le Messager* had pointed to the incident as evidence of weakness in the education of Franco-Americans, because the boys had had six or seven years of schooling, and it had contended: "English-language citizens certainly have reason to rouse themselves and to demand explanations, in the presence of a situation one can without exaggeration qualify as strange." In 1926, however, when the English-language press criticized Franco-Americans because some of their youth had difficulty communicating in English at the local court, *Le Messager* went on the offensive in asserting that they should have been spoken to in French. As a result of *Le Messager*'s actions, the loyalty of Franco-Americans became questioned. The editor of the *Portland Evening Express* argued that English was "the common, the official and the chief language" of the United States, and not knowing it constituted "an affront to the country, an injustice to the child and a silly, short-sighted policy." The editor of the *Journal*, in a fairly balanced article promoting bilingualism, nonetheless argued that francophones should talk "American" in public.[24]

Following the court incident, Maine Commissioner of Education Dr. Augustus O. Thomas visited the schools of Saint-Pierre and Sainte-Marie parishes. According to the *Sun*, Thomas indicated that older students had greater knowledge of English than the younger ones, and he found that the women religious "cannot teach English as well as a prepared lay teacher, as their English is imperfect." He felt that French instruction received too much emphasis at the schools, and he pointed out that the practice of speaking French in the home also hindered the acquisition of English. In early November, *Le Messager* worried that the negative press generated by the court incident and the subsequent visit by the education commissioner would prompt nativists in the Maine state legislature to take further measures to push the Americanization of French speakers. *Le Messager*'s editor, George Filteau, claimed that there was no cause for alarm about English-language acquisition on the part of francophones. The three boys in question were between eight and thirteen years of age, he stated, and two had received less than three years of schooling, while the third could understand English when interviewed by *Le Messager*. Despite the negative comments of the English-language press, Filteau reiterated the argument that the judge should have spoken French to the boys; in a city where a majority of the population spoke French, so should the judge, he contended. Dominican priest R. Ouimet defended the parish schools in the French-language press, arguing that teaching younger children in their mother tongue was an important pedagogical tool, and pointing out that Thomas had found that students from grade four up did as well in English as public school students. Ouimet thus sought to allay any fears among Lewiston Franco-Americans that their parish schools could not meet the language needs of their children.[25] The 1926 court incident and school inspection brought undue pressure to bear on Lewiston's Franco-American community, making francophones uneasy about expressing themselves in their mother tongue.

In 1931, another court incident created tension over the persistence of spoken French. Eleven-year-old Marcel Desjardins had to testify at the Superior Court of Maine in Auburn about an accident during which his father's bread truck had hit a three-year-old child on his sales route. Desjardins had to give some of his testimony in French. "Here is a boy 11 years old," Justice Herbert T. Powers admonished. "He has been to school for four years and he cannot speak English. Lewiston schools better be overhauled." The *Journal* splashed the judge's harsh words on its front page. Embarrassed by the negative publicity surrounding one of their students, the Dominican Sisters privately affirmed in their convent's journal "that instruction in English is not neglected in our classes." Following the court incident, the editor of the *Journal*, Arthur G. Staples, made the case for all citizens to learn good English. Yet he also encouraged bilingualism in English and French by francophones and anglophones alike. *Le Messager* translated Staples's editorial into French for its readers and indicated that it was "very timely, completely sympathetic and brings to light a delicate situation."[26] Unlike the sensational front-page story that brought undue, negative attention to French speakers, Staples's editorial in the *Journal* reflected a more enlightened, tolerant response to the issue of language differences in Lewiston.

In September 1931, another public incident of discrimination took place against Lewiston Franco-Americans. According to *Le Messager*, the new fire commissioner, an Irish-American doctor surnamed Scannell, posted rules in city fire stations forbidding the speaking of French. While *Le Messager* conceded that politeness dictated that francophones should not use French when non-French speakers were part of a conversation, a departmental practice since 1928, it pointed out that Franco-Americans held twenty-six of the thirty-six positions in the fire department, and implied that they should otherwise feel free to speak in their mother tongue.[27] *Le Messager* offered a tempered response to the incident, but the fact remained that the fire commissioner's efforts to limit the use of French represented intensified discrimination against Franco-Americans. As we shall see in the chapters that follow, these efforts were part of a pattern of discrimination against French speakers that took place throughout the twentieth century.

Some of the discrimination against Franco-Americans came from within the Catholic Church of Maine. In his promotion of American loyalties and the use of English, Bishop Louis S. Walsh worried more about the rise of the Ku Klux Klan in the early 1920s than he did about Franco-Americans. Thus he acted like other Irish prelates who dominated the Catholic hierarchy in the United States, and who sought to unify the ethnically diverse Church in the face of nativist hostilities. After Walsh visited Saint-Pierre School in 1922, for example, the Dominican Sisters recorded in their journal that he had urged them to "work English hard." After meeting in October 1923 with the Soeurs de Saint-Joseph de Lyons (Sisters of Saint Joseph of Lyons), a teaching order from France, Walsh recorded in his diary, "I told them plainly that the State law about 'English as [a] basic language' must be followed." The 1919 law to which he referred represented part of the intensified discrimination against Franco-Americans that took place in the aftermath of World War I. Walsh apparently did not tell the sisters that the law applied to high schools, not to elementary schools like the ones they oversaw in South Berwick and Jackman, Maine. The Ku Klux Klan surely was on Walsh's mind. Its state headquarters were in Portland, the episcopal seat of Maine's Catholic Church. Among Walsh's files at the Chancery Archives in Portland are several copies of the *Maine Klansman*—some of the few known copies of this publication. In the December 13, 1923, issue is the report that Klan-backed candidates had won election to the Portland City Council and School Committee. "Portland citizens are, for the first time in decades, represented by a Protestant city government," the newspaper exulted. An

undated, typed note addressed to the bishop from Klan headquarters following the elections underscored the point that Catholics had won no seats.
"It is the 18th place in New England that the Klan has kept Catholics from
holding office," Klansman G. S. Mertell wrote the bishop. "Hereafter no
niggers [sic] catholics [sic] nor Jews will ever hold office in Portland." On
New Year's Eve, Walsh recorded in his diary that the KKK had contributed
to making 1923 his most difficult year.[28]

It was in 1923 that Walsh had launched his offensive against the
Dominican priests. Despite continued communication with Dominican
authorities in Québec over title to the property of Saint-Pierre Parish in
the early 1920s, Walsh still lacked the real-estate deed he earnestly desired.
The conflict between Walsh and the Dominicans became exacerbated when
the bishop learned in the early 1920s that Reverend Thomas M. Gill had
erected a chapel in Sabattus in 1913 on land purchased by his sister of
Montréal without first obtaining the bishop's approval. The Dominicans
had served Catholics in Sabattus on an unofficial basis since 1883, and by
assignment of the bishop since 1905. News of the chapel infuriated Walsh,
who demanded title to the property. The Dominicans resisted, and they were
not entirely forthcoming about how they had financed the chapel's construction. Gill maintained that the Dominicans had never held collections
in Lewiston or other parts of Maine for the chapel. But he acknowledged to
his provincial that they had held raffles to raise from $1,000 to $1,200. "If
the bishop does not know that we had raffles, I will not speak to him about
them; let's let him prove it!" Gill wrote the provincial. Exasperated by the
lack of progress in resolving two property disputes with the Dominicans,
both private extensions of the publicly fought Corporation Sole controversy, Walsh went on the offensive in 1923. According to the Dominicans,
"Monsignor Walsh played his trump card: to divide Saint Peter's." With the
assistance of Lewiston's Irish pastors, Walsh purchased properties in the
southern and eastern sections of Lewiston. Then he carved up Saint-Pierre to
create two new parishes, Holy Cross and Holy Family. *Le Messager* decried
the secrecy surrounding Walsh's property acquisitions, and it bristled upon
learning that Irish priests had negotiated and concluded transactions affecting Franco-Americans. For their part, the Dominicans proved intransigent
about giving up the Sabattus chapel. Tired of the unsatisfactory progress of
continued discussions with the Dominicans, Walsh recorded in his diary on

December 17, 1923: "I see my way now more clearly to solve the situation, even though a radical remedy must be applied." Walsh's "remedy," recorded the Dominicans, was to close the chapel in Sabattus and to reassign its members to Holy Family Parish. Walsh also demanded that Father Gill leave the Diocese of Portland.[29]

When Walsh divided Saint-Pierre to gain the upper hand over the Dominicans, he created Holy Family and Holy Cross as territorial parishes that would serve all Catholics living within their boundaries, unlike Sainte-Marie and Saint-Pierre, which were national parishes designed to serve Franco-Americans. The new pastors Walsh appointed were not of French-Canadian descent: Michael F. Drain of Holy Cross had been born in Ireland, and Vital Nonorgues of Holy Family had been born in France. Given that the population of each of the two new parishes was predominantly Franco-American, Walsh's intention in assigning these priests seems to have been to limit French-Canadian influence and to promote acculturation. Holy Family's demography confounded the bishop's plan: it immediately became a Franco-American institution, because virtually all parishioners were of French-Canadian background. About 10 percent of the parishioners of Holy Cross were Irish and Polish Catholics, so it was not without struggle that the Franco-Americans of Holy Cross shaped their new parish into a Franco-American institution.[30]

In mid-November 1923, Reverend Drain met with about a hundred women to plan a whist party to raise funds for the new parish of Holy Cross. All but seven of the women were Franco-American. After the francophone women saw the tickets for the whist party, they complained to the pastor that the name of the parish did not appear in French. Drain insisted that the parish's name would remain "Holy Cross." All but about twelve women left the meeting in protest.[31] Their actions precipitated another controversy that ultimately pitted Maine's Irish bishop against Franco-Americans.

Following the walkout, francophone men took up the cause of pushing for "Sainte-Croix" as the official name of their parish. In December, from 90 to 125 men held meetings in the halls of Franco-American institutions in Lewiston to discuss the situation and to plan strategy. While they did not object to Drain's making announcements at masses in both English and French, they insisted that the parish be named "Sainte-Croix," that it not become an English-speaking parish, and that their children receive instruction in French. As one family head put it, "The parishioners of Holy Cross are not rebels against religious authority; they want quite simply to obtain justice for their language and recognition for their French origins." Disaffected Franco-Americans attended mass in other parishes and did not contribute funds to Holy Cross during the pastor's visit to their homes. A committee of men met with Drain. He told them that there would be only one hour of French instruction daily at the parish school, and he stated ambiguously that the parish name would be neither English nor French. Dissatisfied with the results of the meeting, the committee traveled to Portland in January 1924 to meet with Bishop Walsh, who conversed with them in French. Following the meeting, over 160 family heads gathered in Lewiston to learn what Walsh had said. He had apparently sympathized with the Franco-Americans. The inscription on the church could read "Sainte-Croix," Walsh had told the committee, because a majority of the parishioners were francophone. He felt, however, that celebrations should include some English for the benefit of the non-francophone members. Walsh assured the committee that instruction at the parish school would be offered equally in French and English. Disaffected parishioners subsequently returned to Holy Cross for religious exercises.[32]

Exultant, Lewiston's French-language newspaper contrasted the Franco-Americans of Lewiston and Sanford, Maine. All but three families in a newly created parish in Sanford were francophone; they had worked to raise $16,000 to build their church, and yet the church bore the English name of "Holy Family." "Evidently the Franco-Americans there do not have the same mentality as those from Lewiston who requested and got their new parish from West Rose Hill to be called *Sainte-Croix*."[33]

But the conflict in Lewiston was not over. Drain remained at odds with his Franco-American parishioners. He informed communicants in late January that the issues that had divided them were still unresolved, and he forbade them from meeting without his permission to discuss parish affairs. A committee of Franco-American men traveled again to Portland to complain to Bishop Walsh. Walsh proved much less receptive during the ten-minute meeting he accorded the delegates. He went back on his word, the committee felt, and he told its members that the United States was neither French nor Canadian, but American, reported *Le Messager*. The following Sunday, few people attended masses at Holy Cross, and over five hundred Franco-

American men from throughout Lewiston met in the afternoon to discuss the controversy. After Drain again insisted from the pulpit that parishioners keep quiet about the conflict at Holy Cross and not discuss it on the trolleys or in the streets, the editor of *Le Messager* chided: "And this is what we call pure Americanism!" Francophone men began a petition to have Holy Cross renamed "Sainte-Croix" and received messages of support from Franco-Americans from throughout New England. Women attended one of the Sunday meetings in early March. Participants at that meeting felt that women should be included in future meetings, too, because they could help increase the intensity of the dispute by circulating petitions and by avoiding involvement in parish projects during the course of the controversy.[34] As francophones used their constitutional rights of petition, assembly, and free speech to preserve their French-Canadian ethnicity in the United States, they provided only further evidence that they had their own brand of Americanism. Their Americanism, in other words, employed U.S. forms, but they used these forms to achieve their own ends.

Tensions abated somewhat after the opening of the chapel-school building in late April 1924, and attendance at masses improved. When Drain surprised parishioners in June 1925 by announcing that there would be a special Saint-Jean-Baptiste Day mass for children, as in the other Franco-American churches of Lewiston and Auburn, *Le Messager* recognized this conciliatory gesture: "Needless to say that Father Drain's gesture will do a great deal to efface the unhappy tension that has existed in this parish since its founding." At masses, Drain gave announcements in French, summarized them in English, and recited communal prayers in French while members of the congregation responded to them in their own language; these arrangements satisfied parishioners, reported *Le Messager* in August 1925. But only after Walsh died and his Irish successor, John Murray, appointed a Canadian-born francophone to succeed Drain as pastor of Holy Cross in January 1926 did the controversy end. Franco-Americans had won. By mid-January, the name "Ste-Croix" appeared on the chapel-school complex, and it remains on the structure to this day.[35]

The controversy at Holy Cross provides further evidence that the road from *Canadien* to Franco-American in Lewiston was not linear. In the face of Americanizing pressures within the Catholic Church, actions Louis-Philippe Gagné termed "false Americanism" on the part of the Irish bishop and Irish pastor, Franco-Americans fought for what they perceived to be in their ethnic interests. For Franco-Americans, true Americanism meant accepting one's civic responsibility in the host society, such as by naturalizing and voting.[36] It meant understanding—and defending—one's constitutional rights. It also necessitated learning English. But it did not entail giving up their ethnic heritage, which the Roman Catholic Church and nativists like the Klan believed.

Even in the presence of the local Ku Klux Klan and the Americanizing pressures that it represented, Lewiston Franco-Americans persisted in their ethnic struggle to see Holy Cross named Sainte-Croix. Louis-Philippe Gagné saw the struggle as part of a larger issue concerning the place in U.S. society of New England's two million Franco-Americans. He argued in 1924 that they represented "a national treasure for the United States," and, given this, he questioned: "Why do they want to take our language away and to treat us as pariahs?" Gagné continued by encouraging Franco-Americans to fight to preserve their identity: "Let us not permit the debasement of ourselves and let us see what we can keep of the heritage of our ancestors."[37] In brief, Gagné felt that Franco-Americans should be proud to speak French, to practice Roman Catholicism, and to participate in French-Canadian celebrations. Just as outside pressures were not primarily responsible for Franco-Americans joining U.S. society, they also did not prevent this population from asserting its identity—and its brand of Americanism—in its country of adoption. Moreover, the Holy Cross affair demonstrates that Franco-Americans actively negotiated their identity in the United States: they set the pace, and their definition predominated.

Until his death in 1924, Walsh continued to press the Dominicans for title to Saint-Pierre Church and the chapel in Sabattus. To force their hand, he threatened to seek a new arrangement between them and the Diocese of Portland or to replace the Dominican order altogether, in which case he would publicize their private conflict. "If I am obliged to mention the maladministration of Father Dallaire in the construction of the new church, it will not take much time to decide the issue," Walsh wrote the Dominican provincial, "but I much prefer the quiet method without publicity, yet my mind is fully made up on this matter," he insisted.[38] Walsh's frustration in dealing with French-Canadian Dominicans, along with his concerns about the Klan in Maine, had probably led him to change course in the Holy Cross controversy in January 1924. Only Walsh's death in May prevented him from carrying out his threats.

Walsh's successors overturned a number of decisions he had made that discriminated against Franco-Americans.[39] Shortly after John Murray became bishop, *Le Messager* stated that "The reign of oppression and injustice that Franco-Americans had to endure for nearly a quarter-century is over." To the great pleasure of Franco-Americans, Murray allowed Catholics to hold midnight masses at Christmas, beginning in 1925, and Murray's successor in 1932, Bishop Joseph McCarthy, granted the same permission. By appointing a *Canadien* as pastor of Holy Cross, and by allowing the parish to be called Sainte-Croix, Murray demonstrated respect for Lewiston Franco-Americans and for their efforts to preserve their language. Fluent in both English and French, Murray encouraged all priests within the Diocese of Portland to become bilingual. He also asked the Dominicans to celebrate masses again at the Sabattus chapel in July 1926, and they did. In 1934, Bishop McCarthy settled the longstanding dispute between the diocese and the Dominicans by signing papers officially giving the order title to the parish property, thus honoring the agreement they had made with Bishop Healy when they had first arrived in Lewiston in 1881. The Dominicans did not record in their monastery's chronicle, however, whether this agreement extended to the property in Sabattus. Through various measures, then, the episcopacy capitulated: the Irish bishops who succeeded Walsh ended the ethnic controversies that had plagued his administration and that had discriminated against Maine's French-speaking Catholics.[40]

The actions of Bishop Walsh in the early twentieth century, and the ensuing conflicts between him and Lewiston Franco-Americans, appear to have made several parishes more resolute about retaining their French-Canadian heritage, and one of them more inclined to pursue acculturation. We can speculate about the long-term effects of his actions in part by looking at the language of masses. Saint-Pierre and Sainte-Croix parishes each continued to offer one weekend mass in French at the start of the new millenium; Sainte-Marie, which Walsh had created as a national parish in Lewiston's Petit Canada, also offered one French mass each weekend before closing during summer 2000. Sainte-Famille, however, dropped its remaining French mass by June 1991, becoming the only Franco-American church in Lewiston to celebrate all masses in English.[41] Unlike the other Franco-American parishes, Sainte-Famille had a French-from-France pastor for nearly four decades during the twentieth century; appointed by Walsh in 1923, Vital Nonorgues served Sainte-Famille until his death in 1961. The pastors of Lewiston's three other Franco-American parishes from the 1920s through the end of the twentieth century (with the exception of Walsh appointee Michael F. Drain at Sainte-Croix) have all been of French-Canadian birth or background.

But it was not solely the ethnic origins of pastors that affected the different parish communities. The orders of men and women religious who taught in the parochial schools determined the speed with which each parish community anglicized over the course of the twentieth century. If asked, older Lewistonians would say that the in-town schools of Sainte-Marie and Saint-Pierre were "more French" than the suburban schools of Sainte-Croix or Sainte-Famille. We can trace differences in the schools to the composition of their teaching orders. Each of the eleven Ursuline Sisters who taught at Sainte-Marie School in 1920 was of French-Canadian birth or background; in fact, nearly three-fourths (eight of eleven) were Canadian-born, which undoubtedly contributed to ethnic retention in the parish community. Among the thirty-one Dominican Sisters who taught at Saint-Pierre in 1920, over one-third (eleven) were French, two-fifths (thirteen) were of French-Canadian birth, one-fifth (six) were Franco-American, and one sister, a music teacher, was Spanish. Given the smaller proportion of Canadian-born sisters teaching at Saint-Pierre, one might have expected the parish to have promoted the acculturation of its children at a more rapid pace than Sainte-Marie. But most (eight out of eleven) of the French Dominican Sisters in 1920 did not speak English, and the novitiate the sisters established in 1927 in Valleyfield, Québec, ensured French-Canadian recruits to their order. Moreover, French-Canadian Dominican pastors administered the parish, and they brought to Saint-Pierre the Frères du Sacré-Coeur (Brothers of the Sacred Heart), a teaching order of men from Victoriaville, Québec, to teach some classes of boys beginning in 1928. The brothers also began teaching boys in grades six through eight at Sainte-Marie School in 1939.[42] Along with the orders of women religious, they surely helped the in-town schools to retain their ethnic heritage.

Sometimes, however, the presence of an Irish teacher in a Franco-American school led to cultural confusion. Lucien Aubé attended grades six to eight at Sainte-Marie School from the early to mid-1930s. In sixth grade, a nun of Irish descent taught him in English in the mornings, while one of French-Canadian descent taught him in French in the afternoons. When discussing the history of colonial Canada, his francophone instructor spoke of the Hurons as good Indians who had allied themselves with the French, and she depicted the Iroquois as enemies. In contrast, his Irish teacher spoke in glowing terms of the Iroquois and "encouraged us to be proud of being Americans." Too shy to question the dichotomous portraits presented by his instructors, Aubé fell victim to what he later termed "cultural fragmentation."[43] Surely students from other parish schools experienced similar cultural confusion as Lewiston's teaching orders became ethnically mixed.

Two different religious orders taught at the suburban parish schools of Lewiston. Les Soeurs de la Présentation de Marie (the Sisters of the Presentation of Mary), an order based in Saint-Hyacinthe, Québec, began teaching at Sainte-Croix in 1927. Each of the eight sisters who lived at the convent of Sainte-Croix during 1927–1928 was of French-Canadian descent. Four were Canadian-born, three were U.S.-born, and the place of birth of one was not known. As evidence of the orientation of the Soeurs de la Présentation de Marie towards Canada, all of them departed to Canada for their religious retreats during the summer following their first school year in Lewiston. Invited to Sainte-Famille by Reverend Vital Nonorgues, the Soeurs de Saint-Joseph de Lyons, a French order, began teaching in Lewiston in 1926. The four founding sisters at Sainte-Famille each represented a different national or ethnic origin: one was Irish-American, one Franco-American, another French-Canadian (i.e., Canadian-born), and the superior was French. The personnel records of the Soeurs de Saint-Joseph make it possible to examine the ethnic composition of the order through the 1920s and 1930s. They reveal that only 12 percent (three out of twenty-five) of the sisters missioned at Sainte-Famille during the twenties and thirties were Canadian-born, 12 percent (three) had been born in France, and 72 percent (eighteen sisters) were U.S.-born. While one of the native-born sisters was Irish-American and another Anglo-American, the other sixteen were Franco-Americans, and they constituted over three-fifths of the personnel at Sainte-Famille from the mid-1920s to the late 1930s.[44]

Given that the Soeurs de Saint-Joseph appear to have had the largest proportion of U.S.-born sisters, we might expect them to have promoted the use of English at a more rapid pace than the other teaching orders, and they did. Unlike the other Franco-American schools of Lewiston, which provided half a day of instruction in French—a practice typical of most Franco-American schools throughout New England until mid-century— Sainte-Famille offered only one hour of instruction in French each day, beginning when the Soeurs de Saint-Joseph arrived in the parish in 1926. According to Sr. Marie Therese Beaudoin, the Soeurs de Saint-Joseph "felt children must first meet the language of the culture." She reported that many of Sainte-Famille's students heard only French at home; their parents probably admonished, as had her mother: "English outside the home; speak French at home." The sisters believed that teaching half a day in French would have been unfair to students trying to pass Lewiston High School's English entrance exam, and they were concerned that students were ridiculed in high school for their French accents and for difficulties they had with the English language. Teaching for only one hour in French was an instructional standard the sisters also followed in their Jackman and South Berwick schools.[45]

In summary, Bishop Walsh's actions may have served to promote ethnic retention in three Lewiston parishes and to facilitate the anglicization of a fourth. Sainte-Marie, created by Walsh as a national parish in the heart of Lewiston's Petit Canada and served by Ursuline Sisters of primarily French-Canadian descent, retained its ethnic character until its closing. Walsh's struggle with the French-Canadian Dominican priests of Saint-Pierre probably made them more determined to safeguard that parish's ethnic identity. A teaching order from France, the Dominican Sisters of the parish had a sizable number of Canadian-born teachers on their staff, and their novitiate in Québec ensured a continued supply of French-Canadian sisters teaching at Saint-Pierre, Lewiston's largest Franco-American school. The French-Canadian order of the Frères du Sacré-Coeur must have helped the Dominican and Ursuline Sisters with the task of ethnic preservation at the in-town parish schools. Walsh's conflict with the Franco-American parishioners of Sainte-Croix appears to have made them more intent upon preserving their ethnic identity. The Canadian-born pastor appointed to Sainte-Croix by Walsh's successor invited the French-Canadian teaching order of the Soeurs de la Présentation de Marie to staff the parochial school, and this helped the parish community to retain its ethnic heritage. Only at Sainte-Famille, then, did Walsh's actions seem to promote anglicization. Appointing a French pastor who, in turn, invited the French order of the Soeurs de Saint-Joseph to teach at the school facilitated this. By teaching primarily in English, the Soeurs de Saint-Joseph promoted more rapid anglicization than the other women religious of Lewiston. The Franco-American parish they served was the only one in Lewiston to have discontinued all of its French masses by the start of the twenty-first century.

During their teaching ministry at Sainte-Famille, the Soeurs de Saint-Joseph did not neglect or discourage activities that promoted French-language acquisition. Students could earn diplomas in both English and French from Sainte-Famille School, as they could at other parish schools. They also participated in French composition contests, sponsored by the Franco-American societies, in competition with children from other Franco-American schools.[46]

But that did not prevent *Le Messager* from publicly criticizing Sainte-Famille for providing less instruction in French than the other parish schools. In 1935, the newspaper singled out the Irish Sr. Saint Agnes (née Donahue) when it contended that the school's francophone staff was insufficient. The founding principal of Sainte-Famille School and a teacher of English, Sr. Saint Agnes was more fluent in English than the other teachers, and she addressed people who visited the school in that language. Parishioner Mrs. Gédéon Jacques defended the sisters and their school by arguing that, while parishioners of Sainte-Famille did not want to lose their French language, "we do not want our children to leave our dear parish school handling the English language insufficiently either." Students had left Franco-American parish schools for the Irish ones in order to learn English, she argued, and some had even come to Sainte-Famille to do the same. Sainte-Famille parishioners who wanted their children to retain their French language had little reason to worry, Roger Bissonnette pointed out, because "there wasn't the danger for loss of language as there is now. Everyone with Canadian ancestors living in the area could speak French." Although *Le Messager* acknowledged the need to learn English in the United States, it maintained that French should not be accorded secondary status. Franco-American schoolchildren should master French before acquiring English, the newspaper insisted. One result of the controversy with *Le Messager*, indicated Sr. Alvina Levesque, was that the sisters were "almost not allowed to talk English outside of school."[47]

Ill feelings towards Sainte-Famille did not pass quickly. When Louis-Philippe Gagné spoke in 1936 about Maine's Franco-American population on Montréal's CKAC radio station, owned by *La Presse* and audible in Lewiston, he told listeners that an Irish nun in a French teaching order of Lewiston would tell her students to "Talk United States!" Gagné's sensitivity about the French language becomes all the more apparent in other parts of his speech. He proudly indicated on the air, for example, that Yankees called Lewiston "the French City," and that it was no longer necessary for businesses to place signs in their windows announcing, "Ici on parle français" (French is spoken here). "It is understood we speak it everywhere and it would be commercial suicide for businessmen not to employ any French-Canadian clerks," Gagné asserted with evident pleasure.[48] The tension that arose between the Soeurs de Saint-Joseph and Gagné/*Le Messager* demonstrates that one parish community in Lewiston was moving faster than the others in reshaping its identity.

The controversy also highlights the presence of intergenerational tension in Lewiston's Franco-American community. Gagné had emigrated to the United States from Québec in 1922 and had naturalized by 1928.[49] His quick naturalization offers no better evidence that joining the host society was not inimical to preserving French-Canadian ethnicity. But, as a representative of the first generation, Gagné was apparently less inclined to accept Sainte-Famille's faster pace of acculturation than were the predominantly Franco-American sisters who taught there during the 1920s and 1930s. As we will see, generational tensions grew in Lewiston as U.S.-born Franco-Americans increasingly used English as their primary language, causing older Franco-Americans to worry about the place of their mother tongue in the community.

Men like Gagné were not the only defenders of the French language and of French-Canadian traditions in Lewiston. As noted earlier, the 1920 census informs us that Lewiston's Franco-American women were more likely than the men to speak only French. The insistence of women that "Sainte-Croix" be the name of their parish adds further weight to the impression that francophone women exercised a central role as cultural hearth-keepers in the Spindle City.[50] The incident at Sainte-Croix suggests that women were as willing as men like Gagné to take proactive measures to preserve their language and their ethnic heritage.

As in previous decades, the evolving identity of Lewiston Franco-Americans in the 1920s and 1930s revealed itself in public celebrations of Saint-Jean-Baptiste Day. On this ethnic feast day, Franco-Americans continued to assert their identity in the face of the Americanization movement. Sometimes they needed a little prodding from *Le Messager*. In 1922, the year that l'Institut-Jacques Cartier celebrated its fiftieth anniversary, *Le Messager* encouraged readers: "Let us not be afraid to show who we are, by wearing a small tricolor ribbon on our lapels, tomorrow, Saint John the Baptist Day and Sunday, the fiftieth anniversary of the Institute." Residents of Petit Canada decorated their homes, and the Franco-American societies paraded to Saint-Pierre Church for mass, during which Dominican prior Arsène Roy emphasized the importance of preserving the French language in order to retain the Catholic faith. The following year, when *Le Messager* reminded readers of the upcoming feast day of Saint-Jean-Baptiste, it asked them to decorate their homes with flags and banners "in the national and American colors, which after all are the same." Thus it made explicit what francophones had conveyed through their symbols since the late nineteenth century, namely that their identities as French-Canadian descendants and Americans were closely intertwined. The French-language newspaper also asked Franco-Americans to sport buttons of the maple leaf or Tricolor. Despite the presence of the Ku Klux Klan in the Lewiston area, one thousand men, women, and children marched in the Saint-Jean-Baptiste Day parade in 1923 to and from Saint-Pierre Church, which was decorated with flags of France and the United States. Pleased by the large parade and fine celebration, the Dominicans noted: "True patriotism awakens." An industrial crisis in Lewiston in 1924, as well as cross burnings and Klan parades in the Lewiston area, probably discouraged the organization of a Saint-Jean-Baptiste Day celebration that year. Other evidence suggests that Franco-Americans did not fear public demonstrations in that tumultuous year, however, for one thousand children paraded through Lewiston's streets in September to celebrate the opening of the new school of Saint-Pierre Parish. From 1925 to 1927, about two to three thousand Franco-American children paraded on Saint-Jean-Baptiste Day, carrying flags of the United States and either a flag or *boutonnière* of the Tricolor. After watching the children pass in 1926, *Le Messager* pointed out the symbolism they expressed when it stated that the U.S. flag "is equally tricolor and consists of blue, white and red." Just as the colors of the French and U.S. flags were the same, so too were the identities of Franco-Americans. The symbolism of the flags spoke volumes. So did the singing of both "O Canada" and the "The Star-Spangled Banner" following the Saint-Jean-Baptiste Day banquet of 1938, anthems that Franco-Americans probably sang at celebrations in other years as well.[51]

In conclusion, the experiences of Lewiston's Franco-Americans in the 1920s and 1930s demonstrate that this population continued to pursue both *survivance* and participation in U.S. society as intertwined goals prior to World War II. Despite the presence of the Ku Klux Klan in the 1920s, Franco-Americans in Lewiston, reinforced by heavy immigration from Québec, did not shed their ethnic identity. The actions of the Irish bishop, Louis Walsh, appear to have spurred one Lewiston parish to move faster than the other Franco-American parishes in refashioning its identity in the United States. But there were forces internal to the community of Sainte-Famille—in, for example, the Soeurs de Saint-Joseph and their defenders—that promoted change. During the interwar period, Franco-Americans of Lewiston reshaped their identity at their own rhythms, rather than to the drumbeats of nativists.

✤

CHAPTER SEVEN

Burying the Elephant

Politics, Gender, and Ethnic Identity
in Lewiston, 1920–1940

Elated by President Franklin D. Roosevelt's re-election in 1936, Franco-American women held a mock funeral for the Republican Party. As we will see, the obsequies began at their workplace in Auburn, Maine, and continued across the river into Lewiston, where most local French speakers resided. Once a Yankee town, Lewiston had evolved into a Franco-American city by 1920. First- and second-generation Franco-Americans made up 46.6 percent of Lewiston's residents, and third- and later-generation Franco-Americans constituted an additional 3.1 percent of the city's population. Thus individuals of French-Canadian descent made up approximately half of Lewiston's total population in 1920. By the third decade of the twentieth century, Lewiston had become a bilingual community in which banks and stores had at least one French speaker. Even signs that forbade spitting on sidewalks appeared in both English and French![1] Increasing immigration, continued naturalization and voter-registration drives, and the rise of Franco-American suffragettes served to challenge Republican Yankees in the 1920s and 1930s.

Heavy immigration from Québec during the 1920s continued to facilitate ethnic retention in the Spindle City, but as we shall see, it did not slow the process of acculturation. The immigration restrictions the United States imposed during the 1920s, principally to stem the tide of immigrants from southern and eastern Europe, were also applied to Canadians in 1930. Until then, the international border between Canada and the United States remained relatively porous. Unlike during the opening decades of the twentieth century, French-Canadian emigration to the United States returned in the 1920s to nearly the same high level that had existed in the late nineteenth century: from 1920 to 1929, the net migration from Québec to the United States totaled 130,000. Mechanization and the productivity of farms in Québec were low, and a recession from 1920 to 1922 precipitated emigration.[2]

Le Messager kept an eye on the massive immigration from Québec. In 1921, the newspaper explained that trainloads of families arriving in Lewiston had come because of a lack of work "in the native country," and it warned readers: "Those who hold good jobs today will do well to keep them, for replacement candidates will be numerous." Citing the Lewiston Journal, Le Messager in June 1923 reported that, due primarily to Canadian emigration, Lewiston's population was growing by about 300 persons each week, and that it had increased by 1,000 in the previous month. Some of the immigrants had formerly lived in Lewiston and had chosen to return to the Spindle City because economic conditions were better in the United States than in Canada, it noted.[3]

Naturalization records from the 1920s and 1930s suggest, however, that few francophones had returned to Canada and then emigrated for a second time to the United States. This information comes from an examination of the places of birth of the children of immigrants who became U.S. citizens. Only twenty of the 1,238 individuals (1.6 percent) who naturalized while living in Lewiston in the 1920s and 1930s had older U.S.-born children as well as younger Canadian-born children at the time of their naturalization. Pierre Therriault was one of the twenty. His two oldest children had been born in Massachusetts in 1911 and 1913, and his next three offspring had been born in the Province of Québec between 1916 and 1920. In 1922, during a period of mass exodus from Québec, Therriault emigrated again to the United States, and in 1924 his youngest child (at the time of his naturalization) was born in Maine.[4] The French Canadians of Lewiston who naturalized, it appears, participated little in such migrations back and forth across the international border.

Naturalization records suggest that more French Canadians migrated to the Spindle City in the 1920s than during any other decade. Thirty (29.5) percent of the 5,551 French-Canadian immigrants of Lewiston who naturalized by 1987 had come to the United States during the 1920s, a proportion more than double that of any other decade in the nineteenth or twentieth centuries.[5] With the influx of new immigrants in the 1920s and the natural rate of increase, French speakers made up an estimated 65 percent of Lewiston's 34,948 residents in 1930—a large concentration that helped considerably with the task of ethnic retention in the Spindle City. The large infusion of French speakers in the 1920s helps explain the cultural persistence of Franco-Americans in Lewiston (and in other cities of New England) for at least another generation. Yet despite its magnitude, the immigration of the 1920s has attracted little attention from historians.[6]

The Province of Québec and the federal government of Canada worried about this mass emigration. Repatriation and colonization agents working for Québec and Canada tried to persuade French-Canadian emigrants to return. Some agents appeared in Lewiston in the 1920s. In 1923, J.-N. Jutras, a repatriation agent for the Province of Québec, and Reverend J.-A. Beauchamp, a pastor and colonization agent from Abitibi, Québec, spoke to a packed room at l'Institut Jacques-Cartier (Jacques Cartier Institute) Hall. They promoted migration to Abitibi, an area of colonization far to the northwest of Montréal. Beauchamp tried to convince his audience that Abitibi was not another Siberia, but was in fact a place suitable for farming. In 1924, over two hundred persons attended a meeting at l'Institut Jacques-Cartier Hall on colonization in western Canada, organized by J.-E. Laforce, a railway agent working for the Canadian government, and Reverend A.-L. Lébel, the former pastor at Prince Albert, Saskatchewan. Lébel spoke of the churches, schools, and banks established in western Canada and expressed his hope that with the migration of more French speakers to the region, they would remain francophone institutions; for his part, Laforce spoke about special railroad fares—at one-third of the usual cost—available to those wishing to travel to western Canada to live or to explore possibilities. Through the late 1920s, francophone agents, often clergymen, continued to visit Lewiston and other Franco-American centers in New England as they tried to recruit potential colonizers to rural Canada. The Canadian government supported their efforts by promoting the country in a 1925 advertisement as the "Country of Butter and Cheese," because of Canada's large export of dairy products; the ad encouraged readers of Le Messager to move either to eastern or western Canada in order to farm.[7]

Few believed that repatriation efforts would succeed, acknowledged the managing director of a Québec City newspaper to Le Messager's Louis-Philippe Gagné in 1925. A complementary strategy was to use propaganda to slow the massive emigration of francophones to the United States. The newspaper director admitted this to Gagné when he wrote that the Colonization Department of Québec had paid newspapers from the province to publish articles laced with propaganda "to try to stop the emigration of our people to the United States."[8] Ultimately, Canadian efforts to stem emigration to the United States or to encourage a large remigration to settle farms in Canada proved unsuccessful.

From occasional, brief reports in Le Messager, it appears that few from Lewiston returned to Canada to colonize new lands in Québec or in the western provinces. Following the recruitment efforts of Jutras and Beauchamp in 1923, about seventeen local families voiced their intention to move to Abitibi; the newspaper did not later indicate how many of these families actually remigrated to Canada. In February 1929, after reading a report prepared by Québec's Minister of Colonization, Le Messager published the names of three Lewiston families that had repatriated. During the same month, using figures obtained from Lewiston's French-language parishes, Le Messager reported that the city's Franco-American population had declined from January 1927 to January 1929. The textile industry had bottomed out well before the Stock Market Crash of 1929, and the resulting industrial crisis had led to an 8.6 percent drop in the Spindle City's French-speaking population. The newspaper believed, however, that only about one-fourth of the approximately 1,600 who had departed Lewiston had returned to Canada, while the rest had moved to other locations in the United States.[9] Even during difficult economic times in Lewiston, remigration to Canada did not appear to be an attractive option for French-Canadian immigrants, something that suggests they were comfortable in the United States.

Only three of the 1,238 (0.2 percent) who naturalized in the 1920s and 1930s later gave up or lost their U.S. citizenship. The two men and one woman were each between sixty-three and seventy-four years of age when U.S. immigration officials notified the court clerk of their expatriation. One lost his U.S. citizenship for having lived in Canada for three years after his naturalization and for not having established a permanent residence in the United States prior to October 15, 1946, thus violating the terms of the Nationality Act of 1940; immigration officials did not disclose the reasons for the expatriation of the other two persons.[10] Like naturalizers in the late nineteenth and early twentieth centuries, those who became U.S. citizens in the 1920s and 1930s tended overwhelmingly to retain their citizenship.

A significant demographic shift had taken place in Lewiston by these decades. By 1920, a majority of the city's francophones were U.S.-born. Data compiled from the 1920 nominal census reveals that while the first generation constituted 46.1 percent of Lewiston's population of French-Canadian descent, the second generation made up 47.7 percent, and succeeding generations, 6.2 percent. Despite heavy immigration from Québec during the 1920s, Canadian-born French speakers remained a minority in Lewiston in 1930. Aggregate data from the 1930 federal census provided the numbers of only first- and second-generation Franco-Americans; the first generation made up 43.0 percent of Lewiston's French-Canadian stock in 1930, and the second generation, 57.0 percent.[11] This demographic shift to U.S.-born Franco-Americans served to accelerate the speed with which Lewiston's French speakers Americanized as the century progressed. Additionally, the immigration restrictions the United States applied to Canada by 1930 caused the proportion of U.S.-born Franco-Americans over time to increase further, thereby serving to quicken the pace of their Americanization.

After 1930, Canadian immigrants needed U.S. visas, jobs, and proof that they could support themselves financially before they could move to the United States. Even before 1930, however, there existed some limitations on the flow of Canadian immigrants to the United States. From June 1906, immigrants had to pay an immigration, or head, tax and had to obtain a certificate of arrival before entering the country. U.S. immigration officials denied entry to Canadians who did not meet these requirements, and they deported those who had managed to enter the country without first obtaining the necessary documentation. Periodic reports in *Le Messager* reminded readers of these immigration requirements, and they revealed that Lewiston residents who had managed to enter the country illegally would make trips back to Canada in order to comply with the entry requirements they had avoided and which were a prerequisite to naturalization. In July 1929, the newspaper informed readers that they no longer had to return to Canada to register legally their U.S. arrival, but could now do so at different locations in Maine, the nearest of which was Portland. During the 1920s, the newspaper occasionally warned readers traveling to Canada that U.S. authorities sometimes hindered Franco-Americans upon their return, and it strongly suggested that they bring identification, including naturalization papers or marriage certificates, to facilitate their reentry.[12] As immigration statistics attest, these limitations on the flow of migrants from Canada hardly impeded the mass movement of French Canadians to the United States before 1930. While Canadians were not subject to the same immigration restrictions as overseas migrants in the 1920s, the entry requirements they had to meet and the periodic problems Lewiston residents had returning to the United States after visits to Canada nonetheless suggest that the large immigration of Canadians concerned U.S. officials.

It certainly concerned U.S. Census Bureau consultant Niles Carpenter, a sociology professor at the University of Buffalo. From the 1840s through the 1880s, and again in the second decade of the twentieth century, Canada had placed among the top five countries sending the largest number of emigrants to the United States, he revealed in his 1927 publication. Like his contemporaries, who viewed European immigrants as invading hordes, Carpenter saw the immigration of Canadians and Mexicans as "invasions." He worried that their concentration along U.S. borders would ultimately lead the United States to cede land to Canada and Mexico. Using data he adapted from another source, which had sampled twenty-eight courts for the period 1913–1914, Carpenter argued that Canadians took longer than other immigrant groups to acquire U.S. citizenship. In fact, Canadians placed last in his table of twenty immigrant groups, because they took an average of 16.4 years from the time of their arrival in the United States until they processed their final naturalization papers. Although the data Carpenter presented does not distinguish between English and French Canadians, he was more worried about francophone immigrants, because he believed they would not Americanize as readily as English speakers.[13]

Carpenter may have been correct in arguing that Canadians took longer than other groups to acquire U.S. citizenship. But my findings suggest that a longer-term, historical perspective, rather than one that relies primarily upon data from a single decade, leads to a more nuanced and ultimately different understanding of French-Canadian participation in U.S. society. Among the French-Canadian men who had arrived in the United States as minors under eighteen, about one-third naturalized within five years of their twenty-first birthday between 1910 and 1919, the decade from which Carpenter drew his data. But over three-fourths had done so within five years of their twenty-first birthday in the late nineteenth century, and just under three-fourths had done so during the first decade of the twentieth. As argued in chapter 4, regulations that lengthened the time to naturalization for immigrants entering the United States as minors appear to account best for the drop noted between 1910 and 1919. The proportion of these men who naturalized by twenty-five remained at one-third (33.7 percent) in the 1920s and dropped to one-fourth (25.7 percent) in the 1930s. To take one example, Joseph Elzear Wilfrid Paradis arrived in the United States in 1923 at the age of seventeen, declared his intention to become a citizen at twenty-one, and naturalized several years later, just a few weeks short of his twenty-fourth birthday. While men like Paradis may have taken longer to naturalize than in previous years, other evidence reveals that they did not wait especially long to become U.S. citizens. As in the past, a majority of the men like Paradis who had arrived in the United States as minors became citizens by their thirty-first birthday. This was true of 60.1 percent of the men in the 1920s and 69.1 percent in the 1930s. Smaller proportions of women who had entered the United States as minors naturalized at a young age, however. During the 1920s, only two-fifths (40.0 percent) naturalized within ten years of their twenty-first birthday, while well over half (57.7 percent) did so during the 1930s. Estelle Labadie Plourde was among them. She arrived in the United States in 1916 at ten years of age and naturalized at thirty-one, hence within ten years of eligibility.[14] Thus, while some French-Canadian immigrants took longer to naturalize in the 1920s and 1930s than they had in the late nineteenth or early twentieth century, the data do not suggest that they were particularly slow to become U.S. citizens.

The naturalization records of French-Canadian immigrants who had arrived in the United States as adults add further evidence of this. Unlike the women who had entered the United States as minors, those who had arrived as adults generally took less time to naturalize. In fact, the data reveals that their naturalization patterns were fairly similar to those of the men. During the 1920s, over three-fifths of the French-Canadian women (68.4 percent) and men (63.8 percent) who had entered the United States at eighteen or older became citizens within ten years of their border-crossing. During the 1930s, however, under one-third (28.9 percent) of the women and about one-third (34.2 percent) of the men became citizens within ten years of their arrival in the United States. This significant drop from the twenties to the thirties reveals that the large majority of men and women who naturalized in the 1930s were not recent immigrants. Yet, most women and men who had arrived in the United States as adults naturalized within fifteen years of crossing the border. Eighty (80.2) percent of the men and 76.3 percent of the women in the 1920s, and 72.7 percent of the men and 72.4 percent of the women in the 1930s, naturalized within fifteen years of arriving in the United States. Louis Philippe Blais, for instance, had crossed the border as an adult at age twenty-four, and he naturalized twelve years later when he was thirty-six years old.[15] Like most other French-Canadian men and women who had entered the United States as adults, Blais had waited some time, but not particularly long, to naturalize.

These findings on the time it took French-Canadian immigrants to become U.S. citizens stand in contrast to the portrait Niles Carpenter painted of francophones hesitant to fulfill the civic requirements for political participation in the United States. Carpenter's 1927 publication highlights how poorly anglophone Americans understood the intentions of individuals of French-Canadian birth and background in the United States. It reveals how trapped they were by received paradigms that postulated a false dichotomy between ethnic retention and participation in the host society.

One might wonder if the post–World War I Americanization movement of the 1920s, including the visible presence of the Ku Klux Klan in the Lewiston area, had any effect on naturalizations during the interwar period. The number of French-Canadian immigrants from Lewiston who became U.S. citizens nearly doubled during the 1920s and 1930s over the first two decades of the twentieth century. Whereas 684 had naturalized from 1900 to 1919, 1,238 did so from 1920 to 1939. But we cannot attribute this increase to the presence of the KKK in the 1920s. Nearly equal numbers naturalized in the 1920s as in the 1930s. While the Americanization movement may have played a role in increasing the number of naturalizers in both decades, the lack of opportunity in Québec, not only during the 1920s but also during the Great Depression of the 1930s, surely motivated large numbers to pursue naturalization. During the Depression, jobs and New Deal benefits went first, if not exclusively, to U.S. citizens, and the Immigration Bureau deported aliens who became public charges; these restrictions on the foreign-born must have propelled French-Canadian immigrants to naturalize in the thirties.[16]

Women also expanded the number of Lewiston francophones who naturalized during the 1920s and 1930s. To exercise the privilege of suffrage obtained in 1920, women had to be citizens. According to the Cable Act, as of September 22, 1922, immigrant women could no longer gain derivative citizenship by marriage to U.S. nationals; like single women, wives had to naturalize on their own. When Estelle Labadie married U.S.-born Lucien Plourde in 1927, for example, she did not automatically become a U.S. citizen; she became a citizen in her own right only when she filed final naturalization papers in 1937. During the 1920s, eighty-eight French-Canadian immigrant women of Lewiston became citizens, and 206 did so in the 1930s. In all, they made up nearly one-fourth (23.7 percent) of the Lewiston francophones who naturalized during these two decades, and they account in part for the increase in the number of naturalizations from the first two decades of the century.[17]

During the 1920s and 1930s, French-Canadian descendants largely joined the host society with little outside help and at their own pace. During the interwar period, *Le Messager* and local francophone elites continued both to promote naturalization and to guide French-Canadian immigrants through the citizenship process. *Le Messager* frequently provided information about naturalization procedures, changes in naturalization laws, and potential questions and answers—in English—that might arise during naturalization exams. The French-language newspaper regularly publicized classes offering instruction in English or which prepared French-Canadian immigrants to become U.S. citizens—classes typically led by Franco-Americans and held in their own institutions. The newspaper strongly encouraged readers to avail themselves of these classes. It also kept track of candidates for naturalization and published the names of those who had taken out first or final naturalization papers, as it had in the past. *Le Messager* used whatever means it could to nudge francophones to naturalize. In June 1923, for instance, it informed readers that individuals who became citizens during the September court session would be eligible to vote in October in favor of a state law limiting the work week to forty-eight hours.[18] In doing this, *Le Messager* sought to connect the identity of Franco-Americans as workers with the opportunity to exercise influence in their adopted country. The acquisition of citizenship could thus facilitate the intersection of working-class and ethnic identities among Franco-Americans.

Sketchy reports in *Le Messager* suggest that Franco-American women enrolled in classes beginning in the 1920s to learn English and to prepare for naturalization. In October 1920, fifty-four women, most of them married, took English lessons from Miss Ernestine Lemaire in the evenings in one of the school buildings of Saint-Pierre (Saint Peter) Parish. The YWCA also offered English and naturalization classes for women, and *Le Messager* encouraged Franco-Americans to attend. Some did. Some women also attended the naturalization classes that a Franco-American man led at l'Institut Jacques-Cartier Hall.[19] *Le Messager*'s brief reports of these classes do not give us a clear sense of the total number of French-speaking women who participated. What they reveal, however, is that francophone women, like the men, were proactive in acquiring citizenship.

Elites continued to propagandize for naturalization. Attorney F. X. Belleau continued to argue in the post–World War I era that, unlike repatriation to Canada, naturalization was a practical option for French-Canadian immigrants, because it offered them the opportunity to increase their influence throughout New England. He saw naturalization as a strategy that served the interests of the group. Mindful of the pressure nativists exerted on U.S. ethnic groups to Americanize in the postwar years, Belleau implied that naturalization did not mean conceding to nativism and giving up one's ethnic identity, and he contended: "It is not necessary to be more American than the American himself."[20] For Belleau, as for other Franco-Americans, naturalization was a step in the process of identity formation in the host society—a process they defined very differently than cultural assimilation.

Belleau was one of a number of speakers who addressed the naturalization classes that Franco-Americans organized in the 1920s and 1930s. He spoke on the history of the naturalization of local Franco-Americans in March 1926. Other francophone speakers included businessmen, journalists, attorneys, and politicians. These speakers discussed such figures as George Washington, topics like the Declaration of Independence, and more generally, the history of the United States. Students in the naturalization classes also studied the U.S. Constitution, and the non-francophone attorneys and politicians invited to address these classes probably spoke on state and local politics as well as naturalization laws. State representative George C. Wing, Jr., for instance, spoke about Maine politics and the issue of respect for laws in April 1928.[21]

But naturalization classes did not consider uniquely American themes. Franco-American mutual-benefit societies supported the classes financially and by providing speakers. In 1927, J.-H. Reny, president of the local Conseil Gabriel (Gabriel Council) of l'Union Saint-Jean-Baptiste d'Amérique (the Saint John the Baptist Union of America), advised candidates for citizenship not only to learn English well but also not to lose their mother tongue. Reny seized the opportunity to promote membership in the Franco-American societies, "to be a valuable contributor to our element," paraphrased *Le Messager*. As candidates became U.S. citizens, they should be proud of their French-Canadian identity, Reny told them.[22] If speeches by other mutualists reflected similar themes, naturalization classes served to promote ethnic retention as well civic participation.

Naturalization records provide us with a wealth of information about the French-Canadian immigrants who became U.S. citizens during the 1920s and 1930s, and in the aggregate, they suggest some of their motivations for becoming citizens. As in the late nineteenth and early twentieth centuries, the francophone immigrants of Lewiston who naturalized from 1920 to 1939 had come predominantly from the Province of Québec. Only 3.2 percent had been born outside of Québec.[23] The overwhelming proportion had come from Québec counties south of the Saint Lawrence River. Two counties to the north of Maine, Témiscouata and Kamouraska, together supplied up to 15.0 percent of the French-Canadian immigrants who naturalized in Lewiston in the twenties and thirties. The western belt of Dorchester, Beauce, Mégantic, Wolfe, and Arthabaska provided as much as 46.2 percent of the naturalizers. In fact, Beauce alone supplied from one-fifth (19.0 percent) to over one-fourth (28.0 percent) of those who naturalized during the 1920s and 1930s. While visiting Beauce County during his honeymoon in summer 1923, Louis-Philippe Gagné reported that the town of Beauceville had no industries, its residents barely made a living, and the town had no youth, for they had migrated elsewhere, such as to the industrial cities of Lewiston and Waterville, Maine. Unlike during the opening decades of the twentieth century, the counties of Lévis and Québec did not supply many (no more than 3.1 percent) of the Lewiston residents who naturalized from 1920 to 1939; the growing cities of Lévis and Québec within those counties must have offered more economic opportunities to French-Canadian residents than did rural towns like Beauceville in the twenties and thirties.[24]

More than pressure from U.S. nativists, the lack of opportunity in Québec must have motivated French-Canadian immigrants to naturalize. Records reveal that nearly two-thirds (64.9 percent) of the francophones who naturalized in Lewiston in the twenties and thirties had emigrated from their place of birth to the United States, while about one-third (35.1 percent) had moved within Canada before crossing the border.[25] Although these proportions are comparable to those from the first two decades of the century, they suggest that a sizable number of francophones who became U.S. citizens (or, in the case of naturalizers who had immigrated as minors, that their parents) had unsuccessfully sought other opportunities in Canada before emigrating to the United States. Better opportunities in the United States surely motivated them to acquire citizenship.

Among the francophone naturalizers of the 1920s and 1930s, virtually no differences existed between the migration patterns of men and women within Canada before their border crossing. In all, 35.2 percent of the men and 35.0 percent of the women had migrated elsewhere in Canada before entering the United States. Lucy Levesque was one of them. Born in Québec, she had emigrated to the United States from the neighboring province of New Brunswick. But her migration pattern was exceptional, for most of the French-Canadian immigrants who naturalized in Lewiston had moved to the United States from their province of birth. Whereas between 1.3 and 1.5 percent of the men had migrated to a different Canadian province before crossing the international border, 1.7 percent of the women had.[26]

Over four-fifths (81.8 percent) of the French-Canadian men and women who naturalized in Lewiston from 1920 to 1939 had entered the United States through Vermont, and only about one-sixth (17.2 percent) had crossed the international border into Maine. Their choice of transportation explains these travel patterns. Like their predecessors, the French-Canadian immigrants who naturalized in Lewiston in the 1920s and 1930s had arrived in the United States predominantly (88.8 percent) by train, and most (77.8 percent) of these individuals had completed all or part of their journey on the

Grand Trunk Railroad that passed through Vermont. To take one example, Estelle Labadie Plourde emigrated to the United States from Montmagny County, Québec, which lies on Maine's western border. Rather than entering the United States in Maine, she first passed through Vermont because she traveled on the Grand Trunk Railway. Under one-tenth (8.2 percent) of those who naturalized in the 1920s and 1930s had arrived in the United States by automobile, whereas none of the persons who had naturalized during the first two decades of the century had done so. This new means of transportation accounts for the increased proportion of Lewiston naturalizers in the 1920s and 1930s who had crossed the international border into Maine. By 1928, there were fourteen "ports of entry" along Maine's borders. Not all who entered the United States through Maine arrived by automobile, however, for some walked across international bridges, others took ferries, and some traveled on railroad lines other than the Grand Trunk. Louis Philippe Blais, for instance, arrived at the "port of entry" of Jackman, Maine, on the Canadian Pacific Railroad.[27]

Available evidence suggests that the time these immigrants spent journeying to the United States was short. Nearly all (98.2 percent) of the naturalizers from 1920 to 1930 (the last year this information is available) had completed their journey to the United States within one day.[28] In terms of time and transportation, then, returning to Québec was not a daunting prospect; that these immigrants became citizens testifies to their willingness to become permanent members of the United States.

Two items on the naturalization forms provide us with a glimpse of the journey that French-Canadian immigrants had taken within the United States prior to their naturalization. Louis Philippe Blais, for example, had filed his first naturalization papers in Augusta, Maine, and his final papers in Auburn. Forty-seven (3.8 percent) of the 1,238 individuals like Blais who became U.S. citizens in the 1920s and 1930s had declared their intention to become citizens outside of Auburn or Portland, Maine, the location of the courts that Lewiston's French-Canadian immigrants used to process their final naturalization papers. These forty-seven persons filed first naturalization papers in other cities or towns of Maine (1.5 percent), other states in New England (2.0 percent), or elsewhere in the United States (0.3 percent). In addition, the two children Louis Philippe Blais had at the time of his naturalization had both been born in Waterville, Maine, located near Augusta.

Ninety-eight (7.9 percent) of the 1,238 naturalizers had children who had been born in the United States in places other than the twin cities of Lewiston and Auburn. As in the early twentieth century, the naturalization data suggests that the men and women who became citizens in the 1920s and 1930s had migrated little within the United States before settling in Lewiston. In their country of adoption, they were not a population "on the move."[29]

Child labor legislation of the early twentieth century probably accounts best for the significant decline in the proportion of men, and for the small proportion of women, who had arrived in the United States as minors under eighteen. Whereas about half of the men who had naturalized during the first two decades of the twentieth century had entered the United States between the ages of ten and eighteen, inclusive, the proportion dropped to 37.7 percent of the naturalizers in the 1920s and to 29.8 percent in the 1930s. By comparison, 30.7 percent of the women who naturalized in the 1920s, and 37.9 percent in the 1930s had crossed the international border between ten and eighteen years of age.[30] Child-labor legislation made immigrating with young children less attractive than in the past, because the children could no longer legally contribute wages to the family economy.

Along with child-labor laws, the regulations of the Bureau of Immigration and Naturalization, such as English-language requirements (see chapter 4), appear to have contributed to the decline in the number of francophones who naturalized shortly after reaching adulthood. The proportion of people naturalizing at age twenty-five and under continued to drop during the 1920s and 1930s, as it had after passage of the Naturalization Act of 1906. During the 1920s, 16.7 percent of the French-Canadian male immigrants were twenty-five or younger at naturalization, and the proportion dropped even further to 8.9 percent in the 1930s. A similar pattern existed among the women who naturalized. In the 1920s, 14.8 percent were twenty-five or younger, and in the 1930s, the number decreased to 9.2 percent.[31] Thus, changing patterns of migration influenced by child-labor legislation and by the naturalization requirements imposed by the federal government (which promoters of Americanization influenced) led to the naturalization of proportionally fewer young francophones in the 1920s and 1930s.

The records suggest some of the variables, including the internal forces, that affected the decision of francophone women and men to become U.S. citizens. Holding Lewiston's better-paying jobs was not central. Only about one-tenth of the French-Canadian immigrant men (12.1 percent) and women (10.2 percent) who naturalized in the 1920s held white-collar jobs. In the 1930s, about one-tenth (11.8 percent) of the men were white-collar workers, while only one-fifteenth (6.3 percent) of the women were. Well over half of the men who naturalized in the 1920s (57.4 percent) and 1930s (57.4 percent) held industrial jobs. The proportion was smaller (40.9 percent) among the women who became citizens in the 1920s, but comparable (55.8 percent) in the 1930s. Estelle Labadie Plourde, a shoe worker, was part of this latter group. Unlike her, a significant proportion of the women who naturalized did not work outside of the home. Over one-third (35.2 percent) of the naturalizing women in the 1920s, and one-fourth (25.7 percent) in the 1930s did not work for wages. In addition, none of the men or women who became U.S. citizens in the 1920s were unemployed at the time of their naturalization; this was not the case during the Great Depression of the 1930s, when a small fraction of the men (1.0 percent) and women (0.5 percent) who became U.S. citizens were unemployed.[32] French-Canadian Lewiston residents without jobs were not the ones demonstrating a commitment to the United States through the affirmative act of naturalization.

Family considerations played a role in naturalization decisions. About three-fourths (74.0 percent) of the men of Lewiston who became U.S. citizens from 1920 to 1939 were married, and more than one-third (37.6 percent) of them had U.S.-born wives. The places of birth of children appeared more consequential to the decision to naturalize than the wife's place of birth, just as during the early twentieth century. The offspring of three-fourths (75.5 percent) of the men with children had all been born in the United States, and an additional one-sixth (16.6 percent) of the men had some children with U.S. birthplaces. Thus, 92.1 percent of the men with issue had children who had been born in the United States. This was the case for Louis Philippe Blais. Not only his two children but also his wife had been born in the United States, considerations that must have propelled him, as other French-Canadian men, to pursue his U.S. citizenship.[33]

The place of birth of children also appears to have influenced the decision of mothers to naturalize. Among the women with issue, over four-fifths (82.2 percent) had children who had all been born in the United States. This was true for Estelle Labadie Plourde: the two children she had at the time of her naturalization had both been born in her country of adoption. An additional small proportion of women (5.6 percent) had some (but not all) children with birthplaces in the United States; only around one-tenth (9.3 percent) had children who had all been born in Canada.[34] Thus, for Estelle Labadie Plourde as for most mothers, the U.S. birth of their children seems to have played a critical role in their decision to naturalize.

So, it appears, did the citizenship status of their husbands. Two-fifths (40.8 percent) of the women who naturalized in the 1920s and 1930s were single, widowed, or divorced, and three-fifths (59.2 percent) were married. Under half (47.1 percent) of the married women had husbands who had been born in the United States, and about one-twelfth (8.0 percent) had Canadian-born husbands who had naturalized. Thus, no less than 55.2 percent of the married women who naturalized in the twenties and thirties had husbands who were U.S. citizens. The proportion may have been significantly higher, because court clerks in the 1920s and 1930s inconsistently reported the naturalization status of the husbands of women pursuing U.S. citizenship.[35] Naturalization regulations of the 1920s and 1930s made it possible for French-Canadian women who married U.S. citizens to naturalize sooner than single women. From September 22, 1922, to May 23, 1934, an immigrant woman who married a U.S. citizen could naturalize after having lived in the United States for only one year; from May 24, 1934, until January 12, 1941, she had to have resided in the United States for at least three years. In either case, she did not have to meet the five-year residency requirement imposed upon men, single women, and women married to noncitizens. Moreover, women who married U.S. citizens did not have to file first papers, something which shortened the naturalization process by at least two years.[36] Given these regulations, it is not surprising that most of the women who naturalized in the 1920s and 1930s were married.

But a closer examination of the records reveals that unattached women, and married women who lived without their spouses, were the first to acquire U.S. citizenship through naturalization. Siblings Octavie and Marie Anna Roberge, both single, were the first French-Canadian immigrant women from Lewiston to naturalize. Both milliners, they had emigrated together to the United States in 1895, and they naturalized on the same day in 1925. Like the Roberge sisters, three-fifths (60.2 percent) of the women who naturalized during the 1920s were either single, divorced, widowed, or married but living apart from their husbands (due, perhaps, to a work situation, separation, or desertion). During the 1930s, however, this group constituted only two-fifths (39.3 percent) of the French-Canadian women who became citizens.[37] Thus, single women and married women living on their own were the ones more likely to naturalize during the first decade in which women could vote in the United States.

One other group of naturalizing women deserves brief mention. These were women who had been born in the United States and who had lost their citizenship upon marriage to a foreign national. When Marie Yvonne Godbout, who had been born in Lewiston in 1895, married her Canadian-born husband in 1913, she lost her U.S. citizenship. From March 2, 1907, until September 21, 1922, U.S. naturalization law followed the dictum *Qui prend mari, prend pays* (Whoever takes a husband takes his nationality). This practice ended in 1922, when women could no longer acquire derivative citizenship from their husbands. Godbout did not automatically become a citizen when her husband naturalized in 1929, but had to naturalize on her own, which she did in 1931. Like her, twenty-seven women of Lewiston who had similarly lost their U.S. citizenship repatriated in the United States during the 1920s and 1930s.[38] These repatriates are not included in the naturalization figures discussed in this chapter, for the data focuses exclusively on the Canadian-born.

After naturalization, the next logical step was voter registration. When women gained suffrage in 1920, *Le Messager* informed readers of the conditions that U.S.- and Canadian-born women had to meet in order to register to vote. Echoing Progressive reformers of the period, the French-language newspaper expressed hope that women would upgrade the quality of politics: "Let us hope that the participation of women in elections will bring honesty back to politics and more civility and decency at the voting places." *Le Messager* encouraged eligible women to appear before the voter-registration bureau at City Hall, telling them, "Our female compatriots can go there without fear, as they are very polite at the Bureau. (They cannot be otherwise because nearly all are French Canadians)." The newspaper's smug parenthetical comment reflected the political strength Franco-Americans had gained by 1920. *Le Messager*, of course, hoped woman suffrage would increase the voting power of Franco-Americans, and it kept an eye on voter registrations. By noon on August 30, 1920, sixty of the one hundred women who had registered to vote were Franco-American, it reported. When the local bureau stopped accepting applications from new voters before the mid-September state elections, *Le Messager* estimated that 1,500 of the 3,811 women who had registered were Franco-American.[39]

In October, when the voter-registration bureau began accepting new registrations for the upcoming elections, *Le Messager* again encouraged women to register, indicating that the Catholic Church supported suffrage, even for women religious. For a cloistered order like the Ursuline Sisters of Sainte-Marie (Saint Mary) Parish, suffrage was a bit overwhelming. After the pastor informed the sisters in August of their right to vote, they recorded their thoughts: "Can you see us, suffragettes discussing politics, ha! ha! What the future yet holds for women." Only in late October, after learning that the bishop wanted them to exercise their right of suffrage, did the four eligible Ursuline Sisters make the trip to City Hall to register. But the voter-registration bureau had closed, and the sisters needed to wait until prior to the next elections to register.[40]

Lewiston Franco-Americans organized their own naturalization and voter-registration drives. Typically the drives did not favor either political party. In 1924, both Republican and Democratic Franco-Americans formed a committee that visited Lewiston francophones from house to house to promote naturalization as well as voter registration. *Le Messager*, of course, strongly supported such efforts to get Franco-Americans to register to vote. After women gained suffrage, the newspaper encouraged them to register, too. It regularly informed readers of the voter-registration bureau's hours, and it reminded them of the requirement that voters had to read and write in English. In 1924, after about fifty Franco-Americans had told members of the committee pushing voter registration that they did not want to "'bother' themselves" with voting, *Le Messager* chastised them in its columns. Individuals like these, the newspaper charged, give adversaries of Franco-Americans ammunition for calling them such names as "Fifty-Fifty Americans," an obvious reference to Robert Cloutman Dexter's 1924 publication by the same title. Disappointed that the drive increased the number of Franco-American voters by only 460 out of a potential 800 new voters, *Le Messager* challenged nonvoters to prove to their critics that they, too, were 100 percent American, because the Franco-American version of Americanism placed considerable emphasis on meeting civic responsibilities.[41] Thus in 1924 the Americanization movement, and the presence of the Ku Klux Klan in the Lewiston area, did concern Franco-American leaders. It did not seem, however, to pressure all Franco-Americans to pursue suffrage.

The discussion on naturalization presented in this chapter suggests that Franco-American women appeared as willing as men to take proactive steps to modify their identity in the United States. This study sheds light, therefore, upon the history of Franco-American women, about which we currently know very little. It demonstrates that Franco-American women negotiated their ethnic identity in the United States, and were historical actors in their own right.

Scholars have neglected to examine the political participation of Franco-American women. Part of the problem is that, to date, they have focused on the pre-1910 period, and women did not gain suffrage until 1920. Brief reports in *Le Messager*, however incomplete at times, provide us with a window onto the experiences of women as they gained and exercised the right of citizenship in the 1920s and 1930s. They suggest that Franco-American women began adopting a political identity during the interwar years. In June 1924, *Le Messager* reported that a Mrs. Côté-Howard of Rockland, Maine, the wife of a prominent Democrat, spoke in French to about fifty women in a meeting room at Lewiston City Hall. The French-language newspaper explained that Côté-Howard was president of a committee organizing women's political clubs that sought to exert influence in state and federal elections. As a result of the meeting, the Franco-American Democratic Women's Club formed. It is not clear how long it survived or how active it became. Before the presidential election in 1936, *Le Messager* reported that a recently founded group, le Club des Femmes Démocrates (the Democratic Women's Club), headed by two Franco-American women, would hold a rally at l'Institut Jacques-Cartier Hall in favor of Franklin D. Roosevelt's reelection.[42] From the scant evidence, we can only infer that the Franco-American women's political clubs of the 1920s and 1930s were ad hoc organizations not unlike those that Franco-American men had created in the late nineteenth and early twentieth centuries, when suffrage for most of them had been a relatively new experience.

Despite the lack of information on the women's political clubs, two pieces of evidence—one quantitative, the other anecdotal—suggest the growing political consciousness of Franco-American women during the interwar years. By February 1928, according to *Le Messager*, there were

5,418 Franco-American voters in Lewiston: 2,117 were women and 3,301 were men. Franco-Americans constituted a majority of Lewiston's 10,580 voters, and they maintained a majority in five of the city's seven wards. While it is not clear whether 1928 was the first year in which francophone voters outnumbered those of other groups, it is evident that women made up a significant portion of the potential voting strength of Lewiston's Franco-American population. Besides registering to vote and joining political clubs, some Franco-American women showed another sign of their political consciousness. To celebrate Roosevelt's reelection in 1936, women at Clark Shoe in Auburn held a mock funeral for the Republican Party. They placed an elephant in a small coffin and paraded it through the factory, hearing hisses from the few Republican stalwarts who worked there. But their fun did not end at the workplace. The women decided that the elephant should lie in state for one month, "as is customary for notables," and they transported the coffin to *Le Messager*'s offices, where passers-by could view it from the front window. "Those who still feel a little compassion for this poor elephant can therefore stop by *Le Messager* and view the coffin," *Le Messager* informed readers. It added: "You are asked, however, not to send flowers."[43] The women who staged the mock funeral almost certainly were Franco-American. This incident illustrates the intersection of their ethnic, political, and working-class identities as they evolved during the 1930s.

There are no indications from *Le Messager* that Franco-American women participated in Republican Party politics in the 1920s or 1930s. Occasional reports in the French-language newspaper reveal, however, that a small group of Franco-American men continued to promote the Grand Old Party during these decades. But they appear not to have attracted many francophones to join them. When Democratic mayoral candidate Louis J. Brann defeated his Republican Franco-American challenger, Arsène Cailler, by over 2,700 votes in 1922, *Le Messager* contended that Lewiston's francophones had kept true to their political principles. In that election, no Republicans won seats in the municipal government. A Franco-American Republican Club existed in Lewiston at least from 1926 to 1931. It had its origins in l'Alliance Civique (the Civic Alliance), formed in the second decade of the century to assist Franco-Americans in gaining local office, and it had helped Dr. Robert J. Wiseman win election in 1914 as the first mayor of French-Canadian descent in Lewiston. In 1926, l'Alliance Civique reorganized itself as le Club Républicain Franco-Américain (the Franco-American Republican Club), ostensibly to promote attorney Patrick Tremblay's expected run for the state senate. The following year, when *Le Messager* learned that Franco-American Republicans were trying to enroll more francophones in the Grand Old Party, still in hopes of electing one of their own to the state senate, it warned readers who switched parties that they would not be able to vote Democratic in the municipal primaries in the spring. The newspaper continued: "Besides, several bit their own thumbs last spring." *Le Messager* did not indicate the actual size of the Franco-American Republican Club, perhaps because it did not know. Sometimes it would give readers a rough idea of the club's size. In December 1929, for instance, the French-language newspaper reported that 330 individuals had appeared before the voter-registration bureau, and that a majority of them had switched to the Republican Party as a result of their membership in the Franco-American Republican Club.[44] Francophone Republicans probably never numbered more than a few hundred in the 1920s and 1930s.

They certainly did not exert much influence in the politics or on the voting behavior of Lewiston during the interwar period. The large majority of Lewiston's Franco-American population became Democratic Party loyalists, and their leaders played a role in building the city's Democratic political machine. Between 1920 and 1939, Democrats won the mayor's office in Lewiston in all but two years; these Democratic mayors were Franco-American in 1920, from 1925 to 1929, and from 1932 to 1939.[45]

Demography helped Franco-Americans to dominate local politics by the late 1920s. Their voting strength concerned their political adversaries, as it did the non-francophones within the Democratic Party. When Franco-Americans embarked upon a naturalization and voter-registration campaign in 1924, people "in certain fanatic circles," *Le Messager*'s euphemism for nativists, became worried because Franco-Americans hoped to increase their voting strength by one thousand, making them a greater political force in Lewiston. When three hundred Franco-Americans attended a naturalization class in November 1926, instructor A.-G. Légendre informed *Le Messager* that some Democrats opposed his efforts to promote naturalization "under the pretext that French-language voters are already numerous enough here."[46] While Légendre did not specify the nationality of these Democrats, they were most likely individuals of Irish descent. As Franco-Americans gained electoral strength in Lewiston, non-francophones worried about their place in local politics.

So did Franco-Americans who were not part of the Democratic political machine. In the 1930s, some Franco-Americans helped bring to an end the machine politics that francophones had played a role in creating. In a direct challenge to the Democratic political machine, Franco-American jeweler Rodolphe Hamel left the Democratic Party in 1930 to run for mayor on the Citizens' ticket. Hamel mounted a vigorous campaign, but died during the election. The Republican candidate, Harold N. Skelton, subsequently picked up the endorsement of the Citizens' movement and won the mayoralty in both 1930 and 1931. When Skelton chose not to seek a third term in 1932, the Democratic machine regained the mayor's office. Political corruption and scandals in the 1930s motivated some Franco-Americans to take action. In August 1936, they formed a new society, called "les Vigilants," open only to Franco-Americans. Promoted as a social organization in the English- and French-language press, les Vigilants had a larger purpose. *Le Messager* hinted at this when it stated that "The chief goal of the 'Vigilants' is the well-being of French-language citizens, and this term 'well-being' says much," and also when it indicated that politicians could not be officers of the organization. By November, les Vigilants had eighty members, "all very well known in social, economic and professional circles," *Le Messager* reported.[47]

This new Franco-American society initiated the drive to revise Lewiston's city charter. Except for eliminating the Common Council, Lewiston had operated under its original charter since 1863. Under the old charter, political machines handpicked candidates for mayor and aldermen, and aldermen used their power to appoint individuals to city positions as a means of rewarding members of their party. After adoption of the new city charter in 1939, local office seekers had to petition to get their names on the ballot, and they had to run for office without political party designation. Run-off elections settled contests in which contenders lacked a majority vote. Under the new charter, the mayor made appointments to municipal boards and required the approval of the aldermen only for appointments to the police department. In addition, city boards could no longer be filled solely by members of the same political party. Reforms such as these essentially brought to an end the Democratic political machine that Franco-Americans had helped create in Lewiston.[48]

Besides supporting Democratic candidates at the local level, Lewiston strongly supported Democrats who ran for governor, congress, and president in the 1920s and 1930s. Democratic contenders for governor won a majority—sometimes over three-fourths—of Lewiston's votes in each gubernatorial election of the twenties and thirties. The same was true of Democratic congressional candidates who ran in presidential election years. Except for assisting Warren Harding in 1920, Lewiston voters threw their support behind Democratic presidential candidates during each of the other contests in the 1920s and 1930s. The Democratic Party reached out to Franco-Americans. In 1928, the Democratic National Committee printed pamphlets in French entitled "Why French-language voters should vote for the Honorable Alfred E. Smith." This gesture, which *Le Messager* applauded, and Smith's background as a Catholic Democrat, must have enamored Lewiston Franco-Americans. When A.-G. Légendre organized a debate in his naturalization class, he had considerable difficulty finding a Franco-American to represent Republican Herbert Hoover and no trouble getting one to play the role of Democrat Al Smith. Smith won nearly three-fourths of Lewiston's vote in 1928. In contrast, Auburn voters backed Hoover by a larger than two-to-one margin.[49] Lewiston's twin city remained a Republican stronghold. For male and female Franco-Americans of Lewiston, Democratic Party affiliation had become an integral part of their identity by the late 1920s.

After the Bureau of Immigration and Naturalization came into existence in 1906 and standardized naturalization procedures, few French-Canadian immigrants ventured from Lewiston to Portland to naturalize. During the 1920s and 1930s, only seven of the 1,238 (0.6 percent) made the thirty-mile trip to Portland to secure their final naturalization papers. All others became U.S. citizens at the Androscoggin County Courthouse in Auburn, even though the city was a Republican bastion.[50] This evidence suggests that national standards of procedure imposed by the federal bureau overseeing naturalization helped to dissipate the local political pressures that formerly had motivated French-Canadian immigrants to naturalize in Portland. Perhaps the growing strength and confidence of Franco-American Democrats fortified them as well.

While becoming naturalized citizens and voters, Franco-Americans exercised whatever political clout they had to retain the ethnic customs they held dear. One Democrat, Jean-Charles Boucher, helped make New Year's Day a legal holiday in Maine. In December 1934, the Franco-American societies of Lewiston and Auburn met to promote the idea of making this French-Canadian day of celebration a legal holiday statewide. Representative-elect Boucher, an active member of numerous Franco-American societies, agreed to support the idea in the state legislature, and he introduced his bill in February 1935. Franco-American Lewiston Mayor Robert Wiseman and members of local Franco-American societies traveled to the state capitol in Augusta to attend hearings on Boucher's bill. In July 1935, the bill to make New Year's a holiday became law in Maine.[51] Enactment of this legislation provided further evidence of how Franco-Americans used American forms to preserve their identity in the United States and, in the process, to reshape practices of the host society—in this case, the state of Maine.

In conclusion, the evidence suggests that Franco-American women and men actively pursued their entry into U.S. society in the 1920s and 1930s. They enrolled in classes to learn English and to prepare for naturalization exams. After becoming U.S. citizens, they joined the ranks of registered voters. During the interwar years, they actively fashioned a Democratic political identity. Along with the men, Franco-American women helped make the city of Lewiston a Democratic stronghold in the state of Maine. In this Republican-controlled state, Democratic candidates for governor, congress, and president typically won a large majority of Lewiston's votes in the 1920s and 1930s.[52] During these decades—both figuratively and literally—Franco-American women helped bury the elephant in Lewiston.

Forging Ethnic Unions

Social, Welfare, and Credit Institutions
in the Spindle City, 1920–1970

In the early twentieth century, French-Canadian descendants of Lewiston
continued to maintain close ties with Québec, and they developed social
and economic institutions in the United States that drew upon models
and inspiration from *la mère patrie* (the native country). In creating social,
welfare, and credit institutions in Lewiston from the 1920s through the
1960s, French-Canadian descendants demonstrated their evolving identity
in the United States.

Lewiston francophones took advantage of Québec's proximity to maintain, and even to expand, contacts in their homeland in the early twentieth
century. Enrollment in Québec's *collèges classiques* (classical schools) by
young Franco-American men of Lewiston serves as a prime example. There
were forty-two enrollments from Lewiston in the first decade of the twentieth century at the Collège de Saint-Hyacinthe and the Séminaire Saint-
Charles Borromée, and sixty-two at these institutions in the second decade.
The number peaked at 162 in the 1920s and dropped to 142 during the
Depression of the 1930s. Until the 1940s, Lewiston Franco-Americans who
wanted to provide a Catholic education for their sons beyond elementary
school either had to send them to Canada or, from 1904, to Assumption

College in Worcester, Massachusetts, the only *collège classique* francophones established in New England.[1] Anecdotal evidence suggests that Franco-Americans from the Lewiston area more often opted to attend *collège* in Canada rather than Worcester. Armand A. Dufresne, who had been born in New Auburn, later practiced law in Lewiston and went on to become chief justice of the Maine Supreme Court. His parents sent him to Séminaire Saint-Charles Borromée in Sherbrooke rather than Assumption, not only because his father had a first cousin teaching at the institution but also because it charged less tuition. Reverend Hervé Carrier, a Lewiston native, indicated that financial considerations were a major reason why Franco-Americans sent their sons to seminary in Canada—often to Sherbrooke, like himself, or to Saint-Hyacinthe, where older priests had trained.[2] This quantitative and anecdotal evidence attests to the continuing ties between French Canadians in Québec and Franco-Americans in the United States, even as the latter population continued sinking roots in the host society.

Robert G. LeBlanc argues that the *collèges classiques* were promoters of *survivance*: "Above all, the classical college was a conservative institution promoting the preservation of the French language, Roman Catholic religion and other aspects of French-Canadian culture." What may be a little-known fact is that Franco-Americans also learned English at the Québec *collèges*. Adelard Janelle, a longtime Lewiston resident who was active in the French-language societies, told an interviewer that boys he knew had attended the *collège* in Sherbrooke "to learn English. Then they would come back, and find it easier."[3] If Janelle's impression is accurate, it suggests the unexpected conclusion that attending a *collège classique* in Québec did not necessarily promote a dichotomy between ethnic retention and acculturation.

Some Lewiston Franco-Americans, like Romeo Boisvert, attended the *collèges commerciaux* (commercial schools) of Québec, where they, too, learned English. In contrast to the *collèges classiques*, these institutions emphasized instruction in science, math, and English over such subjects as Latin and Greek. Boisvert, a former mayor of Lewiston, maintained that he had not learned English at the city's parochial schools but at the *collège commercial* of Berthierville where he had studied for three years. This *collège* had teachers from the United States to instruct the Franco-American students, and it offered them four hours of instruction in English and two in French, Boisvert recalled. Announcements in the local news column of

Le Messager confirm Boisvert's comments about the program of Collège Saint-Joseph de Berthierville. While we do not have detailed enrollment figures for this *collège*, we do know from *Le Messager* that about thirty-five youth from Lewiston-Auburn attended in 1930. Boisvert himself recalled that forty-two of the 210 Franco-Americans at Berthierville one year were Lewiston residents.[4] What we can infer from the limited information on Lewiston is that attendance at Québec's *collèges commerciaux* provided an alternative to classical education that, surprisingly enough, promoted the acquisition of English among Franco-American youth.

Contacts between francophones on both sides of the international border expanded from the mid-1920s with the organization of the American Snowshoe Union in Lewiston. Scattered reports in *Le Messager* reveal that snowshoe clubs existed from time to time in Lewiston in both the late nineteenth and early twentieth centuries, but not until 1925 did snowshoeing become a major sport in the city. Louis-Philippe Gagné was instrumental in organizing le Montagnard (the Mountaineer) snowshoe club, named and modeled after the largest snowshoe club of the Province of Québec. The Lewiston organization adopted the bylaws of le Montagnard of Montréal as well as its motto, *Toujours Joyeux* (Always Happy). The club's original charter indicated that its purposes were "social, to engage in, foster, promote and encourage winter sports," and 150 men joined in its first year.[5]

As secretary and clerk of le Montagnard, Gagné organized the first International Snowshoe Congress, held in Lewiston in 1925. Gagné worked with members of Maine's congressional delegation and U.S. immigration officials to address the concerns of Canadian snowshoe organizations that there might be problems crossing the border and that each snowshoer would have to pay U.S. immigration officials a ten-dollar fee to enter the United States. When Gagné lobbied the different snowshoe clubs in the Canadian Union to vote in favor of holding their 1925 congress in Lewiston, he had already worked through these issues, and he informed them that there would be no fee to pay at the border. Gagné also touted special railway fares and the use of the city armory to save on hotel expenses, and he emphasized to the Canadian clubs: "Needless to tell you that none needs to speak English to come to Lewiston." The Canadian Union voted to hold its congress in Lewiston, and snowshoe clubs came from such cities and towns as Montréal, Québec City, Trois-Rivières, Drummondville, Saint-Hyacinthe, Sherbrooke, Thetford

Mines, and Ottawa. Most snowshoers arrived on special trains run by the Grand Trunk Railroad. Four French-Canadian men traveled to Lewiston on their snowshoes: Two snowshoed 272 miles from Montréal, and two others 172 miles from Sherbrooke![6]

Like Saint-Jean-Baptiste (Saint John the Baptist) Day celebrations, the winter carnival included U.S. dignitaries and reflected the identity of Franco-Americans. Governor Ralph O. Brewster welcomed Canadians to the Lewiston carnival, indicating that he felt the event would encourage ties of friendship between Canada and the United States. Ten U.S. and Tricolor flags flew above the twenty-foot ice castle erected at Lewiston City Park. An estimated 7,000 Lewiston residents took part in the snowshoe races at the park, and 25,000 persons attended the evening torch-light parade. Other activities included two hockey games between members of l'Association Saint-Dominique (the Saint Dominic Association) and a team from Québec City, a Sunday morning parade to mass at Saint-Pierre (Saint Peter) Church, and a banquet at City Hall attended by Lewiston Mayor Louis Brann.[7]

The February 1925 carnival spurred the creation of other snowshoe clubs in Lewiston and other areas of northern New England. Lewiston's l'Institut Jacques-Cartier (Jacques Cartier Institute) founded its own snowshoe club within a couple of weeks of the carnival, and its members decided to contact le Club Commercial de Québec (the Commercial Club of Québec) to adopt the club's bylaws as its own. By the end of March 1925, four Lewiston snowshoe clubs—le Montagnard, l'Institut Jacques-Cartier, le Cercle Canadien (the Canadian Circle), and les Diables Rouges (the Red Devils)—formed the American Snowshoe Union, an idea Louis-Philippe Gagné had proposed, and he became its first president. In 1925, women organized snowshoe clubs of their own, called les Dames Montagnards (the Women Mountaineers), la Gaieté (Cheerfulness), and l'Oiseau de Neige (the Snow Bird), and they gained admission to the American Union in November of that year as auxiliary members. When a woman's snowshoe club had its flag blessed at Saint-Pierre Church in 1928, a Dominican priest commented: "Peculiar sight these women and these girls in men's clothing, in a church, even in the sanctuary!" By 1936, Lewiston had five snowshoe clubs for women and five for men. Other clubs formed in Biddeford, Brunswick, and Rumford, Maine, and in Berlin, Somersworth, and Manchester, New Hampshire, and they all joined the American Snowshoe Union. One of the goals of the organization was to alternate the location of its yearly conventions between Canada and the United States, something it did over the course of the twentieth century.[8] Thus, Louis-Philippe Gagné's efforts in the mid-1920s to foster the growth of snowshoe clubs among Franco-Americans led to the creation of an organizational structure in the American Snowshoe Union that promoted interaction between francophones on both sides of the international border, an interaction that continued throughout the twentieth century. The Americanization movement of the 1920s did not, therefore, discourage Lewiston Franco-Americans from expanding their ethnic ties with Canada.

With one notable exception, the Lewiston clubs that joined the American Union were French-language organizations. In 1926, when the Knights of Columbus snowshoe club had its flag blessed at Sainte-Croix Church, *Le Messager* indicated that members of the American Snowshoe Union attended the ceremony and that the president of the Canadian Union had traveled from Québec to participate. The head of the snowshoe club of the Knights of Columbus was a Franco-American, and Holy Cross had just been renamed Sainte-Croix. The day after the ceremony, *Le Messager* reflected on the ethnic intermixing taking place at the benediction of the club's flag: "An excellent lesson to draw from yesterday's celebration is that the sport of snowshoeing has contributed to uniting in one celebration snowshoers of two languages, for the blessing of the flag of an English-language club directed by a Franco-American."[9] Acculturation in the United States was not a unidirectional process.

Beginning during the 1925 Christmas season, local snowshoe clubs teamed up with the Société Saint-Vincent de Paul (Saint Vincent de Paul Society) to bring the French-Canadian custom of *la Guignolée* to Lewiston. According to *Le Messager*, parishes in Québec first began taking up a collection on Christmas Eve in 1884 for their destitute; while the French-language newspaper did not make clear when *la Guignolée* fell out of practice, it noted that Québec parishes revived the custom in 1903. The idea took root in Lewiston after Louis-Philippe Gagné discussed it with F. X. Marcotte, the president of the Société Saint-Vincent de Paul of Saint-Pierre Parish. Subsequently, the Saint-Vincent de Paul societies from Lewiston's two largest parishes, Sainte-Marie (Saint Mary) and Saint-Pierre, took up the practice with the assistance of members of some of the snowshoe clubs. Yearly reports by

Le Messager at Christmastime reveal that l'Institut Jacques-Cartier and le Montagnard were the snowshoe clubs that most actively participated in *la Guignolée*, a practice that continued through the 1930s. Snowshoers would travel from house to house, collecting cash, clothing, and other goods for the poor of their parish communities.[10] Imported from Québec, *la Guignolée* represented one of the ways in which Franco-Americans took care of the needs of their community before, and during the early years of, the development of the welfare state in the United States.

Franco-Americans created parish societies, such as the men's Société Saint-Vincent de Paul, to help the poor. The formation of les Dames de Charité (the Ladies of Charity) of Saint-Pierre Parish reveals the role men thought women could exercise in charitable work and underscores conceptions of charity before the Great Depression. Conceived by F. X. Marcotte in 1925 as an auxiliary of the Saint-Vincent de Paul society, les Dames de Charité of Saint-Pierre Parish organized women to visit the poor and sew clothes for them. At one of the first meetings of the women's society, F. X. Marcotte "underlined the role that a woman could fill better than a man, near the sick and the poor, keeping in mind that a good word often does more good than material assistance."[11]

Women, of course, had long been active in providing for needy francophones in Lewiston. Les Soeurs de la Charité de Saint-Hyacinthe (The Sisters of Charity of Saint-Hyacinthe) had founded a hospital in Lewiston in the late 1800s, and they provided care for the indigent at no charge, as their annual reports revealed in the 1930s. These Soeurs Grises (Grey Nuns) expanded their social services in the 1920s by building Maison Marcotte (Marcotte Home), a nursing facility for the elderly, and l'Orphelinat Saint-Joseph (the Saint Joseph Orphanage), an orphanage for girls, in different wings of one structure. In donating $120,000 to the project, which would house 200 elderly people and 250 orphan girls, businessman F. X. Marcotte stipulated that the sisters had to accept sixteen elderly Franco-Americans (twenty after the death of himself and his wife) at no charge for up to twenty-five years after he and his wife had passed. In publicizing Marcotte's donation, *Le Messager* indicated that it would help keep indigent Franco-Americans from having to live at the city's poor farm and would prevent the associated shame. Implicit in *Le Messager*'s report was the pride of Franco-Americans in being able to take care of their own. This pride factored into the decision of the Woonsocket headquarters of the Franco-American mutual-benefit society, l'Union Saint-Jean Baptiste d'Amérique (the Saint John the Baptist Union of America), to loan the Soeurs Grises from $200,000 to $300,000 to finance construction of their new institution.[12]

While Franco-Americans built institutions to meet their own needs, they were not strictly ethnic institutions, for they opened them to non-Franco-Americans and to non-Catholics. For example, the Sisters' Hospital, named Hôpital Général Sainte-Marie (Saint Mary's General Hospital) in 1908, continued in the twentieth century to accept patients without regard to religious background or national origin. In fiscal year 1920, while Franco-Americans constituted a majority of the patients treated at the institution, 37.7 percent of the women and 45.1 percent of the men admitted to the hospital did not have French surnames. A French Catholic institution, it welcomed other residents of the Lewiston area. Similarly, Maison Marcotte and l'Orphelinat Saint-Joseph "are open to all, without distinction to religion or to nationality."[13] This practice likely helped the institutions of the Soeurs Grises to procure state subsidies to help finance operations.

Because historians have devoted little attention to such charitable Franco-American institutions (and, for that matter, to other benevolent Catholic institutions), to date we know hardly anything about them. The same is true of the savings institutions of Franco-Americans—notably the credit unions, which they introduced to the United States in 1908. A French Canadian, Alphonse Desjardins, brought the cooperative credit movement from Europe to North America when he opened a *caisse populaire* (credit union) in his home in Québec in 1900.[14] Reverend Pierre Hévey, who had instituted a savings bank in Lewiston during his tenure as pastor of Saint-Pierre Parish in the 1870s, subsequently served as pastor of Sainte-Marie Parish in Manchester, New Hampshire, where he organized la Caisse populaire Sainte-Marie with the assistance of Desjardins in 1908. When incorporated the following year by an act of the New Hampshire legislature, this institution became the first credit union in the United States.[15]

Hévey's savings bank in Lewiston in the 1870s represented one of several attempts to create savings institutions for the city's French speakers. In 1905, *Le Messager* reported that attempts to found a bank for francophones in that year had not succeeded because the state government had denied organizers the necessary charter. The French-language newspaper suspected that banking interests had pressured the state to take this action because local bankers had feared losing up to one million dollars in deposits by Franco-Americans. Ten years later, Franco-Americans F. X. Marcotte, A. G. Gagnon, J. B. Janelle, and A. T. Gastonguay successfully obtained a state charter to create the Mutual Loan Company of Lewiston, designed to provide loans to purchase real estate or to enable borrowers to get out of high-interest loans they held. *Le Messager* informed readers that the savings association had gained its charter despite opposition from banks that feared both losing Franco-American clients and having to compete with the new institution. An ethnic organization, the Lewiston Mutual Loan Society gave credit "exclusively to compatriots." In 1921, the institution lost its charter and had to liquidate its assets, because the state banking commission worried about its declining yearly profits, reported *Le Messager*.[16] The French-language newspaper kept silent about any suspicions it might have had that the action discriminated against Franco-Americans.

Not until 1938, in the midst of the Great Depression, did Lewiston francophones have their own credit union. Four years after President Franklin D. Roosevelt signed the Federal Credit Union Act, Sainte-Famille (Holy Family) opened the first parish credit union in the state of Maine. Interestingly enough, it was the Antigonish Movement, a Catholic social-action movement of Nova Scotia, that had inspired Pastor Vital Nonorgues to found this credit union. Nonorgues had pursued his philosophical and theological studies at Halifax, Nova Scotia, prior to his 1912 ordination and, before becoming pastor of Sainte-Famille in 1923, had served as a priest in northern Maine's Saint John Valley, an area where the Antigonish Movement later influenced the development of cooperatives and credit unions during the Depression. Nonorgues founded the credit union of Sainte-Famille to help parishioners struggling with indebtedness.[17]

Discrimination against Franco-Americans may have played a role in the founding of Sainte Famille Federal Credit Union. In the 1930s, Bates College sociologists A. M. Myhrman and J. A. Rademaker observed that while Franco-Americans held political power in Lewiston, Yankees owned and managed the large companies and banks and held economic and social power in the city. "To describe the social and ecological relationships briefly," they wrote, "it might well be said that the Yankees exploit the French Canadians, and operate on a basis of mutualism with the Irish in most instances."

Longtime Lewiston resident and public school teacher Geneva Kirk informed an interviewer that banking institutions in Lewiston discriminated against Franco-Americans during the Depression by maintaining a quota system. As the victim of such discrimination, a former Franco-American postmaster told Kirk that a bank officer had indicated that he was "well qualified" for a job at his institution, but that the banker could not hire him. When asked to explain, the banker had offered: "We have one Frenchman here now, and that's our quota. That's a token number." Such discrimination against Franco-Americans probably carried over into the lending practices of bankers, thus motivating Franco-Americans to try again to found their own savings institution during the Great Depression, assisted by the passage of the Federal Credit Union Act.[18]

The founding of additional credit unions in Lewiston at mid-century reveals more ethnic institution building in the Spindle City. These institutions supported and reflected the growing economic strength of Franco-Americans. Les Vigilants (the Vigilants) actively promoted the establishment of credit unions by Franco-American parishes. In 1945, Saint-Pierre Parish founded its own credit union, modeled after that of Sainte-Famille. To promote membership, Pastor Hervé Drouin would invite parishioners to the sacristy after mass to obtain information about joining the credit union. Dominican sources reveal that Drouin had been concerned about "some family disasters that lending and credit corporations cause in the parish." In February 1947, *Le Messager* reported that ten professional and business men of Lewiston were considering founding a Franco-American bank, and it explained that "Judge Adrien Côté has declared that this group of men considers the number of French-speaking directors in our local banks unrepresentative of the city's population." While Franco-Americans did not establish their own bank, they did continue founding credit unions. In February 1947, Sainte-Marie Parish organized its credit union, and Sainte-Croix Parish followed suit in 1950. The Franco-American parish credit unions, several of which had accumulated assets of over one million dollars by 1959–1960, helped members gain economic strength in the postwar era. Drouin credited his parish financial institution with facilitating the economic and social progress of its members: "We developed an economic pride that permitted our French Canadians to ascend the social ladder."[19]

The credit-union movement spread beyond Lewiston's francophone parishes to other entities to which Franco-Americans belonged. In 1944, city employees founded the Lewiston Municipal Credit Union, modeled after the credit union of Sainte-Famille Parish. Mayor Jean-Charles Boucher, the founding president of Sainte Famille Credit Union, was one of the seven individuals to sign the organization certificate of the municipal credit union. Bates Mill in 1956 organized a credit union for its employees. In 1959, the Men's Club of the Irish church of Saint Joseph, headed by Franco-American John M. Lavertu, organized a credit union for the parish.[20] Lewiston credit unions, it appears, sprang up where Franco-Americans could be found.

Not only did credit unions begin springing up in Lewiston during the Great Depression, but also the French-language media grew. As other French-language newspapers folded in different New England cities, *Le Messager* became a daily publication, beginning in January 1934. While *Le Messager* had sold about 5,500 subscriptions in 1925, its circulation peaked at between 9,000 and 10,000 during the 1930s. *Le Messager*'s increased circulation and its evolution to a daily newspaper demonstrate that the Depression did not necessarily weaken ethnic identification and ethnic institutions in the Spindle City. The newspaper did refashion itself, however. In 1934, *Le Messager* dropped without explanation the words *religion*, *nationalité*, and *patrie* (country) from its masthead and replaced them with *franchise* (openness) and *vérité* (truth).[21] Perhaps the change signified a shift in *Le Messager*'s outlook from the values its founders had brought from Québec to those it wished to promote amidst the political corruption of 1930s Lewiston.

Le Messager's president, J. B. Couture, founded the Twin City Broadcasting Corporation and gained a Federal Communications Commission license for a radio frequency. In August 1938, WCOU (COU for Couture) went on the air. Established in *Le Messager*'s building, it was the only radio station in Lewiston-Auburn, Maine. While much of WCOU's programming was in English, and three of its first four announcers had English surnames, it offered daily programs in French. One was *le Club Matinal* (*The Morning Club*) from 6:00 to 7:00 each morning, Monday through Saturday, featuring songs and local, national, and international news, as well as periodic announcements of the time of day. There were Sunday radio programs, also featuring news and entertainment in French.[22] Programming in English and

French on WCOU provides only further evidence of the intertwining of ethnic retention with the realities of living in an anglophone country.

The technology of radio may have intensified the transborder relationship of French Canadians and Franco-Americans in the 1930s. As early as October 1929, emissions from Montréal's CKAC radio station could be heard in the Lewiston-Auburn area. In December 1938, *Le Messager* announced that WCOU would broadcast the *réveillon* (dinner party, usually after the midnight mass at Christmas) organized by les Vigilants from 2:00 to 4:00 on Christmas morning; because other radio stations did not operate during those hours, the newspaper speculated that the broadcast would be heard not only in other parts of the United States, but in Canada as well. Given the proximity of Lewiston to the Canadian border, and the Franco-American ownership of WCOU, it would seem that the advent of radio could not necessarily draw Franco-Americans from the Spindle City into a more homogeneous, U.S. mass culture—unless they chose that to happen.[23]

As demonstrated by the institution building of French speakers, neither the Americanization movement of the 1920s nor the Great Depression of the 1930s served to unravel the intertwined identity of Lewiston Franco-Americans. During these decades, francophones continued to maintain ties with Québec while creating institutions in the Spindle City that reveal their continued efforts to plant roots in their country of adoption. As we will see in the next chapter, they also developed workers' unions over the course of the twentieth century that drew upon U.S. models and inspiration.

We Will Earn a Living and Not Merely an Existence

Franco-American Workers Assert Their Rights, 1920–1970

In 1943, Dominican Pastor Hervé Drouin of Lewiston's Saint-Pierre (Saint Peter) Parish made a grand departure from the past: He supported the trade unionism of his Franco-American parishioners.[1] At mid-century, clergymen like Drouin had to acknowledge reality and accept the growing working-class identity of their Franco-American parishioners. In the twentieth century, Franco-Americans developed workers' unions that drew their inspiration from U.S. models. Their efforts revealed the intersections of their ethnic and working-class identities.

Franco-Americans had far more agency than they have been credited with. An oft-repeated stereotype is that they were a priest-ridden population. The origins of this stereotype are difficult to pinpoint, but it appears to have followed their ancestors from Québec. In the United States, the characterization of Franco-Americans as clergy-dominated may have come from their religious leaders and from nativists. In December 1881, for example, the French Dominican Alexandre-Louis Mothon, who had remigrated from Saint-Hyacinthe to become pastor of Lewiston's Saint-Pierre Parish, penned a letter to his order describing the role of the parish priest: "The latter [the priest] must occupy himself here with many things that our pastors in France would not themselves dream of doing; it is he who must lead everything, the temporal like the spiritual." Mothon elaborated: "He is, furthermore, the peacemaker, the counselor, the universal arbiter, and nothing important takes place, in most families, without his advice or his direction." For his part, nativist Robert Cloutman Dexter wrote in 1924 of the French Canadian in Québec: "So far as the individual habitant is concerned, his personal and family life is almost entirely controlled by the Church. He is obedient to his curé, who is for him not only the religious leader, but also the political, social, educational, and moral guide." Dexter continued: "His own ignorance and superstition only place him the more definitely under the influence of the priest." Dexter believed that the same was true of Franco-Americans, asserting that "the Canadian Church remains essentially the same in the United States as in the villages of Canada. In the fundamental matters of church doctrine, religious ascendency, [and] the control of the priest, . . . there has been no change."[2] The participation of Franco-Americans in trade unions and labor protests in the twentieth century provide perhaps the clearest evidence that they did not follow submissively the dictates of their religious leaders.

The trade-union activities of Franco-Americans reveal how their identity evolved in the United States from the 1920s through the 1960s. During the 1920s, Lewiston Franco-Americans increasingly joined textile unions, for salary reductions and unpleasant working conditions motivated them to organize. In February 1922, competition from textile mills in the South, which paid workers lower wages, led the cotton mills of New England to reduce the salaries of their workers. Unlike in other towns of the region, mill workers in Lewiston swallowed a 20 percent pay cut rather than risk striking during a depression in business. Although a majority of Lewiston's textile workers were not unionized in 1922, 90 percent of the loom fixers and enough weavers belonged to unions, reported Le Messager, that they could have forced the mills to close by going on strike. Following the failed strike vote, about six hundred men and women from different departments in the mills joined the local textile union, which was part of the American Federation of Textile Operatives.[3]

After textile manufacturers cut wages about 10 to 15 percent in late 1927, anglophone and francophone labor organizers from outside of Lewiston descended upon the city to sign up members for their competing unions.

They represented the American Federation of Textile Operatives and the United Textile Workers of America, the latter associated with the American Federation of Labor. *Le Messager* expressed concern about their rivalry and the possible consequences for Lewiston: "There is no doubt that a serious rivalry exists between the two workers' organizations for control of the local situation. The sort that in organizing we disorganize ourselves." During a meeting of a men's society at Saint-Pierre Parish, a Dominican priest told weavers not to rush to join these two unions, which could adversely affect local industries and social conditions in Lewiston, but to consider forming instead Catholic worker unions like those that existed in Québec. There is no indication that Lewiston Franco-Americans pursued the priest's recommendations. By February 1928, the United Textile Workers, which conducted meetings in French and English, had organized eight hundred people from Lewiston. While *Le Messager* did not provide updated membership figures for the American Federation of Textile Operatives, it appears from one brief report in the newspaper that this organization might have had less success in attracting Franco-Americans because it held its meetings in English.[4]

The cheating and arbitrariness of employers during the Great Depression embittered Franco-Americans. Mélanie Côté recalled mill bosses stealing five to ten dollars from the weekly pay envelopes of workers. "We'd go over there and tell them. 'I'm supposed to have this much.' Mill bosses would respond: 'You have enough.' And we'd go back—nobody to report it to. That's what the bosses did in those days." Romeo Boisvert followed his father into the mills at age sixteen and discovered that foremen arbitrarily selected who would work during the Depression: "In the mill, on each floor, there was a space where all the employees would be standing. The foreman would pick out employees, 'O.K., you work today,' regardless of your years of service to the company." Bosses also replaced male family heads who had worked at the mill for years with young women to whom they paid lower wages. Such experiences led Boisvert and other Lewiston Franco-Americans to join trade unions.[5]

Labor protests erupted in the Lewiston-Auburn area in the 1930s. In mid-August 1932, over two hundred cutters and stitchers at Cushman-Hollis Shoe Company of Auburn left their jobs to protest a 15 percent wage reduction (another of several cuts they had experienced over recent months), paralyzing other departments in the factory of two thousand employees. They returned to work within days as their demands went to arbitration. When arbiters adjusted the wage reduction to 9 percent in late August, cutters protested the decision as "unjust and inexcusable," reported *Le Messager*, but they continued working. In early September, over three hundred leather cutters formed a union called the Lewiston and Auburn Shoe Cutters Social and Protective Association.[6] *Le Messager* did not specify whether Franco-Americans joined either the shoe strike or the union.

Franco-Americans were heavily involved in the shoe strike that began in mid-September. Following a blacklisting agreement among shoe manufacturers, a factory fired a Franco-American surnamed Croteau for distributing union cards in a shop other than the one in which he worked, and the manufacturers also fired another ten members of an employee committee. About two thousand shoe workers, 80 percent "of the French language," went on strike and paraded from downtown Lewiston across the bridge to the shoe shops in Auburn. Several days later, about two thousand men and women paraded again from Lewiston to Auburn, some carrying signs in French: "Do away with the Black List," and "We want Justice." The French-language newspaper empathized with the strikers. Perhaps sharing more about itself than about popular opinion, *Le Messager* indicated that the public supported the strikers because they were not seeking a wage hike. About one week into the strike, following the report that Cushman-Hollis would close if its employees did not return to work, *Le Messager* urged Franco-Americans: "Return to work." For their part, the Dominicans worried that Franco-Americans participating in the strike were giving Lewiston a bad reputation. At Sunday mass in late September, Dominican pastor Mannès Marchand told parishioners of Saint-Pierre: "I bitterly deplore that the strikers have not followed the wise directions given them yesterday (Saturday) by governor-elect Brann." Brann, a former mayor of Lewiston who served as an intermediary between workers and management in this dispute, had urged the strikers to return to work because manufacturers were losing orders. The supplications of *Le Messager*, the pastor of Lewiston's largest Franco-American parish, and civic leader Brann weighed on the Franco-American strikers. Two other factors did as well. The strike organizer was an anglophone from England, and some francophones told *Le Messager* that they no longer wanted to attend meetings conducted in

English. In addition, grocers decided not to extend further credit to strikers. The strike ended in late September with manufacturers maintaining the right to an open shop, but giving partial recognition to an employee association or union. When nearly three thousand shoe factory employees returned to work, *Le Messager* complimented the individuals who had lost their jobs—the action that had precipitated the strike—for not standing in the way of its resolution.[7]

In 1933, President Franklin D. Roosevelt signed legislation creating the National Recovery Administration (NRA). Although it shortened the work week and improved wages, problems arose that eventually led to further unionization among Franco-Americans. Mill employee Cecile Lebel earned from seven to nine dollars each week during the Depression. "Then Roosevelt came in and gave us forty hours and fourteen dollars a week. We thought we were rich." But manufacturers sped up machines so that employees ended up working as hard as when they had put in fifty-four hours weekly, she indicated. "We weren't independent. We were *dependent*," she stated emphatically. "We wanted a job. We needed the money."[8]

In 1934, the Franco-American clergy of Lewiston used the pulpit to dissuade the city's shoe and textile workers from participating in strikes. In May, pastors Eugène Gauthier of Sainte-Marie (Saint Mary) and Mannès Marchand of Saint-Pierre warned parishioners at Sunday masses against heeding outside organizers encouraging shoe workers to strike; this followed the firing of Wilfred Therrien from Venus Shoe Company of Auburn after he had engaged in union activity—activity legalized by the National Labor Relations Act.[9] The shoe workers did not strike.

In late August and September 1934, all pastors of Lewiston's Franco-American parishes discouraged textile workers from joining an industry-wide strike that took place from Maine to Texas. Franco-American Mayor Robert Wiseman denied strike organizers permission to meet at City Hall, and he summoned the National Guard to watch over the city's textile mills and to ensure that those who wanted to work could do so. Only about forty workers from the Androscoggin Mill took part in the sympathy strike; they did so for less than one week. Thus nearly six thousand textile workers of Lewiston and Auburn avoided participating in the industry-wide strike. They were not uninterested in organizing, however, for *Le Messager* reported in November that mill workers were forming the L. & A. Local Textile Workers

Association, which would cooperate with other unions, including the American Federation of Labor, in the event of future labor problems.[10]

A couple of years later, when Saint-Pierre Parish hosted a festival to raise money for its new church (still only partially built following the struggles of the Dominicans with Bishop Louis Walsh), the Dominican Sisters noted in their chronicle the participation of Americans and Jews at the festival and attributed it to the pastor's role in discouraging Franco-Americans from taking part in the 1934 textile strike: "Father Marchand is very popular since his very successful intervention in October [sic] 1934 to hinder French-language workers from joining the strike. A good number of industrialists have remained very grateful to him and have proved it." The sisters expected the festival to bring to the parish coffers about $5,000, a sizable sum in those days.[11]

In 1937, Franco-American clergy again cautioned parishioners against striking. Representatives of the Committee for Industrial Organization (CIO) came to Lewiston-Auburn to organize shoe workers to help them achieve higher wages and better working conditions. When the strike began in late March, Le Messager reported that the meeting of strikers at Lewiston City Hall featured singing, music, and dancing: "It appeared to be a big family reunion and there was not any hint of disorder." At Easter Sunday in late March, Pastor Marchand reminded parishioners of the hardships other strikes had brought to the community. What distinguishes this strike from others in the 1930s, something that other accounts have not emphasized, is that some Franco-Americans became openly critical of their clergy. Mrs. Alexina Leclair of Lewiston spoke frequently and in French at meetings of strikers at City Hall and often led them in song. At one meeting shortly after the strike began, she voiced her support for the CIO and spoke against local clergy. "We will earn a living and not merely an existence," Leclair asserted. "Mrs. Leclair then said she did not think it proper for priests to talk against the strike as they did in most churches. She said they should preach; that they . . . should not seek to keep laborers at work merely to get 15 cents from them on Sunday," reported the Lewiston Journal. Unlike the English-language press, Le Messager sided with the strikers. This apparently led pastor Eugène Gauthier of Sainte-Marie to advise his parishioners to read some articles in the English-language newspapers as they decided whether or not to join the strike. In April, priests from the four Franco-American parishes of Lewiston asked shoe workers to return to their places of work. Subsequently, an unspecified number of Franco-Americans did return to work.[12]

Not all followed the advice of their clergy. W. J. Lessard responded in *Le Messager* to a letter that Pastor Edouard Nadeau of Sainte-Croix (Holy Cross) had published in the French-language newspaper in early April. Lessard argued that strikers did not view the situation the same way as the priest. He suggested that Nadeau tend to his affairs and not meddle with the strike, contending that the CIO was working to help poor people. Wrote Lessard: "We know very well that it is not the Catholic Church that feeds us and gives us sufficient wages when we do not earn enough money to feed and clothe our children that you insist we have under penalty of hell." Perhaps Philippe Gilbert best symbolized the change he wished to see effected in the perception of Franco-Americans. "They told you and repeated that you, French Canadians, you were not capable of holding together," he said at a meeting at City Hall. "But the French Canadian is becoming a lion. We are beginning to get mad. Show them that the lamb has changed into a lion," Gilbert cried out to loud applause. During the strike, Auburn police, businessmen, the courts, Lewiston's Franco-American pastors, and the English-language press all sided with manufacturers against the CIO and the largely Franco-American membership it represented. After three months, the shoe strike—involving nineteen factories and six thousand workers, protest marches across the bridge to Auburn, and the eruption of violence—ended unsuccessfully in late June. "The *poverty* of the Lewiston-Auburn shoe workers forced them finally to submit," concluded historian Richard Condon.[13]

Unsuccessful or not, what the organizing and protests of the 1920s and 1930s reveal is that the identity of Franco-Americans as workers continued to evolve during the difficult economic times they experienced during the interwar years. This worker identity had its roots in the late nineteenth century, when French-Canadian descendants first joined the Knights of Labor and participated in strikes despite the opposition of their clergy. Even when Franco-Americans opted not to strike to resolve workplace conflicts in the 1920s and 1930s, they joined trade unions in order to improve their working conditions. While the strikes may not have yielded positive results, the involvement of Franco-Americans helps to dispel notions about their passivity in the world of work. Moreover, the anticlerical sentiments Franco-Americans openly expressed during the strike demonstrate that they were not as docile or as submissive to clergy as some have been wont to say.[14]

The same appears true concerning the issue of limiting family size. As W. J. Lessard noted in his letter to *Le Messager*, Catholic clergy insisted that their parishioners not practice birth control. Antoinette Boucher, a senior citizen, indicated in 1981 that priests would not grant absolution in the confessional to women who did. Other than advocating the rhythm method and prolonged nursing, the only advice clergy would give couples who wanted to limit the size of their families was to "live as sister and brother," she pointed out. Former restaurant owner Juliette Filteau made the same observation when she stated that priests would advise separate bedrooms for couples who wanted to limit their family size. Otherwise, priests expected women to continue bearing children, even during the Great Depression, Filteau discovered, when one threatened to withhold communion from her. "So I got mad. I says, 'Can't have communion, uhn? Are you gonna support my kid if I can't support him?'" she shot back. When the priest responded, "No," she told him to keep the host![15] We can infer from such comments as Filteau's that Franco-American women did challenge the teachings of the Catholic Church and were not as submissive to clergy as generally believed.

Like other working-class Americans, French speakers benefited from the New Deal programs of Franklin Roosevelt during the Great Depression. Lewiston Franco-Americans had special reason to celebrate passage of the National Recovery Act in 1933, because they took credit for the legislation. William Bourassa, the Franco-American founder of the American Bobbin Shop in Lewiston, had circulated his idea for the NRA among other industrialists, members of Congress, and through financial publications, before a Massachusetts senator introduced the legislation. Roosevelt aide Louis Howe contacted Bourassa for a history of the idea, and the president subsequently pushed for the plan in a radio address. After passage of the NRA, about ten thousand Lewistonians—including Bourassa, textile and shoe workers, public and parochial school children, and members of Maine's congressional delegation—took part in the city's October 1933 parade. Roosevelt's New Deal programs won him widespread acclaim among Franco-Americans. In February 1934, *Le Messager* reported: "Everywhere, people speak of the good works of our President Roosevelt. . . . Even his photograph pleases [people] to see. Exclamations heard at the bazaar currently underway at Saint Mary's confirm this." *Le Messager* did periodically complain, however, that Lewiston Franco-Americans were subject to discrimination in the award of government jobs and benefits. In January 1934, the French-language newspaper argued that while Franco-Americans constituted more than half of Lewiston's voters, only ten francophones had posts in the Civil Works Administration, compared to twenty-seven anglophones. In 1937, the newspaper published a series of articles that identified deserving Franco-Americans who had been denied old age pensions; it asserted that the Augusta agency overseeing the federal awards discriminated against Franco-Americans because they were Democrats.[16] The effect of the New Deal on Franco-Americans is a subject that merits additional research. Despite discrimination they may have endured in reaping its benefits, Lewiston Franco-Americans probably became more solidly Democratic in political identity as a result not only of the employment and pecuniary benefits they reaped from the New Deal, but also because of the legislation Roosevelt enacted to support the right of workers to organize during the Great Depression. Roosevelt's leadership as president appears to have cemented the allegiance of Franco-Americans to the Democratic Party. His tenure helped Franco-Americans continue to evolve more solidly in their identity as Democratic voters and members of the working class.

Republicans made up only a small fraction of Lewiston's Franco-American population at mid-century. In 1949, estimated Bates College student Glenn Kumekawa, they made up a mere 15 percent of Lewiston's Franco-Americans. In 1969, slightly over one-tenth (11.9 percent) of Lewiston's registered voters were Republicans, one-seventh (14.6 percent) were Independents, and about three-fourths (73.5 percent) were Democrats. As a result of the staunchly Democratic political identity of Franco-Americans, Democratic presidential contenders carried Lewiston from 1940 through 1968; in fact, Franklin D. Roosevelt in the 1940s, and John F. Kennedy, Lyndon B. Johnson, and Hubert Humphrey in the 1960s each won 80 percent or more of Lewiston's vote. Indicative of Lewiston's Democratic fervor, an estimated fifteen thousand people turned up before midnight, two days before Kennedy's election as president, to hear the Catholic candidate speak for forty-five minutes at Lewiston's municipal park, despite both his four-hour delay and the frigid temperature. During presidential election years,

Democratic congressional candidates pulled over 60 percent of Lewiston's vote from 1940 to 1952, and over 80 percent from 1956 to 1968. Similarly, Democratic gubernatorial contenders won from 62 to 71 percent of Lewiston's vote from 1940 to 1952, and over 80 percent from 1956 to 1966.[17] Franco-Americans had made Lewiston the fortress of Democratic candidates.

At mid-century, the working-class identity of Lewiston's Franco-Americans grew more solid. In the 1930s, Julian Cloutier's sympathies had not been with trade unionists. "In those days if you belonged to a union or were strongly in favor of a union you might be called a Commy or . . . a Socialist. You were called names and then the clergy also was against the union and so you had many people critical of you." Cloutier continued: "I had a provincial upbringing heavily influenced by the church and these union people were outsiders coming in and often not even church people." But while serving in the Merchant Marine during World War II, Cloutier learned of the advantages of unionization from shipmates involved in the Maritime Union, and his thinking changed. Not only did he join a union, but he also became president of the local at Bates Mill, a position he had held for twenty years at the time of his 1975 interview.[18]

Like Cloutier, many other Franco-Americans joined union ranks at mid-century. By the end of October 1941, workers at the Androscoggin, Continental, Hill, and Bates mills—Lewiston's largest textile mills—had voted to accept union representation. The union elections underscored the intersection of ethnic and working-class identities in the Spindle City as well as the federal government's acknowledgement of that intersection. For example, when Bates Mill employees accepted the Textile Workers Union of America (TWUA) of the Congress of Industrial Organizations (CIO) as its union in an October 1941 election mandated by the Federal Labor Relations Board, they voted at l'Institut Jacques-Cartier (Jacques Cartier Institute) Hall on ballots that appeared in both English and French. Delighted, *Le Messager* proclaimed, "French is the language of adaptation even for what concerns the official government of Washington."[19] The ballots in this election, the voting site, and the acceptance of union representation all highlighted the intersection of Franco-American and working-class identities in Lewiston.

Franco-American clergy had to come to terms with this reality. When the TWUA held a banquet in February 1943, pastors Hervé Drouin of Saint-

Pierre and Félix Martin of Sainte-Croix both attended. Franco-American clergy, it seems, finally recognized that they had to support the trade union affiliation of their parishioners. In fact, a couple of weeks after the banquet, Drouin delivered a sermon entitled "A New Beginning," in which he argued that trade unions had served as friends of the working class, pointing to their efforts to eliminate sweat shops, end child labor, and shorten work days. Drouin connected these gains in the labor movement to the pursuit of liberty in the ongoing world conflict: "Let us take seriously our war effort, but let us not lose on the domestic front the liberties for which our soldiers are sacrificing today."[20] Drouin's words must have resonated with Franco-American workers.

Clergy support for trade unions did not necessarily lead to support for striking, however. In late October 1945, workers from six Lewiston mills voted to join a regional strike on the first of November if management did not grant their demands for a wage increase, a paid vacation, and a closed shop. At Sunday mass, Marcel Charbonneau, the assistant pastor of Saint-Pierre, expressed his view that the impending strike "certainly will not settle anything." He did not stop there. "It is out of harmony, peace and mutual concessions that life in society becomes possible and stable," he stated, before admonishing: "[It is up to] you to show that you are true, intelligent and reasonable Christians. [It is up to you] to demonstrate that you understand the true liberty that we make use of in this country and for which so much blood has been spilt."[21] Charbonneau's conception of "liberty" apparently excluded the right to strike.

Le Messager ostensibly agreed with Reverend Charbonneau, for it introduced his remarks with the comment that he "has faithfully translated the sentiments of thoughtful people." On October 31st, the newspaper contended that the decision of 1,300 union members to strike would affect 6,000 local workers. It expressed the concerns of workers who did not want to strike because they worried about unemployment, the high cost of living, and the approach of winter. *Le Messager* further argued that the manufacturers had agreed to all of the demands of workers except supporting further unionization. After the strike began, *Le Messager* affirmed that it supported the rights of workers. But it repeated that the textile mills had agreed to all of their demands except one—an issue that was more important to the union than to the workers, it asserted. This was not solely a local strike, however. In all, 10,000 textile workers from Maine and 20,000 from the New England states of Maine, Rhode Island, Connecticut, and New Hampshire participated in this CIO-organized regional strike. In Lewiston, 6,000 textile workers struck, and 4,000 of them were Franco-American, estimated *Le Messager*. During the strike, Lewiston unionists from four of the six targeted mills took turns meeting at l'Institut Jacques-Cartier Hall, with Androscoggin Mill workers meeting at 10:00 A.M., those from Continental Mill at 11:00 A.M., the Hill Mill at 1:00 P.M., and the Bates Mill at 2:00 P.M., because the hall could not accommodate them all in one sitting. The strike was not resolved in Lewiston. Company representatives, CIO leaders, and a federal mediator negotiated its end in Boston. When *Le Messager* reported the resolution of this labor dispute in late November, it highlighted the gains workers had made—noting, for example, that their hourly wage had increased, that those working for the same firm for five years would receive a paid vacation of two weeks, and that employers would provide accident and health insurance. But it also pointed out that the strike's successful conclusion had depended upon dropping the request for a closed shop.[22]

In April 1955, 23,000 textile workers from throughout New England went on strike when manufacturers wanted to reduce wages and benefits to those paid to workers in the textile mills of the South. As in 1944, about 10,000 of the strikers were from Maine's industrial cities, including Lewiston. While *Le Messager* did not specify how many of Lewiston's Franco-Americans participated, it is clear from various reports that they were heavily involved in the strikes that took place at the Bates, Pepperell, and Continental mills. In late April, strikers held a dance at l'Institut Jacques-Cartier Hall to raise funds for needy workers. They had to generate some of their own monies because the Lewiston Welfare Department only aided strikers who did not receive assistance from the CIO, who had no possessions of value that they could sell to generate cash, and who declared themselves "paupers"—a situation that cost them their right to vote.[23] As had become usual, *Le Messager* sympathized with the workers, indicating that "these restrictions are distressing, although they signify a little hope of aid for certain large families." The strikes at the three mills ended between early May and mid-July 1955, with workers from each company accepting salaries and contracts comparable to what they had before the strike.[24]

Franco-Americans successfully won concessions from their employers during both the 1945 and 1955 strikes. As in the past, the trade union activity and labor protests of Franco-Americans at mid-century revealed their commitment to improving the conditions of their lives in the United States. Participation in the regional textile strikes of 1945 and 1955 demonstrated their solidarity as workers. Their use of l'Institut Jacques-Cartier Hall for union meetings, elections, and fundraisers underscored their ethnic identification. In short, these activities in the world of work at mid-century demonstrated that Franco-American identity was inextricably tied to working-class identity, something their newspaper and their clerical leaders had to accept, whatever their aversion to strikes.[25]

With ninety-two manufacturers of cotton, wool, rayon, shoe, brass, iron, and electronic products, Lewiston continued to promote itself as the "Industrial Heart of Maine" in 1960. It remained predominantly a working-class community, and Franco-Americans held most of the blue-collar jobs, particularly the city's industrial jobs. In fact, men with French names doubled the proportion of other men who did industrial work, and nearly twice as many Franco-American women held industrial jobs as did other women in the city (see table 4). Although Franco-Americans had experienced some upward occupational mobility since 1920, individuals with non-Franco-American family names still held Lewiston's best jobs in 1960.[26]

The concentration of Franco-American men in blue-collar jobs probably explains why so many of their wives worked outside of the home. Over half (54.4 percent) of married women with French surnames worked outside the home in 1960, compared to two-fifths (40.7 percent) of married women with non-French surnames. The prevalence of working wives among Franco-Americans, a pattern begun early in the twentieth century, thus appears to have persisted into mid-century. These Franco-American women possibly contributed to trade unionism at mid-century, just as women like Mrs. Alexina Leclair had in the 1930s. Perhaps the wages the wives contributed to their family economies helped Franco-Americans to achieve the same level (33.8 percent) of homeownership as non-Franco-Americans (33.7 percent) by 1960.[27]

The upward occupational mobility some Franco-American women experienced by mid-century occasionally led to amusing exchanges with the non-Franco-Americans they befriended who did not understand their ethnic traditions, as the experience of les Enfants de Marie (Children of Mary) illustrates. As a parish society for single women that also existed in Québec, les Enfants de Marie's chief objective probably was to keep young women chaste. When its members married, they had to include at least one representative from the society in their bridal party; after walking down the aisle, the bride and representative(s) would proceed to the statue of Mary, kneel before the Blessed Virgin, and the bride would read a statement in French indicating her intention to leave les Enfants de Marie. Explained Theresa Marcotte, who married in the mid-1940s: "I had to renounce myself as an Enfant de Marie in order to become a wife." The bride and her representative(s) then returned to the altar, and the wedding began. When Claire Lagace married in the mid-1950s, she walked up the aisle of Sainte-Famille Church, then halfway back into the church to reach the statue with the representative of les Enfants. Watching this procession, non-Catholic friends with whom Lagace worked in the personnel department of a Lewiston mill wondered if she had suddenly taken ill or had developed cold feet![28] Besides highlighting a difference in traditions between Franco-American and non-Franco-American women of the period, Lagace's experience gives evidence of the intermixing that took place when Franco-American women experienced upward occupational mobility.

The decline of Lewiston's textile industry at mid-century pushed Franco-American men and women into other jobs. Whereas the industry had employed 8,000 persons in 1951, it provided only 4,000 to 5,000 jobs by 1961. This structural change in Lewiston's economy had the effect of promoting the integration of French speakers with non-francophones. As Franco-Americans moved out of the textile mills into jobs other than those provided by the shoe factories, they often intermixed with non-Franco-Americans and spoke English, particularly if they found white-collar employment.[29]

Self-employment provided some Franco-Americans an avenue to upward mobility by mid-century, largely in the construction and building trades for men and in hair dressing for women. Proportionally more Franco-American women than men had salaried, professional jobs in 1960. Ten of the fourteen French-surnamed women with such positions were nurses, while the other four were teachers or principals.[30] It may be that the Soeurs Grises (Grey Nuns) had trained most of these nurses at the nursing school of Sainte-Marie Hospital and had thus facilitated their mobility. Future

Table 4. Occupational Distribution in Lewiston in 1960 (in percentages)[a]

	MEN WITH NON-FRENCH SURNAMES	MEN WITH FRENCH SURNAMES	WOMEN WITH NON-FRENCH SURNAMES	WOMEN WITH FRENCH SURNAMES
WHITE COLLAR				
Self-governing professional	2.9%	1.0%	0%	0%
Salaried professional	2.9	1.7	11.9	4.8
Small business and managerial	12.4	8.5	2.5	2.4
Semiprofessional	1.8	0.5	1.7	1.4
Clerical and sales	12.4	5.6	22.9	10.0
BLUE COLLAR				
Self-employed	1.8	2.7	1.7	1.7
Nonindustrial	37.1	30.0	16.9	5.5
Industrial	21.2	42.4	35.6	67.6
Primary sector	0.6	0.7	0	0
Unable to determine	7.1	6.8	6.8	6.6
NUMBER	170	410	118	290

Source: Derived from every twenty-fifth entry in Manning's Lewiston Auburn (Maine) Directory for Year beginning November, 1960, vol. 57 (Springfield, Mass.: H.A. Manning, 1960).
a. Columns may not add up to 100.0 percent on account of rounding.

research could provide insight into whether the charitable institutions of francophone women religious enabled Franco-American women over the course of the twentieth century to pursue options for waged work outside of the textile mills and shoe factories.

In conclusion, Franco-Americans forged a stronger working-class identity from the 1920s through the 1950s as they increasingly joined trade unions and labor protests, asserting their rights as workers in the United States. For many, the closing of textile mills from the 1950s necessitated movement into occupations that required greater facility in English and more integration with non-French speakers. At mid-century, external events and forces internal to the community propelled the evolution of Lewiston francophones from Franco-American to American.

The Quiet Evolution

Franco-Americans Become Americans, 1940–1970

On July 2, 1947, three anglophones precipitated a brawl in an Auburn café because they heard men and women speaking French there. Police arrested Glendon, David, and Annie Moody for assault and battery on Emery Samson, the owner of the café; Alliette Therriault, a waitress; and Lionel Beaulieu, whom the press did not identify. "According to officials, the Moodys were in the café and strongly objected to other persons using the French language in view of the United States being an English-speaking country," reported the *Lewiston Journal*. An argument ensued; then a fight broke out. During the fracas, a bottle hit Beaulieu in the head, Glendon and David Moody each sustained a bruised eye, and Therriault "had her dress torn off," indicated the *Journal*. Incredulous, *Le Messager* commented: "And there we believed that this kind of fanatic was extinguished with Hitler."[1]

Religious, class, and language differences still distinguished Franco-Americans from Yankees at mid-century. In a term paper discussing jokes collected from the Lewiston area that poked fun at Catholics and French speakers, University of Maine student Richard Clark wrote in 1966: "The anti-French feelings of the Protestants are based on the concept that the

Lewiston French as a group are of low intelligence. This view is supported by the fact that most of the menial jobs are held by members of the French population, mill jobs, for instance." But he also felt that ethnic retention on the part of Franco-Americans annoyed Protestant Yankees: "Another contributing factor to this idea is the reluctance of the French popilation [sic] to give up the last vestiges of thier [sic] Canadian heritage." That Franco-Americans did not speak standard French also caused Yankees to look upon them with disdain: "Most of them speak the local patois, a corrupt version of French as it was spoken in Canada a hundred years ago, with a few frenchified [sic] modern English words thrown in. Conversely, few of them speak good English, while some speak no English at all," he added. Clark's statements underscore the cultural hostility that Franco-Americans still faced two decades after World War II. Not surprisingly, as attorney Robert Couturier explains, "For some people [in the postwar era] having a French name and being of Canadian background was like having to wear a scarlet letter."[2] This caused increasing numbers of Franco-Americans after World War II to separate the previously intertwined goals of ethnic preservation and acculturation. This chapter examines the evolving identity of French-Canadian descendants in Lewiston from the 1940s through the 1960s.

The advent of the Second World War had a dramatic impact upon the naturalization of French-Canadian immigrants of Lewiston, Maine. When housewife Marie Rose Emelie Lepage became a U.S. citizen in 1941, she joined a large pool of unnaturalized Lewiston residents who rushed to become United States citizens during World War II. During the 1940s, 1,787 women and men became U.S. citizens, a figure surpassing that of any previous decade; in fact, those who naturalized from 1940 to 1949 represented nearly one-third (32.2 percent) of the 5,551 French-Canadian Lewiston residents who acquired their U.S. citizenship during the period from 1877 to 1987.[3] After the 1940s, naturalizations declined significantly. It would seem that there were few French-Canadian immigrants left to naturalize. During the 1950s, only 436 French-Canadian immigrants of Lewiston became U.S. citizens, and this number dropped to 146 during the 1960s. Like Lepage, the unnaturalized immigrants who remained in the United States after the imposition of immigration restrictions in 1930 apparently rushed to become citizens during World War II.[4]

In Lewiston, the number of French-Canadian immigrants who naturalized jumped to the triple digits in 1939, the year that Canada entered World War II, and they remained in the triple digits each year until 1945, the year the war ended. Although Canada did not impose a general conscription until November 1944, its passage of the National Resources Mobilization Act (NRMA) in 1940 increased the possibility that it would draft unnaturalized French-Canadian males from the United States to serve in Canada's military. Unlike in the past, at mid-century *Le Messager* was not as good a source on happenings in Canada; consequently, it is difficult to assess the effect of the NRMA on Lewiston's French-Canadian immigrant population. Passage of the U.S. Alien Registration Act of 1940, a war measure that required noncitizens to submit fingerprints and to register yearly with the Immigration and Naturalization Service, motivated previously reluctant French-Canadian immigrants to give up their British citizenship. Only a couple of weeks after *Le Messager* explained the alien-registration law to readers, the newspaper reported in early July 1940 that 1,500 individuals had requested first or final naturalization papers.[5]

While *Le Messager* specified neither the ethnicity nor the gender of those making requests, a large number must have been francophone women. Each year from 1941 to 1949, the number of naturalizing French-Canadian immigrant women exceeded the number of men. While the number of naturalizing French-Canadian men and women of Lewiston usually was close in the 1950s and 1960s, naturalizations by women tended to exceed those of the men in each year. This pattern was not unique to Lewiston's francophone population, for immigrant women from throughout the country naturalized in greater numbers than men beginning during the Second World War and continuing into the postwar era.[6]

Because the immigration restrictions the United States imposed on Canadians in 1930 ended their mass migration to the United States, those who naturalized in each successive decade disproportionately represented individuals who had delayed acquiring U.S. citizenship. While well over half of the women who had entered the United States as minors under eighteen naturalized within ten years of their twenty-first birthday in the 1930s, that proportion dropped to 36.4 percent in the 1940s, to 13.6 percent in the 1950s, and to 9.8 percent in the 1960s. Whereas over two-thirds of the men who had arrived in the United States as minors under eighteen had naturalized within ten years of turning twenty-one in the 1930s, that proportion dropped sharply to under half (45.7 percent) in the 1940s, and it declined even more dramatically to one-seventh (14.3 percent) in the 1950s, before climbing to around one-fourth (26.1 percent) in the 1960s.[7]

The naturalization records of women and men who had entered the United States as adults present a more complicated picture. They reveal that while close to three-fourths of the women who naturalized in the 1930s had acquired citizenship within fifteen years of their immigration to the United States, the proportion dropped dramatically to 32.5 percent in the 1940s, before rising slightly to 40.0 percent in the 1950s, and rising more sharply to 65.9 percent in the 1960s. What these figures reveal is that the forties and fifties were "catch-up" decades for the French-Canadian immigrant women who had delayed acquiring their U.S. citizenship. Marie Rose Emelie Lepage, for example, had arrived in the United States in 1923 at the age of twenty; although her husband naturalized in 1936, she waited until 1941, eighteen years after immigrating to the United States, before becoming a citizen. Among the men who had arrived in the United States as adults, close to three-fourths in the 1930s naturalized within fifteen years of their immigration to the United States; this proved true of slightly over one-fourth (26.8 percent) in the 1940s, under half (47.3 percent) in the 1950s, and over four-fifths (83.9 percent) in the 1960s.[8] Thus, only in the 1940s and 1950s had more than half of the francophone women and men who naturalized waited more than fifteen years to become U.S. citizens. The French speakers of Lewiston who naturalized during these decades, in other words, had been much slower than those of other periods to obtain their U.S. citizenship.

Consequently, francophones who naturalized at mid-century tended to be older than those who had become U.S. citizens in the 1920s and 1930s. Among women, those over age forty constituted 40.5 percent of those who naturalized in the 1940s, and this proportion increased dramatically to 60.9 percent in the 1950s, before dropping to 45.7 percent in the 1960s. Among men, 41.3 percent of those naturalizing in the 1940s were above the age of forty, and the proportion escalated dramatically to 71.8 percent in the 1950s, before plummeting to 38.9 percent in the 1960s. Those who naturalized in the 1950s represented a unique group. To take one example, Arcles Lafreniere had immigrated to the United States in 1887 at the age of six; he naturalized only in 1952 at the ripe age of seventy-one, half a century after reaching the age of eligibility. French-Canadian immigrants like Lafreniere, who had put off naturalizing through the Second World War and the years immediately following it, perhaps finally resigned themselves in the 1950s to the fact that they would not return to Canada to live out their final days. Equally significant, the Nationality Act of 1952 exempted elderly persons and those who had resided in the United States for a long time from having to demonstrate any English-language skills in order to naturalize. In March 1952, *Le Messager* informed readers that men and women age fifty and older, who had resided in the United States for at least twenty years as of September 1950, could naturalize in French; it announced plans by l'Association des Vigilants (the Association of Vigilants) to offer a naturalization class in French to meet their needs.[9] While the newspaper did not report on the results of the course, we can infer from the naturalization data of the 1950s that a sizable proportion of senior Franco-Americans probably naturalized in French.

In summary, naturalization data from the 1940s through the 1960s illustrates that even the holdouts in Lewiston's francophone community took steps to become civic participants in U.S. society at mid-century. The data particularly reveals that the community's cultural hearth-keepers—its women, and especially the housewives among them—turned out in large numbers to acquire their U.S. citizenship during and after the Second World War. While we have no way of knowing from currently available sources how many French-Canadian immigrants of Lewiston never did naturalize, we can speculate from the naturalization patterns at mid-century that the overwhelming majority of Lewiston's French-Canadian immigrant population naturalized by the late 1950s.[10] For these first-generation holdouts, and especially for those who naturalized in French, participation in U.S. society and ethnic retention presumably still represented intertwined goals.

The contribution of Lewiston Franco-Americans to World War II gave evidence that they still regarded the two goals as intertwined in the early 1940s. In 1942, state senator Jean-Charles Boucher of Lewiston argued in a radio address on Saint-Jean-Baptiste (Saint John the Baptist) Day that Franco-Americans did not have to give up their language, traditions, or faith to be good citizens of the United States. Boucher encouraged Franco-Americans to contribute to the war effort in whatever capacity they could. "And when we will have won the war, we will be glad to write in the pages of the history of the French race in America," proclaimed Boucher, "the glorious military feats of our Franco-Americans which will once again prove to our enemies that we can be as patriotic as anyone, all the while conserving our faith and our language." Franco-Americans enthusiastically supported the war effort. In the United States, there was no conscription crisis dividing English and French speakers as there was in Canada beginning in 1944.[11] In the 1940s, good citizenship remained an important component of Franco-American identity, and it demanded supporting U.S. objectives in the world conflict.

Besides serving in the armed forces, Lewiston Franco-Americans contributed financially to the war effort. In 1943, at the invitation of Treasury Secretary Edward B. Hitchcock, Franco-Americans from throughout New England organized a campaign to purchase war bonds, hoping to raise six million dollars to finance three Liberty ships to be named after Franco-Americans. Not coincidentally, the ten-week campaign began and ended on days important to the identity of Franco-Americans: it started on the feast day of Saint-Jean-Baptiste, June 24, and concluded on Labor Day, September 6. In all, New England's Franco-Americans raised over $12,000,000, double their original goal; Lewiston alone raised more than a half-million dollars. In December, *Le Messager* proudly informed readers that the U.S. government had accepted the six names Franco-Americans had proposed for the ships their funds would finance. At the same time, the jubilant French-language newspaper announced on its front page in big bold letters that Maine's cargo ship would carry the name of the late Jean-Baptiste Couture, owner of *Le Messager* for a half-century, who had died in April. The federal government moved too slowly, however. By February 1945, Liberty ships carried the names of clergymen Joseph-A. Chevalier of New Hampshire and Charles Dauray of Rhode Island, journalist Ferdinand Gagnon of Massachusetts, and politician Aram J. Pothier of Rhode Island—but not Couture's. On February 27, *Le Messager* complained that none of the twelve ships the United States had recently launched, eight of which had been built at the shipyard in South Portland, Maine, carried a Franco-American name. The implication, of course, was that Franco-Americans of Maine still did not have a ship named after one of their own. "No one regrets having contributed the $2,000,000 for the war bonds, but we demand [equally] for ourselves what we gave to others! No more, and NO LESS!" *Le Messager* insisted. Lewiston Mayor Jean-Charles Boucher, who had coordinated the successful bond drive in Maine, and Franco-American Waterville resident Harold Dubord, a member of the Democratic National Committee, pressed the federal government on this matter.[12] But the war ended before the U.S. government could honor its pledge to Maine Franco-Americans. This World War II episode reveals persistent efforts by Lewiston's French speakers to carve a place for themselves in the United States. Like francophones from throughout New England, they used the campaign to finance Liberty ships as a means to assert their ethnic identity in their country of adoption. Franco-Americans of Lewiston thus continued in the 1940s to negotiate the terms of their participation in U.S. society.

One of the terms they could not insist upon, of course, was the use of French by Franco-American soldiers. Reports in *Le Messager* nonetheless demonstrate that it kept an ear to the French-language expression of servicemen. Prior to U.S. entry into World War II, *Le Messager* reported news from Reverend Leonard LeClair, a Lewiston native and chaplain of Maine's 103rd infantry, stationed at Camp Blanding, Florida. While Franco-Americans at the camp used English to learn combat techniques and to speak to nonfrancophone soldiers, LeClair indicated that they prayed and confessed in French.[13]

If this experience was common among Franco-American servicemen, it would suggest that the adage *La langue est la gardienne de la foi* (Language is the guardian of the faith) continued to have meaning. But it may have been during the Second World War that Franco-American soldiers first recognized the fallacy of that much-repeated saying. During an interview in 1977, World War II veteran Clem Bernier dismissed the connection between language and faith, contending that "God listened just as well in English as he [*sic*] did in French."[14] If not during World War II, Bernier surely acquired this opinion during the postwar years, when English increasingly became the dominant language in Lewiston.

During World War II, *Le Messager* commented on the use of French by servicemen in France. It derided in October 1944 the non-Franco-Americans who spoke so-called "Parisian French" in wartime France. "English-speaking Americans who pride themselves for having learned a little French in school or in college like to shout from rooftops that they have learned a French very different from that which Franco-Americans speak," stated *Le Messager*. "And they deduce from this fact that we speak only gibberish." Based upon letters Lewiston parents had received from their sons, *Le Messager* delighted in informing readers that French military officers better understood the French of Franco-Americans than that of other Americans.[15] Franco-Americans, this account reveals, continued to see themselves as an ethnic group in opposition to Yankees. As tensions over language continued to divide the two ethnicities in the 1940s, *Le Messager* sought to prove that the French spoken by Franco-Americans was not inferior to "Parisian French." Its comments reflected ongoing efforts to preserve the mother tongue of Lewiston's Franco-American community at mid-century.

Issues of ethnic retention preoccupied Franco-American elites from the 1940s through the 1960s. They worried particularly about the declining use of French among younger generations of Franco-Americans for whom English became the dominant language. They engaged in what historian Yves Roby has called a "cult of remembrance" in their efforts to instill ethnic pride.[16]

One of these efforts was le Festival de la Bonne Chanson (the Festival of the Good Song), inspired by the Congrès de la Langue Française (Congress of the French Language), held in Québec City in 1937. Lewiston Mayor Donat Lévesque, Pastor Mannès Marchand of Saint-Pierre (Saint Peter), Pastor Edouard Nadeau of Sainte-Croix (Holy Cross), state legislator Jean-Charles Boucher, as well as local doctors and attorneys, attended the congress, which urged the adoption of the songbook *La Bonne Chanson*, by Reverend Charles-Emile Gadbois of the Séminaire de Saint-Hyacinthe. When Gadbois toured New England's Franco-American cities in 1939 to promote his work, he called upon les Vigilants of Lewiston. This Franco-American society subsequently organized North America's first Festival de la Bonne Chanson in 1940, attended by over five thousand francophones, including Gadbois, representatives of the Québec societies Saint-Jean-Baptiste and le Comité Permanent de la Survivance Française en Amérique (the Permanent Committee of French Survival in America), as well as by officials of New England's largest Franco-American societies, l'Union Saint-Jean-Baptiste d'Amérique (the Saint John the Baptist Union of America, based in Woonsocket, Rhode Island) and l'Association Canado-Américaine (the Canado-American Association, based in Manchester, New Hampshire). At the Lewiston armory, decorated in the colors of the United States, France, and Canada, the audience sang "The Star-Spangled Banner" and "O Canada," and students from the local Franco-American parochial schools competed against each other in their interpretation of songs from Gadbois's publication. This event, *Le Messager* asserted, revealed a population that still wished "to live in French while associating with what is best in its country of adoption, the United States."[17]

Lewiston delayed sponsorship of another Festival de la Bonne Chanson until 1946 because of U.S. entry into World War II. Organized again by les Vigilants, the 1946 festival entertained an audience of over four thousand people. Students from Franco-American schools in Lewiston, Auburn, and Brunswick opened the event by singing the national anthems of the United States and Canada. Boys taught by les Soeurs Grises (Grey Nuns) of Healy Asylum won first prize: $150 in cash and a trip to Montréal to take part in the city's Saint-Jean-Baptiste Day celebration. When the boys returned from Montréal, the sisters publicly thanked les Vigilants and expressed their hope that the boys from their orphanage "will be in the future a little more French Canadian and no less good American citizens" as a result of the trip.[18] The sisters understood the goal of the festival: the continued definition of *survivance* (ethnic preservation) and civic participation as intertwined goals.

Comments such as those by les Soeurs Grises reveal that Franco-American discourse in the 1940s continued to emphasize the importance of being good citizens of the United States. During this decade, naturalizing and contributing to the war effort were the principal ways by which Franco-Americans could demonstrate good citizenship. The French language and French-Canadian culture also remained integral to Franco-American identity during this decade, something elites promoted by twice organizing le Festival de la Bonne Chanson. Franco-American discourse surrounding the 1940 and 1946 festivals conveyed the message that retaining French-Canadian ethnicity took nothing away from U.S. citizenship; ethnic identification enhanced the qualities of Franco-American citizens of the United States. Better Franco-Americans would be better Americans.

Various Franco-American institutions remained active following the Second World War. The snowshoe clubs, for example, continued to participate in international conventions in Canada and the United States—conventions that offered francophones on both sides of the border the opportunity for ongoing contact. Judging from the bylaws of le Montagnard (the Mountaineer), the snowshoe clubs continued to function as ethnic organizations. Le

Montagnard's 1957 bylaws, for instance, spelled out the ethnic qualification for membership: "To be French Canadian or Franco-American or to be recognized as such."[19] While delimiting membership, this statement implicitly acknowledged that ethnic identity could be socially constructed and that ethnic boundaries were permeable.

Associated with the snowshoe clubs, the holiday collection, *la Guignolée*, last took place in Lewiston in 1940. This ethnic tradition appears to have been a casualty of World War II. In fact, in 1943, *Le Messager* announced that there would (again) be no *Guignolée* at Saint-Pierre Parish on account of the war, because many parishioners were working away from the city in shipyards.[20] Although the snowshoe clubs remained active after the war, there is no evidence that they resumed *la Guignolée*.

While the Second World War seems to have curtailed at least one French-Canadian tradition, it did not prevent or discourage the founding of additional ethnic institutions in Lewiston. In 1944, funeral director Napoleon Pinette established the Aroostook Social Club for Lewiston area residents like himself who had migrated from Maine's northernmost county. In its first year, the club had over one hundred members.[21]

The presence of the Aroostook Social Club in Lewiston reveals two major points. First, not only Acadians from New Brunswick but also Acadians from northern Maine had migrated to Franco-American Lewiston. Second, the club appears to have blended into the Franco-American fabric of Lewiston while introducing some Acadian elements. To illustrate, *Le Messager* indicated in February 1950 that the club had "a tradition quite Franco-American," suggesting that the newspaper's definition of Franco-American at mid-century was elastic enough to include Acadians. In that same month, the Acme Aroostook Club, as the association came to be called, organized a large Mardi Gras party, perhaps Lewiston's first, and at least two other Franco-American societies organized Mardi Gras parties that month. Providing further evidence of the inclusion of Acadian themes in Franco-American Lewiston, les Dames de Sainte-Anne (the Ladies of Saint Anne) of Saint-Pierre Parish entered into the 1957 Saint-Jean-Baptiste Day parade the allegorical chariot "Evangeline and her father, episode of Acadian history."[22]

Perhaps a more inclusive definition of "Franco-American" at mid-century explains why the keynote speakers on Saint-Jean-Baptiste Day in 1940 and

1955 were New Brunswick Acadians. After all, Acadians since the colonial era had developed an identity distinct from that of the francophones who had settled Québec, for both geography and history had separated them. Moreover, Saint-Jean-Baptiste Day was not an Acadian holiday: from the 1880s, Acadians had their own patron saint and feast day. Although French-Canadian and Acadian descendants had different histories, their immigration to Lewiston led at mid-century to the appropriation of themes and traditions from the other group and to a broadening of "Franco-American" identity in the Spindle City. This may have represented a step in the Americanization of these francophones. Dino Cinel has argued, for example, that Italian immigrants in San Francisco broadened regional identities from their pre-migration experiences to form a national identity in the United States prior to their Americanization.[23] Franco-Americans similarly appeared to enlarge their identity at mid-century.

During this period, elites founded additional local clubs and regional associations to preserve ethnic traditions. In 1943, Mrs. Eugène Langelier established la Survivance Française in Lewiston as a woman's subcommittee of the Comité de la Survivance Française de Québec (Committee of French Survival of Québec) to preserve the Roman Catholic faith and the French language. The club organized lectures, conferences, and social activities for its members. In 1947, prominent Franco-American men created at a Boston meeting le Comité d'Orientation Franco-Américaine (the Franco-American Orientation Committee) to promote the preservation of French Catholic lifeways. The men's organization founded at its second congress, held in Lewiston in 1951, la Fédération Féminine Franco-Américaine (the Federation of Franco-American Women). La Fédération sought to bring together existing associations of Franco-American women from the northeastern United States, and its formation served to acknowledge the role they had to play in *la survivance*. In addition to sponsoring public-speaking contests among students of Franco-American parochial schools, the women's association organized concerts, art exhibits, and festivals—all to promote French language and culture in the postwar era.[24]

When *Le Messager* learned in 1946 that Franco-Americans of Manchester, New Hampshire, planned to hold their own Festival de la Bonne Chanson, the newspaper crowed that Lewiston had started a movement among New England francophones. But Lewiston's 1946 festival was the last musical competition of record between students of the city's Franco-American parochial schools. There were other French-language competitions, however. Franco-American societies continued to sponsor essay contests in French on such topics as "the Franco-American press." Beginning around 1949, and continuing through the late 1960s, Lewiston's French-language societies also organized French spelling bees, "in the goal of encouraging youth from the parish schools to learn their French well," indicated *Le Messager* in 1961. As the French spelling contests grew, Lewiston students competed against youth from other Franco-American schools in Maine. Organized by la Fédération Féminine Franco-Américaine, French public-speaking competitions in the 1950s and 1960s also pitted Lewiston students against those from other schools in Maine. State winners competed in a regional contest against Franco-American students from throughout New England. In 1953, the first year the women's society organized the contest, eighth-grade students spoke on "The Parish," and high school students on "A historic figure [of] French America." Local winners from Saint-Pierre and Sainte-Croix schools took first and second prizes in 1959 for their speeches on Franco-American newspaperman Ferdinand Gagnon, and French explorer and fur trader La Vérendrye.[25] Designed to encourage Franco-American youth to develop and retain their French-language skills, these oral and written contests represented an active response on the part of elites to the declining use of French by young Franco-Americans in the postwar era.

Lewiston's Franco-American community was in transition after World War II. The immigration restrictions the United States imposed upon Canadians in 1930 ended the mass migration of francophones to Lewiston and to other industrial centers of the northeastern United States. With each successive decade, the proportion of Canadian-born Franco-Americans declined; as the ratio of U.S.-born Franco-Americans increased in Lewiston, the pace of their Americanization quickened. In particular, the francophone community vigorously pursued anglicization, and its youth became unilingual English speakers. The pressure towards English was so strong in 1949 that the Dominican Sisters called it the "invasion of English." Previously intertwined, the goals of ethnic preservation and acculturation unraveled at mid-century, such that each became a divergent aim. While discrimination against Franco-Americans contributed to reorienting the process of acculturation, by the 1950s and 1960s, forces internal to the community increasingly promoted acculturation over ethnic retention. Franco-Americans more often married non-Franco-Americans, they increasingly read English-language newspapers and canceled their subscriptions to *Le Messager*, and they more frequently intermixed with anglophones in secular and religious associations. At mid-century, the identity of French-Canadian descendants broadened: they evolved from Franco-American to American. If what we call "assimilation" is the last stage of the process of acculturation, and if "assimilation" represents the loss of group identity, it would appear that Franco-Americans at mid-century were in fact moving from acculturation to "assimilation" in U.S. society.[26]

Le Messager worried about this decline in ethnic identity. It indicated in March 1951: "Today, in many homes, Franco-American life has nothing Franco-American [in it]." In a March 1950 editorial, *Le Messager* expressed its belief that more and more Franco-American families felt that anglicization served as an avenue to social mobility: "We unfortunately believe that we enhance ourselves by cultivating only the English language." While acknowledging the value of learning to read, write, and speak English, the newspaper contended: "A nationality that loses its language degrades itself." It appeared to acknowledge the perception of inferiority on the part of some francophones when it suggested in 1951 that speaking French caused embarrassment, resulting in the language being spoken less and less often.[27]

The French-language newspaper deplored the exclusive use of English among francophones. In March 1952, *Le Messager* took la Survivance Française to task for hosting a fashion show in English at l'Hospice Marcotte (Marcotte Home). The program chair was a French-speaking Franco-American woman, the audience consisted of women "all French-speaking," and the commentator served as director of a French radio program. Yet, except for the opening remarks, the French-language society conducted the entire program in English, *Le Messager* complained, and it underscored the irony of this action by a society with *survivance française* as its name.[28]

During the 1950s and 1960s, forces within the Franco-American community promoted a more rapid pace of anglicization than in past decades. To counter the momentum towards the exclusive use of English, *Le Messager* extolled the advantages of bilingualism at every opportunity. Often, it encouraged parents to continue speaking French to their children at home. In August 1954, it editorialized: "Before it is too late parents should make a rigorous effort to speak French in the home, to their children and to demand of them that they speak without shame, without fear, without timidity."[29]

It was a theme often expressed at Saint-Jean-Baptiste Day celebrations. In 1956, Sacré-Coeur (Sacred Heart) Parish of Auburn offered the Saint-Jean-Baptiste Day mass, and Pastor Théodore Bouthot "exhorted parents to speak and to have their children speak French within the family." At the evening banquet, Bouthot spoke, as had so many Saint-Jean-Baptiste Day orators before him, of preserving the French language, Catholic faith, and French-Canadian traditions. Like him, Pastor Wilfrid Ouellette of Auburn's Saint-Louis Parish argued on Saint-Jean-Baptiste Day in 1959 that a significant problem for *survivance* was that too many Franco-American children no longer heard the French language spoken in their homes. Romeo Boisvert, state senator from Lewiston and president of *Le Messager*, asked those who attended the Saint-Jean-Baptiste Day banquet in 1961 to help youth to develop their French-language skills through reading and conversation.[30]

During the 1963 Saint-Jean-Baptiste Day celebration, Pinette Funeral Home president Raoul Pinette argued that in the aftermath of World War II, a time of great scientific progress, Franco-Americans were losing their language and their culture. Technological advances had brought radios, phonographs, and televisions into the homes of Franco-Americans. French-Canadian descendants pointed particularly to the role of television in effecting the changeover from French to English in Franco-American communities like Lewiston. "Television has done a lot for the [French] language being extinct here, I think," opined Cecile Lebel. Children in the Lewiston community lost the ability to speak French as a result of watching television, offered Cecile Boisvert. She added: "I found that that so changed the families." In 1964, Norman Fournier underscored this point: "The influence of television, in the last 10 years, has done perhaps more to Americanize the French Canadians than anything else the pro-assimilationist [*sic*] have tried in the past." He continued: "To a large extent, television has killed French Canadian [*sic*] culture in such centers as Biddeford and Lewiston," because it supplanted Franco-American plays and musical productions as family entertainment. Additionally, television gave Franco-Americans greater exposure to the English language and to different lifestyles. One effect of technological progress, Pinette pointed out in his Saint-Jean-Baptiste Day speech, was that children attending Franco-American schools in 1963 spoke English in the courtyards, quite unlike what they had done twenty and forty years previously.[31]

Lewiston's Franco-American schools anglicized at mid-century. As one marker of that anglicization, beginning in the 1950s Franco-American youth competed in English against students from the Irish parochial schools, and sometimes against students from the public schools, in speech contests, essay competitions, and spelling bees. Participation by Franco-American parochial-school students in these English-language contests signified that Lewiston's francophone youth had acquired the English-language skills with which to compete. Contributing in no small measure to this development, Lewiston's Franco-American schools anglicized their curricula. It seems likely that parents who had received bilingual training in the schools pushed for this change. So quietly did the changeover take place in the schools that it evoked no comment from *Le Messager.* By the 1950s and 1960s, students even received religious instruction in English; only their French-language course was not offered in English.[32]

The anglicization of Lewiston's second and third generations in part explains why attendance at Québec's *collèges classiques* (classical schools) dropped markedly after the 1940s. Enrollments at the Collège de Saint-Hyacinthe and the Séminaire Saint-Charles Borromée totaled 140 in the 1940s, remaining at essentially the same level as in the 1930s, but in the 1950s enrollments at the two *collèges* dropped dramatically to forty-one. If enrollments by Lewiston students paralleled those of other New England Franco-Americans, they dropped even further during the first half of the 1960s, when the provincial government took control of Québec's educational institutions from the Roman Catholic Church.[33] The declining enrollments of Franco-Americans at the Québec *collèges* at mid-century provided evidence of their decreasing connection with Canada.

One reason for this loss of connection was that Lewiston Franco-Americans established their own high school in 1941. Concerned about the rapid anglicization of Saint-Pierre Parish, the consequent weaknesses in the oral and written French-language skills of its youth, and the lack of opportunity for French-language instruction after grammar school, Dominican pastor Hervé Drouin founded a Franco-American high school in his parish. Ironically, his efforts at ethnic preservation encouraged a loss of connection with Québec. Building a high school, Drouin argued, would help ensure a francophone elite in Lewiston: "To let these children sink into these American high schools is to deny ourselves of a French elite capable of taking leadership roles in our civic life." Ethnic tensions in the Catholic Church also motivated the pastor, who wrote: "We maintain that without a secondary educational institution for our boys we are defeated and we will have worked for many years to prepare the way for Irish pastors." Drouin also wanted to encourage more Franco-American youth to stay in school. He told an interviewer in 1985 that when he had arrived in Lewiston in 1940, he had found that "Franco-American kids would finish eighth grade and be pushed into the mills to work." Although organized primarily for students from Saint-Pierre Parish, Saint-Dominique High School accepted students from other parishes, opening one grade in the fall of 1941 and adding one each year until it became a four-year high school. State law since World War I had required the provision of secondary-level instruction in English, so the Brothers of the Sacred Heart who staffed the school taught all classes except religion and French in the English language. The Lewiston community nonetheless viewed Saint-Dominique as a Franco-American school. For instance, a woman religious who taught at the Irish grammar school of Saint Patrick indicated in the 1940s that Saint-Dominique did not meet the needs of all Catholic youth, because of the French courses and because instructors spoke with a French accent when teaching in the English language. In 1946, the Dominican Sisters, who had long provided Franco-American girls with two years of instruction beyond the eighth grade in their *cours supérieur* (upper course), began offering a four-year program for them as part of Saint-Dominique High School. Judging from the surnames of male and female graduates, Franco-Americans made up over 90 percent of Saint-Dominique's student body in each decade from the 1940s through the 1960s.[34]

Most of Lewiston's Franco-American youth did not attend Saint-Dominique, however. They attended Lewiston High School. Saint-Dominique was small, it charged tuition, and parents preferred to send their children to Lewiston High School for the English-language training they received there. There was little opportunity to speak French at the public high school. According to Geneva Kirk, who began teaching at Lewiston High in 1945, teachers had instructions to stop francophone youth from conversing in

French between classes or during recess.[35] By sending their children to Lewiston's public high school, Franco-American parents contributed to the anglicization of the city's francophone youth.

Support from unexpected sources did not stem the tide of anglicization and a loosening of ethnic identification. Surprisingly enough, Maine's Irish bishop promoted the French language during the Cold War. When Bishop Daniel Feeney addressed men and women religious of the Portland diocese at their annual convention of educators in 1956, he spoke in English, Latin, and French. Moreover, "Monsignor encourages our bilingual cities to conserve in this way the culture so laudable of English and French," recorded the Ursuline Sisters of Lewiston. The following year, Feeney promoted bilingualism in English and French in a Waterville, Maine, speech to the regional convention of la Société l'Assomption (the Assumption Society, an Acadian mutual-aid association with headquarters in New Brunswick). Attendees enthusiastically applauded his remarks.[36] Fragmentary as it is, the above evidence on the prelate's support for bilingualism suggests that Franco-Americans of Maine had maintained the gains they had won earlier in the century during their conflicts with other Irish bishops. If ethnic disputes between the bishops and Lewiston's Franco-Americans occurred at mid-century, the sources hid them well.[37]

The U.S. government also supported French-language acquisition at mid-century. Concerned about the threat of Communism after World War II, the United States increasingly competed against the Soviet Union in military and scientific endeavors during the Cold War. Following the 1957 launching of the satellite Sputnik by the Soviets, Congress passed the National Defense Education Act (NDEA) of 1958, which, among other measures, increased support for education and promoted the acquisition of foreign languages.[38] This led to a profusion of committees and workshops on the French language. After attending a workshop on modern French teaching in 1965, les Soeurs de la Présentation de Marie (the Sisters of the Presentation of Mary) noted in their chronicle: "In her final speech, the president of the meeting encouraged all the French teachers to hold firm in their devotion to the cause of speaking French. Despite the numerous difficulties to overcome there is still hope for success."[39] The tide had changed in Lewiston well before the mid-1960s, however. The validation of the French language through federal initiatives during the Cold War represented an effort that was too little and too late for Lewiston's francophone community. Its identity at mid-century was evolving rapidly, if quietly, from Franco-American to American.

Among younger generations, Franco-American identity no longer required an attachment to the French language or to French-Canadian traditions. Against the redefinition taking place at mid-century, *Le Messager* in 1954 publicized five elements it considered essential to Franco-American identity:

> A FRANCO-AMERICAN is a person of French or French-Canadian descent, born in the United States, or in Canada or in France, [who] subsequently came to live in America.
>
> A FRANCO-AMERICAN, truly to be one and to honor this title, must be proud of his parents, proud of himself, proud of his ancestors and of the history of the race in which he is born.
>
> A FRANCO-AMERICAN does not truly have the right to this title of honor unless he is born of Catholic parents, he is himself a proven Catholic, he attends his national Catholic parish church and he guides his children in the ways of the [Roman Catholic] Church.
>
> A FRANCO-AMERICAN is not ashamed to speak French on each occasion that presents itself, publicly or other[wise], above all in the family home and particularly in the meetings of our religious, parish, patriotic and civic associations.
>
> A FRENCH NAME does not suffice to say that someone is a Franco-American. It takes more than that! One is not Franco-American only when it helps the pocketbook or [one's] pride![40]

This article may or may not have originated in the editorial offices of *Le Messager*; by publishing it without attribution or disclaimer, the newspaper expressed these sentiments as its own. Through this article, *Le Messager* appeared to emphasize the distinction between "being" and "feeling" Franco-American.[41] For *Le Messager*, "feeling" Franco-American was insufficient to warrant wearing the ethnic label; ethnic identity depended upon active measures. The newspaper apparently had not felt it necessary to make such a declaration in earlier decades. By the middle of the twentieth century, *Le Messager*'s definition of Franco-American did not seem to prevail in the Lewiston community.

The growing membership of Lewiston Franco-Americans in the city's Irish Catholic parishes reveals one dimension of the changing identity of the community at mid-century. In 1960, husbands and wives who both had non-French names headed less than two-fifths (38.6 percent) of the 176 families that baptized their children at Saint Joseph Parish in that year; three-fifths (60.8 percent) of the children baptized at Saint Joseph in 1960 had a father, mother, or both parents who were Franco-American. The changing composition of Saint Joseph Parish surprised even the Irish pastor. After reading the marriage banns at Sunday mass around 1957, Reverend James F. Savage remarked that all names were French. "Sometimes, I wonder what parish I'm in!" he exclaimed.[42]

Ethnic intermixing also took place at Saint Patrick Parish. Of the 104 families baptizing children at Saint Patrick's in 1960, only 27.9 percent were headed by parents who both had non-French names. Thus, nearly three-fourths (72.0 percent) of the families baptizing children at Saint Patrick Parish in 1960 had one or both heads who were Franco-American.[43]

The large Franco-American membership of Lewiston's Irish parishes in 1960 highlights several points. First, it reveals a measure of intermarriage between Franco-American and other (notably Irish) Catholics. Second, more often than Franco-American men, Franco-American women at both parishes accepted spouses from outside of their ethnic group, perhaps as an avenue to social mobility. Third, that one-sixth to one-fifth of the families of each parish had heads who were both of French-Canadian descent reveals the increasing anglicization of members of the Franco-American community and suggests, perhaps, a desire for social mobility that anglicization and membership in an English-speaking parish conferred.

While a significant degree of endogamy continued among Franco-Americans, ethnic intermarriage increasingly took place in Lewiston at mid-century. Of the 312 marriages involving Franco-Americans recorded at the Office of the Lewiston City Clerk in 1960, over two-fifths (42.3 percent)—more than double the proportion from 1920—were between a Franco-American and a non-Franco-American.[44] In slightly more than half (51.5 percent) of these mixed marriages, Franco-American brides took non-Franco-American grooms. While revealing a significant measure of ethnic intermixing since 1920, the marriage records underscore the fact that Lewiston Franco-Americans at mid-century continued to choose Franco-American spouses a majority of the time. Lewiston's demography did not discourage this practice. Indeed, approximately two-thirds of Lewiston's residents were Franco-American in 1960: 68.7 percent of the men and 65.9 percent of the women listed in the city directory had French surnames.[45] That so many exogamous marriages took place in 1960 testifies to the declining ethnic identity of the Franco-American community at mid-century. It also reveals the agency of Franco-Americans in integrating further into the larger community.

The automobile and Vatican II facilitated additional integration. The automobile made possible a postwar migration of young Franco-American families from Petit Canada (Little Canada) and other parts of downtown Lewiston to the Irish and Yankee suburbs of Sainte-Famille (Holy Family) and Sainte-Croix, which in turn encouraged the intermixing of Franco-Americans with other Lewiston residents. In addition, the Second Vatican Council, which met from 1962 to 1965, encouraged better relations between Catholics and Protestants and led to greater intermixing between the two groups.[46]

One response to the intermixing of Franco-Americans with non-Catholic anglophones appears to have been the 1958 establishment of the Lewiston-Auburn Richelieu Club, named and modeled after the organization founded in 1944 by Franco-Ontarians in Ottawa. Richelieu clubs had sprung up in the provinces of Ontario, Québec, and New Brunswick before crossing the border to the United States in 1955, when Manchester, New Hampshire, organized its own club. Like the founding of the organization in Ottawa, the establishment of the Lewiston Richelieu Club probably represented a reaction on the part of elites to the growing practice of French-Canadian descendants of joining anglophone secular associations, such as the Kiwanis, Rotary, and Lions service clubs. In 1949, Bates College student Faith Seiple observed that Franco-Americans made up 16 percent of the membership of the Lewiston-Auburn Kiwanis, 28 percent of the Rotary Club, and 37 percent of the Lions Club. Unlike them, Richelieu organizations had an explicitly Christian character, and their regulations stipulated that "the official language of the clubs is the French language."[47] Lewiston's Richelieu Club thus served in the late 1950s to resist the tide toward assimilation.

While ethnic voting characterized local political contests at mid-century, it declined in the 1960s. Franco-Americans won the mayoral contest each year from 1940 until 1970 in a nonpartisan election, as prescribed by the 1939 city charter. Franco-Americans also controlled the City Council until 1964. In that year, when non-Franco-Americans won four of the seven seats on the Board of Aldermen, the *Portland Sunday Telegram* argued that it was the first time in four decades that Franco-Americans would not dominate the City Council. Observers cited by the *Telegram* contended that Lewiston voters were finally exercising independent political judgment and were not voting strictly on the basis of ethnic background. According to one unidentified source, the Franco-American Lewiston voter was "rebelling against the idea that only Franco-Americans should rule here." "The caliber of some of the Franco-Americans elected here in recent years proves the fallacy of such a policy," the person added. The 1964 election results did not mark a temporary change, for non-French-surnamed aldermen won a majority of seats on the City Council in additional elections in the 1960s.[48] As they evolved from Franco-American to American, French-Canadian descendants of Lewiston began to look beyond ethnic boundaries when selecting some of their local government leadership.

Like ethnic politics, ethnic celebrations declined in Lewiston. By the mid-1950s, Saint-Jean-Baptiste Day celebrations attracted few youth, and the programs became smaller with each passing year. A lackluster parade in 1966 appears to have been the last public demonstration of Saint-Jean-Baptiste Day in Lewiston. By 1969, a mass and banquet were the only means by which Lewiston Franco-Americans celebrated the feast day of French Canadians.[49]

Lewiston's Franco-American parochial schools also declined. Gerard Brault points to four reasons for this development throughout New England in the 1960s and 1970s: high costs due to inflation, a drop in the number of women religious, decreasing birthrates following the postwar baby boom, and declining Catholicism. The Lewiston experience suggests a fifth reason: the anglicization of—or the desire to anglicize—Franco-American youth, whose parents increasingly sent them to the public schools. To some extent, by teaching in English, the men and women religious of Lewiston's Franco-American schools had worked themselves out of their jobs. In 1968, the Dominican Sisters withdrew from Lewiston's Saint-Pierre and Saint-Dominique (Saint Dominic) schools. While those schools remained open, Sainte-Marie (Saint Mary) parochial school closed when the Ursuline Sisters withdrew in the same year. In April 1969, the school board of Sainte-Famille estimated that only between 35 and 40 percent of the parish children of school age attended their parochial school.[50]

In 1964, Sainte-Famille led Lewiston's Franco-American churches in the introduction of English masses. While Petit Canada's Sainte-Marie Church still celebrated all of its masses in French in 1967, Sainte-Famille offered two weekend masses in English, and Saint-Pierre and Sainte-Croix each introduced one English mass in that year. At Saint-Pierre, Canadian-born Pastor Louis-Philippe Fiset had to acknowledge cultural realities. Unable to change the tide, he informed his provincial in Québec in March 1967 that Saint-Pierre had to offer bilingual services to keep anglicizing youth in the parish: "We can do nothing [to stop] this anglicizing evolution." In a letter to parishioners in June, Fiset argued that Saint-Pierre's survival depended upon introducing English masses; the parish was losing families to the Irish parishes because its youth functioned in English, he contended. Eighty-six percent of the parishioners surveyed a few years back had supported the introduction of at least one mass in English, Fiset indicated, before concluding: "We are at a crossroads and we no longer have a choice." In late September, before introducing one weekly mass in English, Fiset pointed out that Franco-American youth could not gain much from attending mass if they did not understand French, and he emphasized that the Second Vatican Council had promoted the idea of communicating in relevant languages. Maine's Catholic churches had begun celebrating parts of baptism, marriage, and funeral ceremonies in vernacular languages in the mid-1950s, but only after Vatican II did the change from Latin to vernacular languages accelerate.[51]

At Sainte-Croix, the parish council (a byproduct of Vatican II) voted to start offering an English mass only in November 1967. That decision must have pained Reverend Félix Martin, a native of the Aroostook county town of Fort Kent who had attended *collège classique* and seminary in Québec, and who had served as pastor of Sainte-Croix since 1939. Newspaper accounts from the 1950s portray Martin as a vigorous defender of the French language and culture. On Saint-Jean-Baptiste Day in 1951, Martin argued the need to continue speaking and reading French in order to preserve the language. He contended that mixed marriages threatened cultural survival: "In these marriages, the one who gives in is not the English-speaking spouse but the French-speaking one." In 1953, Martin proudly indicated that Sainte-Croix students still received a half-day of French instruction and not a half-hour, and that children and women religious still spoke French in the schoolyard. At the 1958 Saint-Jean-Baptiste Day celebration, which Sainte-Croix hosted, Martin spoke of the need to remain French. Martin must have supported only reluctantly the parish council decision to introduce an English mass at Sainte-Croix in 1967. Still under the leadership of Martin, Sainte-Croix in October 1969 was the sole Franco-American parish in Lewiston to celebrate only one weekend mass in English; in that year, Saint-Pierre and Sainte-Marie parishes each offered two weekend masses in English, while Sainte-Famille offered three.[52]

More than simply reflecting existing cultural realities, Sainte-Famille had facilitated the anglicization of the parish community since 1926, when les Soeurs de Saint-Joseph de Lyons (the Sisters of Saint Joseph of Lyons) began teaching in the parochial school and offering only one hour of instruction in French each day. The sisters continued promoting English at mid-century. Third-generation French-Canadian descendant Marc Boisvert spoke no English when he entered first grade at Sainte-Famille in the mid-1950s; consequently, the sisters asked his parents to purchase a television set to help him learn the language, and they did. As late as the mid-1960s, les Soeurs de Saint-Joseph asked the parents of francophone children to speak English at home so that their offspring could develop a facility in English. When Reverend Josaphat P. Sevigny, born in Québec but raised and educated in the United States, became the second pastor of Sainte-Famille in 1961, the parish had for decades led Lewiston's Franco-American community in the promotion of English. Following the introduction of English masses under Sevigny's stewardship, Irish families joined Sainte-Famille, which promoted ethnic intermixing in the parish community.[53] At mid-century, not just Sainte-Famille, but all of Lewiston's Franco-American community was in transition. Sainte-Famille simply moved at a faster pace than the other parishes of the Spindle City.

Ironically, as Québec premier Jean Lesage ushered in the Quiet Revolution in 1960 to modernize provincial institutions, strengthen the economy, and improve the position of francophones—measures to assert the French identity of Québec—Franco-American communities like Lewiston were losing their French identity. As the brother-in-law of Dominican pastor

Alexandre DesRochers of Saint-Pierre, Lesage visited Lewiston with his family in 1960.[54] But there is no record that he spoke to the city's residents about changes he envisioned for Québec at that time.

Le Messager, in fact, did not follow the progression of Québec's Quiet Revolution. Possibly, *Le Messager*'s struggles to stay alive preoccupied it to such an extent that it looked inward and, for that reason, offered no coverage of Québec's evolution in the 1960s. More likely, Franco-Americans and French Canadians had so far diverged that the newspaper felt its readers were not interested. *Le Messager* probably accepted the reality that Lewiston was losing its connection with Canada. Franco-Americans were making fewer trips than in the past to Québec, they seldom had speakers from Québec presenting the keynote address at the annual Saint-Jean-Baptiste Day banquet, and they opted to educate their children locally. As the proportion of first-generation French-Canadian descendants declined, and as Franco-Americans increasingly chose to intermix with non-francophones in the host society, they less often looked to Canada than they had in the past. At the same time, they less often looked at their local French-language newspaper.

At mid-century, the French-language newspaper appeared to be an anachronism, and it struggled for its life. In the 1930s, the decade when *Le Messager* became a daily publication, it had a circulation of between 9,000 and 10,000 newspapers; Franco-American identity in Lewiston appeared to have been the most intense during this period. But *Le Messager*'s circulation dropped sharply to 5,300 by 1940, and it declined more gradually to 4,760 by 1951, the year that a member of the Couture family sold the newspaper to a group of one hundred stockholders. *Le Messager* struggled financially during the 1950s, changing hands in November 1954, and ending daily production to become a weekly newspaper in September 1955. Its subscriptions declined because third-generation Franco-Americans preferred to read the *Lewiston Evening Journal* or the *Lewiston Daily Sun*, noted a contemporary. By 1958, *Le Messager* had a circulation of 3,200. In February, it resumed twice-weekly publication, but that lasted only until November 1962, when it had to revert to weekly publication to cut costs.[55]

During the 1960s, *Le Messager* tried everything it could to survive. While in the past students had written columns in French for the newspaper, during 1961 they appeared in English and French, and students from both parochial and public schools submitted articles for publication. Although the bilingual page "The Student Reporter/La Voix de l'Étudiant" appeared only during calendar year 1961, its appearance signified *Le Messager*'s resignation to the fact that Lewiston youth no longer possessed the French-language skills of years past. The bilingual section represented an effort on the part of the newspaper to capture the interest of the community's youth. But it did not succeed. Still eking out issues in 1966, *Le Messager* became *Le Nouveau Messager* (*The New Messenger*) on August 25, when two of the five columns on its front page carried local news in English. Explained the editor: "We will direct our efforts to provide you with a French newspaper sprinkled a bit with English to permit [access to] certain family members who would have difficulty reading French fluently." The newspaper's management distributed free copies of the refashioned newspaper after Sunday masses in order to increase subscriptions, but it attracted few new customers. *Le Nouveau Messager* complained in September that local youth appeared uninterested in retaining the French language or culture, even at a time when the rest of the nation exhibited growing interest in bilingualism. It asked point blank in the September 22nd issue: "Do the Franco-Americans of Lewiston-Auburn want a French-language newspaper?" *Le Messager* concluded its editorial by telling local Franco-Americans that if they wanted their newspaper to survive, they had to subscribe. The newspaper dropped *Nouveau* from its name in February 1967, and in mid-June it appeared entirely in French again. A lack of subscriptions and paid advertisements finally took its toll. Its resources exhausted, the longest-running French-language newspaper in the United States published its last edition on May 9, 1968.[56]

In conclusion, the identity of Lewiston's French-Canadian descendants changed from 1940 to 1970. During the early 1940s, ethnic retention and participation in U.S. society still represented intertwined goals. After World War II, however, these goals became disconnected as the Franco-American community, particularly the younger generations, increasingly anglicized. The pace of change quickened in the 1950s, and it accelerated even more rapidly in the 1960s. External forces, such as television, the closing of textile mills, changes in the Catholic Church initiated by the Second Vatican Council, and continued discrimination against francophones in the postwar era, all had an adverse impact upon Lewiston's Franco-American community. These external forces did not precipitate change; they merely spurred a process already under way. They helped Franco-Americans to view their desired place in U.S. society and ethnic preservation as incompatible objectives. When these goals diverged, Franco-Americans loosened their connection with Québec, younger generations became unilingual English speakers, their schools declined, the Franco-American parishes introduced English masses, Saint-Jean-Baptiste Day parades ended, and that venerable defender of French-Canadian ethnicity, *Le Messager*, ceased publication. These significant developments were the result of a long, historical evolution.[57] By mid-century, much of Lewiston's Franco-American population had grown ambivalent about the ethnic community. It had actively, if quietly, pursued a change in identity from Franco-American to American.

Contemporary Identity

Americans of French-Canadian Descent, 1970–2007

In the mid-1980s, Ernie Gagné, an office-products salesman from Lewiston and grandson of the late Louis-Philippe Gagné, took on the persona of "Frenchie" for WBLM radio of Auburn. During the morning program, Gagné would phone the radio station to banter in French-accented English with the disc jockeys. During one routine, "Frenchie" could not complete the task of counting the station's record albums because he kept losing count after three. After moving to Portland, WBLM had a listening audience of 188,000 in Maine, Massachusetts, and New Hampshire. It had aired the morning show with "Frenchie" for over seven years when attorney Jed Davis, a director of the Holocaust Human Rights Center of Maine, filed a complaint with the Maine Human Rights Commission. Davis took issue with the negative stereotyping "Frenchie" perpetuated of a sizable population that had endured prejudice in Maine. WBLM claimed that the program represented satire and refused to take it off the air. Davis and Lewiston native Paul Paré of l'Association Canado-Américaine (the Canado-American Association) both countered that programs that made fun of blacks would not be viewed as acceptable; neither should WBLM's show making fun of Franco-Americans. Eugene Lemieux, president of l'Association Canado-Américaine, argued: "If a young person listens to 'Frenchie' and they recognize their father or grandfather has the same accent, they might become embarrassed and submerge their identity." Eighty members from the Augusta, Biddeford, Waterville, and Lewiston councils of l'Association Canado-Américaine met in Lewiston to petition to have "Frenchie" taken off the air.[1]

Journalist Paul Carrier situated the "Frenchie" controversy in the context of discrimination against Franco-Americans. A native of Southbridge, Massachusetts, he argued that Franco-Americans in Maine endured greater prejudice than those in Massachusetts because so many other ethnic and racial minorities existed as targets in Massachusetts. While WBLM might air the "Frenchie" program, it "wouldn't dream of reviving 'Amos and Andy,'" he asserted. In Maine, "'dumb Frenchmen' jokes are so commonplace that even the most 'politically correct' among us feel free to tell them," he complained. "Franco-American cashiers who make an honest mistake have been conditioned to apologize for being French, as if their errors are genetic," he contended. In Maine, he continued, "misguided Franco-Americans laugh louder than anyone else at mean-spirited insults that are thinly disguised as humor."[2] This self-deprecation seemed to bother Carrier the most.

When reporters learned "Frenchie's" identity and contacted him at home and at work, he quit the radio program. Ernie Gagné nonetheless defended his use of "self-deprecating humor." He complained: "It is highly distressing to me that, in a country that prides itself on freedom of speech and expression, that [sic] so few people can impose their standards of correctness on so many." Franco-Americans from the Lewiston area wrote letters to the editor to defend "Frenchie." Like him, a woman from Sabattus decried the loss of First Amendment rights resulting in "Frenchie's" coming off the air, and she suggested that "the snobs in Lewiston" happened to "think they are better than anyone else." Without reflecting on the distinction between ascribed and voluntary ethnic identification, she further contended that the late Lewiston mayor Ernest Malenfant "used to speak like 'Frenchie,' and no one seemed to find it offensive." A man from Auburn who had enjoyed "Frenchie's" program offered "a suggestion for those folks who took offense to Frenchie: Lighten up and learn to laugh at yourself!" A man from Lewiston wrote: "I, for one, tell lots of French jokes and stories and will continue to do so. I could easily change the lines to Polish or Italian." A woman from Lisbon complained that "Frenchie's" detractors had deprived her of the enjoyment of listening to him in the morning. Reflecting an inaccurate knowledge of history, she continued: "The Franco-Americans (along with many other ethnic groups) fled to the new world to escape persecution. Now they've turned on one of their own." These letter writers all had French surnames. Other Franco-Americans publicly supported "Frenchie," including his cousin, Louis-Philippe Gagné, who carried their grandfather's name. Louis-Philippe Gagné founded a group called "Francos for Frenchie" to try to get his cousin back on the air.[3]

The controversy over "Frenchie's" radio program reveals the extent to which Franco-Americans had grown ambivalent about their ethnic identity and ethnic community. The discourse of "Frenchie's" defenders reflected an ignorance of the historic circumstances French-Canadian descendants had experienced during the previous century and a half. Gone with older generations of Franco-Americans like journalist Louis-Philippe Gagné was the firm resolve to fight against discrimination. Franco-Americans have tended to go along with ethnic jokes that put them down rather than doing something to end them, wrote Franco-American author Denis Ledoux during the controversy. That a non-Franco-American had filed the complaint with the Maine Human Rights Commission over "Frenchie's" radio program underscores his point. In Ledoux's analysis, "young people cannot learn to take pride in their heritage when all around them their ethnicity is openly portrayed as lacking in intelligence and sophistication." Donat B. Boisvert argued that divisions in the Franco-American community over the program reflected generational differences. He pointed out that younger Franco-Americans had not been subject to "Dumb Frenchmen" and "Frog" jokes. (The term "frog" had long been used as an ethnic slur against Franco-Americans.) "Frenchie had no reason to assume that his cultural badge of honor would be called into question; he was simply going for laughs," Boisvert wrote. "Critics of his performances, however, felt that his younger audience on a rock station was vulnerable. Without an appropriate historic context, these listeners might find it acceptable to laugh at Franco-American culture."[4] This lack of "historic context" distinguishes contemporary Franco-Americans from their ancestors. In the past, *Le Messager*, Franco-American clergy, and speakers on Saint-Jean-Baptiste (Saint John the Baptist) Day, who knew the lessons of history well, would communicate them to readers and listeners with whom they bonded as a result of a shared language, religion, and culture. Third- and later-generation Franco-Americans lacked this historical perspective.

Yet, they did not abandon all vestiges of their ethnic identity from the 1970s through the 1990s. In fact, curves in the road from Franco-American to American during the final decades of the twentieth century challenge notions we have of the process of assimilation in the United States. Less evidence is available on the experiences of Franco-Americans during the last several decades of the twentieth century than there was for earlier periods of their history. Three reasons account for this. Lewiston no longer had a daily or weekly French-language newspaper in the late twentieth century. Fewer Catholic records exist for this period, because orders of men and women religious declined in number and ended their ministries in Lewiston. In addition, there were fewer naturalization records.

Indeed, there were few French-Canadian immigrants to naturalize. During the 1970s, forty-nine French-Canadian Lewiston immigrants became U.S. citizens, and during the 1980s, a mere twenty-three did. Naturalization records suggest that most of the seventy-two French-Canadian naturalizers were probably postwar immigrants to the United States. Naturalization forms indicate the year of arrival in the United States only until 1976. Thirty-nine of the forty-one persons for whom we have this information (out of seventy-two persons) had immigrated to the United States between 1947 and 1968. Forty of the seventy-two were women, and thirty-two were men, continuing a postwar pattern whereby naturalizing women slightly outnumbered men.[5]

About two-thirds (65.3 percent) of the persons who naturalized in the 1970s and 1980s did so at the federal court in Portland. Political machinations at the local courthouse did not lead to this outcome, however, as they had one century earlier. When the Superior Court of Maine in Auburn stopped processing naturalization petitions in 1974, French-Canadian immigrants of Lewiston had to use the U.S. District Court in Portland.[6]

While not one of the seventy-two who naturalized in the 1970s and 1980s anglicized his or her French name, considerable anglicization took place in the Lewiston community during the last several decades of the twentieth century. When parents and grandparents spoke to their children and grandchildren in French, they often responded in English. Sadly enough, French became a foreign language to Franco-American youth. In fact, in 1986 half of the 368 students enrolled in French courses designed expressly for non-francophones at Lewiston High School had French surnames. At Saint Dominic High School, students hesitated to speak French because their skills were not strong enough, or because they spoke nonstandard French. Putting the latter point differently, French teacher Sr. Solange Bernier offered: "They don't want to identify with what they hear in their surroundings."[7]

What Lewiston youth heard in the city often was a mixture of French and English, sometimes in the same sentence. They also heard French sentence structures applied to the English language, resulting in awkward constructions. One twenty-two-year-old university student from Lewiston told her interviewer in 1991 that her grandmother, rather than saying, "Throw my shoes down the stairs," might say "Throw me down the stairs, my shoes." This student had negative feelings about her background and "does not like to talk about her Franco-American ancestry. She is embarrassed at the stereotype [*sic*] that are placed on her because of her background," noted Amy Bither, her interviewer. "She has worked hard to put herself through college. She does not want to be associated with the typical image of an uneducated 'Frenchie,'" Bither continued.[8] Given that Franco-American youth could have such strong negative feelings about their culture, it is not surprising that the Lewiston community continued to anglicize rapidly in the late twentieth century.

Despite the negative feelings some contemporary Franco-Americans have about their culture, and despite the community's anglicization, traces of French-Canadian ethnicity persist in Lewiston. The language of masses reflects this. In 2000, Saint-Pierre (Saint Peter), Sainte-Croix (Holy Cross), and Sainte-Marie (Saint Mary) before its closing during the summer each still offered one weekend mass in French, while Sainte-Famille (Holy Family) conducted all masses in English, as it had since 1991. But when Sainte-Famille Parish celebrated its seventy-fifth anniversary in 1998, the mass's opening song and second reading were in French, while all else was in English.[9] The language of masses at Lewiston's Franco-American churches thus reveals two tendencies in the late twentieth century: anglicization on the one hand, and cultural persistence on the other.

So does aggregate census data. When census takers came around in 1970, three-fifths (59.9 percent) of Lewiston's population reported having French as a mother tongue. In 1980, just over two-fifths (43.0 percent) of those age five and above spoke French at home. Not surprisingly, the city's youngest residents were the least likely to speak French in 1980: only 18.4 percent of youth between five and seventeen years of age spoke French at home, while 49.6 percent of persons eighteen and over did. The proportion of Lewiston's population, age five and over, that spoke French at home dropped to one-third (34.0 percent) in 1990.[10] While the above figures suggest considerable anglicization among members of Lewiston's Franco-American community in the late twentieth century, they also reveal that a sizable proportion of the city's residents still spoke French.

In fact, Lewiston was one of three New England cities in 1990 that had more than 10,000 francophone residents. Only Boston surpassed Lewiston. The 19,530 French speakers of Boston made up 4 percent of its population, and the 10,960 French speakers in Manchester, New Hampshire, made up 12 percent of that city's population. With 12,590 francophones in 1990, Lewiston ranked second in New England in the number of residents who spoke French at home; among the three cities, Lewiston had by far the highest proportion (34.0 percent) of French speakers.[11]

Data compiled from the 1992 city directory provides a late twentieth-century portrait of Lewiston's community and underscores the continued high concentration of Franco-Americans in the city. Three-fifths (59.2 percent) of the listings represented French-surnamed residents.[12] Those with non-French family names remained a minority in Lewiston in the late twentieth century.

Women married to Franco-American men were no more likely to work outside of the home in 1992 than were those wedded to men with non-French family names. Specifically, 47.1 percent of the married women with French last names worked outside of the home, and 47.6 percent of those with non-French surnames did.[13] This change from 1960 suggests one way in which Franco-American households had become more like those of non-Franco-Americans by the end of the century.

Similarly, the data suggests that the family sizes of Franco-Americans and non-Franco-Americans had become comparable by 1992. In 98.3 percent of the households with French family names, there were three or fewer children under the age of eighteen living at home. This was the case in 90.0 percent of the households with non-Franco-American surnames.[14]

Homeownership statistics reveal that Franco-Americans had made significant economic gains by century's end. Over half (51.7 percent) of the Franco-Americans in the sample owned their homes, compared to two-fifths (39.1 percent) of the non-Franco-Americans. The differential between Franco-American- and non-Franco-American-surnamed individuals may in part be explained by persistence patterns, for 17.9 percent of the non-Franco-Americans in the sample were new to the Lewiston area, compared to 7.2 percent of the Franco-American households.[15]

Occupational data compiled from the 1992 Lewiston directory reveals a tremendous drop since 1960 in the proportion of French-surnamed men and women in industrial employment. In 1960, 42.4 percent of the men with French family names earned their living in industrial jobs, while only 13.2 percent did in 1992 (see table 5). The decrease among French-surnamed women was even more striking. While 67.6 percent had industrial jobs in 1960, only 12.3 percent did in 1992. The closing of textile mills and shoe factories in Lewiston and Auburn eliminated many of the jobs Franco-Americans had long held.[16] In 1992, a greater proportion of men with French surnames could be found in nonindustrial and self-employed blue-collar positions as well as in clerical, sales, and semiprofessional white-collar jobs; in that same year, nearly double the proportion of men held small business and managerial jobs than was the case in 1960. Women with French surnames expanded their ranks the most in clerical and sales positions. But they also moved into nonindustrial blue-collar jobs, as well as into semiprofessional, small business, and managerial white-collar positions. As Franco-Americans moved out of the textile mills and shoe factories, especially as they entered white-collar positions, they had more occasion and greater need to speak English.[17] Structural changes in Lewiston's economy thus promoted English-language use among the francophone community, particularly among the women, its cultural hearth-keepers.

The institutions of the Soeurs Grises (Grey Nuns) may have helped Franco-American women to achieve a measure of upward mobility in Lewiston. Among the nine French-surnamed women at the salaried, professional level, four were nurses. Three of the four nurses worked at the institutions of the Soeurs Grises, or Sisters of Charity, such as Saint Mary's Hospital or the nursing home, D'Youville Pavillion.[18] This suggests that the institutions of

Table 5. Occupational Distribution in Lewiston in 1992 (in percentages)[a]

	MEN	WOMEN	UNKNOWN [b]
Persons with Non-French Surnames (*N* = 233)			
WHITE COLLAR			
Self-governing professional	3.1%	2.4%	0%
Salaried professional	11.6	16.9	19.0
Small business and managerial	17.1	9.6	14.3
Semiprofessional	3.1	8.4	14.3
Clerical and sales	7.8	16.9	23.8
BLUE COLLAR			
Self-employed	0.8	0	0
Nonindustrial	29.5	21.7	9.5
Industrial	7.8	7.2	0
Primary sector	0.8	0	0
Unable to determine	18.6	16.9	19.0
NUMBER	129	83	21
Persons with French Surnames (*N* = 353)			
WHITE COLLAR			
Self-governing professional	0%	0%	0%
Salaried professional	1.1	5.8	0
Small business and managerial	15.8	7.1	0
Semiprofessional	3.2	4.5	0
Clerical and sales	7.9	31.2	33.3
BLUE COLLAR			
Self-employed	5.3	0.6	0
Nonindustrial	35.8	18.8	22.2
Industrial	13.2	12.3	22.2
Primary sector	0	0	0
Unable to determine	17.9	19.5	22.2
NUMBER	190	154	9

Source: Derived from every fifteenth entry in the 1992 Catalist: Business and Household Digest of Lewiston-Auburn (Loveland, Colo.: USWest Marketing Resources, 1991).
a. Columns may not add up to 100.0 percent on account of rounding.
b. The gender of a number of individuals could not be determined because of the use of initials in the city directory and because some names are given to members of both genders.

women religious may have facilitated some of the mobility that Lewiston's Franco-American women enjoyed by 1992.

Considerable ethnic intermixing took place in Lewiston in the late 1990s. In 1998, the Lewiston City Clerk's office recorded 228 marriages in which one or both individuals had a French family name. The data reflects a significant amount of ethnic intermarriage: just under three-fourths (73.2 percent) of these marriages took place between couples where one member did not have a French family name. Conversely, only about one-fourth (26.8 percent) of the marriages were between French-surnamed persons and therefore probably endogamous. Because mixed marriages had taken place between Franco-Americans and non-Franco-Americans throughout the twentieth century, relying solely upon French family names to discern ethnicity is problematic; yet, there is no feasible alternative. However imperfect, the evidence suggests that endogamous marriages celebrated among Franco-Americans in Lewiston in 1998 had declined by more than half since 1960. As in prior periods, the data suggests that Franco-American women were somewhat more inclined than Franco-American men to take spouses of another ethnic background, for slightly more than half (52.1 percent) of the mixed marriages involved French-surnamed brides, and under half (47.9 percent) involved grooms with French family names.[19]

Judging by the Franco-American composition of Lewiston's former Irish parishes, ethnic intermixing also increased within the city's Catholic institutions. The directory of Saint Joseph Parish reveals that half of its membership was Franco-American in 1999: 526 (50.2 percent) of the 1,047 families listed had Franco-American surnames. Under half of the members of Saint Patrick Parish were Franco-American in the same year: 236 (44.8 percent) of the 527 families listed in that parish's directory had French surnames.[20]

A 1996 development may have served as a cause or consequence of Saint Patrick's changing demographics. When the Irish pastor of Saint Patrick resigned due to ill health, the bishop, faced with a shortage of priests, appointed the Franco-American pastor and vicar of Saint Peter's to take over the ministry of Saint Patrick's. Both parishes had declining populations. Without addressing ethnic differences specifically, Bishop Joseph Gerry remarked, "I am asking the parishioners to work together in developing a greater sense of a Catholic community rather than simply a parochial one."[21] Although the bishop's decision to "twin" the administration of the two parishes led to a flurry of newspaper articles and letters to the editor, none focused explicitly on ethnic differences between the two parishes; while those differences may have been the subtext over which community members expressed their concerns, it is likely that the increased intermixing of Irish and Franco-American Catholics since mid-century had tempered members of both Saint Peter and Saint Patrick.

As the Franco-American community Americanized even further during the final decades of the twentieth century, it made some attempts to instill ethnic pride, to retain French-Canadian lifeways, and to preserve the French language. The 1970s were a time of apparent ethnic resurgence in Maine. The federal government funded bilingual education programs through the Elementary and Secondary Education Act, Saint Francis College in Biddeford founded its Institute of French-Canadian Culture, and the Orono and Portland-Gorham campuses of the University of Maine offered courses in French-Canadian literature. In the early 1970s, Lewiston founded its Centre d'Héritage Franco-Américain (Franco-American Heritage Center) in a classroom at Saint-Dominique (Saint Dominic) High School. It collected articles, pictures, books, and other memorabilia on French-Canadian descendants. Funding from the Maine Arts and Humanities Commission supported the cultural programs and art exhibits of the center, as well as symposia.[22] Today, Lewiston-Auburn College houses the Franco-American Collection, an important resource for the local community as well as researchers, and the college continues to organize French-Canadian cultural programs and exhibits.

Several bilingual newspapers appeared in Lewiston in the 1970s to fill the void left by Le Messager's dissolution. The first, Vérité (Truth), gained its funding from the Model Cities Administrative Budget around 1971, but came to an end in 1972 after local officials tried to exercise control over its content. Its reincarnation, Observations (Observations), appeared in June 1972, after securing funding independent of Lewiston city officials, but it only lasted six months.[23]

A controversial publication, Observations brought to light problems francophones had gaining access to public services. For example, it complained about the practice of the Lewiston office of the Maine Department of Health and Welfare of turning away French speakers and telling them to return with interpreters. Employees at the local bureau, the newspaper alleged, were bilingual, but either could not or would not translate information. "It took them a great deal of courage to apply [for benefits] in the first place," the newspaper contended, "and several, unable to find an interpreter because they do not know one or really because they are ashamed to admit that they cannot speak English correctly, will never return to Health and Welfare." This humiliation, charged *Observations*, resulted in francophones being denied the benefits they deserved. To take one other example, *Observations* complained that the sergeant answering calls at the Lewiston police station from 1:00 A.M. to 9:00 A.M. could not communicate in French, unlike the two daytime sergeants, and he had to resort to a dictionary or to an interpreter, resulting in precious time lost. While anglophones had twenty-four-hour police protection, francophones only had sixteen, *Observations* protested.[24]

The third bilingual newspaper launched in Lewiston in the 1970s, *L'Unité* (*Unity*) began publication in May 1976 and lasted until 1984. It received federal and local funds to finance operations. During the late 1970s, *L'Unité* appeared quarterly, and in the early 1980s, nearly monthly. In June 1981, *L'Unité* distributed about six thousand copies at no charge. It discussed the activities of Franco-American clubs in Lewiston and Auburn, French-language events and contests at Saint Dominic High School, and other news relating to Franco-American culture. It also reported on events taking place in Québec.[25]

This renewed interest in Québec marked a change from the 1950s and 1960s; it provides a clear example of the nonlinearity of the process of assimilation in the United States. For its part, Québec, which experienced intense nationalism in the late twentieth century, sought to reestablish ties with Franco-Americans. To this end, the Government of Québec opened an office in Boston in 1969. The Québec Bureau worked with Franco-Americans to bring French-language programs to cable television stations in New England and New York; it must have been through such collaboration that Lewiston could first tune in to a Québec television station in the 1970s. Québec's Ministry of Culture also donated books to support Lewiston's Centre d'Héritage Franco-Américain in the early 1970s.[26]

Both technology and Canada's cancer-care crisis have promoted contact between the *Québécois* and Franco-Americans. By 1999, cable television viewers in Lewiston could tune in to three French channels from Québec.

Phil Nadeau, Lewiston's assistant city administrator, indicated in 1999 that he watched these channels to maintain his French-language skills and to keep current on Québec's separatist movement. Another connection between Franco-Americans and French Canadians stems from the crisis in Canada's health-care delivery system, which led to a huge backlog of cancer patients awaiting treatment at Québec hospitals. By January 2000, Central Maine Medical Center (CMMC) of Lewiston was one of five U.S. hospitals with which Québec's Ministry for Health and Social Services had contracted to provide cancer treatment. A French-speaking social worker at CMMC assisted francophone patients; volunteers from the Franco-American community also helped, whether by offering rides in the local area or a meal in their home. Ironically, Central Maine Medical Center (formerly Central Maine General) was the hospital founded in the late nineteenth century in opposition to the French hospital of the Soeurs Grises.[27]

Other efforts have taken place during the past several decades to promote ethnic retention in Lewiston. Some, like the bilingual-education program, were of limited duration. In 1970, Lewiston secured federal funding to provide bilingual instruction in English and French at three elementary schools, but the city's Board of Education dropped the program after two years. *Observations* offered several reasons for its discontinuance. Because of the lack of turnover among faculty and the absence of local funds to create new positions, the school system used bilingual aides in the classrooms and not bilingual teachers as federal guidelines required; not only did teachers complain that the work of the aides disrupted their classrooms, but the federal government also would no longer accept Lewiston's remedy of utilizing only bilingual aides. The Bilingual Program chafed the Franco-American school superintendent, the newspaper suggested, by its "militant" advocacy in spring 1972, during which it distributed stickers advocating "Frog Power." An ethnic slur, the term "frog" was turned around and used in this case as an assertion of French-Canadian ethnicity. In the final analysis, *Observations* attributed the end of the Bilingual Program to the lack of community support and to the pressure to assimilate: "If growing up French in Lewiston has, in fact, had negative overtones, then it is little wonder that Francos were slow to support the program. Many of them have spent most of their lives rejecting their 'Frenchness' in favor of assimilation by an Anglo environment." Suggested *Observations*: "What was needed, then, was a driving force to reverse the trend toward assimilation and establish positive feelings about French language and culture. Right or wrong, it appears that the School Department was not prepared to take on the role of missionary."[28]

A decade later, Lewiston's Franco-American community still expressed little interest in the possibility of establishing a bilingual-education program. When the Maine Department of Educational and Cultural Services conducted a study in 1984–1985 to gauge interest in establishing such a program for third-grade students, it found a "more negative (attitude toward French) among the Francos than the non Francos [sic]," reported Barney Berube, a department official. This led him to conclude that bilingualism in Lewiston in the future would probably be found primarily among non-Franco-Americans and would be tied to intellectual rather than ethnic interest in the French language.[29]

Founded in the fall of 1974, l'Unité Franco-Américaine (Franco-American Unity), a federation of nearly thirty societies from Lewiston and Auburn, worked to promote Franco-American culture and to unite Franco-Americans. It succeeded in getting a second French-language cable television station for the Lewiston-Auburn community as its first project, and it published the aforementioned newspaper, *L'Unité*. In 1975, l'Unité Franco-Américaine organized a Saint-Jean-Baptiste Day celebration at Our Lady of the Rosary Church in Sabattus, which the Franco-American societies of Lewiston and Auburn attended. Assisted by Franco-American pastors from the local area, Canadian-born Dominican pastor Raymond Laframboise offered an outdoor mass to 500 people; following the mass, 350 persons stayed to enjoy a bean supper and evening program of dance and music, marking the only public celebration of the feast day of French Canadians in the 1970s.[30]

Not until the early 1980s was there another public celebration of Saint-Jean-Baptiste Day in the Lewiston area. In 1983, the Canadian-born Dominican pastor of Saint Peter's Church, Roger Gabriel Blain planned a special mass for this feast day. Le Centre d'Héritage cosponsored the celebration, which included a social hour, buffet, and evening program.[31] Surely it was no coincidence that French-Canadian pastors helped Lewiston-area Franco-Americans to organize public celebrations of Saint-Jean-Baptiste Day in 1975 and 1983. The Canadianization of the Dominican order in the early

1900s had led to a steady supply of French-Canadian pastors to Lewiston, and they had helped the city preserve its ethnic identity. The 1983 activities constituted, however, the last public celebration of Saint-Jean-Baptiste Day in Lewiston.

But the feast day reappeared as a private celebration in the 1990s. At the request of Franco-American residents, Maison Marcotte (Marcotte Home), founded by the Sisters of Charity and now functioning as an independent living center, commemorated Saint-Jean-Baptiste Day in the 1990s with ethnic food like *tortière* (meat pie, usually made with pork), the singing of French songs, and waltzing. The journalist reporting on Maison Marcotte's 1997 celebration, while somewhat trivializing it in her conclusion, hinted at how far Franco-Americans had diverged from French Canadians in Québec: "Although the holiday has evolved to focus on separatist aspirations in Quebec, at Maison Marcotte it seems to have become a time for eating birthday cake and reminiscing."[32] Most importantly, the public celebration of Saint-Jean-Baptiste Day in 1975 and 1983, and the private celebrations at Maison Marcotte in the 1990s suggest modest attempts at ethnic renewal.

Other efforts do also, including renewed contact with Québec, the attempt to promote bilingual education in the local schools in the early 1970s, the founding of bilingual newspapers, the establishment of Le Centre d'Héritage, and the formation and activities of l'Unité Franco-Américaine. In 1976, this federation organized Lewiston's first Franco-American festival. The festival's purpose, recorded the Dominican priests, was one "where the Franco-American spirit will be re-immersed in its warm and familiar traditions and will rekindle its contemporary culture." The Franco-American festival became an annual event attracting tens of thousands of people. In 1979, for example, 130,000 persons attended. Held at Kennedy Park, the eight-day celebrations featured music, French-Canadian foods, exhibits, and open-air French classes, as well as non-French-Canadian activities such as carnival rides. The festivals, with their beery, carnival atmosphere, ended in the late 1980s. After a hiatus of about five years, a refashioned festival, called the Festival de Joie (Festival of Joy), came to Lewiston in 1993 and has since returned yearly. While featuring French-Canadian foods, Cajun and French-Canadian music and entertainment, and opening with the national anthems of the United States, Canada, and France, the Festival de Joie has evolved into a multicultural festival. In 1998, it also featured Italian,

German, Scandinavian, Irish, Mexican, Greek, Israeli, and country and western music, as well as exhibits by Israeli, Scottish, Greek, and Native American groups.[33] While retaining French-Canadian flavor and a French name, the Festival de Joie is now a multicultural event.

The evolution of Lewiston's Festival de Joie symbolizes the changing identity of the city's Franco-American population. The continued existence of the festival suggests that interest in French-Canadian culture has not died out in Lewiston as Franco-Americans have evolved. The multicultural theme reflects that Franco-Americans see themselves as "one piece in the great American mosaic."[34] In short, they view themselves as Americans of French-Canadian descent.

Lewiston's Franco-American festival facilitated the founding of another ethnic organization in the city. In 1986, a Franco-American from outside of Maine attended Lewiston's festival to recruit veterans to start a local post of the Franco American [*sic*] War Veterans, Inc., an organization that existed in other New England states. Beginning with about twenty members, Lewiston Post #31 grew to 124 members by 1998. Although one need not be Franco-American to join, most members are of French-Canadian descent.[35]

Despite having made allowances for the use of English at their meetings, or having in fact changed their language from French to English, most Franco-American clubs have been unsuccessful in attracting youth to their organizations, and their membership is both aging and declining. In the past, most of the Franco-American organizations had snowshoe clubs, and they organized sports events and other activities for their members. As ethnic ties have loosened, they have lost vitality. Franco-American clubs today lack a clear sense of purpose around which to organize and attract new members.[36]

The foregoing suggests an ambivalence about Franco-American identity in the late twentieth century. It is rooted in the problem of low self-image. In 1986, Paul Carrier noted having heard numerous anecdotes of Lewiston Franco-Americans calling themselves—or being called—"dumb Frenchmen" after having made mistakes at their places of work. He attributed the self-deprecatory remarks to a lack of pride and even to an element of "self-loathing."[37] Divisions within the Franco-American community over "Frenchie's" radio program in the early 1990s underscored their ambivalence and low self-image.

Persistent discrimination against Franco-Americans has contributed to these problems. In 1991, Bates College students protested against the college policy forbidding francophone food-service and maintenance employees from speaking French at work. "The policy constitutes gross hypocrisy on the part of the College, which prides itself on both fostering a diverse atmosphere at Bates and on encouraging a healthy relationship with the Lewiston-Auburn community," contended the editor of the *Bates Student*. The editor continued: "The language ban obstructs diversity and favorable relations with the community, since it sends a message that Bates disapproves of the culture that surrounds us." A Franco-American student whose first language was French, but who in 1991 was learning it as a foreign language, argued that the college policy contributed, perhaps unwittingly, to "the relentless extinction of a once proud culture." In reversing the policy, Bates College administrators indicated that they had not been aware of the unwritten rule forbidding French in the presence of non-francophones. Despite the reversal, Franco-American employees still felt uneasy about speaking French at work, complained a student of French-Canadian descent in January 1992. He elaborated: "Tonight while an elderly French Canadian [*sic*] woman served me noodles, I heard a younger worker reminding her she had to say everything in English." In the student's view, "it was as if someone [had] insulted my own Memere [grandmother]!" Despite the policy change, "many of the older women still feel they cannot speak French and if they do or if they complain they will lose their jobs," the student contended.[38]

By the late twentieth century, Franco-Americans had evolved into an amorphous population, one without a clear cultural identity. Language, faith, and traditions no longer united French-Canadian descendants as an ethnic group, nor did employment in the mills following the decline of Lewiston's textile industry. For the most part, younger generations increasingly distanced themselves from their ethnic roots and expressed embarrassment because their elders spoke French-accented English. Not only did Yankees and other English speakers poke fun at francophones, but Franco-Americans themselves did. Franco-Americans also appeared to lack the resolve to fight against prejudice. According to Carol (Lajoie) Tracy, "Historically, the majority in this area has been treated as a minority, and that was because we allowed that to happen to ourselves." She also suggested: "A lot of it was self-inflicted."[39]

One development augurs well for Lewiston. In 1981, the American-Canadian Genealogical Society of Manchester, New Hampshire, formed the Father Léo E. Bégin Chapter in Lewiston-Auburn.[40] Now called the Maine Franco-American Genealogical Society, the chapter survives to this day, providing a collection of resources to aid French-Canadian descendants in the quest to trace their roots. This genealogical society is but one effort in the late twentieth century that has raised the interest of the Lewiston community in its ancestry. The arrival of the genealogical society has given Lewiston a boost at a time when its Franco-American institutions are in decline.

A major reason for their decline lies in the shortage of men and women religious. One of the changes the Second Vatican Council inspired in the Roman Catholic Church was greater choice for women religious. Previously, sisters received assignments (called "obediences") from their superiors. Following Vatican II, women religious had more latitude to pursue different callings, which they did after engaging in a "discernment" process in conjunction with their communities to determine how they might best serve. The magnitude of the change permitting the sisters a choice of assignments is best revealed by contrasting it with descriptions of the former system from the journal of the convent at Holy Family:

11 June 1965

After the evening Veni Sancte, our Mother [Superior] handed each sister an envelope in which there was a letter from the Mother Provincial if we were changing [assignments] or a note from our Mother if we were staying here next year. Our sacrifice or our joy remained concealed amongst the good Lord, our Mothers and each of us in our small chamber.

12 June 1965

Our Mother [Superior] revealed all the secrets of the reassignments of sisters before breakfast. All ears strained and what surprises we had upon learning that our Mother and ten of our sisters would leave!

9 June 1967

Mother Anne-Marie, our Provincial, sent us our obediences for the 1967–1968 year. Our family sorrows begin.

As a result of the discernment process, women religious have opted for ministries outside of education and have pursued work in such areas as pastoral counseling, social services, and foreign missions. Consequently, the number of women religious educating children in Maine's parish schools continued to decline from the 1970s, requiring replacement by lay faculty, which increased the operational costs of the schools. These problems led Holy Family to close its parochial school in 1973.[41] Today, Saint Dominic High School continues, and the remaining elementary schools have merged in order to survive; men and women religious no longer administer or staff these institutions, although the faculty of each may contain one or two religious in any given year.

A shortage of priests led the Dominicans to withdraw from both Sabattus and Lewiston. No longer able to staff the Sabattus mission, the Dominicans turned it over to the Diocese of Portland in 1975, more than half a century after Bishop Louis Walsh had struggled with them for title to the property. In 1986, the Dominicans also withdrew from Saint Peter's Parish and turned its assets over to the Diocese of Portland.[42]

Today, only three Franco-American parishes remain in Lewiston. Following the decline of the textile and shoe industries, and the movement of families to the outskirts of Lewiston, the population of Saint Mary's Parish dropped to under three hundred families by 2000. The parish no longer had the resources to support itself. Created when Bishop Louis Walsh divided Saint-Pierre Parish in 1907, Saint Mary once again forms part of Saint Peter's. The Franco-American Heritage Committee purchased the church from the Diocese of Portland for one dollar and has converted the structure into a Franco-American museum and cultural center. Like Saint Mary's population, that of Saint Peter's also declined from mid-century as youth moved from downtown Lewiston to the city's outskirts. Once Lewiston's largest Franco-American parish, Saint Peter trailed both Holy Family and Holy Cross in the number of families in 1996. Only the suburban parishes of Holy Family and Holy Cross thrive today.[43]

Lewiston's Franco-American parish credit unions evolved in the late twentieth century into institutions whose common bond expanded beyond the parishes they served and included non-Franco-Americans. In December 1969, Sainte Famille Federal Credit Union amended its charter so that anyone living within the boundaries of the parish, whether or not they were members of Holy Family Church, could join the credit union. As the parish aged and Saint Pierre Credit Union attracted few young members, it expanded its field of membership in 1981 to the entire city of Lewiston, and in 1985 changed its name to Community Credit Union to reflect that modification. Sainte Famille Credit Union similarly changed its name to designate that it was no longer a parish or Franco-American institution, becoming Maine Family Federal Credit Union in 1993. In 1994, Sainte Marie Credit Union merged with Rainbow Federal Credit Union, the former parish credit union of Saint Joseph, and is now a branch of that financial institution. Sainte Croix Parish Federal Credit Union had planned to adopt a new, non-French name in 1996, but learned that another credit union in the country had already adopted the name it desired. Consequently, the credit union substituted "Regional" for "Parish" in its name in the hope of attracting more business to its institution.[44] While still serving Franco-Americans, Sainte Croix, Maine Family, Community, and Rainbow credit unions are no longer strictly ethnic institutions, but ones that reflect the integration of Franco-Americans into the larger, non-Franco-American, non-Catholic community.

Some Franco-Americans have, of course, felt conflicted about these changes. In the early 1970s, the board of directors of Sainte Famille Credit Union changed the language of its meetings from French to English to accommodate several new directors elected by the membership who could understand but not speak French. Subsequently, when credit-union president Maurice Fontaine asked the members at an annual meeting if they would object to conducting their meetings in English, one shareholder responded emphatically, "On est tous des canadiens; on restera français," ("We are all French Canadians; we will remain French"), to which the audience applauded. Nonetheless, because the president and other directors found it difficult to continue translating reports from English to French for these annual meetings, they introduced English gradually, with one report delivered in English one year, two the next, and so on until the mid-1970s, when the meetings were held almost entirely in English.[45]

Franco-Americans and their institutions have evolved to such a degree in Lewiston that today an outside observer might not easily discern their French-Canadian roots. Contemporary Franco-American identity no longer depends upon the ability to speak French, the practice of Roman Catholicism, or the celebration of French-Canadian traditions, as it had in the past.

French-Canadian descendants in Lewiston have intermixed considerably with other ethnic groups through intermarriage, as the result of occupational changes, by joining the former Irish churches, and even by continuing to bank at their credit unions. Ethnic identity in Lewiston from mid-century to the present has evolved from an ascribed to a voluntary identification, from "being" to "feeling" Franco-American. After visiting Lewiston in 1998, writer Peter Behrens contended: "Lewiston represents the great American melting pot and also, for Québécois nationalists, the nightmare come true. Ethnically, the city is overwhelmingly 'Franco-American' but hardly anyone under the age of 50 speaks French." Yet, traces of French-Canadian ethnicity and culture persist in the former Spindle City. In Lewiston today, cultural identity represents a personal strategy, rather than a group effort as it had in the past.[46] Lewiston Franco-Americans have evolved into individual Americans of French-Canadian descent.

Conclusion

Whenthe 119th Maine legislature convened in January 1999, a newly elected Republican lawmaker from Auburn, Dr. Thomas F. Shields, introduced a bill to make English the official language of the state. Born in Arkansas and raised in Missouri, Shields had lived in the Lewiston-Auburn area for over thirty years and had practiced medicine at Lewiston's two hospitals. Nonetheless, he was startled by the controversy his bill precipitated, and by the strength of the opposition of Maine's Franco-Americans. According to one journalist, the bill catapulted Shields "from being virtually an unknown freshman to one of the most talked-about members of the Maine legislature"—one whose efforts even attracted the attention of the media in Canada. Shields argued that he merely wanted to make official a practice Maine had employed for two centuries, whereby the state government would continue to produce documents and records only in English. His goal, he indicated, was to promote a common language among immigrants and to prevent the possibility of state documents having to be translated into Spanish. Shields's efforts fed into the contemporary political movement to make English the official language of the United States; U.S.ENGLISH, Inc., a Washington-based political-action group, supported his proposed legislation. Shields's bill hit a raw nerve among Franco-Americans. They perceived L.D. 264 as a discriminatory measure not unlike the 1919 law requiring English as "the basic language of instruction" in Maine's schools—a measure the state had repealed only in 1969. Upon learning of Shields's bill, a seventy-three-year-old Franco-American woman asked her son why French-Canadian descendants were so despised. Conveyed during state legislative hearings, such reactions contributed to the measure's defeat. Shields's bill died in committee on Saint Patrick's Day, 1999.[1]

This community study of French-Canadian descendants in Lewiston, Maine, challenges our understanding of the process of Americanization and has implications for policymakers. The most prominent debate in U.S. immigration history has centered on whether immigrants were "uprooted" or "transplanted."[2] Relatively little debate has focused on the process of Americanization—a process many assume takes place in a straight-line fashion leading to what we call "assimilation."[3] This study questions whether "assimilation" actually takes place in the immigrant-receiving society.[4] The persistence of the French language in Lewiston and the efforts of French-Canadian descendants at cultural renewal during the final decades of the twentieth century reveal that this population has not given up or lost all of the traits that make it distinctive. In short, the term "acculturation" rather than "assimilation" better describes the way in which this ethnic group has joined the host society.

This study also illustrates that the process of Americanization does not occur in a linear fashion. It thus corroborates some of the recent scholarship on the immigrant experience in the United States.[5] In particular, the ethnic conflicts between Franco-Americans and Irish clergy early in the twentieth century, and the cultural rebound and renewed contact with Québec during the final decades of the century, demonstrate curves in the road from *Canadien* to American.

With their proclivity for emphasizing binary opposites, historians and policymakers have perpetuated the view that ethnic preservation and participation in the receiving society necessarily represent dichotomous aims. What this monograph reveals, however, is that an ethnic group may in fact seek to retain its mother tongue and cultural traditions at the same time that it seeks to join the host society. Lewiston's French-Canadian immigrants did not exhibit in the United States a process that historian Dirk Hoerder has described as "a gradual withering of old roots while sinking new ones at the same time."[6] They did not allow their ethnic roots to wither or die. From the late nineteenth century to the middle of the twentieth, French-Canadian descendants maintained close ties with Québec and expanded their ethnic institutions in the United States, all the while demonstrating a strong willingness to become political participants in their country of adoption by becoming naturalized citizens and voters. They created agency for themselves amidst the tension between their homeland and local politics. Rather than struggling between *survivance* (ethnic preservation) and joining the host society, individuals of French-Canadian birth and background actively negotiated their identity in the United States. They challenged, rejected, or redefined some of the norms of the United States as they pursued their own ends. Subject to discrimination by Yankee nativists and by Irish clergy in the Roman Catholic Church, French-Canadian descendants showed considerable agility, courage, agency, and flexibility in maintaining their interconnected French and American identities from the late nineteenth century until the middle of the twentieth.

Their experience refutes the classic three-generation thesis of assimilation and cultural rebound set forth by historian Marcus Lee Hansen in 1937. Hansen argued that second-generation ethnics had difficulty "inhabit[ing] two worlds at the same time" and consequently sought to distance themselves from their ethnic roots. He further contended that ethnic renewal took place among the third generation: "The theory is derived from the almost universal phenomenon that what the son wishes to forget the grandson wishes to remember."[7] Until the mid-twentieth century, first- through third-generation French-Canadian descendants in Lewiston successfully "inhabit[ed] two worlds at the same time." They could do so because for them ethnic retention and civic participation in the host society were closely intertwined. Only when these goals unraveled did (primarily) third- and later-generation Franco-Americans of Lewiston distance themselves from their ethnic heritage.

Today, the movement to promote the English language among new immigrants in the United States and to make it the official language of the country is gaining ground. Three-fifths of the states have adopted laws making English their official language, and U.S.ENGLISH, Inc., has been lobbying Congress to enact federal legislation to make English the official language of the country. Arguing against the promotion of cultural diversity in contemporary U.S. society, journalist Georgie Anne Geyer contends that the acceptance of languages other than English amounts to "reverse colonization," and that efforts to promote multiculturalism weaken U.S. citizenship, leading to "a dangerous watering-down of the levels of passion and commitment to nation."[8] This study suggests that the opposite is true. Lewiston's French-Canadian descendants put a premium on modeling good citizenship in their country of adoption. It was integral to their interconnected identity as ethnic Americans. In fact, better Franco-Americans made better citizens, they fervently believed and effectively demonstrated.

When French-Canadian immigrants began arriving in the United States in droves in the late nineteenth century, they were as foreign as any other immigrant group. They spoke French in a country whose unofficial language was English. They maintained their Catholic faith in a nation dominated by Protestants. They celebrated in a public and grandiose way their cultural traditions, such as Saint-Jean-Baptiste (Saint John the Baptist) Day, that the native-born had never before observed. They also composed the working class of their communities. So different did they appear that the Massachusetts Commissioner of the Bureau of Statistics of Labor labeled them in 1881 the "Chinese of the Eastern States." But, as this study of Lewiston, Maine, reveals, French-Canadian immigrants and their descendants demonstrated great willingness to join U.S. society and to learn its unofficial language. That they became political and cultural members of the United States beginning in the late nineteenth century challenges the contemporary notion that such membership is a post–World War II phenomenon.[9] This monograph illustrates that French-Canadian descendants became political and cultural members of the host society at their own pace, on their own terms, and largely with their own resources.

In light of the experience of French-Canadian descendants in Lewiston over the past century and a half, modern-day concerns over the practice of ethnic groups to remain hyphenated Americans appear to be greatly misplaced. Generalizing from the experience of French-Canadian immigrants and their Franco-American offspring, groups that retain their mother tongue and their ethnic traditions while joining U.S. society are no less American than other groups, including the native stock. Policymakers concerned about the contemporary large-scale immigration of Hispanics across the southern

U.S. border would do well to consider the experiences of the large immigrant population that entered the United States from its northern border. In the host society, these French speakers demonstrated convincingly that they could be "Loyal but French."

Sources, Methodology, and Additional Statistics

Much of the literary evidence used in this study came from *Le Messager*, the French-language newspaper of Lewiston, Maine. The descriptive statistics came from three principal sources: federal censuses, city directories, and naturalization records. Below is an explanation of how I utilized each source; also included are some of the descriptive statistics I moved from the narrative in order to lighten it. The appendix ends with a description of the occupational classification and ranking system I used to analyze information on jobs provided by the censuses, directories, and naturalization records.

Le Messager

Founded in 1880 by Dr. Louis J. Martel, this weekly French-language newspaper of Lewiston changed hands at least four times during the first decade of its existence. Canadian-born J. D. Montmarquet, who had previously worked for *Le Travailleur* of Worcester, Massachusetts, served as the newspaper's editor from its founding until 1883; editorial committees subsequently directed the newspaper, probably until Québec-born Jean-Baptiste Couture purchased the newspaper in 1891 and became its owner-editor. Proprietor of *Le Messager* until his death in 1943, Couture published the newspaper twice weekly from August 1891, three times weekly from December 1905, and daily from January 1934. Besides Couture, the most notable journalist at *Le Messager* was Louis-Philippe Gagné, who had worked five years for *Le Soleil* of Québec before emigrating to Lewiston in 1922; Gagné served thirty-eight (nonconsecutive) years on the staff of *Le Messager*. Following Couture's death, his sons Valdor and Faust either owned *Le Messager* together or individually (passing it from one to the other) until 1951, when a group of one hundred stockholders purchased the newspaper. *Le Messager* changed hands again in 1954, its management scaled back production from daily to weekly in 1955, and except for a four-year stint from 1958 to 1962 as a biweekly newspaper, *Le Messager* remained a weekly until ceasing publication in 1968.[1]

My reading of this French-language newspaper of Lewiston centered on the local news, focusing on the lives of ordinary French Canadians and Franco-Americans. Microfilm produced during bankruptcy proceedings in the early 1950s of the period from 1880 to 1946 is of poor quality and contains significant gaps in coverage of up to two years. Page numbers of citations, possible only when supplied by the newspaper and visible on microfilm, are provided in the endnotes of this monograph. Some articles from *Le Messager* have survived as clippings that the Dominican priests inserted into the chronicle they maintained at their Lewiston monastery; they are so acknowledged in the endnotes. Fortunately for me (and for other scholars), the Maine State Library's Maine Newspaper Project recently produced a new microfilm of this French-language newspaper, covering the period from 1917 to 1968. While it, too, contains some gaps, they are significantly fewer, and the quality of the new microfilm is superior to the microfilm produced a half-century ago. For this study, I have examined all microfilmed copies of *Le Messager* for the period from 1880 to 1968.

Federal Censuses, 1880 and 1920

The data sample compiled from the 1880 federal manuscript census for Lewiston (Androscoggin County), Maine, represented every twentieth household. Because the residents of institutions (such as hospitals) and mill housing blocks were not grouped according to households, and there was no indication of the relationships between the residents, I did not include them in the data. In all, the sample yielded 182 households containing 848 individuals.

The 1880 census did not indicate whether Canadian immigrants were English or French speakers. In this study, individuals with French surnames who had been born in Canada, or whose parents had been born in Canada, were classified as French Canadians. Similarly, Canadian immigrants and their children bearing English surnames were considered English Canadians. Of the 182 households in the sample, Americans headed 54.9 percent, French Canadians 18.1 percent, and the Irish 17.0 percent; other groups headed the remaining households in the following proportions: English 5.5 percent, English Canadians 3.8 percent, and African-Americans 0.5 percent.

Lewiston's households varied considerably in size and composition in 1880. Among the French-Canadian households, 63.6 percent had six or more members, compared to 38.7 percent of the Irish and 21.0 percent of the American households. French Canadians extended their households with kin in 15.2 percent of the cases in the sample, compared to 19.4 percent of the Irish and 22.0 percent of the Americans; in addition, 36.4 percent of the French-Canadian households took in boarders, compared to 15.0 percent of the American and 6.5 percent of the Irish households. Only Americans extended their households with servants or farm laborers.

An examination of the age structure of all of Lewiston's residents in 1880 provides evidence that French Canadians married young. In 35.5 percent of the Irish households, the oldest single, never-married child was nineteen years of age or older; this was true in 25.0 percent of the American households but in only 21.2 percent of the French-Canadian households. Alternatively, the proportion of married, male, French-Canadian household heads in their twenties more than doubled that of all non-French-Canadian heads in Lewiston, and this pattern also held true for the wives of these household heads. In all, 35.5 percent of married male French-Canadian household heads were in their twenties, compared to 15.9 percent of the non-French-Canadian male heads; in households headed by French Canadians, 43.8 percent of their wives were in their twenties, compared to 20.6 percent of the spouses of the rest of Lewiston's household heads.

Due to inconsistencies in the recording of data on unemployment, compilers of the 1880 census never tabulated and published the results.[2] Unemployment data for Lewiston appears to have been collected reasonably well, however, and the results compiled from my sample are reported in the narrative.

Ethnicity did not account for any appreciable difference in the length of unemployment among Lewiston's working women. On average, unemployed American women in 1880 had been out of work for 4.3 months during the year prior to the census taker's visit, compared to 4.4 months for French-Canadian women and to 4.5 months for Irish women. Similarly, ethnicity did not affect substantially the amount of time American and French-Canadian men were out of work, for the unemployed among them averaged, respectively, 6.0 and 5.9 months without work; Irish men fared better, averaging only 4.5 months of unemployment during the previous year.

The sample taken from the 1920 federal manuscript census came from every thirtieth household and did not include institutions. The data represents 224 households containing 974 individuals. Unlike the 1880 census, the 1920 census indicated the mother tongue of enumerated persons and their parents, making it easier to distinguish between French- and English-Canadian descendants of both the first and second generations. Third- and later-generation individuals of French-Canadian descent were identified by their French surnames.

Data from the 1920 census reveals the extent to which differences between Lewiston's francophone population and the city's other large ethnic groups either had narrowed by, or continued to persist in, the early twentieth century. Unless otherwise noted, the figures provided for Irish and Franco-American Lewiston residents represent only individuals from the first and second generations, the only two generations specifically identified in the census.

By 1920, Lewiston had become an immigrant city; immigrants and their immediate offspring made up nearly 70 percent (68.8) of its population. Most of the immigrants had entered the United States after the turn of the century. Vénérand and Léontine Vallé, for example, had arrived in 1911, as had seven of the nine children who lived with them in 1920. None of the Irish in the sample had entered the United States in the twentieth century;

as Lewiston's oldest immigrant population, the Irish consisted primarily of third and later generations by 1920. Unlike them, individuals from southern and eastern Europe were among Lewiston's newest residents, and most of them had arrived in the United States in the first and second decades of the twentieth century.

The large differences that existed in 1880 between the households of Lewiston's French speakers and those of the city's Irish and American residents had narrowed by 1920; in fact, most of the differences in the size and composition of the Franco-American households and those of their Irish coreligionists had all but disappeared. In 1920, over one-third (37.1 percent) of the Franco-American households (including relatives and boarders) had six or more members, a proportion comparable to the Irish (36.8 percent) but significantly larger than the American households (12.9 percent). The eleven members of the nuclear family of Vénérand and Léontine Vallé made their household one of Lewiston's largest in 1920; sizable Franco-American families like theirs especially stood out from the American households. Unlike in 1880, Lewiston's French speakers in 1920 took in relatives about as often as they did lodgers. In 1920, they expanded their homes with relatives in nearly the same proportion as the Irish, but less often than the American household heads. In all, 31.4 percent of the American heads took in relatives, compared to 26.3 percent of the Irish and 23.7 percent of the Franco-American heads. As in 1880, Franco-Americans continued in 1920 to expand their households with boarders more often than Lewiston's other large ethnic groups. To wit, one-fourth (24.7 percent) of the Franco-American households took in boarders in 1920, compared to under one-sixth of both the Irish (15.8 percent) and the American (15.7 percent) households. In addition, two (2.9 percent) of the American, two (2.0 percent) of the Franco-American, and none of the Irish heads extended their households in 1920 with housekeepers, servants, or hired help.

Some other differences persisted between the Franco-American, Irish, and American households of Lewiston in 1920. As in 1880, Franco-American men and women tended to marry at a younger age than the Irish or Americans living in Lewiston. In close to half (47.4 percent) of the households headed by the Irish in 1920, for example, the oldest single, never-married child was nineteen years of age or older, whereas this was the case in only one-fourth (25.8 percent) of the Franco-American households. American households had an even smaller proportion (17.1 percent) where the oldest never-married child was over eighteen, but other data suggests that Franco-Americans married younger than Americans. While 21.8 percent of the married Franco-American male household heads were in their twenties, 9.8 percent of the American and none of the Irish heads was in his or her twenties. Similarly, 34.6 percent of the married Franco-American female heads were in their twenties, while 17.4 percent of the American and none of the Irish were. Given that the Irish represented an older immigrant stock in Lewiston, the finding that no married Irish heads were in their twenties is not surprising; in fact, a closer examination reveals that the married Irish household heads were all between their forties and sixties, unlike the Franco-American and American heads, whose ages ranged from the twenties to the seventies. While the cultural practice of Franco-Americans to marry young does not explain why their family size approached that of the first- and second-generation Irish who were at the end of or beyond their childbearing years in 1920, it does help account for the larger size of Franco-American families over those of the Americans. Religious practice likely explains the comparable family size of Catholic Irish and Franco-American Lewiston residents in 1920 and in part accounts for the difference between the sizes of their families and those of Protestant Americans.

City Directories, 1960 and 1992

Data compiled from the 1960 Lewiston city directory came from every twenty-fifth entry; if that entry was a business, however, I skipped to the next Lewiston resident. Unlike the 1880 and 1920 censuses, the directory did not enumerate each member of the household, but only provided the name of a male or female resident and the name of that person's spouse. The 922 entries I examined yielded a total sample of 1,455 residents. Each entry supplied only the occupation of the main person listed; I obtained information on the occupations of their spouses by tracking their names in the resident directory. In addition, I compiled data on homeownership by tracking the names and addresses of all household heads in the numerical street directory.[3]

For a portrait of the Lewiston community in the 1990s, I relied upon the 1992 city directory. Although the most recent Lewiston city directory was published in 1996, it did not provide sufficient information on the occupations, spouses, and homeownership of residents to be useful to this study. Data compiled from the 1992 directory came from every fifteenth entry; if the entry listed a business or an Auburn resident, I passed to the next Lewiston resident. In all, the sample comprised 889 listings that yielded information on 1,270 persons.[4]

Naturalization Records

To compile the naturalization data used in this study, I examined all of the naturalization records of the courts of Lewiston, Auburn, and Portland, Maine, from 1790 to 1991. These records, stored in courthouses and in state and federal archives, are available for public inspection; it was not necessary to submit Freedom of Information/Privacy Act request forms to view them, as is the case with records from 1991, which are in the possession of the Immigration and Naturalization Service. The data comprised all Canadian immigrants living in Lewiston who had French maiden names or surnames, as well as those with non-French names whose naturalization records identified them as French Canadians. The sources reveal that 5,551 French-Canadian immigrants in Lewiston acquired their U.S. citizenship through 1991 (see table 6). The information court clerks compiled on these individuals varied at different points in time, as naturalization forms changed. Before the Bureau of Immigration and Naturalization came into existence in September 1906, the information even varied by courthouse, for there was no standardization of naturalization forms. Nonetheless, naturalization records serve as a rich source on U.S. immigrants, a source that historians have rarely tapped.[5]

Among the valuable information they provide is the place of birth of immigrants. But the records are seldom as complete as the researcher would like. Court clerks processing naturalization records in Lewiston, Auburn, and Portland typically recorded the town in which the immigrant had been born, but rarely the county; sometimes they even omitted the name of the province. Of the 5,551 French-Canadian immigrants of Lewiston

Table 6. Naturalization of Lewiston's French-Canadian Immigrants by Decade from the 1860s until the 1990s

DECADE	NUMBER	DECADE	NUMBER
1860–1869	0	1940–1949	1,787
1870–1879	2	1950–1959	436
1880–1889	519	1960–1969	146
1890–1899	667	1970–1979	49
1900–1909	488	1980–1989	23
1910–1919	196	1990–1991	0
1920–1929	626	TOTAL	5,551
1930–1939	612		

Source: Compiled from the naturalization records of the courts of Lewiston, Auburn, and Portland, Maine, for the period from 1790 to 1991: Supreme Judicial Court, Androscoggin County, Records, vols. 1–27.5, 1854–1894, Maine State Archives [hereafter MSA], Augusta, Maine; Supreme Judicial Court, Androscoggin County, Naturalization Records, vols. B, B-2, C-1, E, 1–21, 1895–1930, Office of the Clerk of the Superior Court of Maine, Auburn, Maine; Supreme Judicial Court, Androscoggin County, Naturalization Records, vol. D-1, 1903–1906, National Archives and Records Administration, Waltham, Massachusetts [hereafter NARA-Waltham]; Superior Court of Maine at Auburn Naturalization Records, vols. 22–47, 1930–1974, Auburn, Maine; Lewiston Municipal Court Naturalization Records, vols. 4–8, 1882–1893, MSA; Auburn, Maine, Municipal Court Naturalization Records, 1893, NARA-Waltham; U.S. District Court, Portland, Maine, Naturalization Records, vols. 1–2, 6–8, 1790–1845, vols. 1–11, 1851–1906, vols. 1–76, 1912–1991, Overseas Military Petitions and Records, 1942–1945, NARA-Waltham; U.S. Circuit Court, Portland, Maine, Naturalization Records, vols. 1–10, 1851–1912, NARA-Waltham; Superior Court, Cumberland County (Portland, Maine), Naturalization Records, 1868–1903, MSA.

who naturalized, only 226 had been born in a Canadian province other than Québec, three more had probably been born outside of Québec, and the province of birth of twenty-nine others could not be determined. Alternatively, 5,079 immigrants (91.5 percent) had been born in Québec, and another 214 (3.9 percent) had probably been born in the province. Thus, up to 95 percent of the 5,551 French-Canadian immigrants who naturalized while living in Lewiston had been born in the Province of Québec.

Determining the county in which these French-Canadian immigrants had been born proved difficult, however. There were over fifty counties in Québec at the turn of the century. Numerous Québec towns began as parishes and, when they incorporated, took the parish name as their own. Consequently, a number of municipalities in different counties of Québec shared the same name, particularly the names of saints. Sainte-Hélène, for example, appeared in Kamouraska, Arthabaska, and Bagot, all potential sources of Lewiston's French-Canadian population, for the Grand Trunk Railway passed through each of these counties. I was able to match 3,769 of the Québec towns listed in naturalization records to counties in the province. Such considerations as proximity to Lewiston, the place of emigration (if different from the place of birth), the dates that similarly named towns incorporated, as well as the migration patterns of Lewiston's French-Canadian population suggested the county from which another 1,077 had *probably* originated. Insufficient or conflicting information prevented assignment of the remaining 447 (a figure which includes the 214 who had probably been born in Québec and not in another Canadian province). In the narrative of this work, wherever a range indicates the proportion of naturalizers from a given county, the larger figure includes those who had *probably* been born in the county, while the smaller figure represents those for whom the assignment is nearly certain.[6] For the sake of consistency, I have employed throughout this monograph Québec county names and divisions as they existed around the turn of the last century.

The Naturalization of French Canadians during World War II and the Postwar Era

Because the naturalization process was not as critical to the story of French-Canadian immigrants in Lewiston from the middle to the end of the twentieth century, much of the analysis of the naturalization records from the period is represented here in the appendix rather than in the narrative.[7] As in the past, only a small minority (up to 4.4 percent) of the francophones who naturalized in Lewiston in the 1940s had been born in Canada outside of the Province of Québec. During the 1950s and 1960s, however, that proportion jumped to one-tenth (10.0 percent). As in prior decades, the Province of New Brunswick supplied most of these non-*Québécois* francophones.

Consistent with prior periods, a preponderance of the Québec-born immigrants came from counties south of the Saint Lawrence River. No more than 3.0 percent of the individuals who naturalized in the 1940s had been born in counties north of this arterial waterway; the proportion climbed to 8.1 percent in the 1950s and 1960s, reflecting a wider migration field than in earlier periods. As in the past, a majority of the immigrants who had been born north of the Saint Lawrence came from the three largest cities on the river. Madeline Landry, for instance, a housewife who naturalized in 1952, had been born in Québec City. Among the places of birth south of the Saint Lawrence, roughly the same regional patterns surfaced again in the naturalization records, patterns which revealed premigration concentrations near Maine's northern and western borders. Beauce County alone provided the greatest proportion of naturalizers—as much as 29.6 percent in the 1940s and up to 24.7 percent in the 1950s and 1960s.[8] Beauce sent so many francophones to Lewiston, in fact, that *Le Messager* periodically published in the late 1940s and 1950s a column entitled "Chronique des Beaucerons" ("Chronicle of the Beaucerons") featuring news from different towns in the county; no other region of French Canada received as much coverage in this newspaper.

Like the French-Canadian immigrants who naturalized in the 1920s and 1930s, over three-fifths of the men (65.7 percent) and women (61.9 percent) who acquired U.S. citizenship in the 1940s had emigrated from their place of birth to the United States. In contrast, a greater proportion of the men who naturalized from 1950 to 1952 (the last date for which we can discern this information from naturalization forms) had migrated within Canada before entering the United States, while the opposite was true for women. The numbers reflect that 54.8 percent of the men and 67.2 percent of the women who became U.S. citizens in the early 1950s had emigrated from their place of birth to the United States. Napoleon Eudore Poirier was one of the men who migrated within Canada before crossing the border to the United States. Poirier had been born in Bonaventure, a county in eastern Québec north of the Province of New Brunswick; he moved south to New Brunswick before migrating further south to Maine in 1928. Poirier's experience was atypical, however. Only a tiny proportion of the naturalizing men (2.6 percent) and women (up to 2.2 percent) of the 1940s had migrated to a different Canadian province before journeying to the United States; in the early 1950s, a slightly larger proportion of men (3.2 percent) than women (1.6 percent) had done so.[9]

Among the French-Canadian immigrants of Lewiston who naturalized in the 1940s, three-fourths (74.3 percent) had crossed the international border in Vermont, and one-fourth (24.1 percent) had entered the United States in Maine. While the large majority (76.4 percent) had arrived in the United States on trains, most on the Grand Trunk Railway, an increasing proportion had entered the United States on highways, using automobiles as their means of immigration. A change in transportation explains why increasing

numbers of naturalizers from 1950 to 1966 (the last date for which naturalization forms provide information on the journey of immigrants) had entered the United States in Maine. Jeannine Yvette Mathieu was one of these
individuals; born in Beauce County, she crossed the international border by
car at Jackman, Maine, in 1957 and became a U.S. citizen in 1961.[10] We do
not know whether French-Canadian immigrants like Mathieu owned the
automobiles that transported them to the United States; we can speculate,
however, that the increase in this form of transportation suggests that naturalizers of the 1960s had arrived in the United States with more capital than
those of prior decades whose passage to the United States had required only
the purchase of a train ticket.

After crossing the international border, the francophones who eventually became U.S. citizens did not demonstrate much geographic mobility.
Only 1.3 percent of the naturalizers in the 1940s and 1.1 percent in the
early 1950s had filed their first naturalization papers at courts other than in
Auburn or Portland, Maine, suggesting that very few had lived elsewhere in
the United States before settling in Lewiston. These small percentages may
understate the actual situation, because most of those who naturalized in
the 1940s and early 1950s did not need to file Declarations of Intention to
become U.S. citizens; spouses of U.S. citizens, minors who had arrived in
the United States under the age of sixteen and who filed papers within one
year of reaching twenty-one, and veterans of World War II needed only to
file final naturalization papers. Other evidence suggests that a larger proportion of naturalizers had migrated within the United States before becoming
citizens. One-tenth (10.7 percent) of those who naturalized in the 1940s
had children who had been born outside of the Lewiston-Auburn area. Between 1950 and 1962 (after which naturalization forms no longer provided
the places of birth of children), that proportion jumped to one-sixth (16.6
percent). Although French speakers who became citizens at mid-century had
evidenced greater migration within the United States than those who had
naturalized in earlier periods, significantly fewer had migrated within their
country of adoption than within the sending society.[11]

There was also little migration back and forth across the international
border. As in the past, the places of birth of the children of those who
naturalized in the 1940s suggest that only a minuscule proportion (1.8
percent) of French-Canadian immigrants had returned to Canada and then

emigrated to the United States for a second time before becoming citizens. At least 3.1 percent of those who naturalized in the 1950s and early 1960s had emigrated to the United States from Canada for a second time before naturalizing. While this reflects a small increase over the 1940s, it nonetheless demonstrates that only a tiny proportion of those who naturalized in Lewiston had participated in such migrations back and forth between Canada and the United States before acquiring U.S. citizenship.

Franco-Americans steadfastly retained their citizenship. Letters from Immigration and Naturalization Service (INS) officials attached to naturalization records reveal that only four of the 1,787 (0.2 percent) who naturalized in the 1940s later became expatriated. Among the naturalizers of the 1950s and 1960s, only two out of 582 (0.3 percent) later gave up or lost their U.S. citizenship. On only one of the six letters did INS officials supply the reason for the person's expatriation: Joseph Lorenzo Alfred Ouellette lost his U.S. citizenship in 1950 for having lived in Canada for three consecutive years following his naturalization in 1941.[12]

More than half of the women (55.0 percent) and men (52.3 percent) who naturalized in the 1940s had entered the United States as minors under eighteen. Whereas over half (53.1 percent) of the women who naturalized during the 1950s and 1960s had also arrived in the United States under the age of eighteen, only about one-third (36.7 percent) of the men had done so. Napoleon Eudore Poirier was not one of them. Naturalized in 1951, Poirier had crossed an international bridge between New Brunswick and Maine in 1928 while already in his mid-twenties. Just as in the 1930s, a majority of the men like Poirier who naturalized in the fifties and sixties had immigrated to the United States as adults.

Discrimination against Franco-Americans in the postwar era appears not to have led to much name changing in Lewiston. During the 1940s, only three (0.2 percent) of the 1,787 individuals who naturalized anglicized their given names, and none anglicized family names. While the number of persons who changed their French names increased in the fifties and sixties, the overall proportions remained small. Only 1.4 percent in the 1950s and 4.1 percent in the 1960s anglicized their given names at the time of naturalization, and under one percent in either decade anglicized their family names. Typically, the new surnames reflected spelling rather than phonetic alterations. For example, Francis Therriault changed his name in 1952 to Frank

Terrio, and Joseph Louis Philippe Beaulieu both shortened and anglicized his name in 1961 to become Philip Bolyer.[13]

As in the past, mid-century naturalization records suggest some of the motivations for acquiring U.S. citizenship. During the 1940s, four-fifths (79.5 percent) of the men who naturalized were married, and nearly half (47.6 percent) of their wives were U.S.-born, a proportion larger than in previous decades.[14] This must have motivated the men to become U.S. citizens. But, as in prior decades, the place of birth of their children appears to have been the more salient consideration. Over four-fifths (81.2 percent) of the men with issue had children who had all been born in the United States; about one-tenth (11.9 percent) had some children, but not all, who had been born in the United States. In sum, over nine-tenths (93.1 percent) of the naturalizing men with issue had some children who had been born in the United States.[15] Three-fourths (74.4 percent) of the women who naturalized in the 1940s were married at the time of their naturalization. The husbands of 42.9 percent were U.S.-born, and an additional 40.1 percent of the husbands had derived their U.S. citizenship from their parents or had naturalized on their own; thus, the husbands of 83.0 percent of the women who naturalized in the 1940s were U.S. citizens. This undoubtedly propelled immigrant wives to become citizens themselves. As with the men who naturalized in the 1940s, over four-fifths (83.2 percent) of the women with issue had children who had all been born in the United States; another tenth (11.3 percent) had some, but not all, children who had been born in the United States. Well over nine-tenths (94.5 percent) of the francophone mothers who naturalized in the 1940s, then, had delivered some or all of their children in their adopted country. In short, both the external force of World War II and the internal force manifested in family considerations appear to have motivated large numbers of French-Canadian men and women to acquire their U.S. citizenship during the 1940s.

In the postwar era, family considerations, it seems, continued to propel francophone men and women to naturalize. To take one example, Madeline Landry's three children and her husband had all been born in the United States, something that must have motivated her in 1952 to acquire her citizenship papers. Three-fourths of the men who naturalized during the 1950s (75.4 percent) and 1960s (75.9 percent) were married, whereas smaller proportions of the women who naturalized in the fifties (68.0 percent) and sixties (62.0 percent) were married at the time they acquired their U.S. citizenship. The naturalization records provide the places of birth of their spouses until 1966, and of their children until 1962. What these records reveal for married male naturalizers is that slightly over half (51.8 percent) had U.S.-born wives, and the overwhelming majority with issue (87.0 percent) had children who had been born in the United States. For wedded female naturalizers, these records reveal that under half (47.2 percent) had husbands who had been born in the United States, and over one-third (36.0 percent) had foreign-born husbands who had acquired their U.S. citizenship from their parents or through the naturalization process. Thus, like Landry, over four-fifths (83.2 percent) of the married women who naturalized through 1966 had husbands with U.S. citizenship. Also like her, as with the men, the overwhelming majority (93.1 percent) of the women with issue had children with places of birth in the United States.

Naturalizations did not necessarily correlate with higher occupational status. Only a small proportion of the men (8.5 percent) and women (3.4 percent) who naturalized in the 1940s held white-collar jobs, whereas half (50.8 percent) of the men and nearly half (48.2 percent) of the women were industrial workers. Greater numbers of housewives like Marie Rose Emelie Lepage acquired their citizenship during World War II and in the years immediately following it. Specifically, while one-fourth of the women who had naturalized in the 1930s were not working outside of the home at the time of their naturalization, the proportion rose to two-fifths (41.9 percent) in the 1940s.[16]

These occupational patterns changed somewhat in the 1950s and 1960s.[17] Beginning in the 1950s, a majority of the men and women who naturalized were not industrial workers. Under one-third of the naturalizing men in the 1950s (29.6 percent) and about one-third (32.5 percent) in the 1960s held industrial jobs; over one-third (38.4 percent) of the women who naturalized in the 1950s and one-third (33.3 percent) in the 1960s had industrial positions at the time of their naturalization. The proportion of naturalizing men with white-collar jobs climbed to one-fifth (19.7 percent) in the 1950s but dropped to one-twentieth (5.0 percent) in the 1960s. During the 1950s, one-twentieth (4.8 percent) of the naturalizing women had white-collar jobs, and this proportion doubled to one-tenth (10.3 percent) in the 1960s. Marielle Gaetane Roy, for instance, was a department-store clerk when she naturalized in 1963.

Housewives continued to make up a significant proportion of the women who acquired their citizenship in the postwar decades: half (50.3 percent) of the women who naturalized in the 1950s, and under half (44.9 percent) in the 1960s, did not work outside of the home.[18]

As in prior periods, the overwhelming majority of the French-Canadian immigrants who naturalized in the 1970s and 1980s had been born in Québec counties south of the Saint Lawrence River. Only about one-seventh (13.9 percent) of the naturalizers had been born outside of the Province of Québec, a proportion slightly higher than in previous periods, and most of them had come from New Brunswick. A tiny proportion (4.2 percent) of the naturalizers had been born in Québec counties north of the Saint Lawrence River. As in the past, counties south of the river furnished most of the naturalizers, and Beauce county again sent the largest proportion—from 26.4 to 37.5 percent. Together Beauce and Compton, neighboring counties on Maine's western border, supplied from one-third (34.7 percent) to nearly one-half (47.2 percent) of Lewiston's French-Canadian naturalizers of the 1970s and 1980s.

Because of changes in naturalization forms, we have considerably less information about the French-Canadian immigrants who acquired U.S. citizenship in this period. We can, for example, determine the age of immigrants at the time of their border crossing only until 1976. Under half (46.2 percent) of the women and over half (53.3 percent) of the men who naturalized from 1970 to 1976 had arrived in the United States as minors under the age of eighteen. One-half (50.0 percent) of the twelve women who had immigrated as minors naturalized within ten years of turning twenty-one. Under two-thirds (62.5 percent) of the eight men who had arrived in the United States as minors under eighteen naturalized within ten years of reaching age twenty-one. Thus, what little data we have on the length of time it took French-Canadian immigrants to naturalize from the early to mid-1970s suggests that women had waited longer than men to become U.S. citizens.

This was not the case among the immigrants who had arrived in the United States as adults. The women among them waited no longer than the men to naturalize. Over half (57.1 percent) of the fourteen women and under half of the seven men (42.9 percent) who had crossed the international border as adults naturalized within fifteen years of their immigration.

Naturalization forms provide little information about the families of petitioners. Only until 1977 do they indicate their marital status. From 1970 to 1977, nearly three-fourths (73.3 percent) of the men and slightly over three-fourths (76.9 percent) of the women were married at the time of their naturalization. We do not know whether the spouses of these naturalizers were U.S. citizens, potentially motivating the petitioners to become citizens themselves.

We have more complete information on the age of naturalizers. During the 1970s, slightly more than one-fourth (26.7 percent) of the women were over forty. The proportion more than doubled in the 1980s, reaching the same high level (60.0 percent) as in the 1950s. One of the women who naturalized in the 1980s, Marie Laure Simone Marquis, had been born in Beauce County and became a U.S. citizen while in her mid-fifties; her naturalization form does not indicate whether she had waited a considerable length of time to naturalize, as had so many of the French-Canadian immigrants who had become U.S. citizens in the 1950s. In contrast to the women, the proportion of men over forty remained under one-third in both the 1970s (31.6 percent) and 1980s (30.8 percent). Judging from the absence of INS letters attached to the naturalization papers of French-Canadian petitioners from the 1970s and 1980s, none appears to have given up or lost his or her U.S. citizenship.[19]

Occupational Classification and Ranking System

The occupational classification and ranking system used in this study allowed me to examine changes in Lewiston, particularly among its population of French-Canadian descent, over nearly a century and a half of historical time. The categories and rankings I have utilized vary in the following ways from Stephan Thernstrom's classic scale of three decades ago.[20] Rather than being lumped together into one group, professionals are characterized as self-governing or salaried. Small business, managerial, and semiprofessional jobs are ranked above clerical and sales positions. Types of occupation, not levels of skill, distinguish blue-collar employment categories; these classifications better reflect the nature of Lewiston's economy during the period under study and demonstrate more clearly how it changed over time.

Assigning self-employed tradespeople to blue-collar rank reflects the way in which the community defined itself. No effort was made to determine whether independent contractors or grocers had capital and employees, thus meriting ranking as small-business owners. Contractors in Lewiston typically worked for themselves rather than for wages and, if they had any employees, usually oversaw small operations; for these reasons, they are categorized as having self-employed, blue-collar occupations. Grocers are lumped together with merchants. Laborers often worked for the mills and factories of Lewiston and Auburn; those who did are classified as industrial employees. Because mills and factories dominated the local economy until the mid-twentieth century, persons identified in the sources simply as "laborers" through 1960, the last occurrence, are also classified as industrial workers.[21] Laborers employed by nonindustrial concerns are ranked as nonindustrial, blue-collar workers. Listing primary-sector employment as a separate category allows us to trace more easily the continuities or changes over time in the proportion of French-Canadian descendants employed in farming and lumbering—occupations this group engaged in before and after the immigration experience. In addition, this classification system, unlike Thernstrom's, includes occupations that women have usually filled. Although somewhat arbitrary, the classification and ranking system detailed below better suits the Lewiston community, while still preserving elements that would make comparisons possible with other communities. For example, the categories of self-governing and salaried professionals correspond to Thernstrom's "High White-Collar" jobs, and the remaining white-collar categories correspond to Thernstrom's "Low White-Collar" classification.

Occupational Rankings

- WHITE COLLAR
  - *self-governing professional*: doctors, lawyers, dentists, professors; persons with advanced degrees, specialized training, usually licensed by the state, and often self-employed
  - *salaried professional*: teachers, accountants, social workers, engineers, registered nurses, editors; occupations requiring college training; state officials; managers (and the few owners) of large businesses

— *small business and managerial*: people in supervisory positions and local officials

— *semiprofessional*: embalmers, journalists, photographers, librarians, opticians, music teachers, medical technicians, licensed practical nurses, and certified nurses' aides

— *clerical and sales*: cashiers, bank tellers, bookkeepers, secretaries, adjusters, auditors, agents, merchants, and grocers

- BLUE COLLAR

— *self-employed*: persons in manual trades, including barbers and beauticians, contractors and builders; mechanics with their own garage; cobblers, tailors, and dressmakers working for themselves; owners of rooming houses

— *nonindustrial*: providers of domestic, personal, and protective services, including food preparers and servers, laundry workers, janitors, servants, letter carriers, and providers of fire and police protection; persons involved in transport or in servicing means of transportation, including teamsters, gas station attendants, and mechanics; people in the building trades, such as carpenters, painters, and plumbers; those in other trades, such as blacksmiths, meat cutters, bakers, printers, lithographers, haircutters, ice cutters, nurses' aides, and dressmakers (who typically worked from home); and laborers employed by nonindustrial concerns

— *industrial*: mill and factory employees; people involved in manufacturing, processing, and assembly in the textile, shoe, metal, box making, and sanitary napkin industries; machinists; saw- and grist-mill workers; and laborers employed by mills and factories

— *primary sector*: persons engaged in farming, fishing, and lumbering

⚜

Notes

Introduction

1. Typescript notes of Reverend Philip Desjardins on Saint Joseph Parish, Lewiston, Maine, Chancery Archives, Roman Catholic Diocese of Portland, Maine; *Lewiston Democratic Advocate*, 13 December 1855.

2. John Herd Thompson and Stephen J. Randall, *Canada and the United States: Ambivalent Allies* (Athens, Ga.: University of Georgia Press, 1994), 51–55, 128–129; Yolande Lavoie, *L'émigration des Canadiens aux États-Unis avant 1930: Mesure du phénomène* (Montréal: Les Presses de l'Université de Montréal, 1972), 63, 76–77. Randy William Widdis argues that while English-Canadian immigrants may have appeared "invisible or not clearly discernable" in the United States, high rates of endogamy, their reluctance to acquire U.S. citizenship, and their continued interest in Canada suggest that they had some distinctive traits. See *With Scarcely a Ripple: Anglo-Canadian Migration into the United States and Western Canada, 1880–1920* (Montreal and Kingston: McGill-Queen's University Press, 1998), 179–289, 350–351.

3. Yolande Lavoie, *L'émigration des Québécois aux États-Unis de 1840 à 1930* ([Québec]: Éditeur officiel du Québec, 1981), 65. Not all French-Canadian immigrants

worked in the textile industry. On their experiences in lumbering and in the woods industries of Old Town, Maine, and in the granite industry of Barre, Vermont, see C. Stewart Doty, *The First Franco-Americans: New England Life Histories from the Federal Writers' Project, 1938–1939* (Orono: University of Maine at Orono Press, 1985), 46–118.

4. Ralph Dominic Vicero, "Immigration of French Canadians to New England, 1840–1900: A Geographical Analysis" (Ph.D. dissertation, University of Wisconsin, 1968), 343; Laureat Odilon Bernard, "A Political History of Lewiston, Maine (1930–39)" (master's thesis, University of Maine-Orono, 1949), 6.

5. The one notable exception is John F. McClymer, "The Paradox of Ethnicity in the United States: The French-Canadian Experience in Worcester, 1870–1914," in Michael D'Innocenzo and Josef P. Sirefman, eds., *Immigration and Ethnicity: American Society—"Melting Pot" or "Salad Bowl"?* (Westport, Conn.: Greenwood Press, 1992), 15–23.

6. Historian Dirk Hoerder similarly questions the use of the term "assimilation" to describe the immigrant experience in the United States in "From Migrants to Ethnics: Acculturation in a Societal Framework," in Dirk Hoerder and Leslie Page Moch, eds., *European Migrants: Global and Local Perspectives* (Boston: Northeastern University Press, 1996), 211–262.

7. François Weil, *Les Franco-Américains, 1860–1980* ([Paris]: Belin, 1989), 177–178.

8. *Le Messager*, 9 December 1918, p. 8. In this work, all quotations from French-language sources are represented in English. All translations are my own. Readers interested in the French quotations are encouraged to consult the dissertation upon which this monograph is based.

9. Yves Frenette, "Understanding the French Canadians of Lewiston, 1860–1900: An Alternate Framework," *Maine Historical Society Quarterly* 25 (Spring 1986): 205.

Chapter One.
Creating a Mosaic: Catholic Immigrants in a Protestant Mill Town, 1850–1880

1. *Lewiston Weekly Journal*, 15 May 1873, p. 26; *Lewiston Evening Journal*, 26 December 1882.

2. Geneva Kirk and Gridley Barrows, *Historic Lewiston: Its Government* (Lewiston, Maine: Lewiston Historical Commission, 1982), 1, 3; James S. Leamon, *Historic Lewiston: A Textile City in Transition* (Lewiston, Maine: Lewiston Historical Commission, 1976), v, 4, 6–7, 9; Georgia Drew Merrill, ed., *History of Androscoggin County, Maine* (Boston: W.A. Fergusson, 1891), 38; A. M. Myhrman and J. A. Rademaker, "The Second Colonization Process in an Industrial Community" (typescript, Lewiston Public Library, n.d.), 5; Edmund S. Hoyt, comp., *Maine State Year-Book and Legislative Manual, for the Year 1872* (Portland, Maine: Hoyt, Fogg & Breed, 1871), 168–169; N. Dingley, Jr., *Historical Sketch of Lewiston* (Lewiston, Maine: Lewiston Journal [1872]), 15.

3. Leamon, *A Textile City in Transition*, 6, 14, 28–34, 43; Secretary of State, comp., *Statistics of Industries and Finances of Maine for the Year 1883* (Augusta, Maine: Sprague and Son, 1883), 4–5; Myhrman and Rademaker, "The Second Colonization Process in an Industrial Community," 5.

4. Leamon, *A Textile City in Transition*, 14–15; Myhrman and Rademaker, "The Second Colonization Process in an Industrial Community," 1; James H. Mundy, *Hard Times, Hard Men: Maine and the Irish, 1830–1860* (Scarborough, Maine: Harp Publications, 1990), 54. Leamon's interpretation differs from mine in that he views the Irish as posing not an economic threat, but primarily a social and cultural threat to Lewiston's Yankee population. As in Lewiston, Yankee women initially dominated the labor forces of New England's textile-mill communities; by the 1860s, Irish workers supplanted them. On this change from a native-born to an immigrant-dominated work force in the textile mills, see Thomas Dublin, *Women at Work: The Transformation of Work and Community in Lowell, Massachusetts, 1826–1860* (New York: Columbia University Press, 1979).

5. Allan R. Whitmore, "'A Guard of Faithful Sentinels': The Know-Nothing Appeal in Maine, 1854–1855," *Maine Historical Society Quarterly* 20 (Winter 1981): 165, 170, 172–176; Fergus Macdonald, *The Catholic Church and the Secret Societies in the United States* (New York: The United States Catholic Historical Society, 1946), 29–30; Alexander Keyssar, *The Right to Vote: The Contested History of Democracy in the United States* (New York: Basic Books, 2000), 84; William Leo Lucey, S.J., *The Catholic Church in Maine* (Francestown, N.H.: Marshall Jones Co., 1957), 100, 124–125, 130–131, 155; James Paul Allen, "Catholics in Maine: A Social Geography" (Ph.D. dissertation, Syracuse University, 1970), 104–109; Mundy, *Hard Times, Hard Men*, 147; Diocese of Portland Centenary Year Edition, *Portland Sunday Telegram*, 6 November 1955, p. 6. Internal conflicts, increasing

public opposition, and the rise of the Republican Party helped lead to the collapse of the Know-Nothing movement in Maine in 1856. Know-Nothings became absorbed into Maine's Republican Party, something that led the state's Irish population to lean towards Democratic Party membership. Whitmore, 183–184, 189–190; Mundy, 189.

6. Typescript notes of Reverend Philip Desjardins on Saint Joseph Parish, Lewiston, Maine, Chancery Archives, Roman Catholic Diocese of Portland, Maine; T. Edward Conley, "Lewiston's Pioneer Catholic Parish," in *Fiftieth Anniversary of St. Josephs [sic] Church, Lewiston, Maine: Catholic Guide and Reference Book* (unidentified publisher, [1908?]), 11; *Lewiston Evening Journal*, 4 March 1901, p. 2; *Lewiston Falls Journal*, 15 and 22 December 1855; letter by "An Irish Catholic" to the editor of the Lewiston, Maine, *Democratic Advocate*, 13 December 1855; *Democratic Advocate*, 13 December 1855; Mundy, *Hard Times, Hard Men*, 21; Margaret J. Buker, "The Irish in Lewiston, Maine: A Search for Security on the Urban Frontier, 1850–1880," *Maine Historical Society Quarterly* 13 (Special, 1973): 7; Leamon, *A Textile City in Transition*, 15–16.

7. Myhrman and Rademaker, "The Second Colonization Process in an Industrial Community," 3–4; Dingley, *Historical Sketch of Lewiston*, 6; *Lewiston Evening Journal*, 4 March 1901, p. 2; Conley, "Lewiston's Pioneer Catholic Parish," 11; *Church World*, 18 February 1955, p. 13.

8. Supreme Judicial Court, Androscoggin County, Records, Maine State Archives [hereafter MSA], Augusta, Maine, vol. 17, pp. 139–140; Lewiston Municipal Court Naturalization Records, MSA, vol. 4, p. 503; *U.S. Census, 1860; Le Messager*, souvenir issue, 24 June 1892, p. 2, souvenir issue, 2 July 1895; *Paroisse Canadienne-Française de Lewiston (Maine): Album historique* ([Lewiston, Maine]: Les Pères Dominicains, 1899), 11–12; *U.S. Census, 1850*.

9. *Le Messager*, 23 January 1890, p. 4, souvenir issue, 24 June 1892, p. 2, souvenir issue, 2 July 1895.

10. James P. Allen, "Migration Fields of French Canadian Immigrants to Southern Maine," *Geographical Review* 62 (July 1972): 369–371. In an unsigned letter to the editor of the Portland, Maine, *Eastern Argus*, a promoter of U.S. investment in Canada indicated that one could potentially travel the 212-mile road between Québec City and Augusta, Maine, in two days. *Eastern Argus*, 4 July 1834, p. 2.

11. Allen, "Migration Fields of French Canadian Immigrants to Southern Maine," 372–373; Myhrman and Rademaker, "The Second Colonization Process in an Industrial Community," 5; Department of the Interior, Census Office, *Report on the*

Social Statistics of Cities, George E. Waring, Jr., comp., part 1, *The New England and the Middle States* (Washington, D.C.: Government Printing Office, 1886), 26; Yves Frenette, "La genèse d'une communauté canadienne-française en Nouvelle-Angleterre: Lewiston, Maine, 1800–1880" (Ph.D. dissertation, Université Laval, Québec, 1988), 151A; James P. Allen, "Franco-Americans in Maine: A Geographical Perspective," *Acadiensis* 4 (Autumn/automne 1974): 40; Ralph Dominic Vicero, "Immigration of French Canadians to New England, 1840–1900: A Geographical Analysis" (Ph.D. dissertation, University of Wisconsin, 1968), 343; U.S. Department of Commerce, Bureau of the Census, *Fifteenth Census of the United States, 1930*, vol. 1 (Washington, D.C.: Government Printing Office, 1931), 472.

12. Frenette, "La genèse d'une communauté canadienne-française en Nouvelle-Angleterre," 340–341; U.S. Department of the Interior, Census Office, *Compendium of the Tenth Census (June 1, 1880)*, part 1 (Washington, D.C.: Government Printing Office, 1883), 455; *Greenough's Directory of the Inhabitants, Institutions, Manufacturing Establishments, Societies, Business, Business Firms, Etc., Etc. in the Cities of Lewiston and Auburn, for 1880–81* (Boston: W.A. Greenough, 1880), 209–211, 363–365.

13. Myhrman and Rademaker, "The Second Colonization Process in an Industrial Community," 11–13, 34; *Annual Municipal Report, Fiscal Year Ending February 28, 1937: Lewiston, Maine* (unidentified publisher [1937]), 18.

14. Yves Roby, *Les Franco-Américains de la Nouvelle-Angleterre (1776–1930)* (Sillery, Québec: Septentrion, 1990), 22; *Le Messager*, 19 January 1923, p. 9; Supreme Judicial Court, Androscoggin County, Records, MSA, vol. 18, pp. 757–758.

15. Yves Roby, "L'évolution économique du Québec et l'émigrant (1850–1929)," in Claire Quintal, ed., *L'émigrant québécois vers les États-Unis (1850–1920)* (Québec: Le Conseil de la Vie française en Amérique, 1982), 8, 12–13, 17, 19; Roby, *Les Franco-Américains de la Nouvelle-Angleterre*, 33–45; Paul-André Linteau, René Durocher, and Jean-Claude Robert, *Histoire du Québec contemporain: De la Confédération à la crise (1867–1929)* (Montréal: Boréal, 1989), 168.

16. No women appear in the nineteenth-century data. Women derived their U.S. citizenship from their husbands or fathers and did not naturalize on their own until 1922. Widows, however, whose husbands had declared their intention to become U.S. citizens but who had died before filing final papers, could become naturalized by taking an oath of allegiance. John J. Newman, "American Naturalization Processes and Procedures, 1790–1985" (typescript, Family History Section, Indiana Historical Society, 1985), available at the National Archives and Records

Administration, Waltham, Massachusetts [hereafter NARA-Waltham], pp. 14, 22–23. The following constitute the nineteenth-century naturalization records of the courts of Lewiston, Auburn, and Portland, Maine, from which naturalization data represented throughout this chapter were compiled: Supreme Judicial Court, Androscoggin County, Records, vols. 1–27.5, 1854–1894, MSA; Supreme Judicial Court, Androscoggin County, Naturalization Records, vol. B, 1895–1899, Office of the Clerk of the Superior Court of Maine, Auburn, Maine; Lewiston Municipal Court Naturalization Records, vols. 4–8, 1882–1893, MSA; Auburn, Maine, Municipal Court Naturalization Records, 1893, NARA-Waltham; U.S. District Court, Portland, Maine, Proceedings, vols. 1–2, 6–8, 1790–1845, NARA-Waltham; U.S. District Court, Portland, Maine, Naturalization Records, vols. 1–11, 1851–1899, NARA-Waltham; U.S. Circuit Court, Portland, Maine, Naturalization Records, vols. 1–3, 1851–1899, NARA-Waltham; Superior Court, Cumberland County (Portland, Maine), Naturalization Records, 1868–1899, MSA. Hereafter, these records will be cited more succinctly as "nineteenth-century naturalization records."

17. Allen, "Catholics in Maine," 142, 142n, 145. Fleeting references to Acadians in Lewiston appear not in the city's French-language newspaper, but in the chronicle maintained by the Dominican priests and in the hospital reports of the Sisters of Charity. See, for example, La Chronique du couvent, the series Monasteries and Parishes, the subseries Monastery of the Apostles Pierre and Paul of Lewiston, Maine, Archives of the Dominicans, Montréal, Québec [hereafter la Chronique des Dominicains], vol. 1, 10 September 1883, p. 119; and *Hospital of the Sisters of Charity: Thirteenth Annual Report, 1905* (Lewiston, Maine: Haswell Press [1905], 17.

18. Nineteenth-century naturalization records. See the appendix for an explication of the methodology employed in determining the counties of origin of naturalized males.

19. Nineteenth-century naturalization records. Readers interested in a detailed breakdown of the birthplaces of the French-Canadian immigrants naturalized in Lewiston, Maine, between 1877 and 1987 are urged to consult Mark Paul Richard, "From *Canadien* to American" (Ph.D. dissertation, Duke University, 2001), maps two through seven.

20. Allen, "Migration Fields of French Canadian Immigrants to Southern Maine," 379–380; William N. Locke, "The French Colony at Brunswick, Maine: A Historical Sketch," *Les Archives de Folklore* 1 (1946): 110–111.

21. Nineteenth-century naturalization records; L'Heureux's naturalization record is from the Lewiston Municipal Court, MSA, vol. 4, p. 495.

22. In fact, only three out of 1,188 persons had remigrated to Canada before becoming citizens. Because the information provided on naturalization forms varied by courthouse prior to the creation of the Bureau of Immigration and Naturalization in 1906, we do not have complete details on the migrant journey of French Canadians within the United States. The naturalization records of the Portland courts, for example, which account for about 20 percent of the data from the nineteenth century, furnish only the place of arrival in the United States. Records from the Lewiston and Auburn courts, which do detail the journey of emigrants after the border crossing, reveal that only twenty-five men (a mere 2.1 percent of all nineteenth-century naturalizers) who had emigrated directly from Canada to Lewiston had moved elsewhere before returning to the city to become naturalized citizens. Nineteenth-century naturalization records.

23. Roby, *Les Franco-Américains de la Nouvelle-Angleterre*, 33–45; Yves Frenette, "Macroscopie et microscopie d'un mouvement migratoire: Les Canadiens français à Lewiston au XIXe siècle," in Yves Landry, John A. Dickinson, Suzy Pasleau, and Claude Desama, eds., *Les chemins de la migration en Belgique et au Québec: XVIIe–XXe siècles* (Beauport, Québec: Publications MNH, 1995), 226, 228; Yves Frenette, "Understanding the French Canadians of Lewiston, 1860–1900: An Alternate Framework," *Maine Historical Society Quarterly* 25 (Spring 1986): 205, 213; Frenette, "La genèse d'une communauté canadienne-française en Nouvelle-Angleterre," 162.

24. E. Hamon, S.J., *Les Canadiens-Français de la Nouvelle-Angleterre* (Québec: N.S. Hardy, 1891), 405; *Paroisse Canadienne-Française de Lewiston (Maine)*, 13; Reverend John F. Crozier, ed., *One Hundredth Anniversary of Saint Joseph's Church, Lewiston, Maine, 1857–1957* (unidentified publisher, n.d.), 11; Antonin M. Plourde, O.P., "Cent ans de vie paroissiale: SS. Pierre et Paul de Lewiston, 1870–1970," *Le Rosaire* (August/September 1970): 9–10; notes of Reverend Philip Desjardins; Frenette, "La genèse d'une communauté canadienne-française en Nouvelle-Angleterre," 273; James S. Olson, *Catholic Immigrants in America* (Chicago: Nelson-Hall, 1987), 101, 103–104, 113.

25. Robert E. Park and Herbert A. Miller, *Old World Traits Transplanted* (New York: Harper, 1921), 24, 306–308; Plourde, "Cent ans de vie paroissiale," 9, 11, 13; *Le Messager*, October 1938, cited in Plourde, "Cent ans de vie paroissiale," 10; Hamon, *Les Canadiens-Français de la Nouvelle-Angleterre*, 406; Reverend

Alexandre-Louis Mothon, O.P., 1893, cited in J. Antonin Plourde, *Dominicains au Canada: Livre des documents*, vol. 2, *Les cinq fondations avant l'autonomie (1881–1911)* (unidentified publisher, 1975), 95.

26. Plourde, "Cent ans de vie paroissiale," 14; *Le Messager*, 29 June 1897, p. 5; Florence Marie Chevalier, S.S.A., "The Role of French National Societies in the Sociocultural Evolution of the Franco-Americans of New England from 1860 to the Present: An Analytical Macro-sociological Case Study in Ethnic Integration Based on Current Social System Models" (Ph.D. dissertation, Catholic University of America, 1972), 52–53. On the origins of French-language mutual-benefit societies in Québec and the northeastern United States, see Mark Paul Richard, "Coping before *l'État-providence*: Collective Welfare Strategies of New England's Franco-Americans," *Québec Studies* 25 (Spring 1998): 62–64.

27. *Le Messager*, 29 June 1897, p. 5; Yves Roby, "Émigrés canadiens-français, Franco-Américains de la Nouvelle-Angleterre et images de la société américaine," in Yvan Lamonde and Gérard Bouchard, eds., *Québécois et Américains: La culture québécoise aux XIXe et XXe siècles* ([Saint-Laurent, Québec]: Éditions Fides, 1995), 136; *Paroisse Canadienne-Française de Lewiston*, 95.

28. Plourde, "Cent ans de vie paroissiale," 11, 15; Frenette, "La genèse d'une communauté canadienne-française en Nouvelle-Angleterre," 239, 286–287, 292; la Chronique des Dominicains, vol. 5, p. 396; *Paroisse Canadienne-Française de Lewiston*, 96; *Noces d'Argent de l'Union Saint-Joseph: Programme des Fêtes Jubilaires, 22 et 23 juin 1904* ([Lewiston, Maine]: Le Messager [1904]), 4.

29. *Lewiston Weekly Journal*, 19 December 1872, p. 278 (italics in original), 13 February 1873, p. 344, 15 May 1873, p. 26; *Lewiston Evening Journal*, 5 May 1873, p. 3.

30. *U.S. Census, 1880*. See the appendix for a brief explanation of the methodology employed in using the 1880 census, and for more detailed statistics about Lewiston's population groups in 1880.

31. *U.S. Census, 1880*.

32. *U.S. Census, 1880*. Bradbury suggests that past differences in landholding patterns explained why French Canadians married at a younger age than the Irish. The practice of marrying young, she writes, "was typical in societies where land was available and where inheritance traditions did not constitute a brake on marriage." By contrast, the premigration experiences of the Irish—particularly their poverty and limited access to land in Ireland—had led them to delay marriage, a practice they continued in Canada. See Bettina Bradbury, *Working Families: Age, Gender,*

and Daily Survival in Industrializing Montreal (Toronto: Oxford University Press, 1993), 55–56.

33. *U.S. Census, 1880*; Annales de la Maison Mère, July 1881–September 1882, Archives of the Congrégation de Notre-Dame, Montréal, Québec, 6 November 1881, p. 151. See the appendix for an explanation of the occupational classification and ranking system employed here.

34. *U.S. Census, 1880.* Bradbury makes the same finding about Montréal's married working-class women in the nineteenth century. See *Working Families,* 169–172.

35. *U.S. Census, 1880.*

36. *U.S. Census, 1880.*

37. The youngest person who census takers indicated could not read and/or could not write was ten years old. Of the 674 persons in the sample who were ten years of age and older, 133 lacked the ability to read and/or to write. *U.S. Census, 1880.*

38. *U.S. Census, 1880*; Linteau et al., *Histoire du Québec contemporain,* 273, 616.

39. *U.S. Census, 1880.* On the phenomenon of unemployment prior to the Great Depression of the 1930s, see Alexander Keyssar, *Out of Work: The First Century of Unemployment in Massachusetts* (New York: Cambridge University Press, 1986).

40. *U.S. Census, 1880*; *Eighth Annual Report of the Receipts and Expenditures of the City of Lewiston, for the Fiscal Year Ending February 28, 1871; Together with Other Annual Reports and Papers Relating to the Affairs of the City* (Lewiston, Maine: Journal Steam Press, 1871), 68; *Fifteenth Annual Report of the Receipts and Expenditures of the City of Lewiston, for the Fiscal Year Ending February 28, 1878, Together with Other Annual Reports and Papers Relating to the Affairs of the City* (Lewiston, Maine: Geo. A. Callahan, 1878), 72.

41. *U.S. Census, 1880*; Registre des mariages de la Congrégation canadienne de Lewiston, Saint Peter and Saint Paul Parish Pastoral Center, Lewiston, Maine, vol. M-1, 1880, pp. 65–80; Marriage Register for Saint Joseph Parish and Saint Patrick Parish, Saint Patrick Parish Pastoral Center, Lewiston, Maine, 1880, pp. 26–33; Index of Marriages by Groom's Last Name, Office of the City Clerk, Lewiston, Maine, 2 vols. (1999); Elliott Robert Barkan, "French Canadians," in *Harvard Encyclopedia of American Ethnic Groups,* ed. Stephan Thernstrom (Cambridge, Mass.: Belknap Press, 1980), 399.

42. John F. McClymer has observed the same phenomenon among French Canadians in Worcester, Massachusetts, in "The Paradox of Ethnicity in the United States: The French-Canadian Experience in Worcester, 1870–1914," in Michael

D'Innocenzo and Josef P. Sirefman, eds., *Immigration and Ethnicity: American Society—"Melting Pot" or "Salad Bowl"?* (Westport, Conn.: Greenwood Press, 1992), 15–23.

Chapter Two.
The Rooster Crows: French Canadians Become Naturalized Citizens and Democratic Voters, 1880–1900

1. *Lewiston Evening Journal*, 3 March 1884; *Le Messager*, 6 March 1884.
2. Gerard J. Brault, *The French-Canadian Heritage in New England* (Hanover, N.H.: University Press of New England, 1986), 81; Charlotte Michaud, "Early Franco-American Medical Men," *Lewiston Journal* magazine section, 10 April 1976, p. 1A; Paul-M. Paré, "Les Vingt premières années du *Messager* de Lewiston, Maine," in Claire Quintal, ed., *Le Journalisme de langue française aux États-Unis* (Québec: Le Conseil de la Vie française en Amérique, 1984), 85, 93.
3. *Le Messager*, 26 August 1880, 31 March 1881.
4. *Le Messager*, 17 June 1880, 26 August 1880, 14, 21 and 28 October 1880, 4 November 1880, 14 April 1881.
5. *Le Messager*, 5 August 1880, 16 September 1880, 27 January 1881; *U.S. Census, 1880*; *Greenough's Directory of the Inhabitants, Institutions, Manufacturing Establishments, Societies, Business, Business Firms, Etc., Etc. in the Cities of Lewiston and Auburn, for 1880–81* (Boston: W.A. Greenough, 1880), 39, 60, 120, 130; *The Lewiston and Auburn Directory of the Inhabitants, Institutions, Manufacturing Establishments, Societies, Business, Business Firms, Etc., Etc. for 1883* (Boston: W.A. Greenough, 1883) [hereafter 1883 Lewiston city directory], 111; *Seventeenth Annual Report of the Receipts and Expenditures of the City of Lewiston, for the Fiscal Year Ending February 28, 1880; Together with Other Annual Reports and Papers Relating to the Affairs of the City* (Lewiston, Maine: Journal Office, 1880), 131–132.
6. *Le Messager*, 13 and 20 January 1881, 10 March 1881, 12 May 1881.
7. *Le Messager*, 7, 14 and 21 July 1881; typescript, 17 June 1881, Documents Book 6, Chancery Archives, Roman Catholic Diocese of Portland, Maine.
8. *Lewiston Evening Journal*, 4 February 1882; la Chronique du couvent de Saint-Pierre et Saint-Paul de l'ordre des Frères Prêcheurs, Lewiston, Maine, in the series Monasteries and Parishes, the subseries Monastery of the Apostles Pierre and Paul

of Lewiston, Maine, Archives of the Dominicans, Montréal, Québec [hereafter la Chronique des Dominicains], vol. 1, pp. 1–2; Jules Antonin Plourde, O.P., *Dominicains au Canada: Album historique* (unidentified publisher, 1973), 24, 26, 51–52.

9. Antonin M. Plourde, O.P., "Cent ans de vie paroissiale: SS. Pierre et Paul de Lewiston, 1870–1970," *Le Rosaire* (August/September 1970): 11, 20–21; *Lewiston Weekly Journal*, 15 May 1873, p. 26; typescript notes of Reverend Philip Desjardins, Chancery Archives; diary of Bishop James Augustin Healy, Chancery Archives, vol. 1, May 7, 1875, p. 4; J. Antonin Plourde, *Dominicains au Canada: Livre des documents*, vol. 2, *Les cinq fondations avant l'autonomie (1881–1911)* (unidentified publisher, 1975), 124 n. 58; la Chronique des Dominicains, vol. 1, pp. 2–3. The Dominicans modified the parish name, calling it Saint-Pierre et Saint-Paul (Plourde, "Cent ans de vie paroissiale," 22); following local usage, "Saint-Pierre" will generally be used in this work.

10. *Lewiston Evening Journal*, 4 February 1882; *Le Messager*, 2 July 1885, p. 1. On the Dominican perception of a Puritan climate in nineteenth-century New England, see Alexandre-Louis Mothon, O.P., 1883, in Plourde, *Dominicains au Canada: Livre des documents*, 2:64–65, 101.

11. Ralph Skinner, *Historically Speaking on Lewiston-Auburn, Maine, Churches* (Lewiston, Maine: By the Author, 1965), 99; *Lewiston Evening Journal*, 7 November 1881; *Le Messager*, 17 November 1881, 12 January 1888; la Chronique des Dominicains, vol. 1, 24 January 1884, pp. 143–144; Brault, *The French-Canadian Heritage in New England*, 74.

12. La Chronique des Dominicains, vol. 2, 3 October 1886, p. 69; vol. 3, 30 December 1888, p. 74. *Le Messager*, 18 November 1886, 3 May 1888, 23 June 1896; *Lewiston Evening Journal*, 24 June 1892, p. 5; *Paroisse Canadienne-Française de Lewiston (Maine): Album historique* ([Lewiston, Maine]: Les Pères Dominicains, 1899), 89, 91; *Noces d'Argent de l'Union Saint-Joseph: Programme des Fêtes Jubilaires, 22 et 23 juin 1904* ([Lewiston, Maine]: Le Messager [1904]), 13. While baseball existed in Canada in the late nineteenth century, it is not known whether Lewiston's francophone immigrants brought knowledge of the sport with them from Canada or whether they learned it in the United States. For an account that explores the development of baseball as a community sport in Canada's Maritime provinces and, to some extent, in the northeastern United States from the nineteenth century, see Colin D. Howell, *Northern Sandlots: A Social History of Maritime Baseball* (Toronto: University of Toronto Press, 1995). Relying almost exclusively upon sources published in English, this monograph provides little commentary about

the participation of French speakers in the sport in either Canada or the United States.

13. La Chronique des Dominicains, vol. 1, pp. 1–2, 20 August 1882, p. 34, 8 January 1883, p. 58, 2 February 1883, p. 62, 11 September 1883, p. 120, 11 December 1883, pp. 136–137, 18 December 1883, p. 137, vol. 2, 14 July 1885, p. 8⁶, 5 February 1886, pp. 20, 83, vol. 3, 11 and 18 February 1890, p. 189, 4 March 1890, p. 192; newspaper clipping from the *Auburn Gazette*, 28 December 1889, inserted into la Chronique des Dominicains, vol. 3, pp. 175–180; *Le Messager*, 10 July 1884, 28 June 1888; *séance* program inserted into la Chronique des Dominicains, vol. 3, 1890, p. 219.

14. *Le Messager*, 22 September 1891, 15 September 1896; French-language newspaper clipping inserted into la Chronique des Dominicains, vol. 3, 1891, p. 268; la Chronique des Dominicains, vol. 4, 15 October 1893, pp. 150, 187.

15. Yves Roby, "Quebec in the United States: A Historiographical Survey," *Maine Historical Society Quarterly* 26 (Winter 1987): 126.

16. La Chronique des Dominicains, vols. 1–5, passim, vol. 1, 26 June 1884, p. 180.

17. La Chronique des Dominicains, vol. 1, 2 February 1882, p. 17, 4 February 1882, pp. 17–18, 15 February 1883, p. 64, 18 February 1883, p. 65, 6 March 1883, pp. 74–75; *Le Messager*, 9 February 1882; Supreme Judicial Court, Androscoggin County, Records, Maine State Archives [hereafter MSA], Augusta, Maine, vol. 19, pp. 81–82. The following constitute the nineteenth-century naturalization records of the courts of Lewiston, Auburn, and Portland, Maine, from which naturalization data represented throughout this chapter were compiled: Supreme Judicial Court, Androscoggin County, Records, vols. 1–27.5, 1854–1894, MSA; Supreme Judicial Court, Androscoggin County, Naturalization Records, vol. B, 1895–1899, Office of the Clerk of the Superior Court of Maine, Auburn, Maine; Lewiston Municipal Court Naturalization Records, vols. 4–8, 1882–1893, MSA; Auburn, Maine, Municipal Court Naturalization Records, 1893, National Archives and Records Administration, Waltham, Massachusetts [hereafter NARA-Waltham]; U.S. District Court, Portland, Maine, Proceedings, vols. 1–2, 6–8, 1790–1845, NARA-Waltham; U.S. District Court, Portland, Maine, Naturalization Records, vols. 1–11, 1851–1899, NARA-Waltham; U.S. Circuit Court, Portland, Maine, Naturalization Records, vols. 1–3, 1851–1899, NARA-Waltham; Superior Court, Cumberland County (Portland, Maine), Naturalization Records, 1868–1899, MSA. Hereafter, these records will be cited more succinctly as "nineteenth-century naturalization records."

18. La Chronique des Dominicains, vol. 1, 17 February 1883, p. 65, 2 March 1883, p. 70; nineteenth-century naturalization records; translated letter of attorney F. X. Belleau to the editors of the *Lewiston Journal* and column by J. D. Montmarquet, both in *Le Messager*, 15 March 1882.

19. *Le Messager*, 10 January 1884, 16 and 27 February 1894; nineteenth-century naturalization records. The partisan tactics of Republicans to complicate naturalization procedures were part of a broader strategy to limit the voting strength of immigrants, a strategy that native-born Americans pursued throughout the United States during the period from Reconstruction to World War I. See Alexander Keyssar, *The Right to Vote: The Contested History of Democracy in the United States* (New York: Basic Books, 2000), chapter 5.

20. Nineteenth-century naturalization records. Lacking precise data on the relative growth of Lewiston's French-Canadian population during these decades, it is not possible to detail the relative increase in naturalizations as a proportion of that population.

21. Nineteenth-century naturalization records; French- and English-language newspaper clippings inserted into la Chronique des Dominicains, vol. 3, 1889, pp. 171–172; *Le Messager*, 4 February 1886, 20 February 1890, p. 4, 18 November 1892; *Lewiston Evening Journal*, 12 February 1891. Annual reports of Lewiston officials testify to difficult economic times in the city from 1893 until the turn of the century. See *Thirty-First Annual Report of the Receipts and Expenses of the City of Lewiston for the Fiscal Year Ending Feb. 28, 1894, Together with Other Annual Reports and Papers Relating to the Affairs of the City* (Lewiston, Maine: Daily Sun Publishing Company, 1894), 138; *Thirty-Second Annual Report of the Receipts and Expenses of the City of Lewiston for the Fiscal Year Ending Feb. 28, 1895, Together with Other Annual Reports and Papers Relating to the Affairs of the City* (Lewiston, Maine: Geo. A. Callahan, 1895), 3, 140; *Thirty-Fourth Annual Report of the Receipts and Expenses of the City of Lewiston for the Fiscal Year Ending Feb. 28, 1897, Together with Other Annual Reports and Papers Relating to the Affairs of the City* (Lewiston, Maine: Journal Office, 1897), 103; *Thirty-Seventh Annual Report of the Receipts and Expenses of the City of Lewiston for the Fiscal Year Ending Feb. 28, 1900, Together with Other Annual Reports and Papers Relating to the Affairs of the City* (Lewiston, Maine: Le Messager, 1900), 154. Like Maine, other states imposed literacy requirements to limit the franchise of immigrants. See Keyssar, *The Right to Vote*, table A.13 and chapter 5, especially pp. 136–146.

22. Nineteenth-century naturalization records.

23. Elliott Robert Barkan, "Proximity and Commuting Immigration: An Hypothesis Explored via the Bi-polar Ethnic Communities of French Canadians and Mexican Americans," in Jack Kinton, ed., *American Ethnic Revival: Group Pluralism Entering America's Third Century* (Aurora, Ill.: Social Science and Sociological Resources, 1977), 163–179; Gerard Blazon, "A Social History of the French Canadian Community of Suncook, New Hampshire (1870–1920)" (master's thesis, University of New Hampshire, 1974), 155.

24. John J. Newman, "American Naturalization Processes and Procedures, 1790–1985" (typescript, Family History Section, Indiana Historical Society, 1985), available at NARA-Waltham, p. 23. An exception to the two-step naturalization process existed for men who had served in the U.S. Army. Even if they had entered the United States at eighteen years or older, they needed only to file final naturalization papers, provided they had met the one-year residency requirement. This did not contribute many French-speaking citizens to Lewiston, however. Slightly under two (1.7) percent of the men who naturalized from the 1870s through the 1890s had served in the armed forces, and only one of these individuals was over seventeen when he had entered the country. Newman, p. 22; nineteenth-century naturalization records.

25. *Auburn Gazette*, 28 December 1889, inserted into la Chronique des Dominicains, vol. 3, pp. 175–180; nineteenth-century naturalization records. By comparison, two-thirds (67.6 percent) of the French Canadians from Holyoke, Massachusetts, who naturalized from 1868 to 1899 were between twenty-one and thirty years of age. These figures are derived from data compiled by Peter Haebler, "Habitants in Holyoke: The Development of the French-Canadian Community in a Massachusetts City, 1865–1910" (Ph.D. dissertation, University of New Hampshire, 1976), 144, 263.

26. Nineteenth-century naturalization records; Ouellette's naturalization record is from the U.S. District Court in Portland, Maine, NARA-Waltham, vol. 8, p. 113, and Morin's is from the Auburn Municipal Court, NARA-Waltham, 1893, p. 63.

27. Nineteenth-century naturalization records; Ralph Dominic Vicero, "Immigration of French Canadians to New England, 1840–1900: A Geographical Analysis" (Ph.D. dissertation, University of Wisconsin, 1968), 394–395.

28. Susan Olzak, *The Dynamics of Ethnic Competition and Conflict* (Stanford, Calif.: Stanford University Press, 1992). The same can be said of the Irish in communities across the country. As Radical Reconstructionists tightened voter qualifications

for foreign-born whites in the post–Civil War era, the Irish developed political machines and sought to control patronage. Ethnic competition and conflict resulted. On the development of Democratic political machines by the Irish, see Steven P. Erie, *Rainbow's End: Irish-Americans and the Dilemmas of Urban Machine Politics, 1840–1985* (Berkeley: University of California Press, 1988), especially chapter 2.

29. *Le Messager,* 16 March 1882, 8 and 22 March 1883; 1883 Lewiston city directory, pp. 52, 112–113, 118, 127, 139, 148; U.S. District Court, Portland, Maine, Naturalization Records, NARA-Waltham, vol. 7; *Lewiston Evening Journal,* 27 February 1883; la Chronique des Dominicains, vol. 1, 6 March 1883, pp. 74–75.

30. Brault, *The French-Canadian Heritage in New England,* 67–68; Massachusetts Bureau of Statistics of Labor, *Twelfth Annual Report, 1881,* cited in Brault, p. 68; *Le Messager,* 21 July 1881, 3 November 1881, 8 March 1883.

31. *Le Messager,* 13 and 20 December 1883.

32. Aldermen with the Anglo-American surnames of Parker and Coburn fought in favor of requiring the Dominicans to pay for the use of the city hall, while those with the Irish and French-Canadian family names of Callahan, Marcous, Peltier, and Cloutier opposed the measure. English-language newspaper clipping inserted into la Chronique des Dominicains, vol. 1, 1884, p. 145.

33. English-language newspaper clipping inserted into la Chronique des Dominicains, vol. 1, 1884, p. 145; la Chronique des Dominicains, vol. 1, 3 March 1884, p. 147.

34. *Le Messager,* 21 and 28 February 1884, 6 March 1884; *Lewiston Evening Journal,* 3 and 4 March 1884; Edmund S. Hoyt, comp., *Maine State Year-Book, and Legislative Manual, for the Year 1880–81, from April 1, 1880, to April 1, 1881* (Portland, Maine: Hoyt, Fogg and Donham, n.d.), 204.

35. *Le Messager,* 15 November 1883, 19 and 26 June 1884, 7, 14 and 21 August 1884, 11 September 1884, 30 October 1884, 1 January 1885.

36. *Le Messager,* 16 August 1888, 13 February 1894, souvenir issue of 2 July 1895, 3 March 1896, 19 May 1896, 3 July 1896, p. 7, 7 July 1896, 12 January 1897; Lewiston (Maine) *La République,* 17 February 1887, p. 1; Georgia Drew Merrill, ed., *History of Androscoggin County, Maine* (Boston: W.A. Fergusson, 1891), 284; *Lewiston and Auburn Directory of the Inhabitants, Institutions, Manufacturing Establishments, Societies, Business, Business Firms, Etc., 1896* (Boston: W.A. Greenough, 1896), 66, 170, 222, 234.

37. *Lewiston Evening Journal,* 28 December 1889, 4 September 1890.

38. *Le Messager*, 23 and 26 February 1892, 19 December 1893, 9 and 23 February 1894, 2 March 1894. Similar efforts to limit the franchise of other immigrant populations took place throughout the country in the late nineteenth and early twentieth centuries. See Keyssar, *The Right to Vote*, chapter 5.

39. *Le Messager*, 13 September 1888, 11 March 1892, 9 and 20 March 1894. *Le Messager* had attributed Martel's mayoral defeat in the previous year to an Irish clique that had defected to the Republican Party. *Le Messager*, 7 March 1893.

40. *Le Messager*, 9 March 1894.

41. *Le Messager*, 14 October 1886, 11 October 1888, 23 October 1891, 9 August 1893, 3 April 1894, 5 March 1895, [19?] March 1895, souvenir issue of 2 July 1895, [7?] February 1896, 6 March 1896, p. 2, 17 March 1896, 13 April 1897.

42. *Le Messager*, 12 July 1892. In Massachusetts, French Canadians became Democrats or Republicans depending upon which party offered them the influence they desired. See Ronald Petrin, *French Canadians in Massachusetts Politics, 1885–1915: Ethnicity and Political Pragmatism* (Philadelphia: Balch Institute Press, 1990).

43. *Le Messager*, 4 March 1902, p. 6, 21 March 1905, p. 2, 31 March 1905, pp. 7–8, 6 March 1906, p. 7, 31 March 1906, p. 2, 8 March 1916, p. 1.

Chapter Three.
Not Foreigners but Americans: French Canadians Negotiate Their Identity in the Spindle City, 1880–1900

1. *Lewiston Evening Journal*, 24 June 1897, p. 7; *Le Messager*, 29 June 1897, p. 6.

2. *Le Messager*, 2 July 1885, p. 1; *Lewiston Evening Journal*, 24 June 1892, p. 5, 4 July 1895, p. 12.

3. *Le Messager*, 30 October 1884.

4. La Chronique du couvent de Saint-Pierre et Saint-Paul de l'ordre des Frères Prêcheurs, Lewiston, Maine, in the series Monasteries and Parishes, the subseries Monastery of the Apostles Pierre and Paul of Lewiston, Maine, Archives of the Dominicans, Montréal, Québec [hereafter la Chronique des Dominicains], vol. 3, 4 March 1890, p. 192, 22 August 1890, p. 225; *Annual Reports of the School Committee and of the Superintendent of Schools of the City of Lewiston, for the Year Ending August 31, 1890* (Lewiston, Maine: Geo. A. Callahan, Printer, 1890), 17–19, 23; article signed "Un Canadien-Américain," *Le Messager*, 20 November 1890, p. 4.

5. Alexandre-Louis Mothon, cited in J. Antonin Plourde, *Dominicains au Canada: Livre des documents*, vol. 2, *Les cinq fondations avant l'autonomie (1881–1911)* (unidentified publisher, 1975), 112–113.

6. *Le Messager*, 7 May 1891, p. 4, 4 September 1891; English-language newspaper clipping inserted into la Chronique des Dominicains, vol. 3, p. 259; la Chronique des Dominicains, vol. 3, 1 September 1891, p. 272, 17 September 1891, pp. 272–273, 5 October 1891, p. 275, 21 December 1891, p. 282; French-language newspaper clipping inserted into la Chronique des Dominicains, vol. 4, 1893, p. 82.

7. *Sixth Annual Report of the Receipts and Expenditures of the City of Lewiston, for the Fiscal Year Ending Feb. 28, 1869, Together with Other Annual Reports and Papers Relating to the Affairs of the City* (Lewiston, Maine: Evening Journal, 1869), 9; *Seventh Annual Report of the Receipts and Expenditures of the City of Lewiston, for the Fiscal Year Ending Feb. 28, 1870, Together with Other Annual Reports and Papers Relating to the Affairs of the City* (Lewiston, Maine: Geo. A. Callahan, 1870), 47; *Thirteenth Annual Report of the Receipts and Expenditures of the City of Lewiston, for the Fiscal Year Ending Feb. 29, 1876, Together with Other Annual Reports and Papers Relating to the Affairs of the City* (Lewiston, Maine: Geo. A. Callahan, 1876), 86–87; *Fourteenth Annual Report of the Receipts and Expenditures of the City of Lewiston, for the Fiscal Year Ending Feb. 28, 1877; Together with Other Annual Reports and Papers Relating to the Affairs of the City* (Lewiston, Maine: Journal Office, 1877), 66; English-language newspaper clippings inserted into la Chronique des Dominicains, vol. 2, 1887, pp. 141–142; holographic report inserted into the Comptes Rendus de L'Asile Notre Dame de Lourdes de Lewiston à commencer de l'année 1884–1885, Saint Mary's Regional Medical Center Archives, Lewiston, Maine; la Chronique des Dominicains, vol. 2, 15 November 1887, pp. 130–131, 24 November 1887, p. 133. On the role of the Soeurs Grises as providers of social assistance in Québec and New England, see Mark Paul Richard, "Coping before *l'État-providence*: Collective Welfare Strategies of New England's Franco-Americans," *Québec Studies* 25 (Spring 1998): 60–62. For an account that explores the Sisters' Hospital as an illustration of the contribution of women to healthcare, see Susan P. Hudson, *The Quiet Revolutionaries: How the Grey Nuns Changed the Social Welfare Paradigm of Lewiston, Maine* (New York: Routledge, 2006).

8. Letter of F. X. Belleau, published in the *Lewiston Evening Journal*, 15 February 1889; la Chronique des Dominicains, vol. 3, 21 August 1888, p. 46, 13 January 1889, p. 80, 24 January 1889, p. 85.

9. Letter of F. X. Belleau, published in the *Lewiston Evening Journal*, 15 February 1889; *Auburn Gazette*, 13 March 1889, 28 December 1889, inserted into la Chronique des Dominicains, vol. 3, pp. 115, 175–180; English-language newspaper clipping inserted into la Chronique des Dominicains, vol. 3, pp. 92–93; la Chronique des Dominicains, vol. 3, 6 February 1889, p. 94, 10 March 1889, p. 111, 12 March 1889, p. 112, 24 March 1889, p. 121, 28 March 1889, p. 122; *Le Messager*, 14 March 1889; *Lewiston Evening Journal*, 11 March 1889.

10. La Chronique des Dominicains, vol. 3, [4?] November 1890, pp. 236–237; *Lewiston Evening Journal*, 29 January 1891, p. 1. The Grey Nuns had opened an orphanage for girls at their residence when they arrived in Lewiston in 1878, and they relocated it to the hospital property when they moved there. Holographic report inserted into the Comptes Rendus de L'Asile Notre Dame de Lourdes.

11. *First Annual Report of the Central Maine General Hospital, Lewiston, Maine, July 1, 1891, to July 1, 1892* (Lewiston, Maine: Journal Office, 1893), 8.

12. La Chronique des Dominicains, vol. 4, 13 December 1892, p. 67, 2 January 1893, pp. 77–78; English-language newspaper clipping inserted into la Chronique des Dominicains, vol. 4, 1892, p. 67; *Le Messager*, 27 December 1892, 4 January 1893.

13. La Chronique des Dominicains, vol. 1, November 1882, p. 92, 6 July 1884, p. 187, 17 July 1884, p. 193; vol. 2, 31 August 1886, p. 62; vol. 4, 1 August 1892, p. 30. English-language newspaper clipping inserted into la Chronique des Dominicains, vol. 1, 1884, p. 193; written agreement between Reverend T. H. Wallace and Bishop James Augustin Healy, 17 August 1886, and letter of J. Kennedy to Bishop Healy, 31 October 1894, among "Parish Reports, 1879–," Chancery Archives; Reverend John F. Crozier, ed., *One Hundredth Anniversary of Saint Joseph's Church, Lewiston, Maine, 1857–1957* (unidentified publisher, n.d.), 13; Larry and Carol Marcoux, eds., *St. Patrick's Church, Lewiston, Maine, Celebrates 100 Years, 1890–1990* (unidentified publisher [1990]), 7.

14. Alexandre-Louis Mothon, 1893, cited in Plourde, *Dominicains au Canada: Livre des documents*, 2:101; Sommaire, 1885–1904, Sisters of Charity, Saint Mary's Regional Medical Center Archives, p. 10; Registre, vol. 1, 1880–1901, Sisters of Charity, Saint Mary's Regional Medical Center Archives, pp. 9, 11, 14–17; *First Annual Report of the Central Maine General Hospital*, 7; *Sixth Annual Report of [the] Hospital of the Sisters of Charity, Lewiston, Maine, 1898* (unidentified publisher [1898]), 3, 9; *Sisters' Hospital, 1902: Tenth Annual Report* (Lewiston, Maine: Haswell Press [1902]), 10; *Lewiston Evening Journal*, 6 December

1898, p. 9; English-language newspaper clipping inserted into la Chronique des Dominicains, vol. 5, 1900, p. 358; *Le Messager*, 10 January 1899, p. 6; *Seventh Annual Report of [the] Hospital of the Sisters of Charity, Lewiston, Maine, 1899* (unidentified publisher [1899]), 12.

15. Alexandre-Louis Mothon, 1893, cited in Plourde, *Dominicains au Canada: Livre des documents*, 2:105; *Annual Report, Healy Asylum, 1896* (unidentified publisher [1896]); L. C. Bateman, "The Sisters' Hospital: The Beautiful Structure Now Finished and Thrown Open to the Public," *Lewiston Journal* magazine section, 15 November 1902, p. 11.

16. English- and French-language newspaper clippings inserted into la Chronique des Dominicains, vol. 4, 1893, pp. 94, 96; *Le Messager*, 21 March 1899, p. 3; holographic report inserted into the Comptes Rendus de L'Asile Notre Dame de Lourdes; la Chronique des Dominicains, vol. 5, 1898, pp. 171–172.

17. *Le Messager*, 1885 passim, 3 and 10 June 1886, 5 April 1888, letter to the editor signed "L." on 5 April 1888, 19 November 1895. La Chronique des Dominicains, vol. 2, 2 December 1885, p. 12¹; vol. 3, 3 April 1888, p. 25; French-language newspaper clipping inserted into la Chronique des Dominicains, vol. 2, 2 December 1885, p. 12¹. For particulars of the 1885 insurrection and subsequent trials, see Bob Beal and Rod Macleod, *Prairie Fire: The 1885 North-West Rebellion* (Toronto: McClelland and Stewart, 1994).

18. Paul-André Linteau, René Durocher, and Jean-Claude Robert, *Histoire du Québec contemporain: De la Confédération à la crise (1867–1929)* (Montréal: Boréal, 1989), 307, 320–321; *Le Messager*, 1 and 9 August 1893.

19. Claude Galarneau, *Les Collèges classiques au Canada français (1620–1970)* (Montréal: Éditions Fides, 1978), 46; Robert G. LeBlanc, "A French-Canadian Education and the Persistence of *La Franco-Américanie*," *Journal of Cultural Geography* 8 (Spring/Summer 1988): 50, 52.

20. LeBlanc, "A French-Canadian Education and the Persistence of *La Franco-Américanie*," 51–52, 55, 62. I am grateful to the late Robert G. LeBlanc for having shared his research notes, from which the figures in this paragraph were compiled. Note that all figures represent the number of enrollments and not individual students or graduates.

21. La Chronique des Dominicains, vol. 2, 26 July 1887, p. 116; vol. 4, 10 July 1894, p. 229. *Le Messager*, 22 July 1898, p. 3. When the Androscoggin Mill hired Polish workers, *Le Messager* predicted that "the return from the native country will be disappointing for some," but it reported four days later that ten of the thirty

Polish workers who had been learning to weave at the mill had left Lewiston. The newspaper did not indicate if the others kept their jobs, and it offered no evidence of ethnic conflict due to the employment of the Polish workers. *Le Messager*, 22 July 1898, p. 3; 26 July 1898, p. 3.

22. La Chronique des Dominicains, vol. 4, 15 August 1893, pp. 136–137, 27 September 1893, pp. 146–147, 4 December 1893, p. 177; *Le Messager*, 24 January 1889, 5 December 1893.

23. *Le Messager*, 8 July 1898, p. 3, 12 July 1898, p. 3, 22 July 1898, p. 3.

24. *Le Messager*, 24 June 1880, 2 July 1885, p. 1, 27 June 1889, p. 5, 7 April 1893, 23 June 1896, 26 June 1896, p. 2.

25. *Le Messager*, 5 January 1882, 1 January 1885. La Chronique des Dominicains, vol. 1, 1 January 1883, p. 50; vol. 3, 1 January 1889, p. 77; vol. 4, 1 January 1896, p. 351, 23 December 1896, p. 410. *Lewiston Evening Journal*, 31 December 1880, 1 January 1884.

26. *Le Messager*, 24 May 1888, article signed "F.X.B." in the souvenir issue of 2 July 1895, 7 September 1897.

27. On these efforts, see Robert G. LeBlanc, "Regional Competition for Franco-American Repatriates, 1870–1930," *Québec Studies* 1 (Spring 1983): 110–129; and Robert G. LeBlanc, "Colonisation et rapatriement au Lac-Saint-Jean (1895–1905)," *Revue d'histoire de l'Amérique française* 38 (Winter 1985): 379–408.

28. *Le Messager*, 4 and 18 November 1886, 12 October 1897, p. 2; *Lewiston Evening Journal*, 10 February 1898, p. 5. On the late-nineteenth-century hopes of French-Canadian nationalists to expand the influence of Catholics in the United States, see Robert G. LeBlanc, "The Francophone 'Conquest' of New England: Geopolitical Conceptions and Imperial Ambition of French-Canadian Nationalists in the Nineteenth Century," *American Review of Canadian Studies* 15 (Autumn 1985): 288–310.

29. Fernand Harvey, "Les Chevaliers du Travail: les États-Unis et la société québécoise (1882–1902)," in Fernand Harvey, ed., *Aspects historiques du mouvement ouvrier au Québec* (Montréal: Les Éditions du Boréal Express, 1973), 35, 37, 51, 55–57, 112–113; Charles A. Scontras, *Two Decades of Organized Labor and Labor Politics in Maine, 1880–1900* (Orono: University of Maine Press, 1969), 39; Albert S. Foley, S.J., "Open Foes and Hidden," *Bishop Healy: Beloved Outcaste* (Dublin: Clonmore and Reynolds, 1956), 168–169; diocesan letter of Bishop James Augustin Healy, 18 February 1885, Bishop Healy File, Chancery Archives; *Le Messager*, 2 September 1886; Registre du Grand Séminaire de Montréal, Archives of the

Grand Séminaire, Montréal, Québec, vol. 1: 1840–1900, p. 20; Archbishop of Québec to Mgr. J. A. Healy, 21 May 1885, Bishop Healy File, Chancery Archives; James Aug. Healy, Bishop of Portland, to Mgr. Edouard C. Fabre, Bishop of Montréal, 25 May 1885, correspondence file, and 15 October 1885, file of the Chevaliers du Travail/Knights of Labor, Archives of the Chancellery, Archbishopric of Montréal, Québec.

30. Scontras, *Two Decades of Organized Labor and Labor Politics in Maine*, 51–52; Ossian C. Phillips, District Master Workman of the Maine Knights of Labor, quoted in the *Boston Sunday Globe*, 7 March 1886, p. 10, cited in Scontras, *Two Decades*, 52; *Le Messager*, 18 February 1886, 1 April 1886 (italics in original), 2 September 1886; Lewiston, Maine, *Labor Advocate* ("the semi-official newspaper of the Knights of Labor in Maine," according to Scontras, 88), 25 March 1886; *Lewiston Evening Journal*, 4 and 5 February 1886; la Chronique des Dominicains, vol. 2, 4 February 1886, p. 20, 14 February 1886, p. 21. Lewiston's French Canadians were not the only ones to join the Knights of Labor. In 1886, three hundred French Canadians of Biddeford, Maine, formed their own local council of the Knights of Labor, despite the bishop's opposition to the trade union. Michael J. Guignard, *La foi–La langue–La culture: The Franco-Americans of Biddeford, Maine* (By the Author, 1984), 95.

31. Jacques Rouillard similarly argues against portrayals of French-Canadian workers in Québec from the late nineteenth century to World War II as marginal and clergy-dominated, in *Histoire du syndicalisme au Québec: Des origines à nos jours* (Montréal: les Éditions du Boréal, 1989), 7.

32. *Le Messager*, 27 October 1887, 29 August 1893, 26 September 1893, 20 October 1893, 26 April 18[95], 30 April 1895, 12 July 1895, 2, 8 and 23 August 1895; Scontras, *Two Decades of Organized Labor and Labor Politics in Maine*, 138–139; la Chronique des Dominicains, vol. 4, 7 August 1895, p. 326.

33. *Lewiston Evening Journal*, 17 January 1898, p. 9, 15 February 1898, p. 5, 10 March 1898, p. 9; *Le Messager*, 18 January 1898, p. 2, 4 and 8 February 1898, p. 3, 15 February 1898, p. 3, 11 March 1898, p. 7, 18 March 1898, p. 3, 29 March 1898, p. 2; la Chronique des Dominicains, vol. 5, 27 March 1898, p. 142.

34. *Lewiston Evening Journal*, 31 March 1898, p. 12, 4 April 1898, p. 5; *Le Messager*, 1 April 1898, p. 6, 4 April 1898. On the role of the charivari as an instrument of self-governance among French Canadians, see Allan Greer, *The Patriots and the People: The Rebellion of 1837 in Rural Lower Canada* (Toronto: University of Toronto Press, 1993), especially 69–86, 172–174, 217–218, 239–257, 361–362; for

an interpretation of the charivari as an instrument of the working class in both the United States and Canada in the 1800s, see Bryan D. Palmer, "Discordant Music: Charivaris and Whitecapping in Nineteenth-Century North America," *Labour/Le Travailleur* 3 (1978): 5–62.

35. *Lewiston Evening Journal*, 28 March 1898, p. 7, 7 April 1898, p. 5; *Le Messager*, 8 April 1898, p. 6.

36. William MacDonald, "The French Canadians in New England," *Quarterly Journal of Economics* 12 (April 1898): 265. Historian Peter Haebler reaches a similar conclusion about the commitment of French Canadians to the United States in his study of Holyoke, Massachusetts. See "Habitants in Holyoke: The Development of the French-Canadian Community in a Massachusetts City, 1865–1910" (Ph.D. dissertation, University of New Hampshire, 1976), 206–208.

37. La Chronique des Dominicains, vol. 1, 27 November 1884, p. 229; vol. 4, 21 October 1892, p. 40, 27 November 1892, pp. 52 and 76; French-language newspaper clipping inserted into la Chronique des Dominicains, vol. 4, 1892, p. 40. *Le Messager*, 7 July 1887, 7 October 1892, souvenir issue of 2 July 1895 especially article signed "F.X.B," 7 July 1895; English-language newspaper clipping inserted into la Chronique des Dominicains, vol. 4, 1895, p. 315; *Lewiston Evening Journal*, 26 November 1880.

38. *Le Messager*, 2 July 1885, p. 1, 8 July 1886, p. 1; *Lewiston Evening Journal*, 24 June 1875, 7 October 1889, 24 June 1892, p. 5, 4 July 1895, p. 12.

39. *Lewiston Evening Journal*, 24 June 1875, 22 June 1882, 24 June 1890, 24 June 1897, p. 5; French-language newspaper clipping inserted into la Chronique des Dominicains, vol. 3, 1890, p. 212; *Le Messager*, 13 July 1882.

40. *Le Messager*, 2 July 1885, p. 1, 8 July 1886, p. 1; *Lewiston Evening Journal*, 22 June 1882, 27 June 1893, p. 8, 24 June 1897, pp. 5, 7. English-language newspaper clipping inserted into la Chronique des Dominicains, vol. 4, 1892, p. 27; la Chronique des Dominicains, vol. 2, 28 June 1886, p. 44. After a long search to determine why Catholic French Canadians adopted the Tricolor, the symbol of the godless French Republic, I came upon *Le Messager*'s 1952 account (special Saint-Jean-Baptiste issue, 24 June 1952). Since Canadians lacked national colors, the English in 1854 "imposed upon us the Tricolor of the French Revolution because Napoleon III was allied with England against Russia," *Le Messager* explained. French Canadians, the newspaper added, continued to use the three colors of France in their celebrations even after the English stopped doing so from 1870, following the Franco-Prussian War. Whether accurate or not, the newspaper's

explanation reveals that the *Canadiens* had lacked a flag of their own and had had to choose one. Appropriating the Tricolor in the United States served the purposes of French Canadians, not only in asserting their French identity, but also in arguing for acceptance in their adopted country based upon the historical ties between the French and American peoples.

41. *Le Messager*, 2 July 1897, p. 7.
42. *Le Messager*, 8 July 1886, p. 1; French-language newspaper clipping inserted into la Chronique des Dominicains, vol. 3, 1890, p. 212; English-language newspaper clipping inserted into la Chronique des Dominicains, vol. 4, 1892, p. 27; Alexandre-Louis Mothon, 1893, cited in Plourde, *Dominicains au Canada: Livre des documents*, 2:112.
43. *Lewiston Evening Journal*, 4 July 1895, pp. 7, 12, 13.
44. *Lewiston Evening Journal*, 13 January 1896, p. 8; 20 January 1896, p. 7. John Higham, *Strangers in the Land: Patterns of American Nativism, 1860–1925* (1955; New Brunswick, N.J.: Rutgers University Press, 1992), 62, 81, 84. *Le Messager*, 14 January 1896, p. 3; 4 February 1896. *Boston Daily Globe*, 14 June 1895, inserted into la Chronique des Dominicains, vol. 4, p. 309.
45. *Le Messager*, 12 June 1896, p. 4; article signed "Docteur G.," probably Dr. J. Amédée Girouard, *Le Messager*, 15 December 1893.
46. *Le Messager*, 22 April 1898, pp. 2, 3, 26 April 1898, p. 3, 3 May 1898, p. 3, 2 and 9 September 1898, p. 2; la Chronique des Dominicains, vol. 5, 12 June 1898, p. 198.
47. See, for example, *Le Messager*, 23 August 1895, 13 November 1896, p. 2, 15 January 1897.
48. Examples of historians who emphasize instead the role of twentieth-century developments include Elliott Robert Barkan, "French Canadians," *Harvard Encyclopedia of American Ethnic Groups*, ed. Stephan Thernstrom (Cambridge, Mass.: Belknap Press, 1980), 399–400; and François Weil, *Les Franco-Américains, 1860–1980* ([Paris]: Belin, 1989), 201–214.

Chapter Four.
Playing Chopin: French Speakers Celebrate the Demise of Lewiston's Republican Majority, 1900–1920

1. *Le Messager*, 21 June 1901, p. 6; Ralph Dominic Vicero, "Immigration of French Canadians to New England, 1840–1900: A Geographical Analysis" (Ph.D. dissertation, University of Wisconsin, 1968), 343.

2. Yolande Lavoie, *L'émigration des Québécois aux États-Unis de 1840 à 1930* ([Québec]: Éditeur officiel du Québec, 1981), 53; Yves Roby, *Les Franco-Américains de la Nouvelle-Angleterre (1776–1930)* (Sillery, Québec: Septentrion, 1990), 227–232.

3. Naturalization data from the nineteenth century were compiled from the records of the following courts: Supreme Judicial Court, Androscoggin County, Records, vols. 1–27.5, 1854–1894, Maine State Archives [hereafter MSA], Augusta, Maine; Supreme Judicial Court, Androscoggin County, Naturalization Records, vol. B, 1895–1899, Office of the Clerk of the Superior Court of Maine, Auburn, Maine; Lewiston Municipal Court Naturalization Records, vols. 4–8, 1882–1893, MSA; Auburn, Maine, Municipal Court Naturalization Records, 1893, National Archives and Records Administration, Waltham, Massachusetts [hereafter NARA-Waltham]; U.S. District Court, Portland, Maine, Proceedings, vols. 1–2, 6–8, 1790–1845, NARA-Waltham; U.S. District Court, Portland, Maine, Naturalization Records, vols. 1–11, 1851–1899, NARA-Waltham; U.S. Circuit Court, Portland, Maine, Naturalization Records, vols. 1–3, 1851–1899, NARA-Waltham; Superior Court, Cumberland County (Portland, Maine), Naturalization Records, 1868–1899, MSA. Hereafter, these records will be cited as "nineteenth-century naturalization records." The records of the following courts were consulted to compile data on the naturalization of Lewiston's French-Canadian immigrants for the period from 1900 to 1919: Supreme Judicial Court, Androscoggin County, Naturalization Records, vols. B, B-2, E, C-1, 1–8, 1900–1919, Office of the Clerk of the Superior Court of Maine, Auburn, Maine; Supreme Judicial Court, Androscoggin County, Naturalization Records, vol. D-1, 1903–1906, NARA-Waltham; U.S. District Court, Portland, Maine, Naturalization Records, vol. 11, 1900–1906, and vols. 1–8, 1912–1919, NARA-Waltham; U.S. Circuit Court, Portland, Maine, Naturalization Records, vols. 3–10, 1900–1912, NARA-Waltham; Superior Court, Cumberland County (Portland, Maine), Naturalization Records, 1900–1903, MSA. Hereafter in this

chapter, the latter set of naturalization records will be cited as "naturalization records, 1900–1919."

4. Paul-André Linteau, René Durocher, and Jean-Claude Robert, *Histoire du Québec contemporain: De la Confédération à la crise* (1867–1929) (Montréal: Boréal, 1989), 399–405; naturalization records, 1900–1919. The Naturalization Act of 1906 made naturalization the responsibility of the federal government, and it created the Bureau of Immigration and Naturalization to oversee the naturalization process. In 1913 the agency was renamed the Bureau of Naturalization, and in 1933 it evolved into the Immigration and Naturalization Service. U.S. Department of Justice, Immigration and Naturalization Service, *An Immigrant Nation: United States Regulation of Immigration, 1798–1991* ([Washington, D.C.]: Government Printing Office, 1991), 6; John J. Newman, "American Naturalization Processes and Procedures, 1790–1985" (typescript, Family History Section, Indiana Historical Society, 1985), available at NARA-Waltham, pp. 10, 12.

5. Naturalization records, 1900–1919. The French Canadians who had been born outside of Québec were from the Maritime provinces of New Brunswick (1.8 percent), Nova Scotia (0.4 percent), and Prince Edward Island (0.9 percent), and the central Canadian province of Ontario (1.0 percent).

6. Naturalization records from 1900 to 1906 did not provide the place of emigration, making it impossible to gain some sense of the migration patterns of these naturalizers within their country of origin. Naturalization records, 1900–1919; Arthur Grandmaison's naturalization record is from the Supreme Judicial Court, Androscoggin County, Naturalization Records, vol. 8, p. 41.

7. The place of arrival for the rest (2.9 percent) of the 481 was unknown. Naturalization records, 1900–1919.

8. Naturalization records, 1900–1919; the naturalization records of Alphonse Bilodeau and Philippe Neri Beaudet are from the Supreme Judicial Court, Androscoggin County, Naturalization Records, vol. 5, p. 21, and vol. 6, p. 6, respectively.

9. Naturalization records, 1907–1919; Lachance's record is from the Supreme Judicial Court, Androscoggin County, naturalization records, vol. 6, p. 71.

10. Newman, "American Naturalization Processes and Procedures," 10; naturalization records, 1900–1919.

11. *Le Messager*, 23 August 1901, p. 3, 3 September 1901, p. 3, 27 December 1901, p. 3, 10 July 1903, p. 2, 7 July 1905, p. 3, 2 August 1916, p. 8. La Chronique du couvent, the series Monasteries and Parishes, the subseries Monastery of the Apostles Pierre and Paul of Lewiston, Maine, Archives of the Dominicans, Montréal,

Québec [hereafter la Chronique des Dominicains], vol. 8, 22 June 1903, p. 154; vol. 12, 6 August 1908, p. 258; vol. 13, 6 July 1914, p. 296.

12. *Le Messager*, 14 May 1901, p. 1, 16 July 1901, p. 2, article signed "Siram" of 31 January 1902, p. 2, 26 September 1902, p. 3, 15 May 1903, p. 2, 13 October 1903, p. 2, 9 June 1906, p. 3, 11 August 1906, p. 8, 30 August 1906, p. 1, 28 September 1907, p. 7, 14 March 1910, p. 5, 12 April 1911, p. 8, 16 and 19 May 1913, p. 8, 20 October 1913, p. 8, 21 December 1915, p. 8, 13 August 1917, p. 2.

13. *Le Messager*, 2 April 1901, p. 6, 17 May 1901, p. 6, 14 February 1902, p. 3, 4 June 1902, p. 2, 19 December 1902, p. 2.

14. *Le Messager*, 10 October 1902, p. 3.

15. *Le Messager*, 10 May 1901, 14 and 21 May 1901, p. 3, 11 February 1902, p. 2, supplement of 12 December 1902, p. 3, 17 February 1903, p. 3, 10 November 1903, p. 2, 30 September 1904, p. 6, 13 October 1905, p. 2, 10 July 1906, p. 2, 4 October 1906, p. 7, 14 April 1909, p. 2, 24 May 1909, p. 1, 13 October 1909, p. 2, 21 February 1910, p. 5, 11 September 1911, p. 5, 7 and 17 March 1913, p. 8, 22 October 1913, p. 8, 19 and 26 May 1915, p. 8, 27 September 1916, p. 5, 18 January 1918, p. 1, 16 June 1919, p. 6, 28 July 1919, p. 8, 30 July 1919, p. 1.

16. *Le Messager*, 27 September 1916, p. 5, 17 September 1917, p. 8, 12 November 1917, p. 8.

17. Robert G. LeBlanc, "The Franco-American Response to the Conscription Crisis in Canada, 1916–1918," *American Review of Canadian Studies* (Autumn 1993): 343–372; *Le Messager*, 1 September 1915, p. 8, 10 September 1915, p. 1, 1 April 1918, p. 2, 5 April 1918, p. 3, 27 and 31 May 1918, p. 8, 7 June 1918, p. 6, 25 June 1918, p. 11.

18. *Lewiston Evening Journal*, 12 September 1918, pp. 1, 10; la Chronique des Domini- cains, vol. 13, 12 September 1918, p. 481; *Album-Souvenir, 1872–1922: Cinquante- naire de L'Institut Jacques-Cartier de Lewiston, Maine* ([Lewiston, Maine]: le Comité de l'Album-Souvenir, 1922), 31; *Le Messager*, 25 June 1920, p. 1. Naturalization records reveal that no men who had served in the U.S. armed forces became citizens during World War I. Twelve former servicemen naturalized in 1919, and twenty-five did in 1920. These men accounted for one-fifth of the total naturalizations in both 1919 (21.4 percent) and 1920 (21.0 percent). Naturalization records, 1900–1919; Supreme Judicial Court, Androscoggin County, Naturalization Records, 1920, Office of the Clerk of the Superior Court of Maine, Auburn, Maine.

19. LeBlanc, "The Franco-American Response to the Conscription Crisis in Canada," 344, 365–366.

20. *Le Messager*, 17 January 1902, p. 2, 21 January 1902, 3 February 1903, p. 2, 13 February 1903, p. 7, 21 November 1905, p. 7, 9 December 1905, p. 7, 23 January 1906, p. 5.

21. Nineteenth-century naturalization records; naturalization records, 1900–1919; *Le Messager*, 21 May 1901, p. 3, 21 February 1905, p. 3, 24 February 1906, p. 3.

22. The naturalization laws passed by Congress between 1906 and 1910 had the effect of limiting throughout the United States the number of immigrants eligible to vote, and they continued a pattern of restricting the franchise that marked the period from Reconstruction to World War I. Alexander Keyssar, *The Right to Vote: The Contested History of Democracy in the United States* (New York: Basic Books, 2000), 139, but see also chapter 5.

23. Newman, "American Naturalization Processes and Procedures," p. 23; naturalization records, 1900–1919; *Le Messager*, 10 July 1906, p. 2. From 1900 to 1909, nine-tenths (89.2 percent) of the naturalizing French-Canadian men of Lewiston who had crossed the border as minors naturalized by their thirty-first birthday, whereas under two-thirds (62.7 percent) did so during the second decade. Among the francophone men who had entered the United States at age eighteen or older, the proportion naturalizing within fifteen years of their arrival in the United States (that is, within the first ten years of their eligibility) dropped from 67.9 percent in the first decade to 59.0 percent in the second decade of the twentieth century. Naturalization records, 1900–1919.

24. Naturalization records, 1900–1919; *Resident and Business Directory of Androscoggin County, Maine, 1918–1919* (Auburn, Maine: Merrill and Webber Company, 1918), 503.

25. Naturalization records, 1900–1919.

26. *U.S. Census, 1920*. See the appendix for an explanation of the methodology employed with the 1920 census.

27. *U.S. Census, 1920*.

28. *U.S. Census, 1920*; naturalization records, 1900–1919; Vicero, "Immigration of French Canadians to New England," 394–395; Lavoie, *L'émigration des Québécois aux États-Unis de 1840 à 1930*, 58. On the naturalization rates of French-Canadian immigrant men from each of the New England states in 1920, see Ronald Petrin, *French Canadians in Massachusetts Politics, 1885–1915: Ethnicity and Political Pragmatism* (Philadelphia: Balch Institute Press, 1990), 58.

29. *Le Messager*, 1 May 1903, p. 3, 27 October 1905, p. 2, 23 January 1906, p. 2; *Paroisse Canadienne-Française de Lewiston*, 51.

30. *Le Messager,* 25 October 1898, p. 2 (emphasis in original), 28 October 1898, p. 6, 16 February 1904, p. 3; William MacDonald, "French Canadians in Maine," *The Nation* 63 (October 15, 1896): 286.

31. *Lewiston Evening Journal,* 10 April 1913, p. 6; *Le Messager,* 14 April 1913, p. 1, 6 August 1919, p. 2; *Bates College, Lewiston, Maine, 1915–1916* (unidentified publisher [1915]), 164; Mabel Eaton, ed., *General Catalogue of Bates College and Cobb Divinity School, 1864–1930* (Lewiston, Maine: Bates College, 1931), 290; *City of Lewiston, Maine, Annual Report of the School Department for the Year Ending August 31, 1919* (unidentified publisher [1919]), 14, 29.

32. English-language newspaper clipping inserted into la Chronique des Dominicains, vol. 8, 1903, p. 16; *Le Messager,* 5 February 1904, p. 3, 7 December 1905, p. 3, 26 April 1916, 20 December 1918, p. 13; *Forty-Fourth Annual Report of the Receipts and Expenses of the City of Lewiston for the Fiscal Year Ending February 28, 1907, Together with Other Annual Reports and Papers Relating to the Affairs of the City* (Lewiston, Maine: Le Messager, 1907), 176; *Forty-Fifth Annual Report of the Receipts and Expenses of the City of Lewiston for the Fiscal Year Ending Feb. 29, 1908, Together with Other Annual Reports and Papers Relating to the Affairs of the City* (Lewiston, Maine: Haswell Press, 1908), 141; *Forty-Sixth Annual Report of the Receipts and Expenses of the City of Lewiston for the Fiscal Year Ending February 28, 1909, Together with Other Annual Reports and Papers Relating to the Affairs of the City* (Lewiston, Maine: Le Messager, 1909), 88; *Fifty-Fifth Annual Report of the Receipts and Expenses of the City of Lewiston for the Fiscal Year Ending February 28, 1918, Together with Annual Reports and Papers Relating to the Affairs of the City* (Lewiston, Maine: Royal Press, 1918), 14; *U.S. Census, 1880; U.S. Census, 1920.* Le Messager (26 April 1916) emphasized that Ernestine Lemaire's previous experience as a teacher and particularly her English-speaking ability helped her to obtain the position at the library. Her family connections certainly did not hurt.

33. *Le Messager,* article signed "Citoyen" of 15 December 1903, p. 2, 7 March 1907, p. 2, 5 June 1916; Geneva Kirk and Gridley Barrows, *Historic Lewiston: Its Government* (Lewiston, Maine: Lewiston Historical Commission, 1982), 34, 36. Until the 1970s, Lewiston held annual elections for mayor. Kirk and Barrows, 51.

34. *Le Messager,* 5 December 1902, p. 1, 8 March 1904, p. 2, 15 April 1904, p. 3, 7 June 1904, p. 8, 26 August 1904, p. 2, 1 September 1904, 9 September 1904, p. 6, 13 September 1904, p. 7, 10 November 1913, p. 8, 27 September 1915, p. 8, 26 February 1917; *Le Messager,* 18 December 1900, inserted into la Chronique

des Dominicains, vol. 5, p. 391; *Lewiston Daily Sun*, 18 August 1900, p. 1; la Chronique des Dominicains, vol. 10, 10 February 1905, p. 59, 20 March 1905, p. 114.

35. *Le Messager*, 4 March 1902, p. 6, 5 December 1902, p. 1, 21 March 1905, p. 2, 31 March 1905, pp. 7–8, 6 March 1906, p. 7, 31 March 1906, p. 2, 4 March 1910, p. 5, 3 March 1911, p. 4.

36. *Le Messager*, 4 March 1902, p. 2, 15 February 1906, p. 2; *Lewiston Evening Journal*, 2 April 1902, p. 9, 3 April 1902, p. 8, 5 April 1902, p. 10; la Chronique des Dominicains, vol. 14, 18 March 1919, p. 13.

37. *Le Messager*, 5 December 1902, p. 1, 27 October 1903, p. 3, 15 September 1909, p. 7, 5 March 1913, p. 1, 17 November 1913, p. 1, 19 November 1913, 2 February 1914, p. 8, 27 February 1914, 27 February 1914, p. 4, 4 March 1914, pp. 1, 8, 25 August 1915, p. 8; Yves Frenette, "La genèse d'une communauté canadienne-française en Nouvelle-Angleterre: Lewiston, Maine, 1800–1880" (Ph.D. dissertation, Université Laval, Québec, 1988), 381; Kirk and Barrows, *Historic Lewiston: Its Government*, 34; *Lewiston Evening Journal*, 28 February 1914, p. 7, 2 March 1914, p. 1.

38. Kirk and Barrows, *Historic Lewiston: Its Government*, 36; *Le Messager*, 6 March 1918, p. 1.

39. *Le Messager*, 3 November 1920, p. 1; Ronald L. Bissonnette, "Political Parties as Products of Their Environments: A Case Study of Lewiston, Maine" (honors thesis, University of Maine-Orono, 1977), 27–29.

Chapter Five.
The Winding Road: From *Canadien* to Franco-American, 1900–1920

1. Article signed "F.X.B.," most likely attorney F. X. Belleau, *Le Messager*, souvenir issue of 2 July 1895.

2. *Le Messager*, 1 January 1885, 22 November 1901, p. 2. La Chronique du couvent, the series Monasteries and Parishes, the subseries Monastery of the Apostles Pierre and Paul of Lewiston, Maine, Archives of the Dominicans, Montréal, Québec [hereafter la Chronique des Dominicains], vol. 1, 18 December 1884, pp. 234–235; vol. 4, 25 January 1895, p. 281. James Augustin Healy, Bishop of Portland, to the Very Rev. Father A.-L. Mothon, 22 January 1895, Archives of the Dominicans, Correspondence of Mgr. Healy. On the nineteenth-century conflicts in Massachusetts

and Connecticut between French speakers and their Irish bishops, see Yves Roby, *Les Franco-Américains de la Nouvelle-Angleterre (1776–1930)* (Sillery, Québec: Septentrion, 1990), 162–181.

3. *Le Messager*, 23 June 1903, p. 7, 13 October 1905, p. 2, supplement of 24 November 1905, 24 April 1906, p. 2; Antonin M. Plourde, O.P., "Cent ans de vie paroissiale: SS. Pierre et Paul de Lewiston, 1870–1970," *Le Rosaire* (August/September 1970): 15.

4. *Le Messager*, 14 December 1905, p. 2, 19 December 1905, p. 7, 8 February 1906, p. 2, 10 February 1906.

5. La Chronique des Dominicains, vol. 11, 4 March 1906, p. 50, 9 March 1906, p. 64, 11 March 1906, p. 71.

6. *Le Messager*, 15 March 1906, p. 2.

7. La Chronique des Dominicains, vol. 11, 12 March 1906, p. 71; *Lewiston Evening Journal*, 12 March 1906, p. 3; *Le Messager*, 16 June 1906, p. 2.

8. La Chronique des Dominicains, vol. 11, 5 April 1906, p. 122, 11 April 1906, p. 130.

9. *Le Messager*, 7 June 1906, p. 2, 12 June 1906, pp. 1–2, 6 July 1906, p. 2, 10 July 1906, p. 1; undated copies of *La Quinzaine* inserted into la Chronique des Dominicains, vol. 11, 1906, pp. 219, 239–240. On tensions between Franco-Americans and French Dominicans, also see Yves Frenette, "Vie paroissiale et antagonismes culturels: Les dominicains à Lewiston (1880–1906)," in Claire Quintal, ed., *Religion catholique et appartenance franco-américaine* (Worcester, Mass.: Institut français, Assumption College, 1993), 25–35.

10. *Le Messager*, 3 July 1906, p. 2; Mémorial du Monastère du Sacré-Coeur, Lewiston, Maine, Archives of the Dominican Sisters, Sabattus, Maine [hereafter Mémorial des Dominicaines], vol. 1, 1906, p. 89. Mothon served as pastor of Saint-Pierre Parish from 1881 to 1884, 1887 to 1897, and 1902 to 1906.

11. *Le Messager*, 12 June 1906, p. 2; Henri F. Roy, *Échos d'une démission: Le dernier mot* (Lewiston, Maine: Echo Publishing Company, 1925), 16–17, 19; Lewiston, Maine, *Le Courrier du Maine*, 24 July 1906, p. 1. The Dominicans had been divided over the issue of encouraging publication of *Le Courrier du Maine*, Roy later learned. For that reason, they had offered him only $100 in financial support to start this alternative newspaper, the largest amount they could provide without first gaining the approval of the monastery's council. After the Dominican provincial changed the personnel in Lewiston, Roy found himself lacking support

for *Le Courrier du Maine,* and the newspaper ceased publication five months after it began. Roy, 18–19; French-language newspaper clipping inserted onto the opening page of la Chronique des Dominicains, vol. 12.

12. *Le Messager,* 14 July 1906, p. 2, 4 August 1906, p. 2; la Chronique des Dominicains, vol. 11, 29 July 1906, p. 283, 31 July 1906, p. 284.

13. Plourde, "Cent ans de vie paroissiale," 27–29; J. Antonin Plourde, *Dominicains au Canada: Livre des documents,* vol. 2, *Les cinq fondations avant l'autonomie (1881–1911)* (unidentified publisher, 1975), 16–19.

14. Jules Antonin Plourde, O.P., *Dominicains au Canada: Album historique* (unidentified publisher, 1973), 52, 72–75, 99; Plourde, *Dominicains au Canada: Livre des documents,* 2:251–252, 493–496.

15. *U.S. Census, 1920;* L'Ordre des Frères Prêcheurs, *Les Dominicains: Qui sont-ils? Que font-ils? Où sont-ils?* ([Montréal?: Unidentified publisher, 1986?]), 15.

16. *Le Messager,* 14 August 1906, 25 August 1906, p. 2; Michael Guignard, "The Case of Sacred Heart Parish," *Maine Historical Society Quarterly* 22 (Summer 1982): 21–36.

17. Roby, *Les Franco-Américains de la Nouvelle-Angleterre,* 263–264; Michael Guignard, "Maine's Corporation Sole Controversy," *Maine Historical Society Newsletter* 12 (Winter 1973): 116. Through the *fabriques,* French Canadians in Canada managed the finances of their own parishes; as a result, their parishes functioned as self-governing units in which members took a proprietary interest. See Allan Greer, *The Patriots and the People: The Rebellion of 1837 in Rural Lower Canada* (Toronto: University of Toronto Press, 1993), 68. These parish corporations existed in Québec at least until the middle of the twentieth century.

18. Roby, *Les Franco-Américains de la Nouvelle-Angleterre,* 264–265.

19. Guignard, "Maine's Corporation Sole Controversy," p. 112; la Chronique des Dominicains, vol. 13, 25 and 26 February 1911, p. 136; *Le Messager,* 27 February 1911, p. 5, 1 March 1911, p. 7; Roby, *Les Franco-Américains de la Nouvelle-Angleterre,* 264–265.

20. Roby, *Les Franco-Américains de la Nouvelle-Angleterre,* 265; *Le Messager,* 15 May 1911, p. 4; James A. Carey, Chancellor and Secretary, Diocese of Portland, to "Rev. Father," 9 May 1911, Archives of the Dominicans; la Chronique des Dominicains, vol. 13, 14 May 1911, p. 156.

21. *Le Messager,* 19 June 1911, 8 January 1912, p. 8, 15 January 1912, p. 4.

22. *Le Messager,* 26 June 1911, p. 4, 25 June 1915, p. 1, 26 June 1916, p. 8.

23. Roby, *Les Franco-Américains de la Nouvelle-Angleterre*, 265–267; Guignard, "Maine's Corporation Sole Controversy," 124; *Le Messager*, 23 October 1911, p. 1, 24 and 29 May 1912, p. 3, 3 June 1912, p. 2.

24. *Le Messager*, 19 February 1912, p. 8; letters of Louis S. Walsh to Rev. A. C. Côté, O.P., 29 March 1912, 18 May 1912, 11 May 1917, St. Peter's Parish File, Chancery Archives; Guignard, "Maine's Corporation Sole Controversy," 126.

25. James S. Olson, *Catholic Immigrants in America* (Chicago: Nelson-Hall, 1987), 33–46, 197–202; *Le Messager*, 2 and 9 June 1887, 2 June 1911, p. 1; la Chronique des Dominicains, vol. 2, 25 August 1886, pp. 60–61, 5 June 1887, pp. 108–109, 10 June 1887, p. 109, 22 October 1887, p. 128; James Aug. Healy, Bishop of Portland, to Rev. A.-L. Mothon, O.P., 19 October 1887, Archives of the Dominicans, Correspondence of Mgr. Healy; Gerard J. Brault, *The French-Canadian Heritage in New England* (Hanover, N.H.: University Press of New England, 1986), 76; *La Quinzaine*, no. 10, inserted into la Chronique des Dominicains, vol. 10, 1905, pp. 221, 224.

26. *Le Messager*, 21 June 1911, p. 5, 21 June 1916, p. 8, 25 June 1917, p. 8, 6 June 1919, p. 8, 23 June 1920, p. 6.

27. *Le Messager*, 31 December 1900, inserted into la Chronique des Dominicains, vol. 5, p. 393; A.-L. Mothon to Monsignor [Bishop William H. O'Connell], 1 December 1902, 8 January 1903, Chancery Archives, Roman Catholic Diocese of Portland, Maine, Saint Peter's Parish File; W. H. O'Connell, Bishop of Portland, to Very Rev. A.-L. Mothon, O.P., 2 December 1902, Archives of the Dominicans; *La Quinzaine*, 1 January 1905, inserted into la Chronique des Dominicains, vol. 10, p. 4. La Chronique des Dominicains, vol. 10, 25 December 1905, p. 380; vol. 12, 25 December 1907, p. 214, [25 December] 1908, p. 279; vol. 13, 25 December 1913, p. 281. Louis S. Walsh, Bishop of Portland, to Rev. J. A. Dallaire, O.P., Lewiston, 22 December 1907, Chancery Archives, Saint Peter's Parish File; Cecile Levasseur, comp., *75th Anniversary of the Founding of St. Mary's Parish, Lewiston, Maine, 1907–1982* (unidentified publisher, 1982), 15.

28. *Lewiston Evening Journal*, 5 and 7 April 1890; Ralph Skinner, *Historically Speaking on Lewiston-Auburn, Maine, Churches* (Lewiston, Maine: By the Author, 1965), 103–104. La Chronique des Dominicains, vol. 7, 16 October 1902, p. 193, 26 October 1902, p. 195; vol. 9, 30 October 1904, p. 241, 12 November 1904, p. 250; vol. 11, 5 November 1906, p. 375. Typescript notes of Reverend Philip Desjardins, Chancery Archives. *Le Messager*, 1 November 1904, p. 7, 3 March 1906, p. 2. The results of the parish visit revealed that 380 families of Petit Canada

(Little Canada) supported creating a new parish in Lewiston, 200 did not, and 220 others had no opinion. La Chronique des Dominicains, vol. 11, 18 November 1906, p. 383.

29. *Le Messager,* 4 May 1907, p. 3, 10 May 1907, p. 6; *Programme-Souvenir, 1907–1932: Vingt-cinquième anniversaire de la Paroisse Sainte-Marie* (Lewiston, Maine: Unidentified publisher, 1932), 7; Bishop Louis S. Walsh to V. Rev. Paul Duchaussoy, O.P., Dominican Monastery, Lewiston, 21 June 1907, Chancery Archives, Saint Peter's Parish File; Edgar Allen Beem, "La magnifique eglise [*sic*] gothique SS. Pierre et Paul: The Restoration of Lewiston's Franco-American Mother Church," *Maine Times,* 17 May 1991, p. 3.

30. Louis S. Walsh, Bishop of Portland, to Very Rev. H. Hage, O.P., Vicar General, 22 April 1909, 1 February 1912, Archives of the Dominicans.

31. *Paroisse Canadienne-Française de Lewiston (Maine): Album historique* ([Lewiston, Maine]: Les Pères Dominicains, 1899), 32; Plourde, "Cent ans de vie paroissiale," p. 19; copy of the letter of Fr. A.-L. Mothon to Monsignor Walsh, Bishop of Portland [1912], Archives of the Dominicans; Louis S. Walsh, Bishop of Portland, to Very Rev. H. Hage, O.P., Provincial, 13 May 1912, 30 July 1912, 20 January 1913, Archives of the Dominicans; copy of letter from Louis S. Walsh, Bishop of Portland, to Very Rev. Lewis Theissling, O.P., Master General, 5 August 1914, Archives of the Dominicans; Fr. Lewis Theissling, Master General, to the Bishop of Portland, 19 September 1916, Archives of the Dominicans.

32. Louis S. Walsh, Bishop of Portland, to Rev. A.-L. Mothon, O.P., 24 January 1913, Archives of the Dominicans; undated, unsigned, holographic note in French that begins "Réponse du Revdssm P Procureur Général au T.R.P. Hage vicaire général de la Congrégation St. Dominique, à propos d'une demande faite par l'eveque [*sic*] de Portland (Me) au Rdssme P. Général," Archives of the Dominicans.

33. *Le Messager,* 11 and 18 July 1919, p. 8, 21 July 1919, p. 4; *U.S. Census, 1920.*

34. *U.S. Census, 1920.*

35. The figures may have been higher for each group because census takers provided no indication of the literacy status of 3.2 percent of the Americans, 4.3 percent of the Franco-Americans, 3.5 percent of the Irish, and 2.2 percent of the other ethnics who were eight and older in 1920. *U.S. Census, 1920.*

36. The proportion may have been higher, for census takers provided no indication of the English-speaking ability of 6.5 percent of the Franco-Americans. *U.S. Census, 1920.*

37. *U.S. Census, 1920.*

38. *U.S. Census, 1920.*

39. *U.S. Census, 1920.*

40. *U.S. Census, 1920;* Jacques Rouillard, *Ah les États! Les travailleurs canadiens-français dans l'industrie textile de la Nouvelle-Angleterre d'après le témoignage des derniers migrants* (Montréal: Les Éditions du Boréal Express, 1985), 46–47; Mrs. Lagace, cited in Rouillard, p. 68.

41. *U.S. Census, 1920;* Sylvie Beaudreau and Yves Frenette, "Les stratégies familiales des francophones de la Nouvelle-Angleterre: Perspective diachronique," *Sociologie et sociétés* 26 (spring 1994): 171.

42. *U.S. Census, 1920.* The percentages of school-age persons were compiled from figures provided in the *Report of the School Department, City of Lewiston, Maine, for the Years Ending August 31, 1920 and August 31, 1921* (unidentified publisher, n.d.), 41; Beaudreau and Frenette, "Les stratégies familiales des francophones de la Nouvelle-Angleterre," 175.

43. *U.S. Census, 1920.* See the appendix for information on the household size and composition (including boarders) of Lewiston families in 1920.

44. *Le Messager*, 6 September 1904, p. 3, 2 March 1910, p. 2, 15 May 1911, p. 8, 8 September 1915, p. 1; *Lewiston Evening Journal*, 5 September 1911, pp. 7–8, 7 September 1915, p. 2.

45. La Chronique des Dominicains, vol. 9, 23 November 1904, p. 273; Mémorial des Dominicaines, vol. 1, 24 November, 1904, p. 36; *Le Messager*, 29 March 1909, p. 7, 11 August 1911, p. 5.

46. *Le Messager*, 10 September 1901, pp. 3, 6, 17 September 1901, p. 3. C. Stewart Doty makes the same suggestion that scholars should examine the local news, and not just the editorials, to gain a better understanding of the lives of ordinary Franco-Americans; see "The Future of the Franco-American Past," *American Review of Canadian Studies* 30 (Spring 2000): 14.

47. *Le Messager*, 21 February 1905, p. 7, 24 February 1905, pp. 3, 6, 28 February 1905, p. 7.

48. *Le Messager*, 27 December 1905, p. 6, 29 December 1905, p. 3, unsigned letter of 9 January 1906, p. 3, 9 January 1906, p. 6, 16 January 1906, p. 6; *Lewiston Evening Journal*, 28 and 29 December 1905, p. 9, 9 and 15 January 1906, p. 9.

49. *Le Messager*, 14 July 1906, p. 3, 19 July 1906, p. 6, 21 July 1906, p. 7; Geneva Kirk and Gridley Barrows, *Historic Lewiston: Its Government* (Lewiston, Maine: Lewiston Historical Commission, 1982), 32. Perhaps *Le Messager* reported the

outcome of the strike in subsequent issues that are illegible on microfilm; only one
article on the strike could be found in the *Lewiston Evening Journal.*

50. *Le Messager,* 29 September 1913, p. 8, 3 and 13 October 1913, p. 8.

51. *Le Messager,* 13 October 1913, p. 8, letter signed "XX," 13 October 1913, p. 1.

52. *Lewiston Evening Journal,* 18 October 1913, p. 9, 24 October 1913, p. 14, 28
October 1913, p. 10; *Le Messager,* 17 and 20 October 1913, p. 8, 24 October
1913, p. 1, 27 and 31 October 1913, p. 8.

53. *U.S. Census, 1920;* index of Marriages by Groom's Last Name, Office of the City
Clerk, Lewiston, Maine, 2 vols. (1999).

54. Because there are no extant rosters of church members, one must rely upon parish
registers to reconstruct these lists. On the assumption that the parents of baptized
children would have been members of the parish, I used their names to generate a list of the families belonging to Lewiston's Saint Joseph and Saint Patrick
parishes in 1920. Among the baptized were converts to Catholicism. Because their
parents would not likely have been members of these Catholic parishes, they were
excluded from the data.

55. Baptism Registers, 1875–1892, 1914–1931, Saint Joseph Parish Rectory, Lewiston, Maine; 1880, pp. 173–208; 1920, pp. 29–36. Baptism Registers, 1892–1899,
1910–1921, Saint Patrick Parish Pastoral Center, Lewiston, Maine; 1892, pp.
312–340, 342; 1920, pp. 445–482.

56. In her 1944 study of marriage patterns in New Haven, Connecticut, Ruby Jo
Reeves Kennedy found that while ethnic endogamy declined from 1870 to 1940,
over three-fifths of marriages continued to be endogamous in 1940. Much of
the intermarriage that took place was among coreligionists, she contended in
"Single or Triple Melting-Pot? Intermarriage Trends in New Haven, 1870–1940,"
American Journal of Sociology 49 (January 1944): 331–339. While Josef J. Barton
criticizes aspects of Kennedy's study, he agrees with her conclusions, based upon
his study of the marriage patterns of Cleveland, Ohio. See *Peasants and Strangers:
Italians, Rumanians, and Slovaks in an American City, 1890–1950* (Cambridge,
Mass.: Harvard University Press, 1975), 163–169. For an alternative view, based
upon a reexamination of the New Haven marriage records, see Ceri Peach,
"Which Triple Melting Pot? A Re-examination of Ethnic Intermarriage in New
Haven, 1900–1950," *Ethnic and Racial Studies* 3 (January 1980): 1–16. For a
more contemporary portrait of ethnic intermarriage based upon the 1980 census,
see Stanley Lieberson and Mary C. Waters, *From Many Strands: Ethnic and Racial*

Groups in Contemporary America (New York: Russell Sage Foundation, 1988), chapters 6 and 7.

57. *Le Messager*, 9 April 1901, p. 3, 26 February 1919, p. 6.

58. A.-L. Mothon to Monsignor [William H. O'Connell], 25 September 1903, Chancery Archives, Saint Peter's Parish File. *La Quinzaine*, no. 6, 20 March 1904, inserted into la Chronique des Dominicains, vol. 9, p. 41; and no. 15, 7 August 1904, inserted into la Chronique des Dominicains, vol. 9, p. 156. Mémorial des Dominicaines, vol. 1, 1904, pp. 1, 5, 3, 16, 22, 23; summer 1905, p. 56; 2 July 1906, pp. 88–89. *Album-Souvenir: Vingt-cinquième anniversaire de l'arrivée des Religieuses Dominicaines à Lewiston* (Lewiston, Maine: Le Messager [1929]), 3; *Le Messager*, 26 July 1904, p. 3; la Chronique des Dominicains, vol. 9, 5 August 1904, p. 151; Personnel Conventuel, Lewiston, 1904–1947, Archives of the Dominican Sisters.

59. Typescript, "History, Province of the Northeast United States, 1888–1980" [hereafter Ursuline History], Ursuline Archives, Mount Merici Convent, Waterville, Maine, pp. 3, 10, 11, 12, 51. Two of the Ursulines had been born in Québec, two in New Brunswick, and two in Maine. Compiled from a postcard at the Ursuline Provincialate Archives, Dedham, Massachusetts, Saint Mary's Convent, Lewiston, Maine, file; *50th Anniversary: The Ursulines, St. Mary's School, Lewiston, Maine, 1916–1966* (unidentified publisher [1966]); typescript, Entrances at Mount Merici Convent, Ursuline Archives, Waterville, Maine.

60. Ursuline History, p. 52; circular letter, "Petit Journal de Lewiston," Ursuline Provincialate Archives, Saint Mary's Convent, Lewiston, Maine, file, 20 February 1920, p. 9, 7 May 1920, p. 3.

61. John Higham, for example, emphasizes the effect of outside forces on U.S. immigrant groups in *Strangers in the Land: Patterns of American Nativism, 1860–1925* (1955; New Brunswick, New Jersey: Rutgers University Press, 1992).

62. April R. Schultz draws a similar conclusion about the Americanization process in *Ethnicity on Parade: Inventing the Norwegian American through Celebration* (Amherst: University of Massachusetts Press, 1994).

63. Susan Olzak makes the same kind of argument in *The Dynamics of Ethnic Competition and Conflict* (Stanford, Calif.: Stanford University Press, 1992).

64. John F. McClymer starts down this analytical road in "The Paradox of Ethnicity in the United States: The French-Canadian Experience in Worcester, 1870–1914," in Michael D'Innocenzo and Josef P. Sirefman, eds., *Immigration and Ethnicity: American Society—"Melting Pot" or "Salad Bowl"?* (Westport, Conn.: Greenwood

Press, 1992), 15–23. But I go farther in analyzing and demonstrating how French-Canadian descendants negotiated their identity in their country of adoption.

65. *Acts and Resolves as Passed by the Seventy-Ninth Legislature of the State of Maine, 1919* (Augusta, Maine: Kennebec Journal Co., 1919), ch. 146; *Le Messager*, 25 June 1920, p. 1. During the Americanization campaign of and following World War I, Connecticut in 1918 and Rhode Island in 1922 stipulated that English serve as the language of instruction in public and private schools. Roby, *Les Franco-Américains de la Nouvelle-Angleterre*, 291–292, 299–300. In the nineteenth and early twentieth centuries, Canadian provinces outside of Québec—including Ontario, New Brunswick, Manitoba, Alberta, and Saskatchewan—also enacted legislation to curb or to eliminate bilingual instruction in their schools. Discrimination against the French language in Canada had factored into the decision of many French Canadians not to participate in the "war for democracy."

Chapter Six.
Competing Americanisms: The Bishops, the Klan, and the Intertwined Identity of Franco-Americans, 1920–1940

1. *Le Messager*, 11 August 1924, p. 8; *Lewiston Daily Sun*, 11 August 1924, pp. 1, 12; Lawrence Wayne Moores, Jr., "The History of the Ku Klux Klan in Maine, 1922–1931" (master's thesis, University of Maine-Orono, 1950), 25–26, 28.

2. U.S. Department of Commerce, Bureau of the Census, *Fourteenth Census of the United States Taken in the Year 1920*, vol. 3 (Washington, D.C.: Government Printing Office, 1923), 415; U.S. Department of Commerce, Bureau of the Census, *Fourteenth Census of the United States Taken in the Year 1920*, vol. 1 (Washington, D.C.: Government Printing Office, 1921), 46–47; percentage derived from the U.S. Department of Commerce, Bureau of the Census, *Fourteenth Census of the United States Taken in the Year 1920*, vol. 3 (Washington, D.C.: Government Printing Office, 1922), 415; *Official Catholic Directory for the Year of Our Lord 1920* (New York: P. J. Kenedy and Sons, 1920), 526.

3. Leonard J. Moore, *Citizen Klansmen: The Ku Klux Klan in Indiana, 1921–1928* (Chapel Hill: University of North Carolina Press, 1991), 1–3, 11, 118, 188–190.

4. Julian Sher, *White Hoods: Canada's Ku Klux Klan* (Vancouver: New Star Books, 1983), 23–25, 30, 40, 48; Martin Robin, *Shades of Right: Nativist and Fascist*

Politics in Canada, 1920–1940 (Toronto: University of Toronto Press, 1992), 11, 24.

5. William Walsh, "Bishop Walsh and the Ku Klux Klan," typescript, Chancery Archives, Roman Catholic Diocese of Portland, Maine, 1973, pp. 4–5; Moores, "The History of the Ku Klux Klan in Maine," 25–26; C. Stewart Doty, "How Many Frenchmen Does It Take to . . . ?" *Thought and Action* 11 (Fall 1995): 92. These works are among the very few that have examined the Klan's rise in New England.

6. *Lewiston Daily Sun*, 6 February 1923, p. 12; *Le Messager*, 21 February 1923, p. 3.

7. Pierre Vincent Bourassa, "The Catholic Church in the Franco-American Community" (honors thesis, Bowdoin College, 1978), 54; Moores, "The History of the Ku Klux Klan in Maine," 33–34; Robin, *Shades of Right*, 11; *Lewiston Daily Sun*, 22 March 1923, pp. 1, 10; *Le Messager*, 23 March 1923, p. 8.

8. *Lewiston Daily Sun*, 19 April 1923, pp. 1, 5, 21 April 1923, pp. 1, 4.

9. *Le Messager*, 23 April 1923, p. 1.

10. *Le Messager*, 16 and 18 May 1923, p. 8.

11. *Resident and Business Directory of Androscoggin County, Maine, 1920–1921* (Auburn, Maine: Merrill and Webber Company, 1920), 1101–1102; *Fourteenth Census of the United States*, vol. 3 (1923), p. 413; *Lewiston Daily Sun*, 21 and 28 May 1923, p. 12, 21 September 1923, p. 12, 1 November 1923, pp. 1, 5, 28 November 1923, p. 12; *Le Messager*, 28 May 1923, p. 6, 19 March 1924, p. 6.

12. *Le Messager*, 24 September 1923, p. 1, 7 November 1923, p. 8, 14 December 1923, p. 8, 29 February 1924, p. 6; *Lewiston Daily Sun*, 13 December 1923, p. 1.

13. Doty, "How Many Frenchmen Does It Take to . . . ?," 93; *Lewiston Daily Sun*, 25 April 1924, pp. 1, 11, 29 April 1924, p. 9, 16 May 1924, p. 16, 3 July 1924, p. 1; *Le Messager*, 2 May 1924, p. 8.

14. *Bates Student* (Lewiston, Maine), 16 November 1923, p. 1; *Le Messager*, 23 November 1923, p. 8; *Lewiston Daily Sun*, 22 November 1923, pp. 1, 4, 28 November 1923, p. 12.

15. *Lewiston Daily Sun*, 8 August 1924, p. 14, 11 August 1924, pp. 1, 12; *Le Messager*, 8 and 11 August 1924, p. 8, 10 September 1924, p. 1; la Chronique du couvent, the series Monasteries and Parishes, the subseries Monastery of the Apostles Pierre and Paul of Lewiston, Maine, Archives of the Dominicans, Montréal, Québec [hereafter la Chronique des Dominicains], vol. 14, 10 September 1924, p. 192.

16. *Le Messager*, 10 September 1924, p. 8; *Lewiston Daily Sun*, 15 September 1924, p. 4.

17. *Lewiston Daily Sun*, 23 October 1924, pp. 1, 8, 23 November 1924, p. 12, 11 June 1926, p. 1; *Le Messager*, 21 November 1924, p. 8, 9 and 11 June 1926, p. 8; Moores, "The History of the Ku Klux Klan in Maine," 25–26, 99–100.

18. Bourassa, "The Catholic Church in the Franco-American Community," 58–59.

19. *Le Messager*, 9 February 1925, p. 1, 24 June 1927, p. 1, 2 April 1930, p. 5, 9 June 1930, p. 1.

20. Naturalization data for the period from 1920 to 1939 comes from the Supreme Judicial Court, Androscoggin County, Naturalization Records, vols. 7–21, the Superior Court of Maine at Auburn Naturalization Records, vols. 22–32, Office of the Clerk of the Superior Court of Maine, Auburn, Maine; U.S. District Court, Portland, Maine, Naturalization Records, vols. 8–38, National Archives and Records Administration, Waltham, Massachusetts. Cote's record is from the Superior Court of Maine at Auburn, vol. 29, #2886, and Levesque's is from vol. 25, #2551.

21. Published interviews that include Lewiston Franco-Americans can be found in Dyke Hendrickson, *Quiet Presence: Dramatic, First-Person Accounts—The True Stories of Franco-Americans in New England* (Portland, Maine: Guy Gannett Publishing Co., 1980); and James W. Searles, ed., *Immigrants from the North: Franco-Americans Recall the Settlement of Their Canadian Families in the Mill Towns of New England* (Bath, Maine: Hyde School, 1982). The most extensive collection of taped interviews with Franco-Americans of Lewiston is the result of the ethnographic project "*Notre vie, notre travail*," undertaken in 1981–1982, sponsored by the Maine Council for the Humanities and Public Policy, the National Endowment for the Humanities, and the Western Older Citizens Council; the thirty-two acquisitions are now housed at the Maine Folklife Center, University of Maine-Orono, along with several other interviews of Lewiston Franco-Americans that were not part of the project.

22. Doty makes the same argument about the residual effect of the Klan on New England's Franco-Americans in "How Many Frenchmen Does It Take to . . . ?"

23. *Le Messager*, 19 January 1923, p. 9, 8 April 1925, p. 8; *Maine Register: State Year-Book and Legislative Manual*, no. 56 (Portland, Maine: Portland Directory Company, 1925), p. 319.

24. *Lewiston Evening Journal*, 16 October 1926, pp. 1, 9, 28 October 1926, p. 4; *Le Messager*, 10 July 1925, p. 6, 18 October 1926, p. 4, 3 November 1926, pp. 1,

6; *Portland (Maine) Evening Express*, as reported in the *Lewiston Daily Sun*, 22 October 1926, p. 20.

25. *Lewiston Daily Sun*, 27 October 1926, pp. 1, 4; George Filteau, "Autour d'une sensation," *Le Messager*, 3 November 1926, pp. 1, 6; R. Ouimet, O.P., "La langue anglaise dans nos écoles paroissiales," *Le Messager*, 15 November 1926, p. 3.

26. *Lewiston Evening Journal*, 18 April 1931, p. 1, 25 April 1931, p. 4; Mémorial du Monastère du Sacré-Coeur, Lewiston, Maine, Archives of the Dominican Sisters, Sabattus, Maine [hereafter Mémorial des Dominicaines], vol. 3, April 1931, pp. 175–176; *Le Messager*, 29 April 1931, p. 1.

27. *Le Messager*, 9 September 1931, p. 1; Louis-Philippe Gagné, *Le Messager*, 9 September 1931, p. 1.

28. James S. Olson, *Catholic Immigrants in America* (Chicago: Nelson-Hall, 1987), 15, 33–46, 197–202; Mémorial des Dominicaines, vol. 2, 14 May 1922, p. 310; diary of Bishop Louis S. Walsh, Chancery Archives, Roman Catholic Diocese of Portland, Maine, 24 October 1923, p. 297, 31 December 1923, p. 365; *The Maine Klansman*, 13 December 1923, Chancery Archives, Bishop Walsh File; G. S. Mertell to Bishop [Louis S. Walsh], undated, Bishop Walsh files, Chancery Archives.

29. Louis S. Walsh, Bishop of Portland, to Very Rev. Raymund [*sic*] Rouleau, O.P., Provincial, 12 January 1922; Thomas M. Gill to Raymond M. Rouleau, 2 February 1922; R. M. R. [Rouleau] to Monsignor Louis S. Walsh, 24 March 1922; Louis S. Walsh to Very Rev. R. M. Rouleau, March 30, 1922; Louis S. Walsh to Very Rev. G. Proulx, O.P., Father Provincial, December 31, 1923, all in the Archives of the Dominicans. Antonin M. Plourde, O.P., "Cent ans de vie paroissiale: SS. Pierre et Paul de Lewiston, 1870–1970," *Le Rosaire* (August/September 1970): 42–43; diary of Bishop Walsh, 6 July, 7 July, 8 July, 27 August, 31 August, 11 September, 19 September, and 17 December 1923; la Chronique des Dominicains, vol. 14, 8 May 1920, p. 66, 13 May 1920, p. 67, 27 July 1923, p. 165, 17 December 1923, pp. 173–174; the parish bulletin *La Quinzaine*, 1905, no. 12, in la Chronique des Dominicains, vol. 10, p. 259; Androscoggin County Registry of Deeds, Auburn, Maine, book 332, p. 537, book 337, pp. 300, 301, book 339, pp. 65–67, 233–234, book 340, p. 44; *Le Messager*, 1 October 1923, p. 1, 24 December 1923, p. 1.

30. Register of the Grand Seminary of Montréal, Archives of the Grand Seminary, Montréal, Québec, vol. 1: 1840–1900, pp. 550–551; notes of Reverend Philip Desjardins, Chancery Archives; *Le Messager*, 14 November 1923, p. 1, 17 December 1923, p. 1.

31. *Le Messager*, 14 November 1923, p. 1.

32. *Le Messager*, 17, 21 and 24 December 1923, p. 1, 31 December 1923, p. 6, 7 and 11 January 1924, p. 1, 23 January 1924, p. 8.
33. *Le Messager*, 25 January 1924, p. 8.
34. *Le Messager*, 28 January 1924, p. 6, 30 January 1924, p. 1, 4 February 1924, p. 1, 18 February 1924, p. 6, 25 February 1924, p. 1, 5 March 1924, p. 6, 10 March 1924, p. 1; Louis-Philippe Gagné, *Le Messager*, 22 February 1924, p. 2.
35. *Le Messager*, 21 April 1924, p. 8, 5 May 1924, p. 8, 22 June 1925, p. 8, 17 August 1925, p. 8, 4 and 18 January 1926, p. 1; la Chronique des Dominicains, vol. 14, 24 June 1925, pp. 210–211.
36. *Le Messager*, 8 February 1924, p. 4.
37. *Le Messager*, 5 March 1924, p. 5.
38. Louis S. Walsh to Very Rev. Gonzalve Proulx, 12 January 1924, Archives of the Dominicans.
39. Incidentally, Bishop John Murray also ended an ethnic conflict that had taken place between the Slovaks in Lisbon Falls and Bishop Walsh. The Slovaks had left the town's Catholic church to build one of their own, and Walsh had excommunicated four or five of the central figures in this case. Murray ended the controversy between the Slovaks and the Irish Catholic hierarchy of Portland by giving diocesan recognition to the new church and appointing a Slovak priest as pastor. *Le Messager*, 4 January 1926, p. 1.
40. *Le Messager*, 21 December 1925, p. 1, 4 January 1926, p. 4, 14 July 1926, p. 1, 17 November 1926, p. 8, 27 December 1926, p. 1; Cecile Levasseur, comp., *75th Anniversary of the Founding of St. Mary's Parish, Lewiston, Maine, 1907–1982* (unidentified publisher, 1982), 15. La Chronique des Dominicains, vol. 14, 18 July 1926, p. 247; vol. 15, 22 December 1932, p. 204, 17 January 1934, p. 290. *Lewiston Evening Journal* magazine section, 21 May 1927, p. A3. Elsewhere in the 1920s, an ethnic conflict raged between Franco-Americans and Rhode Island's Irish bishop when he demanded that Franco-American parishes contribute to the cost of a Catholic high school. The controversy spread beyond Rhode Island's borders, dividing the moderate Franco-Americans who supported the bishop's plan from the militants who did not. *Le Messager* chose to remain neutral during this bitter conflict, known as the *Sentinelle* Affair. *Le Messager*, 28 March 1927, p. 1, 29 June 1927, p. 4. For details of the controversy, see Yves Roby, *Les Franco-Américains de la Nouvelle-Angleterre (1776–1930)* (Sillery, Québec: Septentrion, 1990), 303–329.
41. *Lewiston Sun Journal*, 22 and 29 June 1991, p. 6.

42. *U.S. Census, 1920; Le Messager,* 14 November 1927, p. 8; la Chronique des Dominicains, vol. 14, 8 July 1928, p. 316, 12 August 1928, p. 324; Mémorial des Dominicaines, vol. 3, 4 September 1928, p. 44; *The Brothers of the Sacred Heart, Lewiston, Maine: Golden Jubilee of Service, 1928–1978* (unidentified publisher [1978]); Levasseur, *75th Anniversary of the Founding of St. Mary's Parish,* 21. Efforts to determine the ethnic composition of the Brothers of the Sacred Heart who served in Lewiston have thus far proven unsuccessful; presumably, most or all of the brothers who taught in Lewiston in the 1920s and 1930s were of French-Canadian birth or background.

43. Lucien A. Aubé, "From the Parochial School to an American University: Reflections on Cultural Fragmentation," in Claire Quintal, ed., *Steeples and Smokestacks: A Collection of Essays on the Franco-American Experience in New England* (Worcester, Mass.: Éditions de l'Institut français, Assumption College, 1996), 638–639, 644.

44. Annales: École paroissiale Sainte-Croix de Lewiston, Sisters of the Presentation of Mary, Holy Cross Convent, Lewiston, Maine [hereafter Annales de Sainte-Croix], vol. 1, 16 July 1928, supplemented with information provided by Sr. Susan Frederick, P.M., who consulted the records of the Provincial House in Methuen, Massachusetts; Sisters' Register: Sisters Who Have Been Missioned to Holy Family Convent, Lewiston, Maine, index cards [hereafter C.S.J. Sisters' Register], Archives of the Provincialate of the Sisters of Saint Joseph, Winslow, Maine; Liste des Soeurs qui ont passé à la Ste. Famille, Lewiston, Maine, Archives of the Provincialate of the Sisters of Saint Joseph, supplemented with data provided by the late Sr. Germaine Bernier, C.S.J., archivist, who consulted the congregation's profession book for places of birth missing from the Register; *U.S. Census, 1920; Le Messager,* 3 July 1945, p. 6. The place of birth of one of the twenty-five sisters at Sainte-Famille was not known. Not all of the sisters at Sainte-Croix and Sainte-Famille were teachers. While the 1920 census distinguished the Ursulines and Dominicans who taught, the records of les Soeurs de la Présentation de Marie and les Soeurs de Saint-Joseph did not supply enough information to separate the teaching sisters from those who served their order in other capacities, such as housekeeping.

45. Gerard J. Brault, *The French-Canadian Heritage in New England* (Hanover, N.H.: University Press of New England, 1986), 75; personal interview with Roger Bissonnette, who attended Sainte-Famille School from 1926 to 1933, Lewiston, Maine, August 17, 1993; personal interview with Sr. Marie Therese Beaudoin,

C.S.J., who graduated from Saint-Famille in 1936 and served as its principal from 1959 to 1961, Winslow, Maine, August 6, 1993.

46. Sr. Marie Therese Beaudoin, August 6, 1993; Aubé, "From the Parochial School to an American University," 644; Annales de Sainte-Croix, vol. 1, 19 June 1938; *Le Messager*, 21 May 1937, p. 7, 11 June 1938, p. 6.

47. *Le Messager*, 19 December 1935, p. 8, 21 December 1935, p. 6, 24 December 1935, p. 5, 26 December 1935, p. 6; C.S.J. Sisters' Register; *Church World*, 18 February 1955, p. 15; Sr. Marie Therese Beaudoin, 6 August 1993; Roger Bissonnette, 17 August 1993; personal interview with Sr. Alvina Levesque, C.S.J., who taught at Sainte-Famille almost continuously from 1932 to 1965, Waterville, Maine, 20 August 1993.

48. *Le Messager*, 21 October 1929, p. 8, 23 June 1936, p. 5.

49. Supreme Judicial Court, Androscoggin County, Naturalization Records, vol. 17, #1777.

50. Women of other ethnic backgrounds have similarly played a vital role in ethnic retention. See, for example, Frances Swyripa, *Wedded to the Cause: Ukrainian-Canadian Women and Ethnic Identity, 1891–1991* (Toronto: University of Toronto Press, 1993).

51. *Le Messager*, 23 June 1922, p. 8, 26 June 1922, pp. 1, 3, 28 June 1922, p. 4, 22 June 1923, p. 6, 25 June 1923, p. 1, 20 June 1924, p. 6, 8 September 1924, p. 1, 26 June 1925, p. 1, 25 June 1926, p. 1, 24 June 1927, p. 1; *Lewiston Daily Sun*, 25 June 1923, p. 12, 27 June 1938, p. 12; la Chronique des Dominicains, vol. 14, 24 June 1923, p. 164.

Chapter Seven.
Burying the Elephant: Politics, Gender, and Ethnic Identity in Lewiston, 1920–1940

1. *Le Messager*, 6 November 1936, p. 8; *U.S. Census, 1920*; *Cinquantenaire de L'Institut Jacques-Cartier de Lewiston, Maine* ([Lewiston, Maine]: le Comité de l'Album-Souvenir, 1922), 31.

2. Yolande Lavoie, *L'émigration des Québécois aux États-Unis de 1840 à 1930* ([Québec]: Éditeur officiel du Québec, 1981), 53; Yves Roby, *Les Franco-Américains de la Nouvelle-Angleterre (1776–1930)* (Sillery, Québec: Septentrion, 1990), 275–277; Paul-André Linteau, René Durocher, and Jean-Claude Robert, *Histoire*

du Québec contemporain: De la Confédération à la crise (1867–1929) (Montréal: Boréal, 1989), 405.

3. *Le Messager*, 24 August 1921, p. 6; *Lewiston Evening Journal*, as reported in *Le Messager*, 15 June 1923, p. 8.

4. Naturalization data for the period from 1920 to 1939 comes from the Supreme Judicial Court, Androscoggin County, Naturalization Records, vols. 7–21; the Superior Court of Maine at Auburn Naturalization Records, vols. 22–32; Office of the Clerk of the Superior Court of Maine, Auburn, Maine; U.S. District Court, Portland, Maine, Naturalization Records, vols. 8–38, National Archives and Records Administration, Waltham, Massachusetts [hereafter NARA-Waltham]. These records will be cited as "naturalization records, 1920–1939" throughout the rest of this chapter. Pierre Therriault's naturalization record is from the Superior Court of Maine at Auburn, vol. 27, record #2747.

5. The naturalization records from 1877 through 1987 come from the Supreme Judicial Court, Androscoggin County, Records, Maine State Archives [hereafter MSA], Augusta, Maine; Supreme Judicial Court, Androscoggin County, Naturalization Records, Office of the Clerk of the Superior Court of Maine, Auburn, Maine; Supreme Judicial Court, Androscoggin County, Naturalization Records, NARA-Waltham; Superior Court of Maine at Auburn Naturalization Records, Auburn, Maine; Lewiston Municipal Court Naturalization Records, MSA; Auburn, Maine, Municipal Court Naturalization Records, NARA-Waltham; U.S. District Court, Portland, Maine, Naturalization Records, NARA-Waltham; U.S. Circuit Court, Portland, Maine, Naturalization Records, NARA-Waltham; Superior Court, Cumberland County (Portland, Maine), Naturalization Records, MSA.

6. Laureat Odilon Bernard, "A Political History of Lewiston, Maine (1930–39)" (master's thesis, University of Maine-Orono, 1949), 6; U.S. Department of Commerce, Bureau of the Census, *Fifteenth Census of the United States, 1930*, vol. 1 (Washington, D.C.: Government Printing Office, 1931), 472. An exception is the article by Bruno Ramirez, "L'émigration des Canadiens français aux États-Unis dans les années 1920," in Yves Landry, John A. Dickinson, Suzy Pasleau, Claude Desama, eds., *Les chemins de la migration en Belgique et au Québec: XVIIe–XXe siècles* (Beauport, Québec: Publications MNH, 1995), 233–246.

7. *Le Messager*, 21 and 23 May 1923, p. 1, 9 May 1924, p. 8, 17 April 1925, p. 10, 15 June 1927, p. 6, 16 May 1928, p. 8.

8. Letter of Florian Fortin, Managing Director, La Cie de l'Événement, Québec, Québec, to Louis-Philippe Gagné, Lewiston, Maine, 1 September 1925, Correspondence

of Louis-Philippe Gagné, Franco-American Heritage Collection, Lewiston-Auburn College, Lewiston, Maine.

9. *Le Messager*, 1 June 1923, p. 8, 13 February 1929, p. 1, 20 February 1929, p. 8; the data are derived from figures provided in *Le Messager*, 13 February 1929, p. 1.

10. Naturalization records, 1920–1939, and the letters attached to them.

11. *U.S. Census, 1920*; 1930 figures are derived from the U.S. Department of Commerce, Bureau of the Census, *Fifteenth Census of the United States, 1930*, vol. 3 (Washington, D.C.: Government Printing Office, 1932), 1031.

12. Yolande Lavoie, *L'émigration des Canadiens aux États-Unis avant 1930: Mesure du phénomène* (Montréal: Les Presses de l'Université de Montréal, 1972), 13; *Le Messager*, 11 August 1920, p. 6, 14 August 1923, p. 8, 1 February 1926, p. 8, 25 October 1926, p. 8, 4 March 1927, p. 8, 18 March 1927, p. 4, 27 and 29 July 1927, p. 8, 24 August 1927, p. 6, 12 September 1927, p. 8, 18 April 1929, p. 9, 1 July 1929, p. 8.

13. C. Stewart Doty, "How Many Frenchmen Does It Take to . . . ?" *Thought and Action* 11 (Fall 1995): 90; Niles Carpenter, *Immigrants and Their Children, 1920: A Study Based on Census Statistics Relative to the Foreign Born and the Native White of Foreign or Mixed Parentage* (Washington, D.C.: Government Printing Office, 1927), 64, 128–129, 264. For an example of the historiography portraying European migrants as invading hordes, see Marcus L. Hansen, "The Second Colonization of New England," *New England Quarterly* 2 (October 1929): 539–560.

14. Naturalization records, 1900–1919, 1920–1939; Paradis's naturalization record from the Superior Court of Maine at Auburn is vol. 22, #2206, and Plourde's is vol. 28, #2819.

15. Naturalization records, 1920–1939; Blais's record is from the Superior Court of Maine at Auburn, vol. 26, #2613.

16. Naturalization records, 1900–1919, 1920–1939; U.S. Department of Justice, Immigration and Naturalization Service, *An Immigrant Nation: United States Regulation of Immigration, 1798–1991* ([Washington, D.C.]: Government Printing Office, 1991), 12.

17. *Le Messager*, 25 September 1922, p. 1; John J. Newman, "American Naturalization Processes and Procedures, 1790–1985" (typescript, Family History Section, Indiana Historical Society, 1985, available at NARA-Waltham), 22; naturalization records, 1920–1939; Ange Marie Begin, O.P., comp., *Marriages of SS. Peter & Paul, Lewiston, Maine (1869–1979)* (Lewiston, Maine: Dominican Fathers [1980]), 553.

18. *Le Messager*, 22 August 1921, p. 4, 2 September 1921, p. 4, 15 September 1922, p. 8, 6 June 1923, p. 8, 7 April 1924, p. 8, 11 April 1924, pp. 2, 8, 23 January 1925, p. 8, 4 September 1925, p. 8, 22 September 1926, p. 8, 12 August 1927, p. 8, 9 September 1927, p. 8, 23 March 1928, p. 14, 9 October 1929, p. 8, 27 December 1929, p. 8, 14 April 1930, p. 8, 1 December 1930, p. 8, 22 September 1934, p. 6, 23 April 1938, p. 8, 22 September 1939, p. 10, 26 September 1939, p. 5, 28 September 1939, p. 10, 9 October 1939, p. 8.

19. *Le Messager*, 15 October 1920, p. 6, 19 November 1924, p. 6, 21 November 1924, p. 8, 17 December 1924, p. 4, 11 May 1927, p. 4.

20. F. X. Belleau, *Le Messager*, 17 September 1924, p. 4.

21. *Le Messager*, 22 March 1926, p. 8, 27 September 1926, p. 8, 5 November 1926, p. 8, 11 February 1927, p. 8, 28 March 1927, p. 8, 17 and 30 April 1928, p. 8, 23 May 1930, p. 8.

22. *Le Messager*, 18 March 1927, p. 4, 21 March 1927, p. 8, 1 August 1927, p. 8, 13 and 16 January 1928, p. 8.

23. They were from the Maritime provinces of New Brunswick (2.7 percent), Nova Scotia (0.1 percent), and Prince Edward Island (0.2 percent); the central Canadian province of Ontario (0.1 percent); and the western province of Manitoba (0.1 percent). Naturalization records, 1920–1939.

24. Naturalization records, 1920–1939; letter of Louis-Philippe Gagné, *Le Messager*, 11 July 1923, p. 1; Linteau et al., *Histoire du Québec contemporain*, 474.

25. Naturalization records, 1920–1939.

26. Naturalization records, 1920–1939.

27. Naturalization records, 1900–1919, 1920–1939; *Le Messager*, 19 December 1928, p. 2.

28. Naturalization records, 1920–1939.

29. Naturalization records, 1920–1939. The quote refers to the work of Bruno Ramirez, *On the Move: French-Canadian and Italian Migrants in the North Atlantic Economy, 1860–1914* (Toronto: McClelland and Stewart, 1991), which emphasizes the geographic mobility of French Canadians.

30. Naturalization records, 1920–1939.

31. Naturalization records, 1920–1939.

32. Naturalization records, 1920–1939.

33. Naturalization records, 1920–1939.

34. The place of birth of the children of the other 2.8 percent of the women was not indicated on the naturalization forms. Naturalization records, 1920–1939.

35. Naturalization records, 1920–1939. Beginning in November 1940, the reporting was more consistent, because naturalization forms included a line on which court clerks could record the naturalization status of a person's spouse; before then, clerks occasionally inserted the information onto any available blank space on the form.

36. Not until 1934 did this same provision in the naturalization regulations apply to men. Newman, "American Naturalization Processes and Procedures," 22.

37. Naturalization records, 1920–1939; *Le Messager*, 28 October 1929, p. 8; the records of the Roberge sisters are from the Supreme Judicial Court, Androscoggin County, vol. 15, pp. 21–22.

38. Newman, "American Naturalization Processes and Procedures," 23; naturalization records, 1920–1939; Marie Yvonne Godbout's record is from the Superior Court of Maine at Auburn, vol. 22, #2225. If a woman married an alien ineligible to become a U.S. citizen, she could still lose her citizenship after September 22, 1922. Daniel Levy, *U.S. Citizenship and Naturalization Handbook* (St. Paul, Minn.: West Group, 1999), 145.

39. *Le Messager*, 30 August 1920, pp. 1, 6, 10 September 1920, p. 8.

40. *Le Messager*, 22 October 1920, p. 6; circular letter, "Petit Journal de Lewiston," Ursuline Provincialate Archives, Dedham, Massachusetts, Saint Mary's Convent, Lewiston, Maine, file, 29 August 1920, p. 1, 28 October [1920], pp. 2–3. On the role of French-Canadian women religious in the early feminist movement of Québec, see Marta Danylewycz, *Taking the Veil: An Alternative to Marriage, Motherhood, and Spinsterhood in Quebec, 1840–1920*, ed. Paul-André Linteau, Alison Prentice, and William Westfall (Toronto: McClelland and Stewart, 1987).

41. *Le Messager*, 1 September 1922, p. 6, 16 February 1923, p. 8, 15 August 1924, p. 1, 27 and 29 August 1924, p. 8, 31 August 1925, p. 8, 26 April 1926, p. 8, 11 October 1926, p. 8, 9 November 1926, p. 4, 19 November 1926, p. 8; Louis-Philippe Gagné, *Le Messager*, 18 August 1924, p. 6; Robert Cloutman Dexter, "Fifty-Fifty Americans," *World's Work* 48 (August 1924): 366–371. Dexter believed that individuals of French-Canadian birth and background maintained "divided loyalties"; like his contemporaries, he did not comprehend how—or rather, he refused to accept that—ethnic retention and civic participation could be intertwined goals.

42. *Le Messager*, 13 June 1924, p. 8, 31 October 1936, p. 6.

43. *Le Messager*, 10 February 1928, p. 1, 6 November 1936, p. 8; *Manning's Lewiston and Auburn, Turner and Webster (Maine) Directory for Year beginning April, 1936*, vol. 44 (Portland, Maine: H.A. Manning Company, 1936), 696.

44. *Le Messager*, 8 March 1922, p. 1, 5 March 1926, p. 1, 15 March 1926, p. 8, 12 September 1927, p. 8, 16 December 1929, p. 8, 5 October 1931, p. 8.

45. Ronald L. Bissonnette, "Political Parties as Products of Their Environments: A Case Study of Lewiston, Maine," (honors thesis, University of Maine-Orono, 1977), 26. La Chronique du couvent, the series Monasteries and Parishes, the subseries Monastery of the Apostles Pierre and Paul of Lewiston, Maine, Archives of the Dominicans, Montréal, Québec, vol. 15, 8 March 1932, p. 136, 4 February 1935, p. 341; vol. 16, 4 March 1936, p. 18. Geneva Kirk and Gridley Barrows, *Historic Lewiston: Its Government* (Lewiston, Maine: Lewiston Historical Commission, 1982), 13, 39. Franco-American Dr. Robert J. Wiseman served as mayor for most of these years: 1925–1929 and 1933–1935. Kirk and Barrows, 34.

46. Louis-Philippe Gagné, *Le Messager*, 18 August 1924, p. 6; *Le Messager*, 9 November 1926, p. 4.

47. Bernard, "A Political History of Lewiston," pp. 12–21, 33–35, 43–47, 186–187; *Le Messager*, 6 August 1936, pp. 4, 6, 21 November 1936, p. 6; *Lewiston Evening Journal*, 6 August 1936, p. 20.

48. Kirk and Barrows, *Historic Lewiston*, 4; Bernard, "A Political History of Lewiston," 7, 12–21, 163–165, 171, 186–187.

49. Bissonnette, "Political Parties as Products of Their Environments," 27–29, 35, 38; *Le Messager*, 24 October 1928, p. 8, 2 November 1928, p. 8, 7 November 1928, p. 1.

50. Naturalization records, 1920–1939.

51. *Le Messager*, 17 December 1934, p. 6, 1 February 1935, p. 8, 13 February 1935, p. 6, 14 February 1935, p. 8, 6 July 1935, p. 6; *Lewiston Daily Sun*, 18 December 1934, p. 18.

52. Bissonnette, "Political Parties as Products of Their Environments," 27–29, 35, 38.

Chapter Eight.
Forging Ethnic Unions: Social, Welfare, and Credit Institutions
in the Spindle City, 1920–1970

1. Data shared with me by the late Robert G. LeBlanc; interview with Romeo Boisvert by Steffan Duplessis and Raymond Pelletier, Lewiston, Maine, 8 January 1981, for the project "*Notre vie, notre travail*," Maine Folklife Center, University of Maine-Orono, accession #1693; Robert G. LeBlanc, "A French-Canadian Education and

the Persistence of *La Franco-Américanie*," *Journal of Cultural Geography* 8 (Spring/ Summer 1988): 51. Daughters of Franco-Americans could receive schooling beyond the eighth grade by studying with either the Dominican Sisters, who from their 1904 arrival in Lewiston offered an additional year or two of education for girls, or the Ursuline Sisters, who had a convent school in Waterville. Mémorial du Monastère du Sacré-Coeur, Lewiston, Maine, Archives of the Dominican Sisters, Sabattus, Maine [hereafter Mémorial des Dominicaines], vol. 1, 1904, p. 32, 1906, p. 94. There were opportunities for women to pursue higher education in Québec beginning in 1908, but *Le Messager* offered no information about whether Lewiston Franco-Americans sent their daughters to the women's *collèges classiques*.

2. Interview with Armand A. Dufresne, Jr., by Marcella Sorg and Steffan Duplessis, Auburn, Maine, 14 May 1981, for the project "*Notre vie, notre travail*," Maine Folklife Center, accession #1670; interview with Armand A. Dufresne, Jr., by Barry H. Rodrigue, Lewiston, Maine, 28 March 1994, Maine Folklife Center, accession #2351; interview with Reverend Hervé Carrier by Raymond Pelletier and Mark Silber, Lewiston, Maine, 19 March 1981, for the project "*Notre vie, notre travail*," Maine Folklife Center, accession #1697.

3. LeBlanc, "A French-Canadian Education and the Persistence of *La Franco-Américanie*," 51; Janelle, cited in Dyke Hendrickson, *Quiet Presence: Dramatic, First-Person Accounts—The True Stories of Franco-Americans in New England* (Portland, Maine: Guy Gannett Publishing Co, 1980), 5.

4. Romeo Boisvert, 8 January 1981; Paul-André Linteau, René Durocher, and Jean-Claude Robert, *Histoire du Québec contemporain: De la Confédération à la crise* (1867–1929) (Montréal: Boréal, 1989), 273; *Le Messager*, 6 August 1930, p. 8, 16 August 1934, p. 8.

5. *Le Messager*, 20 December 1888, 16 January 1890, p. 4, 17 February 1911, p. 4; *Annual Convention of the Canadian Snowshoe Union, February 7–8, 1925, Lewiston, Maine/Convention annuelle de L'Union Canadienne des Raquetteurs, 7 and 8 février 1925* (unidentified publisher [1925]), 5, 9, 14; Edouard Garand, treasurer of le Montagnard, Montréal, to Louis-Philippe Gagné, Lewiston, 28 May 1924, 6 June 1924, copies from Augustin "Gus" Croteau in the author's possession; Charter of le Montagnard, 6 January 1925, in possession of Gus Croteau, secretary of the organization, Sabattus, Maine.

6. Charter of le Montagnard, 6 January 1925; Raoul Charbonneau, "L'Union Canadienne de Raquetteurs," in le Comité du Club Alpin, ed., *La Raquette* ([Manchester, New Hampshire]: L'Avenir National, 1937), 19; U.S. Congressman

Wallace H. White, Jr., Washington, D.C., to Louis Phillipe [*sic*] Gagné, Lewiston, 4 September 1924, and U. S. Senator Bert M. Fernald to Louis-Philippe Gagné, 12 September 1924, copies given to me by Gus Croteau; Edouard Garand to Louis Philippe Gagné, 1 September 1924, copy of Gus Croteau in author's possession; Louis-Philippe Gagné to G.-H. Montpetit, Montréal, 11 November 1924, in the scrapbook of the L. & A. Montagnard Social Club, in possession of Diane Williams, Litchfield, Maine; *Annual Convention of the Canadian Snowshoe Union, February 7–8, 1925,* passim; *Le Messager,* 2 and 6 February 1925, p. 1.

7. *Le Messager,* 6 February 1925, p. 8, 9 February 1925, pp. 1, 6.

8. Les minutes des assemblées, Archives of the Jacques-Cartier Club [hereafter les minutes du Jacques-Cartier], Sabattus, Maine, vol. 1, 19 February 1925, p. 1; *Le Messager,* 30 March 1925, p. 6; Raymond J. Lévesque, "L'Union Américaine de Raquetteurs," in *La Raquette,* p. 22; *La Raquette,* pp. 34, 43; la Chronique du couvent, the series Monasteries and Parishes, the subseries Monastery of the Apostles Pierre and Paul of Lewiston, Maine, Archives of the Dominicans, Montréal, Québec [hereafter la Chronique des Dominicains], vol. 14, 19 February 1928, p. 303; *Le Messager,* 6 April 1925, p. 8, 27 November 1936, p. 8.

9. *Le Messager,* 18 January 1926, p. 1.

10. *Le Messager,* 11 December 1925, p. 3, 22 and 27 December 1926, p. 8, 23 December 1927, p. 2, 18 December 1929, p. 8, 18 December 1931, p. 14, 15 December 1934, p. 6, 18 December 1937, p. 6; letter of F. X. Marcotte, *Le Messager,* 4 January 1926, p. 3. Les minutes du Jacques-Cartier, vol. 1, 6 December 1926, p. 32; vol. 3, 9 December 1938, p. 49, 8 December 1939, p. 73.

11. Dames de Charité: Compte Rendu des Réunions, Archives of the Dominicans, 24 August 1925, p. 1, 21 September 1925, p. 3.

12. *Report of Saint Mary's General Hospital, Lewiston, Maine for the Fiscal Year Ending June 30th, 1934* (unidentified publisher, 1934), 11; *Saint Mary's General Hospital/Hôpital Général Ste-Marie, Lewiston, Maine: A Voluntary Charitable Institution Counting Fifty Years of Faithful Service to the Community, 1888–1938* (unidentified publisher [1938]), 7, 45; *Le Messager,* 25 May 1927, p. 8, 9 December 1927, p. 2. For more information on the role of Franco-Americans in providing for their own needs before the advent of the welfare state, see Mark Paul Richard, "Coping before *l'État-providence*: Collective Welfare Strategies of New England's Franco-Americans," *Québec Studies* 25 (Spring 1998): 59–67.

13. Charlotte Michaud, "Gray [*sic*] Nuns in Lewiston Build Hospital, Student Nurses' Home, Marcotte Home," *Lewiston Journal* magazine section, 10 December 1938,

A12; *Annual Report of St. Mary's General Hospital, Lewiston, Maine, 1917–1918* (Lewiston, Maine: Royal Press [1918]), 8; *Saint Mary's General Hospital, 1938* report, p. 3; figures for 1920 are derived from the Registre, vol. 5, Sisters of Charity, Saint Mary's Regional Center Archives, Lewiston, Maine, pp. 388–551a; *Album souvenir du 75e anniversaire de la Paroisse Saint-Pierre et Saint-Paul de Lewiston, Maine, 1871–1946* (unidentified publisher, n.d.), 49; *Le Messager*, 26 October 1935, p. 6.

14. Michael B. Katz, *In the Shadow of the Poorhouse: A Social History of Welfare in America* (New York: Basic Books, 1986), 300 n. 10; J. Carroll Moody and Gilbert C. Fite, *The Credit Union Movement: Origins and Development, 1850–1970* (Lincoln: University of Nebraska Press, 1971), 21–22; Joel W. Eastman, *The Credit Union Movement in Maine: A History of the Maine Credit Union League, 1937–1988* (Portland, Maine: Maine Credit Union League, 1988), 9. On the *caisse populaire* movement in Canada, see Yves Roby, *Alphonse Desjardins et les caisses populaires, 1854–1920* (Montréal: Fides, 1964); for a class analysis of the movement, see Ronald Rudin, *In Whose Interest? Quebec's Caisses Populaires, 1900–1945* (Montréal: McGill-Queen's University Press, 1990); for an interpretation emphasizing cultural factors, see Brett Fairbairn, "Social Bases of Co-operation: Historical Examples and Contemporary Questions," in Murray E. Fulton, ed., *Co-operative Organizations and Canadian Society: Popular Institutions and the Dilemmas of Change* (Toronto: University of Toronto Press, 1990), 63–76.

15. Eastman, *The Credit Union Movement in Maine*, p. 9. On the promotion of credit unionism in the United States, see Moody and Fite, *The Credit Union Movement*; Roy F. Bergengren, *Credit Union North America* (New York: Southern Publishers, 1940); and Roy F. Bergengren, *Crusade: The Fight for Economic Democracy in North America, 1921–1945* (New York: Exposition Press, 1952).

16. *Le Messager*, 5 May 1905, p. 6, 16 April 1915, p. 10, 2 August 1915, p. 8, 30 August 1915, p. 4, 11 April 1921, p. 1.

17. Eastman, *The Credit Union Movement in Maine*, p. 11; *Church World*, January 21, 1938, p. 1; Organization Certificate, Sainte Famille Federal Credit Union, March 16, 1938, Maine Family Federal Credit Union, Lewiston, Maine; Juliette Lajoie, *Ste. Famille Federal Credit Union 25th Anniversary, 1938–1963* (unidentified publisher, n.d.); notes of Reverend Philip Desjardins, Chancery Archives, Roman Catholic Diocese of Portland, Maine; C. Stewart Doty, *Acadian Hard Times: The Farm Security Administration in Maine's St. John Valley, 1940–1943* (Orono,

Maine: University of Maine Press, 1991), 58; Mme. Laurent (Juliette) Lajoie, "Histoire de la fondation de l'Union Crédit Fédérale Sainte Famille à l'occasion de son vincinquième [*sic*] anniversaire, 1938–1963, Paroisse Sainte Famille, Lewiston, Maine" (typescript, 1963), available at Maine Family Federal Credit Union, Lewiston, Maine, p. 1. The French name of the credit union appears without hyphenation, reflecting the spelling used on its Organization Certificate as well as the practice of the institution. Readers interested in the Antigonish Movement should consult M. M. Coady, *Masters of Their Own Destiny: The Story of the Antigonish Movement of Adult Education through Economic Cooperation* (New York: Harper & Brothers, 1939); and Malcolm MacLellan, *Coady Remembered* (Antigonish, Nova Scotia: St. Francis Xavier University Press, 1985).

18. A. M. Myhrman and J. A. Rademaker, "The Second Colonization Process in an Industrial Community" (typescript, Lewiston Public Library, n.d.), 28–29; interview with Ms. Geneva A. Kirk by students of the First Year Seminar 187, Bates College, Lewiston, Maine, February 12, 1996, transcribed by Anne D. Williams in Anne D. Williams, ed., "The Experience of the Great Depression in Lewiston-Auburn, Maine: A Report by First Year Seminar 187" (typescript, Bates College, Winter 1996; reprinted October 1997), 87. Discrimination against Franco-Americans had motivated the founding of Rhode Island's first credit union in 1915. Under the leadership of Reverend Joseph H. Béland, who had consulted Alphonse Desjardins and Pierre Hévey, Franco-Americans organized the Central Falls Credit Union because banks had denied them loans. Florence Marie Chevalier, S.S.A., "The Role of French National Societies in the Sociocultural Evolution of the Franco-Americans of New England from 1860 to the Present: An Analytical Macro-sociological Case Study in Ethnic Integration Based on Current Social System Models" (Ph.D. dissertation, Catholic University of America, 1972), 208; Paul M. Paré, "Franco-Americans and Credit Unions," *InformACTION* [*Bulletin de l'Action pour les Franco-Américains du Nord-Est (ActFANE)*], vol. 3 (February/March 1984): 5.

19. *Le Messager*, 5 and 8 March 1945, p. 6, 18 April 1945, pp. 3, 6, 31 October 1946, p. 6, 24 February 1947, p. 6, 2 October 1950, p. 6; Saint Pierre Credit Union Organization Certificate, Community Credit Union, Lewiston, Maine; Jules Antonin Plourde, O.P., in "Notices Nécrologiques des Dominicains Canadiens (1873–1990)," Archives of the Dominicans, Montréal, Québec, p. 847; Sainte-Marie Federal Credit Union Organization Certificate, 23 February 1947, Rainbow Federal Credit Union, Lincoln Street branch, Lewiston, Maine; minutes of the organization meeting of 29 October 1950, Sainte Croix Regional Federal Credit

Union, Lewiston, Maine; *Lewiston Evening Journal*, 21 January 1959, p. 12; *St. Pierre Credit Union 25th Anniversary, 1945–1970* (Lewiston, Maine: Screen Printing [1970]); Tenth Annual Report, 31 December 1960, Sainte Croix Credit Union; Drouin, cited by Plourde in the "Notices Nécrologiques des Dominicains Canadiens," 847.

20. *Le Messager*, 28 November 1944, p. 8; Juliette Lajoie, *Ste. Famille Federal Credit Union 25th Anniversary, 1938–1963* (unidentified publisher, n.d.); *Lewiston Evening Journal*, 12 October 1973, pp. 8–9.

21. Paul-M. Paré, "Les Vingt premières années du *Messager* de Lewiston, Maine," in Claire Quintal, ed., *Le Journalisme de langue française aux États-Unis* (Québec: Le Conseil de la Vie française en Amérique, 1984), 81; *Le Messager*, 10 July 1925, p. 6, 8 January 1934, p. 1; Kenneth E. Carpenter, "The Franco-Americans in Maine" (honors thesis, Bowdoin College, 1958), 49.

22. *Le Messager*, 14 May 1938, p. 1, 17 August 1938, p. 12, 20 August 1938, p. 6; interview with Paul Belanger, a senior citizen, by Mark Silber and Raymond Pelletier, Lewiston, Maine, 18 February 1981, for the project "*Notre vie, notre travail*," Maine Folklife Center, accession #1685; Henry V. Gosselin, "The Franco American Daily Press in Maine and a Content Analysis of *Le Messager*, Lewiston, Maine" (master's thesis, Boston University, 1951), 15; Myhrman and Rademaker, "The Second Colonization Process in an Industrial Community," 28.

23. *Le Messager*, 21 October 1929, p. 8, 13 December 1938, p. 8. The technology of radio did not fashion a common culture in the United States during the 1930s. Lizabeth Cohen, for example, argues that while radio programming gave Chicago listeners of different racial and ethnic backgrounds some common experiences in the 1930s, it did not serve to homogenize the city's different groups. See *Making a New Deal: Industrial Workers in Chicago, 1919–1939* (New York: Cambridge University Press, 1990), 329.

Chapter Nine.
We Will Earn a Living and Not Merely an Existence:
Franco-American Workers Assert Their Rights, 1920–1970

1. *Le Messager*, 11 March 1943, p. 8.

2. Mothon, cited in J. Antonin Plourde, *Dominicains au Canada: Livre des documents*, vol. 2, *Les cinq fondations avant l'autonomie (1881–1911)* (unidentified

publisher, 1975), 48; Robert Cloutman Dexter, "Fifty-Fifty Americans," *World's Work* 48 (August 1924): 369–370.

3. *Le Messager*, 3 and 8 February 1922, p. 1, 31 March 1922, p. 8; la Chronique du couvent, the series Monasteries and Parishes, the subseries Monastery of the Apostles Pierre and Paul of Lewiston, Maine, Archives of the Dominicans, Montréal, Québec [hereafter la Chronique des Dominicains], vol. 14, 13 February 1922, p. 137.

4. La Chronique des Dominicains, vol. 14, 14 December 1927, p. 297; *Le Messager*, 28 November 1927, p. 8, 9 and 12 December 1927, p. 8, 14 December 1927, pp. 1, 8, 16 December 1927, p. 2, 6 February 1928, p. 8.

5. Côté and Boisvert, quoted in James W. Searles, ed., *Immigrants from the North: Franco-Americans Recall the Settlement of Their Canadian Families in the Mill Towns of New England* (Bath, Maine: Hyde School, 1982), 27 and 26, respectively; interview with Romeo Boisvert by Steffan Duplessis and Raymond Pelletier, Lewiston, Maine, 8 January 1981, for the project "*Notre vie, notre travail*," Maine Folklife Center, University of Maine-Orono, accession #16938.

6. *Le Messager*, 15 August 1932, p. 1, 17 August 1932, p. 8, 31 August 1932, p. 1, 7 September 1932, p. 6; la Chronique des Dominicains, vol. 15, 18 August 1932, p. 167.

7. *Le Messager*, 16 September 1932, pp. 9, 14, 19 September 1932, p. 6, 21 September 1932, p. 1, 26 September 1932, pp. 1, 2, 6, 28 September 1932, p. 1; la Chronique des Dominicains, vol. 15, 22 September 1932, p. 174, 31 October 1932, p. 187.

8. Interview with Cecile Lebel by Mark Silber and Raymond Pelletier, Lewiston, Maine, 18 February 1981, for the project "*Notre vie, notre travail*," Maine Folklife Center, accession #1692. Speedups and larger workloads following the passage of the NRA were not unique to Lewiston's textile mills. Labor conflicts occurred throughout the textile industry, in both the North and South, as employers resisted implementation of the NRA industrial codes. One result was the industry-wide textile strike that began on 1 September 1934. Tamara K. Hareven, *Family Time and Industrial Time: The Relationship between the Family and Work in a New England Industrial Community* (New York: Cambridge University Press, 1982), 347–348; Gary Gerstle, *Working-Class Americanism: The Politics of Labor in a Textile City, 1914–1960* (New York: Cambridge University Press, 1989), 129–130.

9. La Chronique des Dominicains, vol. 15, 6 May 1934, p. 305; *Le Messager*, 7 May 1934, p. 6; Gorton James, Maine Compliance Office, National Recovery Administration, to Samuel C. Bartlett, Manufacture Labor Board, Boston, 8 May

1934, box 3, record group 25, National Labor Relations Board, National Archives and Records Administration, Waltham, Massachusetts.

10. *Le Messager*, 27 and 28 August 1934, p. 6, 4 September 1934, p. 8, 11 September 1934, pp. 1, 5, 8, 12 September 1934, p. 6, 14 September 1934, p. 1, 19 November 1934, p. 6; *Lewiston Daily Sun*, 5 and 12 September 1934, p. 1; la Chronique des Dominicains, vol. 15, 11 September 1934, p. 322.

11. Mémorial du Monastère du Sacré-Coeur, Lewiston, Maine, Archives of the Dominican Sisters, Sabattus, Maine [hereafter Mémorial des Dominicaines], vol. 3, 19–25 February 193[7?], pp. 332–333.

12. *Le Messager*, 3 March 1937, p. 8, 4 March 1937, p. 6, 26 March 1937 p. 8, 29 March 1937, pp. 2, 6, 30 March 1937, p. 8, 12 April 1937, p. 2, 20 April 1937, p. 6; la Chronique des Dominicains, vol. 16, 28 March 1937, p. 66, 11 April 1937, p. 67; *Lewiston Evening Journal*, 29 March 1937, p. 2; Mémorial des Dominicaines, vol. 3, 1937, pp. 305–306. The CIO became the Congress of Industrial Organizations in 1938. For a comprehensive history of the CIO as a labor federation independent of the American Federation of Labor, see Robert H. Zieger, *The CIO, 1935–1955* (Chapel Hill and London: University of North Carolina Press, 1995).

13. *Le Messager*, 12 April 1937, p. 4, 20 April 1937, p. 3, 28 June 1937, p. 8; Richard H. Condon, "Bayonets at the North Bridge: The Lewiston-Auburn Shoe Strike, 1937," *Maine Historical Society Quarterly* 21 (Fall 1981): 75, 92 (emphasis in original); Robert J. Branham, Lyn Francoeur, and William Surkis, "Roughing the Uppers: The Great Shoe Strike of 1937," VHS video, 1992.

14. My findings stand in contrast to those of Gary Gerstle. He argues that the participation of Woonsocket's Franco-American workers in a 1927 textile strike represented a departure in which they "had found the capacity to act in direct opposition to their ethnic leaders," namely their clergy. He views the strike as a pivotal event in which Franco-Americans, whom he portrays as clergy-dominated prior to World War I, began distancing themselves from their ethnic leadership to reshape their identity in the United States as members of the working class. See *Working-Class Americanism*, chapter 1; quotation is from p. 57. In contrast, this study challenges long-standing myths of the servility and docility of French-Canadian descendants well before the First World War; moreover, it traces the origins of their working-class identity back to the late nineteenth century, and not to the 1920s and 1930s.

15. Interview with Antoinette Boucher by Steffan Duplessis, Mark Silber, Raymond Pelletier, and Marcella Sorg, Lewiston, Maine, 15 December 1980, for the project

"*Notre vie, notre travail*," Maine Folklife Center, accession #1696; interview with Juliette Filteau by Margaret Lanoue, Lewiston, Maine, 5 November 1982, Maine Folklife Center, accession #1623.

16. *Le Messager*, 27 June 1924, p. 4, 25 September 1933, p. 2, 5 October 1933, p. 1, 25 January 1934, pp. 1, 6, 10 February 1934, p. 6, 11 August 1937, p. 3.

17. Glenn Kumekawa, "Political Factionalism within the Franco-Americans in Lewiston" (term paper [Bates College, 1949], available at the Lewiston Public Library), 17; 1969 figures are derived from data provided in Michael Guignard, "The Franco-Americans: The Relationship between Ethnic Identification and Political Behavior" (honors thesis, Bowdoin College, 1969), 37; Ronald L. Bissonnette, "Political Parties as Products of Their Environments: A Case Study of Lewiston, Maine" (honors thesis, University of Maine-Orono, 1977), 35, 38; la Chronique des Dominicains, vol. 17, 6 November 1960, p. 139, 8 November 1960, p. 139; *Le Messager*, 7 November 1960, p. 1; Louis-P. Gagné, "Kennedy," *Le Messager*, 7 November 1960, p. 3.

18. Lynn Franklin, "Black Calf's Son Views Life in a Mill Town," *Maine Sunday Telegram*, 23 February 1975, p. 3D.

19. *Le Messager*, 30 October 1941, pp. 1, 10.

20. *Le Messager*, 8 February 1943, p. 6; Drouin, 21 February 1943, reproduced in *Le Messager*, 11 March 1943, p. 8. Only in the late 1930s/early 1940s did Franco-American clergy in Woonsocket, Rhode Island, also come out in favor of trade unions. See Gary Gerstle, *Working-Class Americanism: The Politics of Labor in a Textile City, 1914–1960* (New York: Cambridge University Press, 1989), 250.

21. *Le Messager*, 29 October 1945, p. 1, 30 October 1945, p. 1.

22. *Le Messager*, 30 and 31 October 1945, p. 1, 2 November 1945, pp. 1, 3, 3 November 1945, p. 1, 19 November 1945, p. 8, 26 November 1945, p. 1.

23. *Le Messager*, 16 and 27 April 1955, p. 1, 29 April 1955, p. 4, 30 April 1955, p. 1. Two decades earlier, in the midst of the Great Depression, the Republican chair of Lewiston's Board of Registration had breathed new life into an old Maine law, which allowed paupers to be excluded from voting, by disfranchising Lewiston voters who had received public assistance. Alexander Keyssar, *The Right to Vote: The Contested History of Democracy in the United States* (New York: Basic Books, 2000), 238–239.

24. *Le Messager*, 29 April 1955, p. 4, 2 May 1955, p. 1, 13 May 1955, pp. 1, 16, 14 July 1955, p. 1.

25. My findings contradict those of Gary Gerstle, who contends that as the class consciousness of Woonsocket's Franco-Americans grew, their ethnic identification declined. See *Working-Class Americanism*, passim.

26. *Manning's Lewiston Auburn (Maine) Directory for Year beginning November, 1960*, vol. 57 (Springfield, Mass.: H.A. Manning, 1960) [hereafter 1960 Lewiston city directory.] See the appendix for an explanation of the methodology employed with the 1960 directory.

27. These percentages of homeownership reflect 152 out of 450 household heads with French surnames, and 82 out of 243 who did not have French family names; 1960 Lewiston city directory. Several other reasons account for the increase in homeownership. Through savings accumulated from overtime work during the Second World War, Franco-Americans acquired sufficient funds to make down payments on homes after the war ended. The G.I. Bill also helped Lewiston Franco-Americans to purchase their own homes after World War II. So did ethnic networks. A case in point: Politician and general contractor Jean-Charles Boucher built houses in the area immediately north of Sainte-Famille (Holy Family) Church that he sold on bonds for deeds to those who could not otherwise afford their own homes. One of Boucher's clients, Wilfrid Marcoux, paid Boucher twenty dollars weekly for his mortgage, taxes, water, and insurance for five years in the early 1950s, after which he acquired a bank loan. Interview with Reverend Hervé Carrier by Raymond Pelletier and Mark Silber, Lewiston, Maine, 19 March 1981, for the project "*Notre vie, notre travail*," Maine Folklife Center, University of Maine, Orono, Maine, accession #1697; Sylvie Beaudreau and Yves Frenette, "Les stratégies familiales des francophones de la Nouvelle-Angleterre: Perspective diachronique," *Sociologie et sociétés* 26 (Spring 1994): 174; personal interview with Jacqueline LeTendre, daughter of Jean-Charles Boucher, Lewiston, Maine, 25 August 1993; personal interview with Roger Bissonnette of Sainte-Famille Parish, Lewiston, Maine, 17 August 1993; personal interview with Wilfrid T. Marcoux of Sainte-Famille Parish, Lewiston, Maine, 25 August 1993.

28. Personal interview with Theresa Marcotte, Auburn, Maine, 14 August 1993; personal interview with Claire Lagace, Lewiston, Maine, 18 August 1993.

29. Planning Services Group, Part III: "Economic Base Report," *The Comprehensive Plan, Lewiston, Maine, Program Report* (Cambridge, Mass.: Planning Services Group, 1962), 12; James H. Parker, "The Assimilation of French Americans," *Human Organization* 38 (Fall 1979), 311. On the decline of New England's textile

industry in the 1950s and 1960s, see W. Stanley Devino, Arnold H. Raphaelson, James A. Storer, *A Study of Textile Mill Closings in Selected New England Communities* (Orono, Maine: University of Maine Press, 1966).

30. 1960 Lewiston city directory.

Chapter Ten.
The Quiet Evolution: Franco-Americans Become Americans, 1940–1970

1. *Lewiston Evening Journal*, 3 July 1947, p. 5; *Le Messager*, 3 July 1947, p. 6.

2. Collection of Catholic and French jokes from the Lewiston-Auburn, Maine, area by Richard Clark of Lewiston, Maine, Fall 1966, Maine Folklife Center, University of Maine, Orono, Maine, accession #85, p. 32; Couturier, cited in Pierre Vincent Bourassa, "The Catholic Church in the Franco-American Community" (honors thesis, Bowdoin College, 1978), 66.

3. The figure of 1,787 in the 1940s includes four minor girls whose parents filed naturalization petitions on their behalf. Naturalization data for the period from 1940 to 1949 comes from the Superior Court of Maine at Auburn Naturalization Records, vols. 30–43, Office of the Clerk of the Superior Court of Maine, Auburn, Maine; U.S. District Court, Portland, Maine, Naturalization Records, vols. 38–52, Overseas Military Petitions and Records, 1942–1945, the National Archives and Records Administration, Waltham, Massachusetts [hereafter NARA-Waltham]. These records will be cited as "naturalization records, 1940–1949" throughout the rest of this chapter. Lepage's naturalization record is from the Superior Court of Maine at Auburn, vol. 35, #3800.

4. The figure of 146 naturalizers for the 1960s includes four minor girls and two minor boys whose parents filed naturalization petitions on their behalf. Naturalization data for the period from 1950 to 1969 comes from the Superior Court of Maine at Auburn Naturalization Records, vols. 42–47, Office of the Clerk of the Superior Court of Maine, Auburn, Maine; U.S. District Court, Portland, Maine, Naturalization Records, vols. 53–64, NARA-Waltham. These records will be cited as "naturalization records, 1950–1969" throughout the rest of this chapter.

5. Naturalization records for 1939 are from the Office of the Clerk of the Superior Court of Maine, Auburn, Maine; and from the U.S. District Court, Portland, Maine, records, NARA-Waltham. J. L. Granatstein and J. M. Hitsman, *Broken Promises:*

A History of Conscription in Canada (Toronto: Oxford University Press, 1977), 142, 229–230; U.S. Department of Justice, Immigration and Naturalization Service, *An Immigrant Nation: United States Regulation of Immigration, 1798–1991* ([Washington, D.C.]: Government Printing Office, 1991), 15; *Le Messager*, 21 June 1940, p. 10, 5 July 1940, p. 8.

6. Naturalization records, 1940–1949, 1950–1969; Reed Ueda, *Postwar Immigrant America: A Social History* (Boston: Bedford Books, 1994), 125–127.

7. Naturalization records, 1940–1949, 1950–1969. Precise figures of naturalization patterns from the 1930s are provided in chapter 4.

8. Naturalization records, 1940–1949, 1950–1969.

9. Naturalization records, 1940–1949, 1950–1959; Lafreniere's naturalization record is from the Superior Court of Maine at Auburn, vol. 44, #6200; U.S. Department of Justice, *An Immigrant Nation*, 19; *Le Messager*, 31 March 1952, p. 6.

10. We do not have global figures on the proportion of French-Canadian immigrants who naturalized by 1960. Without citing his source, Elliott Robert Barkan claims that 72 percent of the French-Canadian immigrants in the United States in 1950 were naturalized. Barkan, "French Canadians," *Harvard Encyclopedia of American Ethnic Groups*, ed. Stephan Thernstrom (Cambridge, Mass.: Belknap Press, 1980), 397. See the appendix for more detailed information on the pre- and post-migration experiences and motivations of the French Canadians who became U.S. citizens during and after the Second World War.

11. *Le Messager*, 29 June 1942, pp. 1, 6. On Canada's World War II conscription crisis, see J. L. Granatstein and J. M. Hitsman, *Broken Promises: A History of Conscription in Canada* (Toronto: Oxford University Press, 1977), chapters 5 and 6. Jean-Charles Boucher's political career spanned three decades: he entered politics in 1933 by winning election to the Board of Aldermen, a position he held for four years, and he became mayor in 1943 and 1944; he also served in the state House of Representatives for two terms from 1934 to 1938 and in the state Senate for eleven terms from 1938 until his death in 1960. *Le Messager*, 24 March 1960, p. 1; Geneva Kirk and Gridley Barrows, *Historic Lewiston: Its Government* (Lewiston, Maine: Lewiston Historical Commission, 1982), 42.

12. Yves Roby, *Les Franco-Américains de la Nouvelle-Angleterre: Rêves et réalités* (Sillery, Québec: Septentrion, 2000), 377; *Le Messager*, 7 April 1943, p. 1, 21 and 23 June 1943, p. 6, 11 September 1943, p. 6, 16 September 1943, p. 1, 3 December 1943, p. 1, 27 February 1945, p. 6; *Church World*, 25 June 1943, p. 1.

13. *Le Messager*, 23 April 1941, p. 14. As with World War I, probably few French-Canadian immigrants of Lewiston returned to Canada during World War II to enlist in the military. *Le Messager* shed no light on the discourse surrounding enlistment in either Canada or the United States during the Second World War.

14. Bernier, cited in Bourassa, "The Catholic Church in the Franco-American Community," 62, 78.

15. *Le Messager*, 30 October 1944, p. 6.

16. Yves Roby, "From Franco-Americans to Americans of French-Canadian Origin or Franco-Americanism, Past and Present," trans. Alexis A. Babineau, A.A., in Claire Quintal, ed., *Steeples and Smokestacks: A Collection of Essays on the Franco-American Experience in New England* (Worcester, Mass.: Éditions de l'Institut français, Assumption College, 1996), 622–623.

17. *Le Messager*, 3 July 1937, p. 8, 5 January 1939, p. 6, 20 May 1940, pp. 1, 8, 21 May 1940, p. 1, 13 May 1943, p. 8; Annales: École paroissiale Sainte-Croix de Lewiston, Sisters of the Presentation of Mary, Holy Cross Convent, Lewiston, Maine [hereafter Annales de Sainte-Croix], vol. 1, 10 January 1940; Mémorial du Monastère du Sacré-Coeur, Lewiston, Maine, Archives of the Dominican Sisters, Sabattus, Maine [hereafter Mémorial des Dominicaines], vol. 3, 19 May 1940, p. 391. *Le Messager* did not specify which colors of Canada were used to decorate the armory. Possibly it meant the colors of the Union Jack, which would have overlapped those of the U.S. and French flags; more likely, it meant red and white, Canada's official colors since 1921. See Department of Canadian Heritage, *Symbols of Canada* (Ottawa, Ontario: Canadian Government Publishing, 1999), 11.

18. *Le Messager*, 28 January 1942, p. 6, 20 March 1946, p. 6, 2 May 1946, pp. 5, 6, 6 May 1946, pp. 3, 6; Mémorial des Dominicaines, vol. 4, 5 May 1946; the Soeurs Grises of Healy Asylum, *Le Messager*, 29 June 1946, p. 6.

19. *Le Messager*, 6 February 1950, p. 6, 30 January 1961, p. 1; Règlements du Lewiston-Auburn Montagnard Social Club, Inc., 17 November 1957, that the secretary, Augustin Croteau, gave the author, p. 1.

20. *Le Messager*, 10 December 1940, p. 6, 17 December 1943, p. 10.

21. *Le Messager*, 11 September 1944, p. 8, 12 October 1944, p. 6, 29 June 1959, p. 1.

22. *Le Messager*, 16 February 1950, p. 8, 18 February 1950, p. 6, 22 February 1950, p. 6, 23 February 1950, 27 June 1957, p. 11. Despite oral traditions and written accounts characterizing francophones from northern Maine as Acadians, not all were of Acadian descent. Béatrice C. Craig argues that French Canadians from

the lower Saint Lawrence had colonized northern Maine's Saint John Valley along with Acadians from southern New Brunswick beginning in 1785. As large numbers of French Canadians migrated to Madawaska between 1820 and 1850, descendants of the founding families (of whom French Canadians had constituted a minority) practiced endogamy and forged an Acadian identity in order to exclude the new French-Canadian migrants and to preserve their social and economic dominance in Madawaska. Craig further contends that they also imposed their view of history—an Acadian one—on the community. See "Early French Migrations to Northern Maine, 1785–1850," *Maine Historical Society Quarterly* 25 (Spring 1986): 230–247; and "Immigrants in a Frontier Community: Madawaska, 1785–1850," *Histoire sociale/Social History* 19 (novembre/November 1986): 277–297.

23. *Le Messager*, 24 June 1940, pp. 1, 3, 27 June 1955, p. 16; Naomi Griffiths, *The Acadians: Creation of a People* (Toronto: McGraw-Hill Ryerson, 1973), 80; A. I. Silver, *The French-Canadian Idea of Confederation, 1864–1900* (Toronto: University of Toronto Press, 1982), 7–9; Dino Cinel, *From Italy to San Francisco: The Immigrant Experience* (Stanford, Calif.: Stanford University Press, 1982). Toronto's Italian immigrants expanded their "hometown" identities to adopt a national identity in Canada, contends John E. Zucchi; extrapolating Zucchi's argument, the process appears to have been a stage in the Canadianization of these Italian immigrants. See John E. Zucchi, *Italians in Toronto: Development of a National Identity, 1875–1935* (Kingston and Montreal: McGill-Queen's University Press, 1988).

24. *Le Messager*, 11 and 16 January 1943, p. 6, 23 June 1950, p. B7, 8 June 1967, p. 5; Fr. Thomas-M. Landry, O.P., Secretary of the Orientation Committee on the history of the organization and on the "Vocation de la Femme Franco-Américaine," in *2ème Congrès, Le Comité d'Orientation Franco-Américaine, les 9, 10 et 11 Novembre, 1951, Lewiston, Maine* (unidentified publisher [1951]); Florence Marie Chevalier, S.S.A., "The Role of French National Societies in the Sociocultural Evolution of the Franco-Americans of New England from 1860 to the Present: An Analytical Macro-sociological Case Study in Ethnic Integration Based on Current Social System Models" (Ph.D. dissertation, Catholic University of America, 1972), 21; Charlotte Bordes LeBlanc, "History and Mission of the Fédération Féminine Franco-Américaine (1951–1991)," in *Steeples and Smokestacks*, 501–508.

25. *Le Messager*, 6 May 1946, p. 6, 10 June 1946, p. 6, 16 November 1953, p. 12, 3 December 1953, p. 2, 7 June 1956, p. B6, 7 December 1959, p. 1, 25 May 1961,

pp. 1, 5. Mémorial des Dominicaines, vol. 4, 6 May 1948; vol. 5, 28 May 1951, pp. 130–131; vol. 7, 29 October 1961, p. 148, 11 November 1961, p. 149; vol. 8, 15 May 1965, 20 May 1967. Annales de Sainte-Croix, vol. 2, 5 June 1949, 14 November 1953, 5 November 1955, 25 May 1956, 1 November 1959; vol. 3, 8 June 1969. Annals of Saint Mary's Convent, Lewiston, Maine, Ursuline Provincialate Archives, Dedham, Massachusetts [hereafter Annales des Ursulines], 27 May 1951, p. 52; Journal de la Maison, Couvent de la Sainte-Famille, Lewiston, Maine, Archives of the Provincialate of the Sisters of Saint Joseph, Winslow, Maine, 5 May 1957, p. 83, 20 May 1962, p. 108.

26. Mémorial des Dominicaines, vol. 5, 17 June 1949, p. 17; Joan H. Rollins, "Introduction: Ethnic Identity, Acculturation and Assimilation," in Joan H. Rollins, ed., *Hidden Minorities: The Persistence of Ethnicity in American Life* (Lanham, Md.: University Press of America, 1981), 11; Melford E. Spiro, "The Acculturation of American Ethnic Groups," *American Anthropologist* 57 (December 1955): 1244.

27. *Le Messager*, 7 March 1950, p. 2, 22 March 1951, p. 4.

28. *Le Messager*, 28 March 1952, p. 4.

29. *Le Messager*, 27 August 1954, p. 4, 30 June 1955, p. 4, 30 October 1958, p. 6, 23 April 1964, p. 4.

30. *Le Messager*, 28 June 1956, p. B2, 22 June 1959, p. 2, 19 June 1961, p. 12.

31. J. C. Larochelle, "Lewiston et Auburn fêtent La Saint-Jean-Baptiste," *Le Messager*, 20 June 1963, p. 5; interview with Cecile Lebel by Mark Silber and Raymond Pelletier, Lewiston, Maine, 18 February 1981, for the project *"Notre vie, notre travail,"* Maine Folklife Center, University of Maine, Orono, Maine, accession #1692; interview with Cecile Boisvert by Steffan Duplessis, Marcella Sorg, and Mark Silber, Lewiston, Maine, 8 January 1981, for the project *"Notre vie, notre travail,"* Maine Folklife Center, accession #1694; Norman Fournier, "Franco-Americans Beginning New Era," *Portland Sunday Telegram*, 26 January 1964, p. 1C; Michael J. Guignard, *La foi–La langue–La culture: The Franco-Americans of Biddeford, Maine* (By the Author, 1984), 131.

32. Mémorial des Dominicaines, vol. 5, 17 February 1951, pp. 111–112, 27 May 1951, pp. 128–129; Annales des Ursulines, 19 January 1954, p. 83, 22 January 1957, p. 146, 4 January 1961, p. 290; Annales de Sainte-Croix, vol. 2, 14 May 1962, 20 March 1965; *Le Messager*, 6 April 1959, p. 9; Lucien A. Aubé, "From the Parochial School to an American University: Reflections on Cultural Fragmentation," in *Steeples and Smokestacks*, 640–641; personal interview with Sr. Yvette Poulin, C.S.J., who taught at Sainte-Famille School from 1945 to 1958

and later served as Superior of the convent until her departure in the early 1970s, Waterville, Maine, 20 August 1993.

33. Data shared with me by the late Robert G. LeBlanc; the data on enrollments at Saint-Charles Borromée only cover the period to 1956; Robert G. LeBlanc, "A French-Canadian Education and the Persistence of *La Franco-Américanie*," *Journal of Cultural Geography* 8 (Spring/Summer 1988): 59.

34. François-M. (Hervé) Drouin, O.P., "Mémoire sur l'administration de la paroisse S. Pierre et S. Paul. De Janvier 1940 à Janvier 1943" (typescript, deposited at the Archives of the Dominicans, Montréal, Québec, 1943), 7–8; Drouin, cited in Charles Hillinger, "French in Maine Bear Bias Quietly," *Los Angeles Times*, 28 January 1985, part 1, p. 12; *Le Messager*, 22 April 1941, p. 6, 16 October 1942, p. 8; *The Brothers of the Sacred Heart, Lewiston, Maine: Golden Jubilee of Service, 1928–1978* (unidentified publisher [1978]); Fr. F.-M. Drouin, O.P., to the Very Reverend Mother General, Soeurs Grises le la Croix, Ottawa, Ontario, 4 October [19]51, Saint Peter's Parish file, Chancery Archives; Carol Patrell, "The Parochial School System in Lewiston and Auburn" (typescript [1948?]), 2, available in the Lewiston Collection, Lewiston Public Library; *The Spirit Echoes, 1941–1991* [Lewiston, Maine: Saint Dominic Regional High School, 1991].

35. Jacqueline P. Boucher, "The Franco-American in Lewiston" (Senior thesis, Bates College, 1956), 36; interview with Ms. Geneva A. Kirk by students of the First Year Seminar 187, Bates College, Lewiston, Maine, 12 February 1996, transcribed by Anne D. Williams in Anne D. Williams, ed., "The Experience of the Great Depression in Lewiston-Auburn, Maine: A Report by First Year Seminar 187" (typescript, Bates College, winter 1996, reprinted October 1997), 87, 89.

36. Annales des Ursulines, 11 October 1956, p. 137; *Le Messager*, 23 May 1957, p. 1.

37. Ethnicity did, however, continue to define relationships at mid-century. Reports in *Le Messager* reveal that the yearly baseball game between the *Canadiens* and the Irish, begun in the early twentieth century and interrupted during the Second World War, resumed after the war ended. The annual contest, pitting the best Irish and Franco-American ball players of Lewiston-Auburn against each other, often drew 2,000 to 4,000 spectators in the 1940s. The contests lasted at least until the mid-1950s, when their longtime promoter and the coach of the *Canadiens*, Omer Gauvin, decided not to continue organizing them. Lewiston brought back the event in a 1964 summer festival that featured, one evening, a ballgame between Irish and Franco-American teams. That these contests took place as late as the 1950s and

1960s demonstrates the salience of ethnicity in Lewiston. Conversely, their apparent end may serve as a marker of the changing identity of the francophone community. *Le Messager*, 10 August 1941, p. 6, 3 September 1946, p. 4, 6 September 1949, p. 4, 5 September 1950, p. 6, 16 August 1956, p. 5, 13 August 1964, p. 13.

38. One of the federal initiatives was sponsorship of the NDEA Institute, held at Bowdoin College during the 1961 and 1962 summers. Organized for teachers of Franco-American students, the Institute sought to promote French-language retention among New England Franco-Americans as a goal "in the national interest." While acknowledging "French-Canadian speech . . . as a respectable means of communication," the Institute's program focused on the promotion of standard French. Gerard J. Brault, "The Special NDEA Institute at Bowdoin College for French Teachers of Canadian Descent," *Publications of the Modern-Language-Association-of-America* 77 (September 1962): 1–5. On the effects of the Cold War on the domestic front, see Stephen J. Whitfield, *The Culture of the Cold War*, 2nd ed. (Baltimore: Johns Hopkins University Press, 1996). Unfortunately, *Le Messager* provided little information on how the Cold War affected the identity and culture of Lewiston's Franco-American population.

39. Annales de Sainte-Croix, vol. 2, 2 March 1965, 26 November 1965.

40. *Le Messager*, 23 March 1954, p. 4.

41. These are terms that sociologist Anny Bakalian uses to differentiate ascribed from voluntary ethnic identification, particularly among different generations of an ethnic population. See *Armenian-Americans: From Being to Feeling Armenian* (New Brunswick, N.J.: Transaction Publishers, 1993).

42. In 18.8 percent of the families baptizing children at Saint Joseph's in 1960, the husband had a French surname and the wife had a non-French maiden name; in 24.4 percent, the husband had a non-French surname and the wife's maiden name was French; and in 17.6 percent of the families, both the husband's surname and the wife's maiden name were French. In one case (0.6 percent) the husband was non-Franco-American and the wife's maiden name was not provided. The data excludes the parents of converts, for they would probably not have been members of the parish. Baptism Register, 1957–1961, Saint Joseph Parish Rectory, Lewiston, Maine, 1960, pp. 57–79; Savage, cited in Mary Raymond Higgins, R.S.M., *For Love of Mercy: Missioned in Maine and Andros Island, Bahamas, 1883–1983* (Portland, Maine: Sisters of Mercy, 1995), 170. Savage had been born, and had completed his clerical studies, in Ireland. Clergy file, Chancery Archives, Roman Catholic Diocese of Portland, Maine.

43. One-fifth (21.2 percent) of the families had fathers with Franco-American surnames and mothers with non-French maiden names, under one-third (30.8 percent) had fathers with non-French surnames and mothers with French maiden
names, and one-fifth (20.2 percent) had parents who both had French names.
The data for Saint Patrick also excludes the parents of baptized converts. Baptism
Register, August 14, 1955–April 28, 1963, Saint Patrick Parish Pastoral Center,
Lewiston, Maine, 1960, pp. 51–62.

44. Index of Marriages by Groom's Last Name, Office of the City Clerk, Lewiston,
Maine, 2 vols. (1999). Men with French family names and women with French
maiden names were classified as Franco-American. In marked contrast to the
Lewiston figures, the intermarriage rate of Franco-Americans and non-Franco-
Americans reached 80 percent in Fall River, Massachusetts, in 1961, claims Elliott
Robert Barkan, "French Canadians," *Harvard Encyclopedia of American Ethnic
Groups*, ed. Stephan Thernstrom (Cambridge, Mass.: Belknap Press, 1980), 399.

45. City Clerk's Index of Marriages; *Manning's Lewiston Auburn (Maine) Directory
for Year beginning November, 1960*, vol. 57 (Springfield, Mass.: H.A. Manning,
1960).

46. James Paul Allen, "Catholics in Maine: A Social Geography" (Ph.D. dissertation,
Syracuse University, 1970), 273; Michael J. Guignard, *La foi–La langue–La culture: The Franco-Americans of Biddeford, Maine* (By the Author, 1984), 131.

47. *Le Messager*, 16 October 1958, p. 18; Chevalier, "The Role of French National
Societies in the Sociocultural Evolution of the Franco-Americans of New England
from 1860 to the Present," 158; l'avant-propos par Robert Fournier, *Les Clubs
Richelieu: Les premiers 25 ans du Richelieu International* (Montréal: Éditions
du Jour, 1971), 8, 13–14; *Les Clubs Richelieu*, 13–14; Faith Seiple, "Assimila-
tion of French Groups into the Lewiston-Auburn Community" (term paper [Bates
College], 1949), available at the Lewiston Public Library, Lewiston, Maine, p. 4;
"Règlements des Clubs Richelieu," p. 4, Club Richelieu Montréal Inc. Collection,
Archives nationales du Québec, Montréal, Québec, reel 6387.

48. Geneva Kirk and Gridley Barrows, *Historic Lewiston: Its Government* (Lewiston,
Maine: Lewiston Historical Commission, 1982), 13; Norman Fournier, "End to
Bloc Voting Seen in Lewiston's New Council," *Portland Sunday Telegram*, 13 De-
cember 1964, p. 20A; *Maine Register: State Year-Book and Legislative Manual*,
no. 97 (Portland, Maine: Fred L. Tower Companies, 1965), 293; *Maine Register:
State Year-Book and Legislative Manual*, no. 98 (Portland, Maine: Fred L. Tower
Companies, 1966), 304; *Maine Register: State Year-Book and Legislative Manual*,

no. 99 (Portland, Maine: Fred L. Tower Companies, 1967), 306; *Maine Register: State Year-Book and Legislative Manual*, no. 100 (Portland, Maine: Tower Publishing Company, 1968), 310; *Maine Register: State Year-Book and Legislative Manual*, no. 101 (Portland, Maine: Tower Publishing Company, 1969), 330.

49. Boucher, "The Franco-American in Lewiston," 38; *Le Messager*, 23 June 1966, p. 1; *Lewiston Daily Sun*, 20 June 1969, p. 2.

50. Gerard J. Brault, "The Achievement of the Teaching Orders in New England: The Franco-American Parochial School," in *Steeples and Smokestacks*, 277; *Lewiston Daily Sun*, 12 June 1968, p. 8; Mémorial des Dominicaines, vol. 8, 8 November 1967; Annales des Ursulines, 2 July 1968, p. 331; Minutes of the Holy Family Parish School Board, 6 April 1969, Holy Family School File, Chancery Archives.

51. Fournier, *Portland Sunday Telegram*, 26 January 1964, p. 1C; *Lewiston Evening Journal* magazine section, 16 December 1967, p. 7A; bulletin of Saint Pierre and Saint Paul Parish, October 1967, p. 1, Archives of the Dominicans; *Le Messager*, 2 November 1967, p. 4; Jules Antonin Plourde, O.P., *Qui sont-ils et d'où viennent-ils? Nécrologie dominicain, 1965–1990*, tome 2 (Montréal: Les Dominicains au Canada, n.d.), 140; Louis-P. Fiset, O.P., to Very Reverend Father Thomas-M. Rondeau, O.P., Prior Provincial, 23 March 1967, Archives of the Dominicans, Lewiston file; Louis-P. Fiset, "Aurons-nous une messe en anglais?" bulletin of the parish Saint-Pierre et Saint-Paul, June 1967, p. 1, Archives of the Dominicans; *Le Messager*, 28 September 1967, p. 1; *Church World*, 18 February 1955, p. 1.

52. *Le Messager*, 6 October 1953, p. 10, 2 November 1967, p. 4; typescript notes of Reverend Philip Desjardins, Chancery Archives; Marcel Blouin, "Il faut retrouver le climat français dit le curé Martin," *Le Messager*, 25 June 1951, pp. 3, 10; Marcel Raymond, "Echos de la St-Jean," *Le Messager*, 23 June 1958, p. 1; *Lewiston Evening Journal* magazine section, 11 October 1969, p. 6A; *Lewiston Daily Sun*, 11 October 1969, p. 9.

53. *Church World*, 17 March 1972, p. 22, 19 June 1975, p. 4; personal interview with Reverend Real J. Nadeau, assistant at Sainte-Famille from 1962 to 1966, Lewiston, Maine, 23 August 1993. I learned English only after my parents followed the advice of the Sisters of St. Joseph and made English the language of our household.

54. La Chronique des Dominicains, vol. 17, 8 August 1960, p. 134.

55. Kenneth E. Carpenter, "The Franco-Americans in Maine" (honors thesis, Bowdoin College, 1958), p. 49; Paul-M. Paré, "Les Vingt premières années du *Messager* de Lewiston, Maine," in Claire Quintal, ed., *Le Journalisme de langue française aux*

États-Unis (Québec: Le Conseil de la Vie française en Amérique, 1984), 81; *Le Messager*, 9 February 1951, p. 1, 9 June 1954, pp. 1, 4, 23 November 1954, p. 1, 6 September 1955, p. 1, 30 January 1958, pp. 3–4, 21 November 1962, p. 1; Boucher, "The Franco-American in Lewiston," 39. Circulation figures suggest that Franco-Americans probably dropped *Le Messager* in favor of the independent *Lewiston Daily Sun* rather than the Republican *Lewiston Evening Journal*. In 1950, the *Sun* had a circulation of 29,139 and the *Journal* 15,442; by 1960, the *Sun*'s circulation had increased to 31,592, whereas the *Journal*'s had decreased to 14,355. *Maine Register: State Year-Book and Legislative Manual*, no. 82 (Portland, Maine: Fred L. Tower Companies, 1950), 228; *Maine Register: State Year-Book and Legislative Manual*, no. 92 (Portland, Maine: Fred L. Tower Companies, 1960), p. 973.

56. *Le Messager*, 1961, passim, 2 February 1967, p. 1, 9 May 1968, p. 1; *Le Nouveau Messager*, 25 August 1966, p. 1, 15 September 1966, p. 1, 22 September 1966, pp. 1, 4; Paré, "Les Vingt premières années du *Messager* de Lewiston, Maine," 94.

57. The historical evidence does not support the view of sociologist and Auburn, Maine, native James Hill Parker that Lewiston francophones underwent "a cataclysmic shift in cultural orientation" during the 1960s, as he argues in "The Assimilation of French Americans," 309–312, and in *Ethnic Identity: The Case of the French Americans* (Washington, D.C.: University Press of America, 1983).

Chapter Eleven.
Contemporary Identity: Americans of French-Canadian Descent, 1970–2007

1. Alan Clendenning and Greg Gadberry, "'Frenchie' Will Go on the Air to Discuss His Radio Character," *Portland Press Herald*, 11 February 1993, pp. 1A, 12A; Donat B. Boisvert, "'Frenchie' Issue Asks: What Is Humor?" *Lewiston Sunday Sun Journal*, 17 October 1993, p. 3D; Paul F. Davis, "'Frenchie' Releases Cassette," *Lewiston Sun Journal*, 22 December 1993, p. 1; *Sun Journal*, 16 January 1993, p. 1; Elizabeth Edwardsen and Christine Young, "Adieu, Frenchie: WBLM's Self-Proclaimed Comic Quits to Protect His Privacy," *Sun Journal*, 12 February 1993, p. 1; Niki Kapsamblis, "More Francos Are Angry over 'Frenchie,'" *Sun Journal*, 26 January 1993, pp. 1, 8; Lemieux, cited in *Sun Journal*, 6 February 1993, p. 32; Greg Gignoux, "Franco-Americans Petition to Get Rid of 'Frenchie,'" *Sun Journal*, 9 February 1993, pp. 1, 8.

2. Paul Carrier, "Lafayette, Where Are You?" *Portland Press Herald*, 9 February 1993, p. 13.
3. Edwardsen and Young, "Adieu, Frenchie," 1; Gagné, cited in Edwardsen and Young, "Adieu, Frenchie," pp. 1, 8; *Sun Journal*, 20 February 1993, p. 5; *Sunday Sun Journal*, 21 February 1993, p. 3D; Davis, "'Frenchie' Releases Cassette," p. 8.
4. Denis Ledoux, "Francos Have Too Long Acquiesced," *Sun Journal*, 22 March 1993, p. 5; Boisvert, "'Frenchie' Issue Asks: What Is Humor?" p. 3D.
5. Naturalization data for the period from 1970 to 1991 comes from the Superior Court of Maine at Auburn Naturalization Records, vol. 47, Office of the Clerk of the Superior Court of Maine, Auburn, Maine; U.S. District Court, Portland, Maine, Naturalization Records, vols. 65–76, National Archives and Records Administration, Waltham, Massachusetts. These records will be cited as "naturalization records, 1970–1991" throughout the rest of this chapter. It should be noted, however, that the naturalization records of the Superior Court ended in 1974; while the District Court handled naturalization petitions until 1991, no French Canadians of Lewiston naturalized there between 1988 and 1991, after which the Immigration and Naturalization Service (INS) took over the processing of naturalization petitions. In the 1970s three minor girls, and in the 1980s one minor boy became U.S. citizens when their parents filed naturalization petitions on their behalf; they are included in the data. Another five men and three women with French surnames naturalized at the U.S. District Court in Portland, Maine, in the late 1970s, but there was no information on the naturalization form about their places of birth or emigration, nor even about their country of nationality; they were therefore excluded from the data. Naturalization records, 1970–1991. On postwar naturalization trends, see Reed Ueda, *Postwar Immigrant America: A Social History* (Boston: Bedford Books, 1994), 126–127.
6. Naturalization records, 1970–1991. See the appendix for further analysis of the naturalization records from 1970 to 1991.
7. Naturalization records, 1970–1991; Pierre Vincent Bourassa, "The Catholic Church in the Franco-American Community" (honors thesis, Bowdoin College, 1978), 65; Paul Carrier, "The Franco Factor: French Heard Less and Less," *Sunday Sun Journal*, 28 September 1986, pp. 1A, 12A; Bernier, cited in Carrier, 28 September 1986, p. 12A.
8. Amy Bither, "Then and Now: Ste. [*sic*] Jean Baptist Holiday: Lewiston, Maine" (term paper, University of Maine, Fall 1991), Charles Stewart Doty Papers, Special Collections, Fogler Library, University of Maine-Orono, pp. 10–12.

9. *Sun Journal*, 22 June 1991, p. 6; "Holy Family Parish 75th Anniversary, 8 November 1998, Lewiston, Maine," VHS video.

10. Figures are derived from the U.S. Department of Commerce, Bureau of the Census, *Census of Population: 1970*, vol. 1, part 21 (Washington, D.C.: U.S. Government Printing Office, 1973), 185; U.S. Department of Commerce, Bureau of the Census, *1980 Census of Population*, vol. 1, chapter C, part 21 (Washington, D.C.: U.S. Government Printing Office, 1983), 110; U.S. Department of Commerce, Bureau of the Census, *1990 Census of Population, Social and Economic Characteristics: Maine* (Washington, D.C.: U.S. Government Printing Office, 1993) [hereafter 1990 census], 234.

11. Madeleine D. Giguère, "New England's Francophone Population Based upon the 1990 Census," in Claire Quintal, ed., *Steeples and Smokestacks: A Collection of Essays on the Franco-American Experience in New England* (Worcester, Mass.: Éditions de l'Institut français, Assumption College, 1996), 570, 582–583; 1990 census, 234.

12. *1992 Catalist: Business and Household Digest of Lewiston-Auburn* (Loveland, Colo.: USWest Marketing Resources, 1991) [hereafter 1992 Lewiston city directory.] See the appendix for an explanation of the methodology employed with the 1992 city directory.

13. 1992 Lewiston city directory.

14. 1992 Lewiston city directory.

15. The figures include mobile-home ownership. The proportions for new residents may have been higher, for the directory provides no indication of the length of residence of about one-third of either the Franco-American or non-Franco-American households. 1992 Lewiston city directory.

16. *Manning's Lewiston Auburn (Maine) Directory for Year beginning November, 1960*, vol. 57 (Springfield, Mass.: H.A. Manning, 1960); 1992 Lewiston city directory. By 1990, the Lewiston economic area (which included the surrounding cities and towns of Auburn, Mechanic Falls, Poland, Lisbon, Sabattus, and Greene) employed only 1,023 in the textile industry and 1,702 in the leather industry. Maine Department of Labor, Bureau of Labor Standards, *Census of Maine Manufactures, 1990* (Augusta, Maine: Maine Department of Labor, Bureau of Labor Standards, 1991), 35–36, 45.

17. 1992 Lewiston city directory; James H. Parker, "The Assimilation of French Americans," *Human Organization* 38 (Fall 1979): 311.

18. 1992 Lewiston city directory.

19. Index of Marriages by Groom's Last Name, Office of the City Clerk, Lewiston, Maine, 2 vols. (1999).

20. Saint Joseph Parish directory, Saint Joseph Parish Rectory, Lewiston, Maine, July 7, 1999; Saint Patrick Parish directory, Saint Patrick Parish Pastoral Center, Lewiston, Maine, 1999.

21. Bishop Joseph Gerry, O.S.B., "The Time Has Come to Consider a New Style of Ministry in the Lewiston Area," *Church World*, 27 June 1996, pp. 10–11; *SS. Peter and Paul Parish, Lewiston, Maine, 1870–1996, Paroisse Saint Pierre et Saint Paul* (Lewiston, Maine: SS. Peter and Paul Parish, 1996), 31–32.

22. "Le Centre d'Héritage Franco-Américain de l'Etat du Maine," typescript, file on Lewiston, Maine, Bibliothèque Mallet, Union Saint-Jean-Baptiste, Woonsocket, Rhode Island; Lance Tapley, "Franco-American Heritage Movement Is Catching Fire," *Maine Sunday Telegram*, 19 March 1972, p. 3D; brochure entitled "Festival Franco Américain," July 20–27 [1980], file on ethnic groups, Androscoggin County Historical Society, Auburn, Maine.

23. Lewiston, Maine, *Observations*, 23 June 1972, p. 2; Armand Chartier, *Histoire des Franco-Américains de la Nouvelle-Angleterre, 1775–1990* (Sillery, Québec: Septentrion, 1991), 350.

24. Chartier, *Histoire des Franco-Américains de la Nouvelle-Angleterre*, 350; *Observations*, 21 July–4 August 1972, pp. 1, 5; José Léveillé, *Observations*, 1–15 September 1972, pp. 1, 13.

25. *Lewiston (Maine) L'Unité*, May 1976, June 1981, pp. 1, 4. *L'Unité* received federal funding through the Comprehensive Employment and Training Act (CETA) and local funds from clubs that needed a nonprofit sponsor in order to carry out "Lucky 7" gambling activities. Interview with senior citizen Paul Belanger by Mark Silber and Raymond Pelletier, Lewiston, Maine, 18 February 1981, for the project "*Notre vie, notre travail*," Maine Folklife Center, University of Maine, Orono, Maine, accession #1685; discussion with Donat Boisvert, former editor of *L'Unité*, Lewiston, Maine, 25 November 2002.

26. Chartier, *Histoire des Franco-Américains de la Nouvelle-Angleterre*, 366; Tapley, "Franco-American Heritage Movement Is Catching Fire," p. 3D.

27. Daniel Hartill, "Cable TV Adds Third French Channel," *Sun Journal*, 26 October 1999, p. B1; Hope Ullman, "On the Way to Wellness," *Sunday Sun Journal*, 2 January 2000, pp. B1, B5. For background on Québec's separatist movement, a helpful (though dated) study is Kenneth McRoberts, *Quebec: Social Change and Political Crisis*, 3rd ed. (Toronto: McClelland and Stewart, 1988).

28. *Observations*, 23 June 1972, pp. 1, 4, 5.

29. Paul Carrier, "The Franco Factor: Besieged Language, Culture Expected to Survive," *Sunday Sun Journal*, 19 October 1986, p. 10A; Berube, cited in Carrier, 19 October 1986, p. 10A.

30. Paul Paré, "L'Unité Franco-Américaine: C'est pour tout le monde," *L'Unité* (hiver 1977–1978): 1, 7; Gerard J. Brault, *The French-Canadian Heritage in New England* (Hanover, N.H.: University Press of New England, 1986), 239 n. 110; *L'Unité* (printemps 1978): 1; la Chronique du couvent, the series Monasteries and Parishes, the subseries Monastery of the Apostles Pierre and Paul of Lewiston, Maine, Archives of the Dominicans, Montréal, Québec [hereafter la Chronique des Dominicains], vol. 17, 23 June 1975, pp. 290–291; Jules Antonin Plourde, O.P., *Qui sont-ils et d'où viennent-ils? Nécrologe [sic] dominicain, 1965–1990*, vol. 2 (Montréal: Les Dominicains au Canada, n.d.), 222.

31. Tom Robustelli, "French People Should Have a Holiday, Too, Says Sen. Charette," *Lewiston Journal*, 26 March 1982, p. 8; *Lewiston Daily Sun*, 2 June 1983, p. 12; St. Peter's Parish File, Chancery Archives, Roman Catholic Diocese of Portland, Maine.

32. Carol Clapp, "St. Jean Still Remembered in Lewiston," *Sun Journal*, 25 June 1997, pp. 1A, 8A.

33. *L'Unité*, May 1976, p. 1; la Chronique des Dominicains, vol. 17, 8 mai 1976, pp. 297–298; Dennis Hoey, "City to Swell for Franco Festival," *Lewiston Daily Sun*, 15 July 1980, p. 17; "Festival Franco Américain," brochure, 20–27 July [1980], Androscoggin Historical Society; Mark Shanahan, "Franco Fest Is On Again," *Sun Journal*, 6 February 1993, pp. 1, 8; brochure, "6th Annual Festival de Joie, 31 July–2 August 1998," in author's possession.

34. Here, I am echoing the title of an early introduction to French-Canadian heritage by Robert B. Perreault, *One Piece in the Great American Mosaic: The Franco-Americans of New England* (Lakeport, N.H.: André Paquette Associates, 1976).

35. This information comes from a discussion I had with members of the Franco American War Veterans, Inc., Post #31, at the Festival de Joie on 1 August 1998, and from typescript notes providing general information on the organization's history, which the veterans distributed from their booth at the festival.

36. Les minutes des assemblées, Archives of the Jacques-Cartier Club, Sabattus, Maine, vol. 5, 8 June 1984, p. 293; "Franco-American Social Clubs" (audiocassette, Maine Public Broadcasting [1993?]); Paul Carrier, "Clubs Survive, but Change Is in the Wind," *Sunday Sun Journal*, 28 September 1986, pp. 1A, 11A; Jonathan Van Fleet,

"Le Club Richelieu proche fini," *Sun Journal*, 20 July 1998, p. B1; discussion with Russ Merrill, president of the Jacques-Cartier Club, Sabattus, Maine, 12 November 1999.

37. Paul Carrier, "The Franco Factor: Negative Image Takes Heavy Toll on Area Francos," *Sunday Sun Journal*, 21 September 1986, p. 1A.

38. Karlene K. Hale, "Bates Lifts 'Don't Speak French' Rule," *Portland Press Herald*, 21 November 1991, pp. 1A, 12A; *Sun Journal*, 19 November 1991, p. 4, 21 November 1991, p. 14; *Bates Student*, 15 November 1991, pp. 4, 7, 17 January 1992, p. 9.

39. Tracy, cited in Carrier, 21 September 1986, p. 1A.

40. *L'Unité* (January 1981): 1–2.

41. Journal de la maison, Sainte-Famille Convent, Lewiston, Maine, February 1926–December 1965, and le journal de la Sainte-Famille, Sainte-Famille Convent, Lewiston, Maine, January 1966–August 1971, Archives of the Provincialate of the Sisters of Saint Joseph, Winslow, Maine; Yvonne Goulet, "Sisters Play Vital Role in Life of the Diocese," *Church World*, 29 May 1975, pp. 4–5; Reverend William K. McDonough, "Mini-Congress Reveals New Directions for the Sisters of St. Joseph in Maine," *Church World*, 9 July 1971, p. 5; Sr. Theresa Morin, S.C.I.M., "Today's Women Religious: 'Their Ministry Is Integral,'" *Church World*, 1 September 1972, p. 12; Sr. Janet Gagnon, C.S.J., "Sisters of St. Joseph: Return to Founder's Insight, Vision," *Church World*, 1 May 1980, p. 14; Donald C. Hansen, "Maine Catholic Schools Await Supreme Court Decision," *Maine Sunday Telegram*, 21 March 1971, p. 4A; Holy Family School file, Chancery Archives.

42. *Lewiston Daily Sun*, 19 June 1978, p. 15; Paul Badeau, "SS. Peter and Paul Parish: Dominicans Turn Administration over to the Diocese," *Church World*, 19 June 1986, p. 10; Our Lady of the Rosary Parish file, Chancery Archives; Henry Gosselin, "A Parish Only One Year, and Already We've Begotten a Mission!" *Church World*, 2 December 1976, pp. 16–17.

43. Interview with Reverend Hervé Carrier by Raymond Pelletier and Mark Silber, Lewiston, Maine, 19 March 1981, for the project "*Notre vie, notre travail*," Maine Folklife Center, University of Maine, Orono, Maine, accession #1697; Michael Gordon, "Doors Closing at City Church," *Sun Journal*, 26 November 1999, pp. A1, A11; parish bulletin, Saints Peter and Paul Parish, 21 May 2000; Michael Gordon, "Church To Be Cultural Center," *Sun Journal*, 26 June 2000, pp. A1, A7; Jules Antonin Plourde, O.P., *Dominicains au Canada: Album historique* (unidentified publisher, 1973), 59. In 1996, Saint Peter had 1,410 families, Holy Family 1,974, and Holy Cross 2,324. *Sunday Sun Journal*, 1 September 1996, p. 1.

44. *Ste. Famille Federal Credit Union: 50 Years of Service, 1938–1988* (unidentified publisher, n.d.), 7; project of Pauline S. Gallant, Vice President, Community Credit Union, for the Northeast Credit Union National Association Management School, April 1988 summary, p. 2; "Community Credit Union History," undated typescript, Community Credit Union, Lewiston, Maine, pp. 3–4; Ann H. Boyce, "Giving Credit Where Credit Is Due: Spectacular Growth Marks Maine's Credit Unions," *Sunday Sun Journal*, 12 June 1994, p. 13F; Ronald L. Bissonnette, "A New Name," *Maine Family Federal Credit Union Quarterly* 1 (Winter 1993): 1; discussion with Denise T. Ouellette, Vice President for Marketing, Sainte Croix Regional Federal Credit Union, Lewiston, Maine, 28 October 1999; "Chairman's Message," 46th Annual Meeting Report, 23 February 1997, Sainte Croix Regional Federal Credit Union.

45. Personal interviews with Maurice H. Fontaine, Lewiston, Maine, 15 and 29 July 1993.

46. The evolution from "being" to "feeling" ethnic is explored in Anny Bakalian, *Armenian-Americans: From Being to Feeling Armenian* (New Brunswick, N.J.: Transaction Publishers, 1993); Peter Behrens, "Welcome to the Town of Ghosts," *Montreal Gazette*, 10 October 1998, p. B7; François Weil emphasizes the idea that the contemporary Franco-American identity is a personal strategy in *Les Franco-Américains, 1860–1980* ([Paris]: Belin, 1989), 218.

Conclusion

1. *Lewiston Sun Journal*, 2 February 1998, p. 1B, 4 March 1999, pp. 1A, 12A; Bonnie Washuk, "Behind Tom Shields," *Sunday Sun Journal*, 7 February 1999, pp. D1, D5; Liz Chapman, "Group Joins Fracas over English Bill," *Sun Journal*, 11 February 1999, pp. A1, A5; *Acts and Resolves as Passed by the Seventy-Ninth Legislature of the State of Maine, 1919* (Augusta, Maine: Kennebec Journal Co., 1919), ch. 146; Liz Chapman, "English Bill Dies," *Sun Journal*, 18 March 1999, pp. A1, A9.

2. See Oscar Handlin, *The Uprooted: The Epic Story of the Great Migrations That Made the American People*, 2nd ed. (Boston: Little, Brown and Company, 1973); and John Bodnar, *The Transplanted: A History of Immigrants in Urban America* (Bloomington: Indiana University Press, 1985).

3. For an example of this straight-line approach to assimilation, see Milton M. Gordon, *Assimilation in American Life: The Role of Race, Religion, and National Origins* (New York: Oxford University Press, 1964).
4. For a defense of the concept of assimilation, see Richard Alba and Victor Nee, "Rethinking Assimilation Theory for a New Era of Immigration," *International Migration Review* 31 (1997): 826–874.
5. See, for example, April R. Schultz, *Ethnicity on Parade: Inventing the Norwegian American through Celebration* (Amherst: University of Massachusetts Press, 1994); and Matthew Frye Jacobson, *Special Sorrows: The Diasporic Imagination of Irish, Polish, and Jewish Immigrants in the United States* (Cambridge, Mass.: Harvard University Press, 1995).
6. Dirk Hoerder, "From Migrants to Ethnics: Acculturation in a Societal Framework," in Dirk Hoerder and Leslie Page Moch, eds., *European Migrants: Global and Local Perspectives* (Boston: Northeastern University Press, 1996), 212.
7. Marcus Lee Hansen, *The Problem of the Third Generation Immigrant* (1937; Rock Island, Illinois: Swenson Swedish Immigration Research Center and Augustana College Library, 1987), 13–15.
8. U.S.ENGLISH, Inc., "States with Official English Laws," 2005, http://www.us-english.org/inc/official/states.asp (24 May 2007), and "Welcome to U.S.ENGLISH, Inc.," 2002, http://www.us-english.org/inc/ (7 January 2003); Georgie Anne Geyer, *Americans No More* (New York: Atlantic Monthly Press, 1996), 176, 203, 210.
9. See, for example, Yasemin Nuhoğlu Soysal, *Limits of Citizenship: Migrants and Postnational Membership in Europe* (Chicago: University of Chicago Press, 1994).

Appendix
Sources, Methodology, and Additional Statistics

1. Gerard J. Brault, *The French-Canadian Heritage in New England* (Hanover, N.H.: University Press of New England, 1986), 81–82; Georgia Drew Merrill, ed., *History of Androscoggin County, Maine* (Boston: W.A. Fergusson, 1891), p. 284; *U.S. Census, 1880*; Paul-M. Paré, "Les Vingt premières années du *Messager* de Lewiston, Maine," in Claire Quintal, ed., *Le Journalisme de langue française aux États-Unis* (Québec: Le Conseil de la Vie française en Amérique, 1984), 84; *Le Messager*, 15 November 1883, 7 April 1943, p. 1, 27 December 1946, p. 6, 9

February 1951, p. 1, 23 November 1954, p. 1, 6 September 1955, p. 1, 30 January 1958, pp. 3–4, 21 November 1962, p. 1, 16 January 1964, p. 1; Lewiston Municipal Court Naturalization Records, vol. 7, 10 September 1892, MSA; typescript notes of Reverend Philip Desjardins on *Le Messager*, Chancery Archives, Roman Catholic Diocese of Portland, Maine.

2. Alexander Keyssar, *Out of Work: The First Century of Unemployment in Massachusetts* (New York: Cambridge University Press, 1986), 343.

3. *Manning's Lewiston Auburn (Maine) Directory for Year beginning November, 1960*, vol. 57 (Springfield, Mass.: H.A. Manning, 1960).

4. *1992 Catalist: Business and Household Digest of Lewiston-Auburn* (Loveland, Colo.: USWest Marketing Resources, 1991); *Lewiston, Maine, 1996 City Directory* (Brewer, Maine: Maine Marketing Resources, 1996).

5. One of the few historians to make extensive use of naturalization records is George J. Sánchez in *Becoming Mexican American: Ethnicity, Culture and Identity in Chicano Los Angeles, 1900–1945* (New York: Oxford University Press, 1993).

6. I am grateful to historian Brian Young of McGill University for suggesting this procedure. Particularly helpful to the task of assigning Québec towns to counties were James White, *Ninth Report of the Geographic Board of Canada, 1910*, part 2, *Place-Names in Quebec* ([Ottawa: King's Printer], 1910); Hormisdas Magnan, *Dictionnaire historique et géographique des paroisses, missions et municipalités de la Province de Québec* (Arthabaska, Québec: L'Imprimerie d'Arthabaska, 1925); E. R. Smith, "Map of Montreal and the Eastern Townships, also Showing the South Eastern Portion of the Province of Quebec" (St. Johns, Quebec: E.R. Smith and Sons, 1897); Canada, Department of Mines, "Quebec, 1911 [Map] Accompanying 'Place Names in Quebec' by James White," ([Ottawa]: Geographic Board of Canada, 1911).

7. Naturalization data for the period from 1940 to 1949 comes from the Superior Court of Maine at Auburn Naturalization Records, vols. 30–43, Office of the Clerk of the Superior Court of Maine, Auburn, Maine; U.S. District Court, Portland, Maine, Naturalization Records, vols. 38–52, Overseas Military Petitions and Records, 1942–1945, the National Archives and Records Administration, Waltham, Massachusetts [hereafter NARA-Waltham]. Naturalization data for the period from 1950 to 1969 comes from the Superior Court of Maine at Auburn Naturalization Records, vols. 42–47, Office of the Clerk of the Superior Court of Maine, Auburn, Maine; U.S. District Court, Portland, Maine, Naturalization Records, vols. 53–64, NARA-Waltham. Naturalization data for the period from

1970 to 1991 comes from the Superior Court of Maine at Auburn Naturalization Records, vol. 47, Office of the Clerk of the Superior Court of Maine, Auburn, Maine; U.S. District Court, Portland, Maine, Naturalization Records, vols. 65–76, NARA-Waltham.

8. Landry's naturalization record is from the Superior Court of Maine at Auburn, vol. 44, #6098.

9. Poirier's naturalization record is from the Superior Court of Maine at Auburn, vol. 43, #5989.

10. Mathieu's naturalization record is from the Superior Court of Maine at Auburn, vol. 46, #6783. Immigrants like Mathieu who had entered the United States after 1930 would have been subject to the quota system the United States applied to Canada beginning in that year. John Herd Thompson and Stephen J. Randall, *Canada and the United States: Ambivalent Allies* (Athens, Ga.: University of Georgia Press, 1994), 128–129.

11. *Le Messager*, 25 April 1940, p. 12, 11 December 1946, p. 6; John J. Newman, "American Naturalization Processes and Procedures, 1790–1985" (typescript, Family History Section, Indiana Historical Society, 1985; available at NARA-Waltham), 24. After 1952, filing first naturalization papers became optional for everyone. Newman, 19.

12. Ouellette's naturalization record is from the Superior Court of Maine at Auburn, vol. 35, #3888.

13. Therriault's and Beaulieu's naturalization records are from the Superior Court of Maine at Auburn, vol. 44, #6143, and vol. 46, #6787, respectively.

14. Naturalization records did not provide the place of birth for 2.8 percent of the wives of naturalizing men.

15. The proportion may have been higher, for naturalization records did not provide the place of birth of 3.2 percent of the children of the male naturalizers.

16. Lepage's naturalization record is from the Superior Court of Maine at Auburn, vol. 35, #3800.

17. Naturalization records provide information on the occupations of petitioners only until 1966; therefore, the data from the 1960s discussed in this paragraph covers only the years from 1960 to 1966.

18. Roy's naturalization record is from the Superior Court of Maine at Auburn, vol. 46, #6866.

19. Marquis's naturalization record is from the U.S. District Court, vol. 72, #15274.

20. Thernstrom's two white-collar and three blue-collar categories are: I. High White-Collar (divided into two groups: professionals; major proprietors, managers, and officials); II. Low White-Collar (divided into three groups: clerks and salesmen; semiprofessionals; petty proprietors, managers, and officials); III. Skilled; IV. Semi-skilled and Service Workers; V. Unskilled Laborers and Menial Service Workers. See *The Other Bostonians: Poverty and Progress in the American Metropolis, 1880–1970* (Cambridge, Mass.: Harvard University Press, 1973), 290–292.

21. In Lewiston, the term "laborer" seems to have been applied to unskilled factory workers and not primarily to navvies. For example, in the 1920 sample, census takers identified the occupations of eleven of the ninety-four working French-Canadian women as laborers. Seven of these "laborers" were employed by cotton mills, three by shoe shops, and one by a shirt factory. *U.S. Census, 1920.*

Bibliography

Primary Sources

Archival and Personal Collections

Androscoggin County Historical Society, Auburn, Maine.
    Files on Ethnic Groups.
Androscoggin County Registry of Deeds, Auburn, Maine.
    Deed books 332, 337, 339, 340.
Archevêché de Montréal, les Archives de la Chancellerie, Montréal, Québec.
    Dossier: Chevaliers du Travail/Knights of Labor.
    Correspondance-Portland (Maine), 1855–1925.
Archives nationales du Québec, Montréal, Québec.
    Fonds Club Richelieu Montréal, Inc., bobine 6387.
Club Jacques-Cartier, Sabattus, Maine.
    Les Minutes des assemblées, 1925–1984.
Community Credit Union, Lewiston, Maine.
    Miscellaneous records on the history of Saint Pierre Credit Union.

Congrégation de Notre-Dame, Montréal, Québec.

Annales de la Maison Mère, juillet 1881–septembre 1882.

Dominicains, Montréal, Québec.

La Chronique du couvent, 1881–1976. In la série Couvents et Paroisses, la sous-série Couvent des Apôtres Pierre et Paul de Lewiston, Maine.

Dames de Charité: Compte rendu des Réunions, 1925–1971. In la série Couvents et Paroisses, la sous-série Couvent des Apôtres Pierre et Paul de Lewiston, Maine.

Dossier: Lewiston, Maine.

"Notices Nécrologiques des Dominicains Canadiens (1873–1990)."

Dominican Sisters, Sabattus, Maine.

Mémorial du Monastère du Sacré-Coeur, Lewiston, Maine, 1904–1968.

Personnel conventuel, 1904–1947.

Grand Séminaire, Montréal, Québec.

Registre du Grand Séminaire de Montréal, tome 1, 1840–1900.

Holy Cross Convent, Sisters of the Presentation of Mary, Lewiston, Maine.

Annales, 1927–1997.

"Holy Family Parish 75th Anniversary, November 8, 1998, Lewiston, Maine." VHS video. Privately owned.

L.&A. Montagnard Social Club, Inc., records in possession of Augustin Croteau, Secretary, Sabattus, Maine, and copies passed from him to me.

Charter of January 6, 1925.

Photocopies of Correspondence, 1924.

Règlements du Lewiston-Auburn Montagnard Social Club, Inc., 17 novembre 1957.

L.&A. Montagnard Social Club, Inc., scrapbook in possession of Diane Williams, Litchfield, Maine.

Lewiston-Auburn College, Franco-American Heritage Collection, Lewiston, Maine.

Correspondence of Louis-Philippe Gagné, notebook #34.

Lewiston, Maine. Office of the City Clerk.

Index of Marriages by Groom's Last Name, 1880, 1920, 1960, 1998; index dated 1999.

Maine Family Federal Credit Union, Lewiston, Maine.

Organization Certificate for Sainte Famille Federal Credit Union, March 16, 1938.

Maine. Office of the Clerk of the Superior Court of Maine, Auburn, Maine.
  Supreme Judicial Court, Androscoggin County, Naturalization Records,
    1895–1930.
  Superior Court of Maine at Auburn Naturalization Records, 1930–1974.
Maine State Archives, Augusta, Maine.
  Supreme Judicial Court, Androscoggin County, Records, 1854–1894.
  Superior Court, Cumberland County (Portland, Maine), Naturalization
    Records, 1868–1903.
  Lewiston Municipal Court Naturalization Records, 1882–1893.
National Archives and Records Administration, Waltham, Massachusetts.
  Auburn (Maine) Municipal Court Naturalization Records, 1893.
  National Labor Relations Board, Administrative and Other Records of
    Regional Offices, 1933–1935, Record Group 25, box 3.
  Supreme Judicial Court, Androscoggin County (Maine), Naturalization
    Records, 1903–1906.
  U.S. Circuit Court, Portland, Maine, Naturalization Records, 1851–1912.
  U.S. District Court, Portland, Maine, Proceedings, 1790–1845.
  U.S. District Court, Portland, Maine, Naturalization Records, 1851–1906,
    1912–1991; Overseas Military Petitions and Records, 1942–1945.
Rainbow Federal Credit Union, Lincoln Street branch, Lewiston, Maine.
  Organization Certificate for Sainte Marie Federal Credit Union, February 23,
    1947.
Roman Catholic Diocese of Portland, Chancery Archives, Portland, Maine.
  Bishop James Augustin Healy file.
  Bishop Louis S. Walsh file.
  Deceased clergy files.
  Diary of Bishop James Augustin Healy, 1875.
  Diary of Bishop Louis S. Walsh, 1923.
  Documents book 6.
  Holy Family School, Lewiston, Maine, file.
  Notes of Reverend Philip Desjardins (typescripts).
  Our Lady of the Rosary Parish, Sabattus, Maine, file.
  Parish Reports, 1879–.
  St. Mary's Parish, Lewiston, Maine, file.
  St. Peter's Parish, Lewiston, Maine, file.

Saint Joseph Parish Rectory, Lewiston, Maine.
  Baptism Registers, 1880, 1920, 1960.
  Parish directory, 1999.
Saint Mary's Regional Medical Center, Lewiston, Maine.
  Sisters of Charity, Registre, 1880–1901, 1916–1920.
  Sisters of Charity, Comptes Rendus de L'Asile Notre Dame de Lourdes de
    Lewiston à commencer de l'année 1884–1885.
  Sisters of Charity, Sommaire, 1885–1904.
Saint Patrick Parish Pastoral Center, Lewiston, Maine.
  Baptism Registers, 1892, 1920, 1960.
  Parish directory, 1999.
  Marriage Register for Saint Joseph Parish, 1880.
Saint Peter and Saint Paul Parish Pastoral Center, Lewiston, Maine.
  Registre des mariages de la Congrégation canadienne de Lewiston, 1880.
Sainte Croix Regional Federal Credit Union, Lewiston, Maine.
  Minutes of the organization meeting of October 29, 1950.
  Annual reports, 1951–1999.
Sisters of Saint Joseph Provincialate Archives, Winslow, Maine.
  Journal de la maison, Couvent de la Sainte-Famille, Lewiston, Maine, février
    1926–décembre 1965.
  Journal de la Sainte-Famille, Couvent de la Sainte Famille, Lewiston, Maine,
    janvier 1966–août 1971.
  Liste des Soeurs qui ont passé à la Ste. Famille, Lewiston, Maine.
  Sisters' Register: Sisters Who Have Been Missioned to Holy Family Convent,
    Lewiston, Maine (index cards).
Union Saint-Jean-Baptiste, Bibliothèque Mallet, Woonsocket, Rhode Island.
  Dossier: Lewiston, Maine.
University of Maine, Maine Folklife Center, Orono, Maine.
  Collection of Catholic and French jokes from the Lewiston-Auburn, Maine,
    area by Richard Clark of Lewiston, Maine, Fall 1966, accession #85.
Ursuline Provincialate Archives, Dedham, Massachusetts.
  Files on Saint Mary's Convent, Lewiston, Maine.
  Annals of Saint Mary's Convent, Lewiston, Maine, 1946–1968.
Ursuline Sisters, Mount Merici Convent, Waterville, Maine.
  "History, Province of the Northeast United States, 1888–1980" (typescript).
  Entrances to the Ursuline Order at Mount Merici, Waterville, through 1950
    (typescript).

Published Primary Sources

Bates College, Lewiston, Maine, 1915–1916. Unidentified publisher [1915].

Begin, Ange Marie, O.P., comp. *Marriages of SS. Peter & Paul, Lewiston, Maine (1869–1979).* Lewiston, Maine: Dominican Fathers [1980].

Bissonnette, Ronald L. "A New Name." *Maine Family Federal Credit Union Quarterly* 1 (Winter 1993): 1.

Canada. Department of Canadian Heritage. *Symbols of Canada.* Ottawa: Canadian Government Publishing, 1999.

Canada. Department of Mines. "Quebec, 1911 [Map] Accompanying 'Place Names in Quebec' by James White." [Ottawa]: Geographic Board of Canada, 1911.

Canadian Snowshoe Union. *Annual Convention of the Canadian Snowshoe Union, February 7–8, 1925, Lewiston, Maine/Convention annuelle de L'Union Canadienne des Raquetteurs, 7 et 8 février 1925.* Unidentified publisher [1925].

Central Maine General Hospital. *First Annual Report of the Central Maine General Hospital, Lewiston, Maine, July 1, 1891 to July 1, 1892.* Lewiston, Maine: Journal, 1893.

Comité d'Orientation Franco-Américaine. *2ème Congrès, Le Comité d'Orientation Franco-Américaine, les 9, 10 et 11 Novembre, 1951, Lewiston, Maine.* S.é. [1951].

Eaton, Mabel, ed. *General Catalogue of Bates College and Cobb Divinity School, 1864–1930.* Lewiston, Maine: Bates College, 1931.

Greenough's Directory of the Inhabitants, Institutions, Manufacturing Establishments, Societies, Business, Business Firms, Etc., Etc. in the Cities of Lewiston and Auburn, for 1880–81. Boston: W.A. Greenough, 1880.

Healy Asylum. *Annual Report, Healy Asylum, 1896.* Unidentified publisher [1896].

Hospital of the Sisters of Charity. *Annual Report of [the] Hospital of the Sisters of Charity, Lewiston, Maine.* Unidentified publisher [1898, 1899].

Hospital of the Sisters of Charity: Thirteenth Annual Report, 1905. Lewiston, Maine: Haswell Press [1905].

Hoyt, Edmund S., comp. *Maine State Year-Book and Legislative Manual, for the Year 1872.* Portland, Maine: Hoyt, Fogg and Breed, 1871.

———, comp. *Maine State Year-Book, and Legislative Manual, for the Year 1880–81, from April 1, 1880, to April 1, 1881.* Portland, Maine: Hoyt, Fogg and Donham, n.d.

Lewiston and Auburn Directory of the Inhabitants, Institutions, Manufacturing Establishments, Societies, Business, Business Firms, Etc. Boston: W.A. Greenough, 1883, 1896.

Lewiston, Maine, 1996 City Directory. Brewer, Maine: Maine Marketing Resources, 1996.

Lewiston, Maine. *Annual Report of the Receipts and Expenditures of the City of Lewiston, Together with Other Annual Reports and Papers Relating to the Affairs of the City.* Lewiston, Maine: Evening Journal/Journal, 1869, 1871, 1877, 1880, 1897; Geo. A. Callahan, 1870, 1876, 1878, 1895; Daily Sun, 1894; Le Messager, 1900, 1907, 1909; Haswell Press, 1908; Royal Press [1918].

Lewiston, Maine. *Annual Municipal Report, Fiscal Year Ending February 28, 1937: Lewiston, Maine.* Unidentified publisher [1937].

Lewiston, Maine. *Annual Reports of the School Committee and of the Superintendent of Schools of the City of Lewiston, Maine, for the Year Ending August 31, 1890.* Lewiston, Maine: Geo. A. Callahan, 1890.

Lewiston, Maine. *City of Lewiston, Maine, Annual Report of the School Department for the Year Ending August 31, 1919.* Unidentified publisher [1919].

Lewiston, Maine. *Report of the School Department, City of Lewiston, Maine, for the Years Ending August 31, 1920 and August 31, 1921.* Unidentified publisher, n.d.

Maine. *Acts and Resolves as Passed by the Seventy-Ninth Legislature of the State of Maine, 1919.* Augusta, Maine: Kennebec Journal, 1919.

Maine Department of Labor, Bureau of Labor Standards. *Census of Maine Manufactures, 1990.* Augusta, Maine: Maine Department of Labor, Bureau of Labor Standards, 1991.

Maine Register: State Year-Book and Legislative Manual. Numbers 56, 82, 92, 97, 98, 99, 100, 101. Portland, Maine: Portland Directory Company, 1925; Fred L. Tower Companies, 1950, 1960, 1965, 1966, 1967; Tower Publishing, 1968, 1969.

Maine. Secretary of State, comp. *Statistics of Industries and Finances of Maine for the Year 1883.* Augusta, Maine: Sprague and Son, 1883.

Manning's Lewiston and Auburn, Turner and Webster (Maine) Directory for Year beginning April, 1936. Vol. 44. Portland, Maine: H.A. Manning, 1936.

Manning's Lewiston Auburn (Maine) Directory for Year beginning November, 1960. Vol. 57. Springfield, Mass.: H.A. Manning, 1960.

1992 Catalist: Business and Household Digest of Lewiston-Auburn. Loveland, Colo.: USWest Marketing Resources, 1991.

The Official Catholic Directory for the Year of Our Lord 1920. New York: P.J. Kenedy and Sons, 1920.

L'Ordre des Frères Prêcheurs. *Les Dominicains: Qui sont-ils? Que font-ils? Où sont-ils?* [Montréal?: s.é., 1986?].

Planning Services Group. *The Comprehensive Plan, Lewiston, Maine, Program Report.* Cambridge, Mass.: Planning Services Group, 1962.

Plourde, J. Antonin, O.P. *Dominicains au Canada: Livre des documents.* Vol. 2, *Les cinq fondations avant l'autonomie (1881–1911).* Unidentified publisher, 1975.

Resident and Business Directory of Androscoggin County, Maine. Auburn, Maine: Merrill and Webber, 1918, 1920.

Roy, Henri F. *Échos d'Une Démission: Le Dernier Mot.* Lewiston, Maine: Echo Publishing, 1925.

Saint Dominic Regional High School. *The Spirit Echoes, 1941–1991.* [Lewiston, Maine: Saint Dominic Regional High School, 1991].

Saint Mary's General Hospital. *Annual Report of St. Mary's General Hospital, Lewiston, Maine, 1917–1918.* Lewiston, Maine: Royal Press [1918].

Saint Mary's General Hospital. *Report of Saint Mary's General Hospital, Lewiston, Maine for the Fiscal Year Ending June 30th, 1934.* Unidentified publisher, 1934.

Saint Mary's General Hospital/Hôpital Général Ste-Marie, Lewiston, Maine: A Voluntary Charitable Institution Counting Fifty Years of Faithful Service to the Community, 1888–1938. Unidentified publisher [1938].

Sisters' Hospital, 1902: Tenth Annual Report. Lewiston, Maine: Haswell Press [1902].

Smith, E. R. "Map of Montreal and the Eastern Townships, also Showing the South Eastern Portion of the Province of Quebec." St. John, Quebec: E.R. Smith and Sons, 1897.

Union Saint-Joseph. *Noces d'Argent de l'Union Saint-Joseph: Programme des Fêtes Jubilaires, 22 et 23 juin 1904.* [Lewiston, Maine]: Le Messager [1904].

U.S. Census, 1850.

U.S. Census, 1860.

U.S. Census, 1880.

U.S. Census, 1920.

U.S. Department of Commerce, Bureau of the Census. *Fourteenth Census of the United States Taken in the Year 1920*. Vols. 1, 3, 3 (reprinted). Washington, D.C.: Government Printing Office, 1921, 1922, 1923.

U.S. Department of Commerce, Bureau of the Census. *Fifteenth Census of the United States, 1930*. Vols. 1, 3 (part 1). Washington, D.C.: Government Printing Office, 1931, 1932.

U.S. Department of Commerce, Bureau of the Census. *Census of Population: 1970*. Vol. 1, part 21. Washington, D.C.: U.S. Government Printing Office, 1973.

U.S. Department of Commerce, Bureau of the Census. *1980 Census of Population*. Vol. 1, chapter C, part 21. Washington, D.C.: U.S. Government Printing Office, 1983.

U.S. Department of Commerce, Bureau of the Census. *1990 Census of Population, Social and Economic Characteristics: Maine*. Washington, D.C.: U.S. Government Printing Office, 1993.

U.S. Department of the Interior, Census Office. *Compendium of the Tenth Census (June 1, 1880)*. Part 1. Washington, D.C.: Government Printing Office, 1883.

U.S. Department of the Interior, Census Office. *Report on the Social Statistics of Cities*. Comp. George E. Waring, Jr. Part 1, *The New England and the Middle States*. Washington, D.C.: Government Printing Office, 1886.

U.S.ENGLISH, Inc. 2002. http://www.us-english.org/incl (7 January 2003).

U.S.ENGLISH, Inc. 2005. http://www.us-english.org/incl (24 May 2007).

Newspapers

The Bates Student

Church World ("Maine's Catholic Weekly")

Le Courrier du Maine

Democratic Advocate (Lewiston, Maine)

Eastern Argus (Portland, Maine)

Gazette (Montréal, Québec)

Labor Advocate (Lewiston, Maine)

Lewiston Daily Sun

Lewiston Falls Journal

Lewiston Journal (evening and weekly editions)

Maine Klansman

Maine Sunday Telegram
Maine Times
Le Messager (Lewiston, Maine)
Observations (Lewiston-Auburn, Maine)
Portland Press Herald
Portland Sunday Telegram
La République (Lewiston, Maine)
Sun Journal (Lewiston, Maine)
Sunday Sun Journal (Lewiston, Maine)
L'Unité (Lewiston, Maine)

Interviews

Beaudoin, Sr. Marie Therese, C.S.J. By the author, Winslow, Maine, 6 August 1993.

Belanger, Paul. By Mark Silber and Raymond Pelletier, Lewiston, Maine, 18 February 1981. Maine Folklife Center, University of Maine-Orono, accession #1685.

Bissonnette, Roger. By the author, Lewiston, Maine, 17 August 1993.

Boisvert, Cecile. By Steffan Duplessis, Marcella Sorg, and Mark Silber, Lewiston, Maine, 8 January 1981. Maine Folklife Center, University of Maine-Orono, accession #1694.

Boisvert, Romeo. By Steffan Duplessis and Raymond Pelletier, Lewiston, Maine, 8 January 1981. Maine Folklife Center, University of Maine-Orono, accession #1693.

Boucher, Antoinette. By Steffan Duplessis, Mark Silber, Raymond Pelletier, and Marcella Sorg, Lewiston, Maine, 15 December 1980. Maine Folklife Center, University of Maine-Orono, accession #1696.

Carrier, Reverend Hervé. By Raymond Pelletier and Mark Silber, Lewiston, Maine, 19 March 1981. Maine Folklife Center, University of Maine-Orono, accession #1697.

Doty, C. Stewart. *The First Franco-Americans: New England Life Histories from the Federal Writers' Project, 1938–1939.* Orono, Maine: University of Maine at Orono Press, 1985.

Dufresne, Armand A., Jr. By Marcella Sorg and Steffan Duplessis, Auburn, Maine, 14 May 1981. Maine Folklife Center, University of Maine-Orono, accession #1670.

Dufresne, Armand A., Jr. By Barry H. Rodrigue, Lewiston, Maine, 28 March 1994. Maine Folklife Center, University of Maine-Orono, accession #2351.

Filteau, Juliette. By Margaret Lanoue, Lewiston, Maine, 5 November 1982. Maine Folklife Center, University of Maine-Orono, accession #1623.

Fontaine, Maurice H. By the author, Lewiston, Maine, 15 and 29 July 1993.

Hendrickson, Dyke. *Quiet Presence: Dramatic, First-Person Accounts—The True Stories of Franco-Americans in New England.* Portland, Maine: Guy Gannett Publishing Company, 1980.

Kirk, Geneva A. By students of the First Year Seminar 187, Lewiston, Maine, 12 February 1996. Transcribed by Anne D. Williams. In Anne D. Williams, ed., "The Experience of the Great Depression in Lewiston-Auburn, Maine: A Report by First Year Seminar 187," 82–92. Bates College, Winter 1996; reprinted October 1997.

Lagace, Claire. By the author, Lewiston, Maine, 18 August 1993.

Lebel, Cecile. By Mark Silber and Raymond Pelletier, Lewiston, Maine, 18 February 1981. Maine Folklife Center, University of Maine-Orono, accession #1692.

LeTendre, Jacqueline. By the author, Lewiston, Maine, 25 August 1993.

Levesque, Sr. Alvina, C.S.J. By the author, Waterville, Maine, 20 August 1993.

Marcotte, Theresa. By the author, Auburn, Maine, 14 August 1993.

Marcoux, Wilfrid T. By the author, Lewiston, Maine, 25 August 1993.

Nadeau, Reverend Real J. By the author, Lewiston, Maine, 23 August 1993.

Poulin, Sr. Yvette, C.S.J. By the author, Waterville, Maine, 20 August 1993.

Rouillard, Jacques. *Ah les États! Les travailleurs canadiens-français dans l'industrie textile de la Nouvelle-Angleterre d'après le témoignage des derniers migrants.* Montréal: Les Éditions du Boréal Express, 1985.

Searles, James W., ed. *Immigrants from the North: Franco-Americans Recall the Settlement of Their Canadian Families in the Mill Towns of New England.* Bath, Maine: Hyde School, 1982.

Secondary Sources

Alba, Richard, and Victor Nee. "Rethinking Assimilation Theory for a New Era of Immigration." *International Migration Review* 31 (1997): 826–874.

Allen, James Paul. "Catholics in Maine: A Social Geography." Ph.D. dissertation, Syracuse University, 1970.

———. "Migration Fields of French Canadian Immigrants to Southern Maine." *Geographical Review* 62 (July 1972): 366–383.

———. "Franco-Americans in Maine: A Geographical Perspective." *Acadiensis* 4 (Autumn/automne 1974): 32–66.

Aubé, Lucien A. "From the Parochial School to an American University: Reflections on Cultural Fragmentation." In Claire Quintal, ed., *Steeples and Smokestacks: A Collection of Essays on the Franco-American Experience in New England*, 638–651. Worcester, Mass.: Éditions de l'Institut français, Assumption College, 1996.

Bakalian, Anny. *Armenian-Americans: From Being to Feeling Armenian*. New Brunswick, N.J.: Transaction Publishers, 1993.

Barkan, Elliott Robert. "Proximity and Commuting Immigration: An Hypothesis Explored via the Bi-polar Ethnic Communities of French Canadians and Mexican Americans." In Jack Kinton, ed., *American Ethnic Revival: Group Pluralism Entering America's Third Century*, 163–183. Aurora, Ill.: Social Science and Sociological Resources, 1977.

———. "French Canadians." In Stephan Thernstrom, ed., *Harvard Encyclopedia of American Ethnic Groups*, 388–401. Cambridge, Mass.: Belknap Press, 1980.

Barton, Josef J. *Peasants and Strangers: Italians, Rumanians, and Slovaks in an American City, 1890–1950*. Cambridge, Mass.: Harvard University Press, 1975.

Beal, Bob, and Rod Macleod. *Prairie Fire: The 1885 North-West Rebellion*. Toronto: McClelland and Stewart, 1994.

Beaudreau, Sylvie, and Yves Frenette. "Les stratégies familiales des francophones de la Nouvelle-Angleterre: Perspective diachronique." *Sociologie et sociétés* 26 (printemps 1994): 167–178.

Bergengren, Roy F. *Credit Union North America*. New York: Southern Publishers, 1940.

———. *Crusade: The Fight for Economic Democracy in North America, 1921–1945*. New York: Exposition Press, 1952.

Bernard, Laureat Odilon. "A Political History of Lewiston, Maine (1930–39)." Master's thesis, University of Maine-Orono, 1949.

Bissonnette, Ronald L. "Political Parties as Products of Their Environments: A Case Study of Lewiston, Maine." Honors thesis, University of Maine-Orono, 1977.

Bither, Amy. "Then and Now: Ste. [*sic*] Jean Baptist Holiday: Lewiston, Maine." Term Paper, University of Maine-Orono, Fall 1991. Charles Stewart Doty Papers, Special Collections, Fogler Library, University of Maine-Orono.

Blazon, Gerard. "A Social History of the French Canadian Community of Suncook, New Hampshire (1870–1920)." Master's thesis, University of New Hampshire, 1974.

Bodnar, John. *The Transplanted: A History of Immigrants in Urban America.* Bloomington: Indiana University Press, 1985.

Boucher, Jacqueline P. "The Franco-American in Lewiston." Senior thesis, Bates College, 1956.

Bourassa, Pierre Vincent. "The Catholic Church in the Franco-American Community." Honors thesis, Bowdoin College, 1978.

Bradbury, Bettina. *Working Families: Age, Gender, and Daily Survival in Industrializing Montreal.* Toronto: Oxford University Press, 1993.

Branham, Robert J., Lyn Francoeur, and William Surkis. "Roughing the Uppers: The Great Shoe Strike of 1937." VHS video, 1992.

Brault, Gerard J. "The Special NDEA Institute at Bowdoin College for French Teachers of Canadian Descent." *Publications of the Modern-Language-Association-of-America* 77 (September 1962): 1–5.

———. *The French-Canadian Heritage in New England.* Hanover, N.H.: University Press of New England, 1986.

———. "The Achievement of the Teaching Orders in New England: The Franco-American Parochial Schools." In Claire Quintal, ed., *Steeples and Smokestacks: A Collection of Essays on the Franco-American Experience in New England,* 267–291. Worcester, Mass.: Éditions de l'Institut français, Assumption College, 1996.

The Brothers of the Sacred Heart, Lewiston, Maine: Golden Jubilee of Service, 1928–1978. Unidentified publisher [1978].

Buker, Margaret, J. "The Irish in Lewiston, Maine: A Search for Security on the Urban Frontier, 1850–1880." *Maine Historical Society Quarterly* 13 (Special, 1973): 3–25.

Carpenter, Kenneth E. "The Franco-Americans in Maine." Honors thesis, Bowdoin College, 1958.

Carpenter, Niles. *Immigrants and Their Children, 1920: A Study Based on Census Statistics Relative to the Foreign Born and the Native White of Foreign or Mixed Parentage.* Washington, D.C.: Government Printing Office, 1927.

Chartier, Armand. *Histoire des Franco-Américains de la Nouvelle-Angleterre, 1775–1990.* Sillery, Québec: Septentrion, 1991. Translated as *The Franco-*

Americans of New England: A History. Worcester, Mass.: Éditions de l'Institut français, Assumption College, 1999.

Chevalier, Florence Marie, S.S.A. "The Role of French National Societies in the Sociocultural Evolution of the Franco-Americans of New England from 1860 to the Present: An Analytical Macro-sociological Case Study in Ethnic Integration Based on Current Social System Models." Ph.D. dissertation, Catholic University of America, 1972.

Cinel, Dino. *From Italy to San Francisco: The Immigrant Experience.* Stanford, Calif.: Stanford University Press, 1982.

Les Clubs Richelieu. *Les premiers 25 ans du Richelieu International.* Montréal: Éditions du Jour, 1971.

Le Comité Historique du Club Alpin, dir. *La Raquette.* [Manchester, N.H.]: L'Avenir National, 1937.

Coady, M. M. *Masters of Their Own Destiny: The Story of the Antigonish Movement of Adult Education through Economic Cooperation.* New York: Harper and Brothers, 1939.

Cohen, Lizabeth. *Making a New Deal: Industrial Workers in Chicago, 1919–1939.* New York: Cambridge University Press, 1990.

Condon, Richard H. "Bayonets at the North Bridge: The Lewiston-Auburn Shoe Strike, 1937." *Maine Historical Society Quarterly* 21 (Fall 1981): 75–98.

Conley, T. Edward. "Lewiston's Pioneer Catholic Parish." *Fiftieth Anniversary of St. Josephs* [sic] *Church, Lewiston, Maine: Catholic Guide and Reference Book.* Unidentified publisher [1908?].

Craig, Béatrice C. "Early French Migrations to Northern Maine, 1785–1850." *Maine Historical Society Quarterly* 25 (Spring 1986): 230–247.

———. "Immigrants in a Frontier Community: Madawaska, 1785–1850." *Histoire sociale/Social History* 19 (novembre/November 1986): 277–297.

Crozier, Reverend John F., ed. *One Hundredth Anniversary of Saint Joseph's Church, Lewiston, Maine, 1857–1957.* Unidentified publisher, n.d.

Danylewycz, Marta. *Taking the Veil: An Alternative to Marriage, Motherhood, and Spinsterhood in Quebec, 1840–1920.* Ed. Paul-André Linteau, Alison Prentice, and William Westfall. Toronto: McClelland and Stewart, 1987.

Devino, W. Stanley, Arnold H. Raphaelson, and James A. Storer. *A Study of Textile Mill Closings in Selected New England Communities.* Orono, Maine: University of Maine Press, 1966.

Dexter, Robert Cloutman. "Fifty-Fifty Americans." *World's Work* 48 (August 1924): 366–371.

Dingley, N., Jr. *Historical Sketch of Lewiston.* Lewiston, Maine: Lewiston Journal [1872].

Dominicaines. *Album-Souvenir: Vingt-cinquième anniversaire de l'arrivée des Religieuses Dominicaines à Lewiston.* Lewiston, Maine: Le Messager [1929].

Doty, C. Stewart. *Acadian Hard Times: The Farm Security Administration in Maine's St. John Valley, 1940–1943.* Orono, Maine: University of Maine Press, 1991.

———. "How Many Frenchmen Does It Take to . . . ?" *Thought and Action* 11 (Fall 1995): 85–104.

———. "The Future of the Franco-American Past." *American Review of Canadian Studies* 30 (Spring 2000): 7–17.

Dublin, Thomas. *Women at Work: The Transformation of Work and Community in Lowell, Massachusetts, 1826–1860.* New York: Columbia University Press, 1979.

Early, Frances H. "French-Canadian Beginnings in an American Community: Lowell, Massachusetts, 1868–1886." Ph.D. dissertation, Concordia University, 1979.

Eastman, Joel W. *The Credit Union Movement in Maine: A History of the Maine Credit Union League, 1937–1988.* Portland, Maine: Maine Credit Union League, 1988.

Erie, Steven P. *Rainbow's End: Irish-Americans and the Dilemmas of Urban Machine Politics, 1840–1985.* Berkeley: University of California Press, 1988.

Fairbairn, Brett. "Social Bases of Co-operation: Historical Examples and Contemporary Questions." In Murray E. Fulton, ed., *Co-operative Organizations and Canadian Society: Popular Institutions and the Dilemmas of Change,* 63–76. Toronto: University of Toronto Press, 1990.

Foley, Albert S., S.J. "Open Foes and Hidden." *Bishop Healy: Beloved Outcaste,* 166–176. Dublin: Clonmore and Reynolds Ltd., 1956.

"Franco-American Social Clubs." Audiocassette. [Bangor, Maine]: Maine Public Broadcasting [1993?].

Frenette, Yves. "Understanding the French Canadians of Lewiston, 1860–1900: An Alternative Framework." *Maine Historical Society Quarterly* 25 (Spring 1986): 198–229.

———. "Vie paroissiale et antagonismes culturels: Les dominicains à Lewiston (1880–1906)." In Claire Quintal, éd. *Religion catholique et appartenance franco-*

américaine, 25–35. Worcester, Mass.: Éditions de l'Institut français, Assumption College.

———. "La genèse d'une communauté canadienne-française en Nouvelle-Angleterre: Lewiston, Maine, 1800–1880." Thèse de doctorat, Université Laval, 1988.

———. "Macroscopie et microscopie d'un mouvement migratoire: Les Canadiens français à Lewiston au XIXe siècle." In Yves Landry, John A. Dickinson, Suzy Pasleau et Claude Desama, dirs., *Les chemins de la migration en Belgique et au Québec: XVIIe–XXe siècles*, 221–232. Beauport, Québec: Publications, MNH, 1995.

Galarneau, Claude. *Les Collèges classiques au Canada français (1620–1970)*. Montréal: Éditions Fides, 1978.

Gerstle, Gary. *Working-Class Americanism: The Politics of Labor in a Textile City, 1914–1960*. New York: Cambridge University Press, 1989.

Geyer, Georgie Anne. *Americans No More*. New York: Atlantic Monthly Press, 1996.

Giguère, Madeleine D. "New England's Francophone Population Based upon the 1990 Census." In Claire Quintal, ed., *Steeples and Smokestacks: A Collection of Essays on the Franco-American Experience in New England*, 567–594. Worcester, Mass.: Éditions de l'Institut français, Assumption College, 1996.

Gosselin, Henry V. "The Franco American Daily Press in Maine and a Content Analysis of *Le Messager*, Lewiston, Maine." Master's thesis, Boston University, 1951.

Gordon, Milton M. *Assimilation in American Life: The Role of Race, Religion, and National Origins*. New York: Oxford University Press, 1964.

Granatstein, J. L., and J. M. Hitsman. *Broken Promises: A History of Conscription in Canada*. Toronto: Oxford University Press, 1977.

Greer, Allan. *The Patriots and the People: The Rebellion of 1837 in Rural Lower Canada*. Toronto: University of Toronto Press, 1993.

Griffiths, Naomi. *The Acadians: Creation of a People*. Toronto: McGraw-Hill Ryerson, 1973.

Guignard, Michael. "The Franco-Americans: The Relationship between Ethnic Identification and Political Behavior." Honors thesis, Bowdoin College, 1969.

———. "Maine's Corporation Sole Controversy." *Maine Historical Society Newsletter* 12 (Winter 1973): 111–130.

———. "The Case of Sacred Heart Parish." *Maine Historical Society Quarterly* 22 (Summer 1982): 21–36.

————. *La foi–La langue–La culture: The Franco-Americans of Biddeford, Maine.* By the author, 1984.

Haebler, Peter. "Habitants in Holyoke: The Development of the French-Canadian Community in a Massachusetts City, 1865–1910." Ph.D. dissertation, University of New Hampshire, 1976.

Hamon, E., S.J. *Les Canadiens-Français de la Nouvelle-Angleterre.* Québec: N.S. Hardy, 1891.

Handlin, Oscar. *The Uprooted: The Epic Story of the Great Migrations That Made the American People.* 2nd ed. Boston: Little, Brown and Company, 1973.

Hansen, Marcus L. "The Second Colonization of New England." *New England Quarterly* 2 (October 1929): 539–560.

————. *The Problem of the Third Generation Immigrant.* 1937; Rock Island, Ill.: Swenson Swedish Immigration Research Center and Augustana College Library, 1987.

Hareven, Tamara K. *Family Time and Industrial Time: The Relationship between the Family and Work in a New England Industrial Community.* New York: Cambridge University Press, 1982.

Harvey, Fernand. "Les Chevaliers du Travail, les Etats-Unis et la société québécoise (1882–1902)." In Fernand Harvey, dir., *Aspects historiques du mouvement ouvrier au Québec*, 33–118. Montréal: Les Éditions du Boréal Express, 1973.

Higgins, Mary Raymond, R.S.M. *For Love of Mercy: Missioned in Maine and Andros Island, Bahamas, 1883–1983.* Portland, Maine: Sisters of Mercy, 1995.

Higham, John. *Strangers in the Land: Patterns of American Nativism, 1860–1925.* 1955; New Brunswick, N.J.: Rutgers University Press, 1992.

Hoerder, Dirk. "From Migrants to Ethnics: Acculturation in a Societal Framework." In Dirk Hoerder and Leslie Page Moch, eds., *European Migrants: Global and Local Perspectives*, 211–262. Boston: Northeastern University Press, 1996.

Howell, Colin D. *Northern Sandlots: A Social History of Maritime Baseball.* Toronto: University of Toronto Press, 1995.

Hudson, Susan P. *The Quiet Revolutionaries: How the Grey Nuns Changed the Social Welfare Paradigm of Lewiston, Maine.* New York: Routledge, 2006.

Institut Jacques-Cartier. *Album-Souvenir, 1872–1922: Cinquantenaire de L'Institut Jacques-Cartier de Lewiston, Maine.* [Lewiston, Maine]: le Comité de l'Album-Souvenir, 1922.

Jacobson, Matthew Frye. *Special Sorrows: The Diasporic Imagination of Irish, Polish, and Jewish Immigrants in the United States*. Cambridge, Mass.: Harvard University Press, 1995.

Kanzler, Eileen McAuliffe. "Processes of Immigration: The Franco Americans of Manchester, New Hampshire, 1875–1925." Doctor of Arts dissertation, Illinois State University, 1982.

Katz, Michael B. *In the Shadow of the Poorhouse: A Social History of Welfare in America*. New York: Basic Books, 1986.

Kennedy, Ruby Jo Reeves. "Single or Triple Melting-Pot? Intermarriage Trends in New Haven, 1870–1940." *American Journal of Sociology* 49 (January 1944): 331–339.

Keyssar, Alexander. *Out of Work: The First Century of Unemployment in Massachusetts*. New York: Cambridge University Press, 1986.

———. *The Right to Vote: The Contested History of Democracy in the United States*. New York: Basic Books, 2000.

Kirk, Geneva, and Gridley Barrows. *Historic Lewiston: Its Government*. Lewiston, Maine: Lewiston Historical Commission, 1982.

Kumekawa, Glenn. "Political Factionalism within the Franco-Americans in Lewiston." Term paper [Bates College, 1949]. Lewiston Collection, Lewiston Public Library.

Lajoie, Juliette. *Ste. Famille Federal Credit Union 25th Anniversary, 1938–1963*. Unidentified publisher, n.d.

Lajoie, Mme. Laurent (Juliette). "Histoire de la fondation de l'Union Crédit Fédérale Sainte Famille à l'occasion de son vincinquième [*sic*] anniversaire, 1938–1963, Paroisse Sainte Famille, Lewiston, Maine." Texte dactylographié, 1963. Déposé à Maine Family Federal Credit Union, Lewiston, Maine.

Lavoie, Yolande. *L'émigration des Canadiens aux États-Unis avant 1930: Mesure du phénomène*. Montréal: Les Presses de l'Université de Montréal, 1972.

———. *L'émigration des Québécois aux États-Unis de 1840 à 1930*. [Québec]: Éditeur officiel du Québec, 1981.

Leamon, James S. *Historic Lewiston: A Textile City in Transition*. Lewiston, Maine: Lewiston Historical Commission, 1976.

LeBlanc, Charlotte Bordes. "History and Mission of the Fédération Féminine Franco-Américaine (1951–1991)." In Claire Quintal, ed., *Steeples and Smokestacks: A Collection of Essays on the Franco-American Experience in New England*,

501–511. Worcester, Mass.: Éditions de l'Institut français, Assumption College, 1996.

LeBlanc, Robert G. "Regional Competition for Franco-American Repatriates, 1870–1930." *Québec Studies* 1 (Spring 1983): 110–129.

———. "The Francophone 'Conquest' of New England: Geopolitical Conceptions and Imperial Ambition of French-Canadian Nationalists in the Nineteenth Century." *American Review of Canadian Studies* 15 (Autumn 1985): 288–310.

———. "Colonisation et rapatriement au Lac-Saint-Jean (1895–1905)." *Revue d'histoire de l'Amérique française* 38 (hiver 1985): 379–408.

———. "A French-Canadian Education and the Persistence of *La Franco-Américanie*." *Journal of Cultural Geography* 8 (Spring/Summer 1988): 49–64.

———. "The Franco-American Response to the Conscription Crisis in Canada, 1916–1918." *American Review of Canadian Studies* (Autumn 1993): 343–372.

Levasseur, Cecile, comp. *75th Anniversary of the Founding of St. Mary's Parish, Lewiston, Maine, 1907–1982*. Unidentified publisher, 1982.

Levy, Daniel. *U.S. Citizenship and Naturalization Handbook*. St. Paul, Minn.: West Group, 1999.

Lieberson, Stanley, and Mary C. Waters. *From Many Strands: Ethnic and Racial Groups in Contemporary America*. New York: Russell Sage Foundation, 1988.

Linteau, Paul-André, René Durocher et Jean-Claude Robert. *Histoire du Québec contemporain: De la Confédération à la crise (1867–1929)*. Montréal: Boréal, 1989.

Locke, William N. "The French Colony at Brunswick, Maine: A Historical Sketch." *Les Archives de Folklore* 1 (1946): 97–111.

Lucey, William Leo, S.J. *The Catholic Church in Maine*. Francestown, N.H.: Marshall Jones Company, 1957.

McClymer, John F. "The Paradox of Ethnicity in the United States: The French-Canadian Experience in Worcester, 1870–1914." In Michael D'Innocenzo and Josef P. Sirefman, eds., *Immigration and Ethnicity: American Society—"Melting Pot" or "Salad Bowl"?*, 15–23. Westport, Conn.: Greenwood Press, 1992.

Macdonald, Fergus. *The Catholic Church and the Secret Societies in the United States*. New York: United States Catholic Historical Society, 1946.

MacDonald, William. "French Canadians in Maine." *The Nation* 63 (October 15, 1896): 285–286.

———. "The French Canadians in New England." *Quarterly Journal of Economics* 12 (April 1898): 245–279.

MacLellan, Malcolm. *Coady Remembered*. Antigonish, Nova Scotia: St. Francis Xavier University Press, 1985.

McRoberts, Kenneth. *Quebec: Social Change and Political Crisis*. 3rd ed. Toronto: McClelland and Stewart, 1988.

Magnan, Hormisdas. *Dictionnaire historique et géographique des paroisses, missions et municipalités de la Province de Québec*. Arthabaska, Québec: L'Imprimerie d'Arthabaska, 1925.

Marcoux, Larry and Carol, eds. *St. Patrick's Church, Lewiston, Maine, Celebrates 100 Years, 1890–1990*. Unidentified publisher [1990].

Merrill, Georgia Drew, ed. *History of Androscoggin County, Maine*. Boston: W.A. Fergusson, 1891.

Moody, J. Carroll, and Gilbert C. Fite. *The Credit Union Movement: Origins and Development, 1850–1970*. Lincoln: University of Nebraska Press, 1971.

Moore, Leonard J. *Citizen Klansmen: The Ku Klux Klan in Indiana, 1921–1928*. Chapel Hill: University of North Carolina Press, 1991.

Moores, Lawrence Wayne, Jr. "The History of the Ku Klux Klan in Maine, 1922–1931." Master's thesis, University of Maine-Orono, 1950.

Mundy, James H. *Hard Times, Hard Men: Maine and the Irish, 1830–1860*. Scarborough, Maine: Harp Publications, 1990.

Myhrman, A. M., and J. A. Rademaker. "The Second Colonization Process in an Industrial Community." Typescript, Lewiston Collection, Lewiston Public Library, n.d.

Newman, John J. "American Naturalization Processes and Procedures, 1790–1985." Typescript, Family History Section, Indiana Historical Society, 1985. National Archives and Records Administration, Waltham, Mass.

Olson, James. S. *Catholic Immigrants in America*. Chicago: Nelson-Hall, 1987.

Olzak, Susan. *The Dynamics of Ethnic Competition and Conflict*. Stanford, Calif.: Stanford University Press, 1992.

Palmer, Bryan D. "Discordant Music: Charivaris and Whitecapping in Nineteenth-Century North America." *Labour/Le Travailleur* 3 (1978): 5–62.

Paré, Paul M. "Les vingt premières années du *Messager* de Lewiston, Maine." *Le Journalisme de langue française aux États-Unis*, 81–96. In Claire Quintal, dir. Québec: Le Conseil de la Vie française en Amérique, 1984.

———. "Franco-Americans and Credit Unions." *InformACTION* 3 (February/March 1984): 4–5, 7.

Park, Robert E., and Herbert A. Miller. *Old World Traits Transplanted*. New York: Harper, 1921.

Parker, James H. "The Assimilation of French Americans." *Human Organization* 38 (Fall 1979): 309–312.

———. *Ethnic Identity: The Case of the French Americans*. Washington, D.C.: University Press of America, 1983.

Paroisse Canadienne-Française de Lewiston (Maine): Album historique. [Lewiston, Maine]: Les Pères Dominicains, 1899.

Patrell, Carol. "The Parochial School System in Lewiston and Auburn." Typescript [1948?], Lewiston Collection, Lewiston Public Library.

Peach, Ceri. "Which Triple Melting Pot? A Re-examination of Ethnic Intermarriage in New Haven, 1900–1950." *Ethnic and Racial Studies* 3 (January 1980): 1–16.

Perreault, Robert B. *One Piece in the Great American Mosaic: The Franco-Americans of New England*. Lakeport, N.H.: André Paquette Associates, 1976.

Petrin, Ronald A. *French Canadians in Massachusetts Politics, 1885–1915: Ethnicity and Political Pragmatism*. Philadelphia: Balch Institute Press, 1990.

Plourde, Antonin M., O.P. "Cent ans de vie paroissiale: SS. Pierre et Paul de Lewiston, 1870–1970." *Le Rosaire* (août/septembre 1970): 1–56.

———. *Dominicains au Canada: Album historique*. S.é., 1973.

———. *Qui sont-ils et d'où viennent-ils? Nécrologe [sic] dominicain, 1965–1990*. Tome 2. Montréal: Les Dominicains au Canada, s.d.

Programme-Souvenir, 1907–1932: Vingt-cinquième anniversaire de la Paroisse Sainte-Marie. Lewiston, Maine: s.é., 1932.

Ramirez, Bruno. *On the Move: French-Canadian and Italian Migrants in the North Atlantic Economy, 1860–1914*. Toronto: McClelland and Stewart, 1991.

———. "L'émigration des Canadiens français aux États-Unis dans les années 1920." In Yves Landry, John A. Dickinson, Suzy Pasleau, et Claude Desama, dirs., *Les chemins de la migration en Belgique et au Québec: XVIIe–XXe siècles*, 233–246. Beauport, Québec: Publications, MNH, 1995.

Richard, Mark Paul. "Coping before *l'État-providence*: Collective Welfare Strategies of New England's Franco-Americans." *Québec Studies* 25 (Spring 1998): 59–67.

———. "The Ethnicity of Clerical Leadership: The Dominicans in Francophone Lewiston, Maine, 1881–1986." *Québec Studies* 33 (Spring/Summer 2002): 83–101.

———. "From Franco-American to American: The Case of Sainte-Famille, an Assimilating Parish of Lewiston, Maine." *Histoire sociale/Social History* 31 (May 1998): 71–93.

———. "From *Canadien* to American: The Acculturation of French-Canadian Descendants in Lewiston, Maine, 1860 to the Present." Ph.D. dissertation, Duke University, 2001.

———. "Negotiating Ethnic Identity: St. Jean-Baptiste Day Celebrations in Francophone Lewiston, Maine." In Nelson Madore and Barry Rodrigue, eds., *Voyages: A Maine Franco-American Reader*, 211–223. Gardiner and Lewiston, Maine: Tilbury House and the University of Southern Maine Franco-American Collection, 2007.

Robin, Martin. *Shades of Right: Nativist and Fascist Politics in Canada, 1920–1940*. Toronto: University of Toronto Press, 1992.

Roby, Yves. *Alphonse Desjardins et les caisses populaires, 1854–1920*. Montréal: Éditions Fides, 1964.

———. "L'évolution économique du Québec et l'émigrant (1850–1929)." *L'émigrant québécois vers les États-Unis (1850–1920)*, 8–20. In Claire Quintal, dir. Québec: Le Conseil de la Vie française en Amérique, 1982.

———. "Quebec in the United States: A Historiographical Survey." *Maine Historical Society Quarterly* 26 (Winter 1987): 126–159.

———. *Les Franco-Américains de la Nouvelle-Angleterre (1776–1930)*. Sillery, Québec: Septentrion, 1990.

———. "Émigrés canadiens-français, Franco-Américains de la Nouvelle-Angleterre et images de la société américaine." In Yvan Lamonde et Gérard Bouchard, dirs., *Québécois et Américains: La culture québécoise aux XIXe et XXe siècles*, 131–156. [Saint-Laurent, Québec]: Éditions Fides, 1995.

———. "From Franco-Americans to Americans of French-Canadian Origin or Franco-Americanism, Past and Present." Trans. Alexis A. Babineau, A.A. In Claire Quintal, ed., *Steeples and Smokestacks: A Collection of Essays on the Franco-American Experience in New England*, 609–625. Worcester, Mass.: Éditions de l'Institut français, Assumption College, 1996.

———. *Les Franco-Américains de la Nouvelle-Angleterre: Rêves et réalités*. Sillery, Québec: Septentrion, 2000.

Rollins, Joan H. "Introduction: Ethnic Identity, Acculturation and Assimilation." In Joan H. Rollins ed., *Hidden Minorities: The Persistence of Ethnicity in American Life*, 1–34. Lanham, Md.: University Press of America, 1981.

Rouillard, Jacques. *Histoire du syndicalisme au Québec: Des origines à nos jours*. Montréal: Éditions du Boréal, 1989.

Rudin, Ronald. *In Whose Interest? Quebec's Caisses Populaires, 1900–1945*. Montréal: McGill-Queen's University Press, 1990.

Rumilly, Robert. *Histoire des Franco-Américains*. Montréal: Chez l'auteur, 1958.

St. Pierre Credit Union 25th Anniversary, 1945–1970. Lewiston, Maine: Screen Printing [1970].

Saint-Pierre et Saint-Paul. *Album souvenir du 75e anniversaire de la Paroisse Saint-Pierre et Saint-Paul de Lewiston, Maine, 1871–1946*. S.é., s.d.

Ste. Famille Federal Credit Union: 50 Years of Service, 1938–1988. Unidentified publisher, n.d.

SS. Peter and Paul Parish, Lewiston, Maine, 1870–1996, Paroisse Saint Pierre et Saint Paul. Lewiston, Maine: SS. Peter and Paul Parish, 1996.

Sánchez, George J. *Becoming Mexican American: Ethnicity, Culture and Identity in Chicano Los Angeles, 1900–1945*. New York: Oxford University Press, 1993.

Schultz, April R. *Ethnicity on Parade: Inventing the Norwegian American through Celebration*. Amherst: University of Massachusetts Press, 1994.

Scontras, Charles A. *Two Decades of Organized Labor and Labor Politics in Maine, 1880–1900*. Orono: University of Maine Press, 1969.

Seiple, Faith. "Assimilation of French Groups into the Lewiston-Auburn Community." Term paper [Bates College], 1949. Lewiston Collection, Lewiston Public Library.

Sher, Julian. *White Hoods: Canada's Ku Klux Klan*. Vancouver: New Star Books, 1983.

Silver, A. I. *The French-Canadian Idea of Confederation, 1864–1900*. Toronto: University of Toronto Press, 1982.

Skinner, Ralph. *Historically Speaking on Lewiston-Auburn, Maine, Churches*. Lewiston, Maine: By the Author, 1965.

Soysal, Yasemin Nuhoğlu. *Limits of Citizenship: Migrants and Postnational Membership in Europe*. Chicago: University of Chicago Press, 1994.

Spiro, Melford E. "The Acculturation of American Ethnic Groups." *American Anthropologist* 57 (December 1955): 1240–1252.

Swyripa, Frances. *Wedded to the Cause: Ukrainian-Canadian Women and Ethnic Identity, 1891–1991*. Toronto: University of Toronto Press, 1993.

Thernstrom, Stephan. *The Other Bostonians: Poverty and Progress in the American Metropolis, 1880–1970*. Cambridge, Mass.: Harvard University Press, 1973.

Thompson, John Herd, and Stephen J. Randall. *Canada and the United States: Ambivalent Allies*. Athens, Ga.: University of Georgia Press, 1994.

Ueda, Reed. *Postwar Immigrant America: A Social History.* Boston: Bedford Books, 1994.

Ursulines. *50th Anniversary: The Ursulines, St. Mary's School, Lewiston, Maine, 1916–1966.* Unidentified publisher [1966].

U.S. Department of Justice. Immigration and Naturalization Service. *An Immigrant Nation: United States Regulation of Immigration, 1798–1991.* [Washington, D.C].: Government Printing Office, 1991.

Vicero, Ralph Dominic. "Immigration of French Canadians to New England, 1840–1900: A Geographical Analysis." Ph.D. dissertation, University of Wisconsin, 1968.

Walsh, William. "Bishop Walsh and the Ku Klux Klan." Typescript, Chancery Archives, Roman Catholic Diocese of Portland, Maine, 1973.

Weil, François. *Les Franco-Américains, 1860–1980.* [Paris]: Belin, 1989.

White, James. *Ninth Report of the Geographic Board of Canada, 1910.* Part 2, *Place-Names in Quebec.* [Ottawa: King's Printer], 1910.

Whitfield, Stephen J. *The Culture of the Cold War.* 2nd ed. Baltimore: Johns Hopkins University Press, 1996.

Whitmore, Allan R. "'A Guard of Faithful Sentinels': The Know-Nothing Appeal in Maine, 1854–1855." *Maine Historical Society Quarterly* 20 (Winter 1981): 151–197.

Widdis, Randy William. *With Scarcely a Ripple: Anglo-Canadian Migration into the United States and Western Canada, 1880–1920.* Montreal and Kingston: McGill-Queen's University Press, 1998.

Zieger, Robert H. *The CIO, 1935–1955.* Chapel Hill and London: University of North Carolina Press, 1995.

Zucchi, John E. *Italians in Toronto: Development of a National Identity, 1875–1935.* Kingston and Montreal: McGill-Queen's University Press, 1988.

Index

Q

Québec: city of, 11, 14, 58, 154, 177, 178, 210, 276 (n. 10); economic conditions in, 14, 37, 73–74, 152, 158; emigration from, 2, 13, 28, 74, 86, 123, 150, 151–153, 155; as inspiration and model for French-Canadian descendants in United States, 17, 20, 23, 50, 58, 100–101, 103, 177, 178, 179–180, 181, 184, 200, 213, 303 (n. 17); as origin of Lewiston residents, 4, 13, 14, 15, 18, 22, 74–76, 91, 148, 152, 161–163, 225, 256, 262–263, 264, 269, 308 (n. 59); politics in, 46, 48, 54–56, 60, 71, 79, 80, 217, 225–226, 239–240; province of, 4, 12, 14, 15, 16, 28, 30, 60, 66, 67, 94, 99, 110, 121, 126, 138, 144, 145, 146, 153, 187–188, 189, 213, 218, 222; ties with French-Canadian descendants in United States, 56–59, 76, 77, 175–177, 179, 185, 210, 217, 224, 228, 239–240, 242, 250, 251. *See also* colonization; repatriation

Quinzaine, La, 97

R

Rainbow Federal Credit Union, 247
Repatriation efforts of Québec and Canada, 59–60, 74, 76–77, 86, 153–154, 160. *See also* colonization
Republicans, 30, 44, 52, 125, 131, 172, 173, 174, 249, 285 (n. 19), 328 (n. 23); in competition and conflict with Lewiston francophones, 27, 35, 39–40, 41–42, 43, 44–45, 90, 92, 151, 170, 288 (n. 39); francophones as, 36, 42–44, 46, 50–51, 90, 91–92, 133, 168, 170–171, 195. See also *Le Messager,* politics

Reny, Arthur, 39
Reny, J.-H., 161
République, La, 43
Richelieu Club, 222
Riel, Louis, 54–55
Roosevelt, Franklin D., 151, 169–170, 182, 191, 194–195

S

Sabourin, Charles, 29
Sabourin, William, 34, 43–44
Sacred Heart Parish (Auburn, Maine), 130, 216
Sacred Heart Parish (Waterville, Maine), 100, 105
Saint-Charles Borromée, 56, 175–176, 217
Saint-Dominique band, 113, 114
Saint-Dominique High School, 218, 223, 233, 238, 239, 246
Sainte-Anne de Beaupré, 57, 76
Sainte-Croix, Lewiston: church/parish, 138, 146, 148, 179, 183, 197, 210, 222, 224–225, 233, 246; controversy over name, 139–144; convent, 145; school, 145, 214, 225
Sainte Croix Parish Federal Credit Union, 247
Sainte-Famille, Lewiston: church/parish: 138–139, 143–144, 150, 182, 200, 222, 224, 225, 233, 246, 247;

Wing, George C., 161

Wiseman, Robert J., 91–92, 170, 174, 191, 320 (n. 45)

Wolfe County, Québec, 15, 75, 161

World War I, 4, 8, 123; Canada's conscription crisis in, 74, 79; Franco-Americans in, 79–80, 134; naturalizations during, 79, 160, 285 (n. 19), 298 (n. 18)

World War II, 33, 110, 150, 204, 205, 214, 219, 252; changes in aftermath of, 216, 219, 227; changes in Franco-American traditions during, 211, 212, 335 (n. 37); Franco-Americans in, 196–197, 207, 209; naturalization during, 204, 263, 265, 267, 268

Wright, Carroll, 40, 65

Y

Yankees, 4, 7, 10, 63, 128, 129, 148, 182, 203, 210, 222, 275 (n. 4); discrimination against francophones by, 134, 204, 244, 251; politics and, 36, 39, 44, 151

YWCA, 160